W9-AEF-729

WITHDRAWN

by Paul Horgan

OF
AMERICA
EAST & WEST

PS
3515
.O6583
A6
1984

OF
AMERICA
EAST & WEST

SELECTIONS FROM
THE WRITINGS OF

PAUL HORGAN

WITH AN INTRODUCTION BY

HENRY STEELE COMMAGER

Farrar · Straus · Giroux

NEW YORK

Salem Academy and College
Gramley Library
Winston-Salem, N.C. 27108

Copyright © 1935, 1936, 1942, 1950, 1954, 1960, 1961, 1964, 1968,
1972, 1973, 1975, 1976, 1977, 1979, 1984 by Paul Horgan
Renewal copyright © 1962, 1963, 1969, 1977, 1982 by Paul Horgan
Introduction copyright © 1984 by Henry Steele Commager
All rights reserved
First printing, 1984
Printed in the United States of America
Published simultaneously in Canada by Collins Publishers, Toronto
Designed by Cynthia Krupat
Library of Congress Cataloging in Publication Data
Horgan, Paul. / Of America, East & West.
I. Title.   II. Title: Of America, East and West.
PS3515.O6583A6 1984   813'.52   83-16551

With devoted memories of

VIRGINIA RICE

1895–1975

my constant friend &

literary agent of five decades

Contents

II / Biography

III / Notebook Pages and an Essay

Introduction

BY HENRY STEELE COMMAGER

Paul Horgan's long and varied career marks him as a man of the Enlightenment in the Jeffersonian tradition. He is distinguished alike as scholar, teacher, and critic, historian, novelist, man of "letters," and artist. And yet it is not diversity but unity which characterizes him, for all of his careers and activities are illuminated by a consistent philosophy.

It is probably as historian that Horgan is most eminent, and this though some of his novels may well survive even his historical volumes. If there is one explanation of his eminence as an historian more persuasive than any other, it is that, as with most historians who have an impact on their own day and on posterity as well, he brings to the study and interpretation of history the same luminous imagination, the same curiosity about human nature, the same sympathy and compassion that suffuse his novels. History is, after all, the faithful reconstruction of the past. That re-creation of the past can be fully achieved only when devotion to the scholarly principle of knowing "what actually happened" is animated by a creative imagination—something that the *Annales* school of French historians is now busy teaching the rest of us.

For it is imagination that most distinguishes the historians who survive in the affections and the allegiance of later generations—a Froissart, a Gibbon, a Michelet, a Macaulay, a Francis Parkman; it is imagination, rooted in the soil of research, that assures to a Winston Churchill and a Samuel Eliot Morison generations of grateful readers. All these historians of the past knew that if history is to live, it must go beyond science to poetry. It is with this goodly company that Paul Horgan is associated.

Horgan's re-creation of life along the *Great River* combines History as fact, History as narrative, and History as a disciplined and inspired imagination. It is his imagination which enables him, and persuades his readers, to enter into the lives, the minds, perhaps the very souls, of the Indians of the American Southwest who first took over this land and adapted themselves to it; of the Spanish conquistadores who conquered it, and their incongruous associates the padres, who bore not the sword but the cross. And because he is a scholar of broad sympathies, and in a sense a participant in the drama which he recounts, he understands with equal insight, almost with clairvoyance, the American invaders, the successive waves of "Anglos" —those seeking land, those seeking copper and oil and gold, those seeking health, or those (like Bronson Cutting*) seeking only an escape from the East—and describes how they invaded and conquered and ruled and ravaged the ancient land. In a long succession of novels and histories, he has conjured up for us with sympathy and deep insight the story of successive and conflicting rather than harmonious civilizations.

In his talent for portraying contrasting cultures, in the breadth of his literary embrace, and in the delicacy of his moral perceptions, Horgan is a kind of modern-day William Dean Howells. Both Howells and Horgan spent much of their boyhood and youth in what were, at the time, geographical and cultural frontiers—Howells in the Ohio of the eighteen-forties which he has re-created in *A Boy's Town* and *The Leatherwood God*; Horgan in the New Mexico of the early years of this century, a frontier whose artistic aridity he has recalled in the touching "Preface to an Unwritten Book" and, more painfully, in a long series of novels including the almost Faulknerian *Far from Cibola*. Both men headed East—interestingly enough, to Connecticut; both managed to play an important role in the literary and cultural life of both New England and New York—and, finally, of the nation; both were prodigiously productive—and in the most varied fields of letters; both ventured into biography, Howells in his affectionate portrait of Mark Twain and his perspicacious criticism of Henry James, Horgan with interpretations of frontier heroes like Bishop Lamy and Josiah Gregg. As critics both were rooted in the Victorian tradition and comfortable with it, but both proved able to surmount it and to welcome challenges to that tradition—Howells in his appreciation of Zola and Turgenev, Horgan in biographies of

* *Bronson Murray Cutting, member of a prominent New York family, settled in Santa Fe and was a U.S. Senator from New Mexico, 1927–1935.*

Peter Hurd and Stravinsky. Both embraced, in the end, the whole American scene, the American character, and with almost theological sanctions, American morality.

For it is not only history and geography which give unity to Paul Horgan's literary world: the unity is philosophical. As with other traditionalists from Hawthorne to Howells, from Henry James to Willa Cather, it is moral solicitude and moral anxiety that provide unity to Horgan's literary opus. It is this, in turn, which assures him a place not only in the history of American literature but in the study of the American character. Moral solicitude and apprehension is as pervasive in the pages of Horgan as in the pages of Henry James, for consistency is one of his more reassuring qualities. It is there in the history of the Rio Grande, and in the numerous volumes, both of history and of fiction, which are tributaries to that river, such as *The Heroic Triad,* the biographies of Bishop Lamy and Josiah Gregg, the long shelf of novels culminating in the Richard trilogy and, most recently, *Mexico Bay.* How could it be otherwise when the very founding of New Spain and particularly of New Mexico was, in a sense, an act of God, and one which Horgan is peculiarly fitted to understand.

Like other expatriates, if we may invoke that somewhat dubious term—the Virginia-born Willa Cather of *A Lost Lady* and *The Professor's House,* or the Henry James whose original theme of New World innocence and Old World depravity ended up, in *The Ambassadors* and *The Golden Bowl,* with the roles reversed, or like the Norwegian-born Ole Rölvaag, whose *Giants in the Earth* portrayed the spiritual rather than the physical cost of transplanting— Horgan is fascinated by the spectacle of the clash (perhaps only the juxtaposition) of cultures on the same physical stage. In the Spanish Southwest it was a clash which, sometimes ostentatiously, more often unconsciously, found expression in moral rather than in physical conflicts. How does it happen, so Horgan speculates, that the same environment can inspire and exalt spiritual values in one people and corrupt these in others; how does it happen that the same challenges posed by Nature, or by History, can exalt or degrade? He is not wholly prepared to accept the familiar and almost orthodox explanation that

> *No villain need be! Passions spin the plot:*
> *We are betrayed by what is false within.*

It is the nature and the ambiguity of that "betrayal" that fascinated Horgan, as it did Henry James. Horgan sees the betrayal as both personal and social. The personal betrayal is the product, more often than not, of confusions and pressures over which the individual has little control. The social betrayal, in turn, is the product of larger social and economic forces—ambition, greed, passion, racial and national animosities—which impose on both the individual and society a persuasive though false morality. It is the interaction of these dark forces which provides the warp and the woof of so many of Paul Horgan's novels. What are called for here—and what Horgan provides, as in his way Henry James did as well—are understanding and charity. He knows that as men and women are confronted by conflicting loyalties, choices are rarely clear, and he knows, too, that as even the wicked cannot wholly escape the imperatives of a moral society, so those who are committed to virtue and purity cannot escape the pressures of an immoral society, and that a resolution of the most profound moral problems does not so much solve those problems as enable life to go on with them unresolved.

Horgan is generous enough not to impose his standards on mankind, but he is quite prepared to impose them upon himself, and upon those who are the purveyors and the guardians of culture. This attitude is explicit in those aphorisms which, he tells us, "reflect his interest in the artist's own vision, and the inexhaustible legacy of the past." He calls these aphorisms *Approaches to Writing*. They are really not so much approaches as principles, and they are principles relevant not just to writing but to conduct. They conjure up the maxims of a La Rochefoucauld, and, like these, they tell us a good deal about the author. Consider a few (and he has, alas, given us only a few here). "There is no essential difference," he tells us, "between running after fashionable persons and running after fashionable ideas: both are harmless diversions, and either may feed satire"— but he refrains from the satire. Or again, he laments that "the public taste in the United States is so offensive—Muzak, commercial architecture, comic strips, rock music, most television, radio, movies, pornography, that it is enough to raise serious doubts about the stylistic trustworthiness of democracy." This is an old complaint: one of the central questions which Tocqueville raised about the ability of a democracy to nourish a genuine Culture, and a question still unresolved. Other aphorisms are more positive. Thus, "the genius of the novel is to give an effect of life in large traits and in intimate details," or the observation that "the most valuable writers are those in whom we find not themselves, or ourselves, or the fugitive era of their lifetime, but the common vision of all times"—literary judgments, these, which apply to a Turgenev, or a Henry James and, in large measure, to a Paul Horgan.

This bountiful anthology celebrates fifty years of contributions to American history, literature, art, and life. In the prodigious volume of those contributions, in the catholicity of interests which they reflect, in the literary qualities they illustrate and the moral standards they exalt, in their contributions to an understanding of the national culture, in their generosity and magnanimity, they constitute a national treasure—a phrase which applies with equal validity to Paul Horgan himself.

Foreword

In the sixth decade of my life as a writer I have taken a retrospective view of the various modes in which I have worked. For the groupings that make up this volume—history, biography, essay, short story, novel—I have selected what seem to me representative excerpts not only of the individual works from which they are drawn but of the general course of my writing. Out of the twoscore volumes I have published, I have chosen from thirteen titles: in some cases, passages from long books; in others, shorter works entire. Considerations of space obliged me to omit selections from a number of other books I should have liked to include.

In my adolescent years I knew a unifying experience of several arts, all of which I practiced blithely without any sense of contradiction among them—writing, painting, music, and theatre; and it amazed me when members of my family and other well-wishers, frightened of the arts as matters of vocation (though decidedly not in terms of appreciation), made foreboding sounds about the precariousness of scattered interests. But it was to writing that I returned most often, and at the age of twenty-one I made it my life work.

The soundings of American experience that I have taken in history, biography, or fiction have reflected my own life in America both East and West; and I can only be grateful for a personal heritage rich in two broadly distinctive aspects of our national culture. It has always seemed to me that the subjects of my books were in a sense bestowed on me by right of that lyric spirit which affirms, whether in comedy and caricature, or through a sense of life that transcends the tragic by the very recognition of it.

The selections here, with only the most minor of corrections, stand as first published, and with the addition, where sense requires, of a few preliminary lines to induct the reader into situations already off and running.

Middletown, Connecticut   P. H.
June 1983

I

HISTORY

Great River: The Rio Grande in North American History

PROLOGUE

... Since I offered to narrate the story,
I shall start at the beginning, which is as follows.

—PEDRO DE CASTAÑEDA, OF NÁXERA

1. CREATION

Space.

Abstract movement.

The elements at large.

Over warm seas the air is heavy with moisture. Endlessly the vast delicate act of evaporation occurs. The seas yield their essence to the air. Sometimes it is invisible, ascending into the upper atmosphere. Sometimes it makes a shimmer in the calm light that proceeds universally from the sun. The upper heavens carry dust—sea dust of salt evaporated from ocean spray, and other dust lingering from volcanic eruption, and the lost dust of shooting stars that wear themselves out against the atmosphere through which they fly, and dust blown up from earth by wind. Invisibly the volume of sea moisture and dust is taken toward land by prevailing winds; and as it passes over the coast, a new condition arises—the wind-borne mass reflects earth temperatures, that change with the earth forms inland from the sea.

Moving rapidly, huge currents of air carrying their sea burdens repeat tremendously in their unseen movement the profile of the land forms over which they pass. When land sweeps up into a mountain, the laden air mass rolling upon it must rise and correspond in shape.

And suddenly that shape is made visible; for colder air above the mountain causes moisture to condense upon the motes of dust in the warm air wafted from over the sea; and directly in response to the presence and inert power of the mountain, clouds appear. The two volumes—invisible warm air, immovable cold mountain—continue to meet and repeat their joint creation of cloud. Looking from afar calm and eternal, clouds enclose forces of heat and cold, wind and inert matter that conflict immensely. In such continuing turbulence, cloud motes collide, cling together, and in the act condense a new particle of moisture. Heavier, it falls from cold air through warmer. Colliding with other drops, it grows. As the drops, colder than earth, warmer than the cloud they left, fall free of cloud bottom into clear air, it is raining.

Rain and snow fall to the earth, where much runs away on the surface; but roots below ground and the dense nerve system of grasses and the preservative cover of forest floors detain the runoff, so that much sky moisture goes underground to storage, even through rock; for rock is not solid, and through its pores and cracks and sockets precipitation is saved. The storage fills; and nearing capacity, some of its water reappears at ground level as springs which find upward release through the pores of the earth just as originally it found entry. A flowing spring makes its own channel in which to run away. So does the melt from snow clinging to the highest mountain peaks. So does the sudden, brief sheet of storm water. Seeking always to go lower, the running water of the land struggles to fulfill its blind purpose—to find a way over, around, or through earth's fantastic obstacles back to the element which gave it origin, the sea.

In this cycle a huge and exquisite balance is preserved. Whatever the amount of its element the sea gives up to the atmosphere by evaporation, the sea regains exactly the same amount from the water which falls upon the earth and flows back to its source.

This is the work, and the law, of rivers.

2. GAZETTEER

Out of such vast interaction between ocean, sky, and land, the Rio Grande rises on the concave eastern face of the Continental

Divide in southern Colorado. There are three main sources, about two and a half miles high, amidst the cordilleran ice fields. Flowing from the west, the river proper is joined by two confluents—Spring Creek from the north, and the South Fork. The river in its journey winds eastward across southern Colorado, turns southward to continue across the whole length of New Mexico which it cuts down the middle, turns southeastward on reaching Mexico, and with one immense aberration from this course—the Big Bend—runs on as the boundary between Texas and Mexico, ending at the Gulf of Mexico.

In all its career the Rio Grande knows several typical kinds of landscape, some of which are repeated along its great length. It springs from tremendous mountains, and intermittently mountains accompany it for three-fourths of its course. It often lies hidden and inaccessible in canyons, whether they cleave through mountains or wide level plains. From such forbidding obscurities it emerges again and again into pastoral valleys of bounty and grace. These are narrow, at the most only a few miles wide; and at the least, a bare few hundred yards. In such fertile passages all is green, and the shade of cottonwoods and willows is blue and cool, and there is reward for life in water and field. But always visible on either side are reaches of desert, and beyond stand mountains that limit the river's world. Again, the desert closes against the river, and the gritty wastelands crumble into its very banks, and nothing lives but creatures of the dry and hot; and nothing grows but desert plants of thirsty pod, or wooden stem, or spiny defense. But at last the river comes to the coastal plain where an ancient sea floor reaching deep inland is overlaid by ancient river deposits. After turbulence in mountains, bafflement in canyons, and exhaustion in deserts, the river finds peaceful delivery into the sea, winding its last miles slowly through marshy bends, having come nearly one thousand nine hundred miles from mountains nearly three miles high. After the Mississippi–Missouri system, it is the longest river in the United States.

Along its way the Rio Grande receives few tributaries for so long a river. Some are sporadic in flow. Reading downstream, the major tributaries below those of the source are Rock Creek, Alamosa Creek, Trinchera Creek, and the Conejos River in Colorado; in New Mexico, the Red River, the Chama River, and four great draws that are generally dry except in storm when they pour wild volumes of silt into the main channel—Galisteo Creek, the Jemez River, Rio

Puerco, and Rio Salado; and in Texas and Mexico, the Rio Conchos (which renews the river as it is about to die in the desert), the Pecos River, the Devil's River, (another) Rio Salado, and Rio San Juan. The river commonly does not carry a great volume of water, and in some places, year after year, it barely flows, and in one or two it is sometimes dry. Local storms will make it rush for a few hours; but soon it is down to its poor level again. Even at its high sources the precipitation averages only five inches year-round. At its mouth, the rainfall averages in the summer between twenty and thirty inches, but there the river is old and done, and needs no new water. In January, at the source the surface temperature is fourteen degrees on the average, and in July fifty degrees. At the mouth in the same months the averages read fifty and sixty-eight. In the mountainous north the river is clear and sparkling, in the colors of obsidian, with rippling folds of current like the markings on a trout. Once among the pastoral valleys and the desert bench terraces that yield silt, the river is ever after the color of the earth that it drags so heavily in its shallow flow.

Falling from so high to the sea, and going so far to do it, the river with each of its successive zones encounters a new climate. Winter crowns the source mountains almost the whole year round, in the longest season of cold in the United States. The headwaters are free of frost for only three months out of the year, from mid-June to mid-September. Where the river carves its way through the mesas of northern New Mexico, the seasons are temperate. Entering the Texas desert, the river finds perennial warmth that rises in summer to blasting heat. At its end, the channel wanders under the heavy moist air of the tropics, mild in winter, violently hot in summer.

3. CYCLE

Landscape is often seen as static; but it never is static. From its first rock in the sky to its last embrace by the estuary at the sea, the river has been surrounded by forces and elements constantly moving and dynamic, interacting to produce its life and character. It has taken ocean and sky; the bearing of winds and the vagary of temperature; altitude and tilt of the earth's crust; underground waters and the spill of valleys and the impermeable texture of deserts; the cover of plants and the uses of animals; the power of gravity and the perishability of rock; the thirst of things that grow; and the need of the sea to create the Rio Grande.

The main physical circumstances of the Rio Grande seem timeless and impersonal. They assume meaning only in terms of people who came to the river.

BOOK ONE

The Indian Rio Grande

THE STUFF OF LIFE

FORMS

There in that long stretch of New Mexico valley (which even so was but one-seventh of the whole length of the river) the Pueblo Indians ordered the propriety of their life to the landscape that surrounded them. This act was implicit in all their sacred beliefs. It recognized the power, nearness, and blaze of the sky; the clarity of the air; the colors of the earth; the sweep of mountain, rock, plain; and the eternity of the river. Environment directly called forth the spirit and the creations of the people. The weather had direct effects upon vegetable growth, and the life of waterways, and the change in land forms. It had equally direct effect upon the human personality and its various states and views of life. The presence of mountains; the altitude of the very valley itself; the outlying deserts beyond; the effects created by the interchange of influence and response between that particular land and that particular sky—all had effect and expression in the Pueblo world.

The natural forms rising from a landscape created by surface water action, and wind, and volcanic fury—that is to say, river, desert, and mountain—bore intimate fruits in their imitation by the forms of Pueblo life. The cave became a room. The room became part of a butte. The butte, joined with others like it, resembled a mesa, terraced and stepped back. The Pueblo town looked like a land form directly created by the forces that made hills and arroyos and deserts. Daylight upon the face of a pueblo looked the same as daylight upon the face of a cliff. Who knew how much this was accidental, and how much devised by the Indian in his sense of propriety in the natural world, his reverence for all its aspects, and his general application in imitative symbols of all the living and enduring forms he knew about him? Even where his town stood above the river, the river dictated his farming methods; for the irrigation ditch leading from the river to the fields below the town was in itself but a tiny river in form, with the same general laws of flow, and reach, and structure as the big river. People not too long the owners of such a concept would not find it a naïve one, to be taken for granted. It would instead be a grave and reassuring fact, to be thankful for along with all of the other energetic expressions of the landscape, among which the Pueblo Indian prayed passionately to be included as a proper part— not a dominant part, not a being whose houses and inventions and commerce would subject the physical world until he rose above it as its master; but as a living spirit with material needs whose modest satisfaction could be found and harmonized with those of all other elements, breathing or still, in the dazzling openness all about him, with its ageless open secrets of solitude, sunlight, and impassive land.

So every act and relationship of Pueblo life included the intention to find and fulfill such harmony. The whole environment found its way by spiritual means into all of Pueblo life. Works of art captured the animal and vegetable and spiritual world—always in objects meant for use, never display for its own sake. The work of art, in the sense that all elements were brought together—colors, emotions, ideas, attitudes—in harmonious proportion and mixed with fluent skill, the work of art was the act of living, itself. No one part of it had significance alone, just as each feature of the landscape by itself meant less than what all meant and looked like together.

Worship entered into every relation between the people and their surroundings. The mountains were holy places; temples standing forever which held up the sky. Gods lived in them, and other supernaturals. The priests of the people went to the mountains to call upon the deities of the four points of the compass. The various pueblo groups identified their sacred mountains differently. For one of them, the northern one was Truchas Peak; the eastern one was the Lake Peak of the Santa Fe range; the southern one was the Sandia range, which they called Okupi^n, turtle mountain; the western one was Santa Clara Peak of the Jemez range, which they called the mountain covered with obsidian. All of them rose far back and above the Rio Grande, into whose valley they all eventually shed water.

The action of the river upon land forms was recognized at times by the Indians. Near the pueblo of San Ildefonso is a great black mesa on the west of the river, faced across the river on the east by high ground. This place they called P'o-woge, "where the water cut through." In the midst of supernatural explanations of natural conditions this was suddenly a cool and observant conclusion; not, however, to the disadvantage of another idea, which was that in the great cave on the north side of the black mesa there once lived (they said) a cannibal giant. His cave was connected with the interior of the vast, houselike mesa by tunnels which took him to his rooms. His influence upon the surrounding country was heavy. Persons did the proper things to avoid being caught and eaten by him.

Lakes and springs were sacred too, and natural pools. They were doorways to the world below. If everything originally "came up" with the people through the sacred lake Shi-pap, the same action could be imagined for other such bodies of water. Many of these were springs which fed the river. Gods and heroes were born out of springs, and ever afterward came and went between the above and below worlds through their pools. Every pueblo had sacred springs somewhere nearby. There was every reason to sanctify them— physical, as life depended upon water; spiritual, as they had natural mystery which suggested supernatural qualities; for how could it be that when water fell as rain, or as snow, and ran away, or dried up, there should be other water which came and came, secretly and sweetly, out of the ground and never failed?

Some of the rivers that went into the Rio Grande dried up for months at a time. In the Pueblo world, the most important tributaries were Taos, Santa Cruz, Pojoaque, Santa Fe, and Galisteo Creeks on the east, and on the west, Jemez Creek, the Chama River. Of these, only the last one had perennial flow. Its waters were red in melting season and colored the Rio Grande for many miles below their confluence. But the courses of them all bore the valley cottonwood. It was the dominant and most useful tree in all the Pueblo country. Its wood was soft and manageable, and it supplied material for many objects. Its silver bark, its big, varnished leaves sparkling in the light of summer and making caverns of shade along the banks, its winter-hold of leaves the color of beaten thin gold lasting in gorgeous bounty until the new catkins of spring—all added grace to the pueblo world. The columnar trunks were used to make tall drums, hollowed out and resonated with skins stretched over the open ends. The wood was hot fuel, fast-burning, leaving a pale, rich ash of many uses. Even the catkins had personal use—eaten raw, they were a bitter delicacy in some towns. And in that arid land, any tree, much less a scattered few, or a bounteous grove, meant good things—water somewhere near, and shade, and shelter from the beating sun, and talk from trifling leaves.

The feeling, the sense, of a place was real and important to the people. Almost invariably for their towns they chose sites of great natural beauty. The special charm of a place was often commemorated in what they named it. On the river's west bank stood a pueblo called Yu^{n}ge, which meant "Western mockingbird place." The name was a clue to the sense of the place, for above its graces of flowing water, rippling groves, and the high clear valley with its open skies would rise the memory of the May nights when the prodigal songs of the mockingbirds year after year sounded all night long in the moonlight. The birds sang so loudly as to awaken people from sleep. Night after night a particular voice seemed to come from the very same tree with the same song. It was like a blessing so joyful that it made an awakened sleeper laugh with delight, listening to that seasonal creature of the river's life. In the daytime little boys on rooftops caught moths which also appeared in May and whistling to the mockingbirds released the moths which the birds in an accurate swoop caught in midair with their bills.

Everything in the landscape was sacred, whether the forms of nature, or those made by people—altars, shrines, and the very towns which were like earth arisen into wall, terrace, light and shadow, enclosing and expressing organized human life.

PERSONALITY AND DEATH

Imprisoned in their struggle with nature, the people sought for an explanation of the personality they knew in themselves and felt all about them, and came to believe in a sorcery so infinitely distributed among all objects and creatures that no act or circumstance of life was beyond suspicion as evil or destructive. Neighbors might be trusted; but they had also to be watched in secret, for who knew who among them might finally turn out to be a witch? If every object, every animal, every man and woman quivered with the same unseen personal spirit, to whom prayers might be said, and of whom in anxiety blessings could be asked, then they could also and with terrible swiftness turn out to be agents for evil. Long ago, they said, the young war gods Masewi and Oyoyewi, the powerful twins, lived among the people, and protected them by killing witches and giants. Nature was vast and people were little and danger was everywhere. But (in the universal canon of faith which brings to every Goliath his David) there was the very cast of hope in the people who imagined their survival and triumph in the midst of menace, then willed it, and even by implausible means achieved it.

But at great cost.

Anyone suspected of sorcery was put to death, often in secret, often by individuals acting without formal sanction. What would identify a witch? A vagrant idea in someone's head; a dream (for dreams were always seen as truth, as actual life encountered by the spirit freed from the sleeping body); a portent in nature; perhaps a conspicuous act, aspect, or statement, anything too unusual, too imaginative in unfamiliar terms; persistent misfortune or sickness among the people which must be blamed upon someone—the notion could come from anywhere. If only one or two people knew of the witch, he might be secretly killed. If everyone suspected him and knew about him, he would be accused and pressed to confess. In their search for a victim the people sometimes fixed upon an ancient person who had outlived his family and, obtaining a confession through torture, exiled him to another pueblo or simply killed him. Sometimes people in one town would discover a witch in another town who was causing them grief, and would murder him virtuously. Retaliation, inspired by the highest motives, would follow. The killing of witches at times reached such numbers that whole towns were nearly wiped out by it.

Otherwise believers in peace, and calm, measured life, the people sanctioned their only outbreak of violence in connection with punishment of witches, whose machinations, they said, threatened the communal safety of life. Was that very communality itself an expression not so much of the dignity of men and women as their fear—a fear which put them always on guard, created a propriety of the commonplace, and held as its core a poisonous distrust of one another? The old people told the children that no one could know the hearts of men: there were bad people—witches—everywhere. Evil resided in them, and never came from the gods. The gods were exempted from doubt or blame. All believed so and, believing, all

Salem Academy and College
Gramley Library
Winston-Salem, N.C. 27108

followed the same superstitions in the same strength of mind. Such strong beliefs, laced through with such compelling fears, created a personality common to the people as a whole.

Men went out during the night to encounter the spirits at sacred sites. They went in fear and returned trembling, whatever their experience, for they went to garner omens for themselves. Going home from the shrine they must not look behind them, no matter what might seem to be following them. They would consider gravely before they would tell what they had encountered, for what had been gained could be lost if not kept secret. It would not be a sin to tell—there was no guilt in the people since they were not responsible for what nature did to them—but in telling a secret, new power against menace might be lost. Ordeals were spiritual rather than physical. Endurance of torture was demanded only of witches.

The personality had many private faces, each with a new name. A man had his name given at birth as a child of the sun. When he joined a kiva, he received another, and another when he entered any organization, and he was nicknamed after his various duties and kinds of work. The personality was renewed and purified by ritual acts, such as vomiting. Before all ceremonial dances, all taking part were required to vomit in the early morning for four days (four was a powerful number in all ways). They said that those who vomited breathed differently from those who had not. "After you vomit four days you're *changed*." A man thus purged left the daily world and entered the supernatural.

The personality was clever. A man prowling in hostile country wore sandals made of wooden hoops wound with thongs of rabbit-skin. His footprints were round; from them, he was sure, nobody would tell which way he was coming or going.

The personality could be shared: images of men or animals were made in gestures of menace, to frighten trespassers away from property.

And the personality was vain, for the people of this town looked down upon the people of that town, saying that those others did not hunt so well, or farm, or fight, or sing, or dance, or race, so well as we do, the poor crazy things, with their silly ways, and their bad imitations of what we do which they stole by watching us secretly. But this was a pitying superiority, without anger or quarrel.

The most immediate medium of personality was talk. The people of the river world did not all speak the same language, but were divided into two general groups, Keres and Tewa, each of which had its localized variations. But all derived from the same mother tongue long ago far in Mexico, and ventured northward with the farming people and their maize. In spite of differences in language the river pueblos with minor local variations lived under much the same beliefs, customs, and ways of work. Their language was expressive and exact. The men spoke it with voices that seemed to try to escape from smothering. They formed some words deep in the throat. Others were framed lightly on the lips. Some ideas were given through little pauses in a series of sounds, and a tiny round-mouthed silence became eloquent. Their words were never written even though in Mexico the mother tongue of the Aztec people was used in written form. The pueblo people taught all their knowledge by word of mouth. The greatest body of it had to do with ceremony and ritual. "One who knows how"—that was a man of power who remembered all that had been told to him. For the dances those "who knew how" had to memorize tremendous amounts of ritual, word-perfectly. Such men showed great powers of mind which their life in other directions hardly equalled. The great movements of time and the seasons, the acts of life and work, the inherited stories of the gods, the forms of prayers, all had to be stored in mind, along with their many variations and combinations, until a vast body of knowledge rested trembling and precarious on the spoken thread of the generations that was spun from elder to youth. Thus, even the act of literature was not individual but cooperative, since it took one to tell, and another or more to listen, and remember. Much of what was so recorded in memory was to be kept secret among those "who knew how." If a man betrayed them, he was punished. The war captains put him naked within a circle drawn upon the ground. He must not lie down, but stand or sit. If he moved to step across the circle he was shot with arrows by the captains.

People within a language group visited one another's towns. Before he went, a man had his hair washed by the women of his family before sunrise, and his body bathed in yucca suds. They gave him a new name for his venture. At the end of his journey, if he found a friend awaiting him, he took his hand and breathed upon it, and clasping it with both hands lifted it toward the sky without words, for joy muted his speech.

"May I live so long," prayed the people, "that I may fall asleep of old age." The personality ended with death and had to be exorcised from living memory, and become one with all ancestry, impersonal, benign, and beyond fear. When a man lay dying among his relatives they sent for the doctors of the curing society that combated witches. Then doctors came and undressed the dying man to examine him carefully. If he was already dead, they put a cotton blanket over him. His people brought all his clothes to the doctors, who tore little holes in each garment to let its life, too, escape and leave the dead cloth. They folded the arms of the dead across his breast, tying his wrists together. His legs they closed up against his body. They wrapped him in this huddled position with cotton blankets. His clothes were included. A feather robe was folded about him next, and lastly, a yucca matting was bundled over all, and tied with a woman's sash. Crouched in silence within its wrappings the body was a restatement of the attitude of birth, when the unborn infant was folded within the womb; and bound by a mother's cincture to the womb of all it was now returned. The doctors rinsed their mouths and washed their hands, saying to each other,

"Now he is gone."

"Yes, he is gone back to Shipapu."

"The place from where all emerged."

"He is gone back to Shipapu."

The family took the body out of doors to burial in the open ground, or in a rocky crevice, or in a midden. With it were placed water and food. The food was cooked, so the dead could feed on its aroma. The dead man's turquoises, his weapons, his tools were buried with him, for he was now about to set out on his journey to the underworld from which all life had come, and his spirit would need the spirits of all such articles to use in the life that awaited him. He was on his way to be one with the gods themselves. At the end of his journey he would take up again what he did in the world, whether as hunter, farmer, priest, or dancer.

Four days after his burial, his personality was finally expunged with ceremony. The doctors returned to his house and arranged an altar on which they laid sacred ears of corn, bear paws, a medicine bowl, and kachinas. They sang songs and ceremonially cooked food for the ghost to smell. They made a painting on the floor with colored corn meal. He was gone, and to confirm this and help him where he now would be forever, they made a bundle of offerings containing moccasins in which he might journey, a dancer's kilt and turtle-shell rattle and parrot feathers and necklace which he might use to start rain from the ghostly world. They buried this out of doors. Underground, he would find it. Doctors then dipped eagle feathers into the medicine bowl on the altar and sprinkled the meal painting, the sacred implements, and the people. They swept the walls of the dead man's room with the eagle feathers to brush away his spirit, and they went to other houses where he had last been seen and did the same. Returning to the house of the ghost, they sang again, and all settled down to a feast provided by the family. A few morsels were thrown aside by the doctors for the spirits. At the end of the repast, the doctors arose and were given finely ground grain for their services. They destroyed the painting and took up its colored meal in a cloth which they gave to a woman, who carried it to the river. There she threw it into the water which for all his life had flowed by the dead man, had sustained him, purified him, and which now took away his last sign forever, through the shade of cottonwoods and into the sweet blue light of distant mountains beyond the pale desert.

BOOK TWO
The Spanish Rio Grande

POSSESSION

Late one morning in April 1598, a party of eight armed and mounted men came to the river from the south through heavy groves of cottonwoods. They were emaciated and wild with thirst. On seeing the water they lost their wits, men and horses alike, and threw themselves into it bodily. The current was swift. Two of the horses thundered far out into the stream and were carried away and drowned. Two others drank so much so fast that, as they staggered to the bank from the shallows, their bellies broke open and they died.

The men drank and drank in the river. They took the water in through their skins and they cupped it to their mouths and swollen tongues and parched throats. When they could drink no more they went to the dry banks and fell down upon the cool sand under the shade of the big trees. In their frenzied appetite for survival itself, they had become bloated and deformed, and they lay sprawled in exhaustion and excess. One of their company, looking upon himself and them, said they were all like drunkards abandoned on the floor of an inn, and that they looked more like toads than like men.

Numbed with simple creature pleasures they took their ease in the shade. In the bounteous trees overhead many birds sang. There were bees in the wild flowers of spring, and the surviving horses grazed in nearby meadows. The river looked calm and peaceful. All such sounds and sights were deeply restful to the squad of men. Their clothes were ragged, their boots were worn through, and their bellies were hungry; for they had come for fifty days through deserts with thorns, mountains with rocks, and nothing to eat but roots and weeds. For the last five days they had not had a drop of water. In finding the river, they not only saved their lives; they fulfilled their assignment—to break a new trail to the Rio del Norte from the south, that would bypass the Junta de los Rios, to bring the colony directly to its New Mexican kingdom with one hundred and thirty families, two hundred and seventy single men, eighty-three wagons and carts, eleven Franciscan friars, seven thousand cattle herded by drovers on foot, and all commanded by the Governor, Captain General and Adelantado Don Juan de Oñate.

The little advance detachment was headed by Vicente de Zaldívar, sergeant major of the colony, and nephew of the Governor. Among his seven men was Captain Don Gaspar Pérez de Villagrá, from Salamanca, a former courtier of King Philip II, and a scholar with a classical education who later wrote the history of the colony's first year in thirty-four rhymed Vergilian cantos. When they set out on their mission, Villagrá said, they were all without scientific knowledge of the heavens by which to set their course. He doubted if there was one among them who, "once the sun had set, could with certainty say, 'There is east, there is west.'" They marched with hunger and thirst and once were captured by Indians, who freed them unharmed, having enjoyed their fright. But with the next dawn the eight Spaniards charged the large camp of their tormentors from all sides, firing their arms, and scattering all but a handful of Indians, whom they captured, holding two as guides, releasing the others. Now they also had rations—venison, badger, rabbit meat, along with herbs and roots. They moved on to the north, again running out of water. The guides brought them to six shallow water holes where all horses and men drank selfishly and greedily but one—Zaldívar, the leader, who waited till all were done, at the risk of there being no water left; then last in turn by his own choice, he drank his fill. Advancing over a plain where they could see far, they asked the guides where lay the river they sought? One did not understand. The other smoothed the ground and at once drew a circle, and "marked the four cardinal points . . . the two oceans, the islands, mountains, and the course of the river we sought. He seemed to act with the knowledge and experience of an expert cosmographer. As we watched him it seemed as though he was tracing the Arctic and Antarctic seas, the signs of the Zodiac, and even the degrees and parallels. He marked the different towns of New Mexico and the road we should follow and where along the journey we should find water. He then explained to us the direction we should take and where we would be able to ford the mighty river." It was reassuring to have such a guide; but by the next day the Indians had escaped and the Spaniards were adrift in the desert, "trusting in God to bring us with safety to the river's shore." There was always too much water or too little. They passed through a whole week of uninterrupted rain; and then there was thirst again, like that of the last five days that brought them to the river.

But now they rested and recovered their strength. They fished in the river, and shot ducks and geese, and on April 20, saw with pride and joy the best results of their efforts, for then arrived the mounted vanguard of the main body, led by the Governor. The wagons and the herds were following more slowly. That evening the trail blazers and the Governor's great cavalcade celebrated their meeting with a feast. They built a roaring fire, and in it roasted meat and fish. Afterward there were speeches. The Sergeant Major described the adventures of his little party. The Governor then rose to tell of all that his people had endured, and they listened thirstily to his accounts of their heroism, and knew all over again the burning days, the cold nights, the thorns, the hunger, the fear, the bewildered privation of children, the courage of women, and the power of prayer to bring them rain when they were parched. At the end of his speech, the Governor was pleased to make them all a gift which only he could make. It was a whole day of rest in which all might do as they wished, to recover themselves before the journey up the river was resumed.

On April 26 the rest of the expedition arrived. All were re-

united, and moved together up the south bank of the river a few
more leagues.

There was a sense of great occasion in this arrival and encampment at the Rio del Norte. The wastes of northern Mexico were
behind them all now, and the path to the north was more familiar
from this point on. To select the ford to the north bank the Sergeant
Major detailed a party of five men, all good swimmers. They found
a shallow wide place, and returning to make their report met with
an Indian encampment where four friendly Indians agreed to return
with them. The Governor received the Indian visitors, gave them
clothes and many gifts to take back to their people. It was not long
before the Indians were back again, with many of their friends,
bringing fish in quantities, which were welcome for the celebrations
and feasts that were approaching. The river flowed through the gates
of the kingdom of New Mexico. The army would enter through them
only after suitable observances.

Under a river grove they built an altar. There on the morning
of the last day of April in the presence of the whole army and the
families, a solemn High Mass was sung by the Franciscan priests.
Candle flames dipped and shone in the dappled shady light under
the trees that let moving discs of sunlight in upon the gold-laced
vestments, the bent heads of the people, their praying hands. At Mass
the Father Commissary, Fray Alonso Martínez, preached a learned
sermon.

After Mass came an entertainment. It was a play composed for
the occasion by Captain Don Marcos Farfán de los Godos, who came
from Seville and in his forty years had seen much of the theatre.
He understood the drama as a habit of occasion, a proper part of
any festival. He was a man of good stature, with a chestnut-colored
beard, and his sense of amenity was becoming to a soldier who was
also a colonist. His play, hurriedly prepared and rehearsed, showed
how the Franciscan fathers came to New Mexico; crossed the land,
so; met the poor savages, so; who were gentle and friendly, and came
on their knees, thus, asking to be converted; and how the missionaries
then baptized them in great throngs. So the colony showed to themselves a great purpose of their toil. The audience adjourned in high
spirits to prepare for the next episode of the celebrations.

Men with horses now went to mount, and came in formation
shining with arms, armor, and all their richest dress. The rest of the
colony took up formal ranks, and when all was ready the Governor

came forward accompanied by the crucifer, the standard-bearer, the trumpeters, and the royal secretary of the expedition to perform the most solemn of acts.

All knew what a great man the Governor was. He was supposed to be one of the five richest men in Mexico. His father the Count de Oñate had been a governor before him—in New Galicia. During the four years of preparations, delays, starts, and stops which the expedition had already endured, they said the Governor had spent one million dollars of his own fortune, for salaries, supplies, equipment, and running expenses. The Governor was magnificent on both sides of his household, for his wife was a granddaughter of the Marquis of the Valley, Cortés, the conqueror; and the great-granddaughter of the Emperor Montezuma himself. Her father was Don Pedro de Tovar, who had gone and returned with Coronado. As a child she must have heard him tell of his adventures in the north. All such great connections were matters of pride to the colony, but since opinion was always divided in human affairs, there were those who had heard things. They said the Governor had squandered and mismanaged his great patrimony, so that he actually owed more than thirty thousand dollars, all of it borrowed in bad faith, with the creditors evaded by tricks ever since. Everybody knew he was only a private individual, and thus had no place in the government to command respect for him. How would anybody obey him? In fact, once before, leading soldiers, he had been treated disrespectfully and disobeyed. Would anybody but wastrels and thugs enlist to go with him? But for all such opinion there was plenty of the opposite, which held that the delays and frustrations that had so many times during the past four years prevented the Governor from actually marching forth with his army had come from the Devil, whose purpose it was to prevent the colony from going to convert the heathen Indians, and it was plain that those who worked against the Governor worked for the Prince of Darkness. Many said that nobody was better fitted for the command than the Governor, with his virtue, his human understanding, and the nobility of his character; his efficiency and his place in the affections of the soldiers; and the fact that he was the son of his father, who was the beloved "refuge of soldiers and poor gentlemen in this kingdom."

When he now came forward to face the army and with them all to signalize their common achievement, all hearts lifted to him in unity. He was a fine-looking man in middle life, wearing one of his six complete suits of armor. He held many closely written pages of parchment on which were written over three thousand words of solemn proclamation. Bareheaded, in the presence of the cross and the royal standard, he began to read aloud.

He invoked the trinity in "the one and only true God . . . creator of the heavens and earth . . . and of all creatures . . . from the highest cherubim to the lowliest ant and the smallest butterfly." He called upon the Holy Mother of God and upon St. Francis. He set forth the legal basis of his authority, and declared, ". . . finding myself on the banks of the Rio del Norte, within a short distance from the first settlements of New Mexico, which are found along this river . . . I desire to take possession of this land this 30th day of April, the feast of the Ascension of Our Lord, in the year fifteen hundred and ninety-eight. . . ." He commemorated the Franciscan martyrs of earlier years up the river, and showed how their work must be taken up and continued. Turning to other purposes of his colony, he listed many—the "need for correcting and punishing the sins against nature and against humanity that exist among these bestial nations"; and the desirable ends "that these people may be bettered in commerce and trade; that they may gain better ideas of government; that they may augment the number of their occupations and learn the arts, become tillers of the soil and keep livestock and cattle, and learn to live like rational beings, clothe their naked; govern themselves with justice and be able to defend themselves from their enemies. . . . All these objects I shall fulfill even to the point of death, if need be. I command now and will always command that these objects be observed under penalty of death." Mentioning the presence of his reverend fathers and of his officers, and the name of the King, he declared:

"Therefore . . . I take possession, once, twice, and thrice, and all the times I can and must, of the . . . lands of the said Rio del Norte, without exception whatsoever, with all its meadows and pasture grounds and passes . . . and all other lands, pueblos, cities, villas, of whatsoever nature now founded in the kingdom and province of New Mexico . . . and all its native Indians. . . . I take all jurisdiction, civil as well as criminal, high as well as low, from the edge of the mountains to the stones and sand in the rivers, and the leaves of the trees. . . ."

He then turned and took the cross beside him, and advancing to a tree he nailed the cross to it and knelt down to pray, "O holy cross, divine gate of heaven and altar of the only and essential sacrifice of the blood and body of the Son of God, pathway of saints and emblem of their glory, open the gates of heaven to these infidels. Found churches and altars where the body and blood of the Son of God may be offered in sacrifice; open to us a way of peace and safety for their conversion, and give to our king and to me, in his royal name, the peaceful possession of these kingdoms and provinces. Amen."

And the royal secretary then read his certification of the deed, and the trumpets blew a tremendous voluntary, and the harquebusiers fired a salute together, and the Governor planted with his own hands the royal standard in the land near the river.

COLLECTIVE MEMORY

SOURCES

Brown plains and wide skies joined by far mountains would always be the image of home to them, the image of Spain that rose like a castle to inland heights from the slopes of the Mediterranean, and gave to the offshore wind the fragrance of ten thousand wild flowers that mariners smelled out at sea.

The home of the Spanish spirit was Rome. When Spain was a province of the Caesarian Empire her promising youths went to Rome, to make a name for themselves, to refresh the life of the capital with the raw sweetness of the country, and to help form the styles of the day in the theatre, like Seneca of Córdoba, and make wit acid as wine, like Martial of Bilbilis, and elevate the public art of speech, like Quintillian from Calahorra, and even become Emperor, like Trajan, the Spanish soldier. Rome gave the Spaniards their law; their feeling for cliff and wall, arch and cave, in building; and their formal display of death in the arena, with its mortal delights, its cynical aesthetic of pain and chance. Martial said it:

> Raptus abit media quod ad aethera taurus harena,
> non fuit hoc artis sed pietatis opus. . . .

A bull, he said, taken up from the center of the arena rises to the skies, and this was not act of art, but of piety . . . It remained an act of passion when Spanish piety turned to Christianity.

It was an empowering piety that grew through fourteen centuries, the last eight of which made almost a settled condition of life out of war with the Moslems of the Spanish peninsula. It was war both holy and political, striving to unify belief and territory. Like all victors the Spaniards bore lasting marks of the vanquished. Perhaps in the Moors they met something of themselves, long quiet in the blood that even before Roman times flowed in Spanish veins from Africa and the East, when the ancient Phoenicians and the Carthaginians voyaged the Latin sea and touched the Spanish shore and seeded its life. From the Moslem enemy in the long strife came certain arts—numbers, the mathematics of the sky, the art of living in deserts, and the virtue of water for pleasure, in fountains, running courses, and tiled cascades. That had style: to use for useless pleasure in an arid land its rarest element.

Hardly had they made their home kingdom secure than the Spaniards put themselves and their faith across the world. They fought the infidel wherever they could find him, they ranged toward the Turk, and the Barbary Coast, and for them an admiral mercenary in 1492 risked sailing west until he might fall over the edge of the world and be lost. But however mockingly he was called a man of dreams, like many such he was a genius of the practical, and as strong in his soul as in his heart; for he believed as his employers believed.

BELIEF

They believed in God, the Father Almighty, Creator of heaven and earth; and in Jesus Christ His only Son their Lord, Who was conceived by the Holy Ghost, born of the Virgin Mary, suffered under Pontius Pilate, was crucified, died and was buried. He descended into hell; the third day He rose again from the dead; He ascended into heaven to sit at the right hand of God the Father Almighty from thence to come to judge the living and the dead. They believed in the Holy Ghost, the Holy Catholic Church, the communion of saints, the forgiveness of sins, the resurrection of the body, and life everlasting. Amen, they said.

So believing, it was a divine company they kept in their daily habit, all, from the monarch to the beggar, the poet to the butcher. The Holy Family and the saints inhabited their souls, thoughts, and words. They believed that, with the love of God, nothing failed; without it, nothing prospered. Fray Juan of the Cross said it for them:

Buscando mis amores,
Iré por esos montes y riberas,
No cogeré las flores,
Ni temeré las fieras,
Y pasaré los fuertes y fronteras.

Thus seeking their love across mountain and strand, neither gathering flowers nor fearing beasts, they would pass fortress and frontier, able to endure all because of their strength of spirit in the companionship of their Divine Lord.

Such belief existed within the Spanish not as a compartment where they kept their worship and faith, but as a condition of their very being, like the touch by which they felt the solid world, and the breath of life they drew until they died. It was the simplest and yet most significant fact about them, and more than any other accounted for their achievement of a new world. With mankind's imperfect material—for they knew their failings, indeed, revelled in them and beat themselves with them and knew death was too good for them if Christ had to suffer so much thorn and lance and nail for them— they yet could strive to fulfill the divine will, made plain to them by the Church. Relief from man's faulty nature could be had only in God. In obedience to Him, they found their greatest freedom, the essential freedom of the personality, the individual spirit in the self, with all its other expressions which they well knew—irony, extravagance, romance, vividness and poetry in speech, and honor, and hard pride.

If they were not large men physically, they were strong, and their bodies which the King commanded and their souls which God commanded were in harmony with any task because both God and King gave the same command. It was agreed that the King held his authority and his crown by the grace of God, communicated to him by the sanction of the Church. This was clear and firm. Thus, when required to serve the King in any official enterprise, great or small, they believed that they would likewise serve God, and had doubled strength from the two sources of their empowerment.

But if the King was divinely sanctioned he was also a man like all; and they knew one another, king and commoner, in the common terms of their humanity. To command, to obey; to serve, to protect— these were duties intermixed as they faced one another. The King

was accountable to the people as well as to God; for they made the
State, and the State was in his care. *Del rey abajo ninguno,* they said
in a proverb: Between us and the King, nobody. So they spoke to him
in parliaments. Representative government began with the Spaniards.
All, noble or commoner, had equality before the law. They greatly
prized learning and respected those who owned it, such as lawyers.
Indeed, the law was almost another faith, with its own rituals and customs, and even its own language, closed to uninitiated eyes and ears.
Learning, being scarce, must also have seemed precious, and beyond
the grasp of many a hungry mind. Yet with other peoples of the
Renaissance, the sixteenth-century Spanish had intimations of world
upon world unfolding, and they could not say what their children
would know except that it would be greater than what they the
fathers knew, watching the children at play with their little puppets
of friars made from bean pods, with the tip broken and hanging
down like a cowl, and showing the uppermost bean like a shaven
head.

THE KING AND FATHER

Not all Spaniards had seen the King, but in every large company
there was always one who had seen him, or knew someone who served
him closely, and remembered much to tell. Anything they could hear
of the King was immensely interesting and important. He was their
pride even as he was their master. He commanded them by the power
of God, and yet, as they were, so was he, a man, their common image,
but with the glory and dignity of the crown over his head, and so,
over theirs. What he was had greatly to do with what they were, as
in all fatherhood. So, his image passed through them to the Indies,
wherever they went, beyond cities and maps, however far along
remote rivers. Even the gossip about great kings created the character of their subjects.

King Charles, who was also the Holy Roman Emperor, lived and
worked in hard bare rooms with no carpets, crowding to the fire in
winter, using the window's sunshine in summer. The doctors of
medicine stated that the humors of moisture and of cold dominated
his quality. His face was fixed in calm, but for his eyes, which moved
and spoke more than his gestures or his lips. His face was pale and
long, the lower lip full and forward, often dry and cracked so that
he kept on it a green leaf to suck. His nose was flat and his brows
were pitted with a raised frown that appeared to suggest a constant

headache. He held his shoulders high as though on guard. He would seem to speak twice, once within and fully, and then outwardly and meagerly. But his eyes showed his mind, brilliant, deep, and always at work. He loved information for its own sake, was always reading, and knew his maps well. They said he saw the Indies better than many who went there, and held positive views on all matters concerning the New World and its conquerors.

But if his opinions were strong, so was his conscience. He said once that it was his nature to be obstinate in sticking to his opinions. A courtier replied that it was but laudable firmness to stick to good opinions. To this the Emperor observed with a sigh that he sometimes stuck to bad ones. Much contemplation rested behind such a remark. He was in poor health for most of his life, and as a result considered himself in many aspects. In his young days he was a beautiful rider, with his light legs and his heavy lifted shoulders. He once liked to hunt bear and boar; but illness and business put an end to it. He worked all day and much of the night, until his supper at midnight, at which he received ambassadors, who were amazed at his appetite. Matters of state went on even then, by candlelight, as the platters were passed, and the baskets of fruit, and the water bowls. He wore his flat black cap, his black Flemish velvet doublet and surcoat with the collar of Germany-dressed marten skins, and his chain of the Golden Fleece. The letters of Cortés from New Spain had good talk in them, and the Emperor later had them published in print.

Whether or not America, so far away, was a matter of policy instead of feeling, Charles required justice for the Indians of the New World. Before 1519 he was sending people to the Indies to study and report to him upon the conditions of the natives. Uppermost was his desire that their souls be saved through Christianity. It was of greater moment that Indians became Christians than that they became Spaniards. So as the conquerors made cities in the New World they made schools, colleges, and universities for the Indians, in which to teach them—often in Latin but more often in the Indian tongues, which the friars learned rapidly—salvation in Christ. The Emperor held that through such salvation all else of life must naturally take its course and would come. He strongly supported the missioners in the Indies, and inspired them and many laymen to build the Church in the New World even as ominous cracks ran up its walls in the Old.

But from the first, and increasingly, another spirit worked against the Indians. The military, the landowners, the civil officials believed that conversion was a proper thing, but once out of the way, let the natives be useful to them in labor and arms. But the priests meant what they preached, just as much as the men of the world meant what they ordered. Both said they served the Crown as it desired to be served. Both appealed to the King.

His Holy Caesarian Catholic Majesty (for so he was addressed in documents) wished to know an all-determining truth. Was the Indian a man, as many claimed? Or was he an animal, as many others insisted? Could he understand Christianity? Did he deserve better than the yoke of slavery?

Commissions investigated, passions rose, and humanity triumphed. The Cardinal Adrian in Spain preached that the Indians were free and must be treated as free men, and given Christianity with Christian gentleness. The Emperor acted, and the laws for the Indies were decreed in that spirit. The Crown gave its approval to the ideals of the missionary priests, who ever afterward, over new land, went with the armies not only to convert but to protect Indians.

When he left Spain for Germany, and after his retirement from the throne in mid-century, the Emperor kept the problem in mind, for he wrote to his son Prince Philip to caution him that he must be vigilant to prevent oppressions and injustices in the Colonies, saying that only through justice were sound business and prosperity possible. It was a cold and impassive statement of policy, but in it (as in the brilliant black-and-white flash of those eyes in his pallid face that found it so difficult otherwise to express itself) true humanity shone behind expediency.

When the Emperor abdicated to become a country gentleman at Yuste near Placencia, there was still much to hear about him, even as he invented ways to pass the time. He made a garden. He designed and fashioned mechanical works, including a hand mill to grind meal, and a marvellous set of little clockwork soldiers that performed military drills. Visitors brought him watches and clocks upon which he delighted to work. The joke went around that one time when he complained of his food, he was told by the majordomo that the only thing that would please his palate then would be a stew of watches. He laughed heartily at this.

From his early days in the Italian campaigns he loved the arts of music and painting. In his military travels, even to Africa, he took along his choir—the best choir in Europe—and pipe organs. His ear was true, he remembered music as well as he did facts, and he loved to sit and listen to a French air, *Mille regrets*. At Placencia he had his nine favorite paintings by Titian with him.

With a few guests in his party, he would go wandering through the woods with his harquebus in hand, watching for game. But the joy he took from this sport in his old age was more that of watching birds, and little animals, and their quick mysterious commerce, than that of killing them. He would shoot now and then, but his friends said that the pigeons pretended out of courtesy to be frightened of his blasts, and perhaps he was an old man hunting for life, not death.

But his piety kept death before him. He was read aloud to from the *Confessions of St. Augustine*, and he could nod in recognition of anybody who turned sharply away from the great world to lead a modest life of outer trifles and inner mysteries of faith and conscience. It was talked of everywhere, for thousands were there, when he had a Requiem Mass sung to rehearse his own funeral. It was just as though it were the actual funeral. There before the altar was the catafalque swept in black draperies and silver lace, with thousands of candles burning at all the altars and shrines, and the prelates and priests singing the pontifical Mass, and the Emperor's wonderful music in the stalls with the organ, and there in the middle of it wearing a black mantle was the Emperor himself, praying for the repose of his soul before it left his body.

The Spaniards knew the same thing in themselves—the strength and the countenance to stare upon contrition and death. For, in their belief, what could anyone do enough to mortify himself, if he was to be worthy of salvation by the sufferings of the Son of Man upon the cross? The Emperor had a flail with which he would whip himself so hard that the thongs showed his blood. After his death it became known that in his will he left this flail to his son Philip, for him to prize all his life and in turn to pass on as a beloved heirloom, a relic of the blood of the father . . .

Philip II spared himself no less, and left his image no less in the Indies, though in somewhat different manner. People missed the occasional humor and grace of the Emperor, even though under him they had had to work just as hard as under his son. But there was as it were a darkening of life that came when the Emperor retired and, dying in retirement, left all power to the new King. But the King demanded more of himself than of anyone else. New Spain and all the other Indies became greater, quieter, richer, and as the conquests receded, the work of government grew enormously. The whole world wrote to Spain. Her ships carried not only the treasure of the New World, they took also reports, contracts, budgets, petitions, court records, confidential intelligence, complaints, and all manner of papers to Madrid. And there, the King himself read them, all of them, and marked his wishes upon their margins.

Secretaries came to him in the morning as he dressed, and after dinner at midday, and again to spend the long evening, while he dictated, initialled, weighed, decided; held in abeyance, revived for discussion, or postponed again; examined for policy or referred for further study dozens, and hundreds, and tens of thousands of papers through a lifetime of late-working nights. Besides all that, there were the endless committees to receive, who sat through hours of giving all aspects proper consideration. Minutes of such meetings were kept, and, doubling the ecstasy of administrative indulgence, could always be referred to later. It was a poor business if anyone sought to relieve the King of any small details of his official burden. Some of the best men in the land were called to court for appointment to important posts, and then denied the use of their faculties of originality and initiative. No detail was too small to interest the King. If he was King and was to sign, then what he signed must be exquisitely proper; and he would put all the power, weight, and style of his office into a debate upon the nicety of a word to employ in a certain phrase to be written down in a state paper. He would refuse to be hurried, but would spend himself twice over on a matter rather than settle it out of hand. Don Pedro Ponce de León (he was Governor Oñate's most serious rival for the appointment) wrote to the King from Mexico asking for the command of the entry into New Mexico to colonize the Rio del Norte, and as the ocean passage of letter and reply would take eight months more or less, he expected to hear nothing for a while. But time passed, and no answer came to him from the King, whereupon he wrote again, begging in all respect for a reply to his earlier petition. The reply when it came said, "Tell him it will take a year to decide."

There was much to decide at home. The King saw with sorrow the disorderly and frivolous nature of the populace, and, asking less actually of them than of himself, issued decrees of prohibition upon conduct, possessions, and belief. It was unseemly and therefore forbidden by royal edict to wear luxurious dress; to live amid lavish surroundings; to use private carriages or coaches except under certain stated conditions; to employ courtesy titles; to seek education beyond the frontiers of Spain; to open the mind to the inquiries of science; or otherwise fail in proper humility and self-discipline. It was a grief to Philip that despite his endless efforts to guide his great family of subjects in ways of piety and decorum all manner of license grew and continued. Rich and clever people found ways to evade the laws, while poor people could not even qualify under them to commit the crimes of indulgence they forbade. Orders might come in a stream of papers from the palace, but Madrid remained a mudhole, the filthy streets choked with carriages and palanquins, bearing rich ladies who accosted men unknown to them, and of whom they invited proposals of shame. How could this be in a land where women were previously sacred and guarded within the family walls as the very Moors had done before them?

How could it be when any man worked so hard that he should be visited with so many sorrows and reverses? The King bent his head and spoke of the will of God. There were endless tales of his natural piety, which sustained him in the hours of humiliation that came to Spain. The Dutch wars went against the Spanish forces. They were defeated in France. The English under an infidel Queen broke Spain's greatest fleet and a year later raided, burned, and robbed Cádiz, Spain's richest city. Spanish ships were attacked homeward bound from the Indies. The King suffered all with courage, determined to be an example to all in adversity, that they might keep their faith. He declared that it was better not to reign at all than to reign over heretics. Of these there were not many, then, and those few learned or vanished, though the question remained whether the delicate seed of faith that could grow to such mighty power could truly prosper through the habits of brutality of all agencies of discipline, such as the army, the constabulary, the office of the Inquisition, and the law courts alike. And still the King worked, writing orders to govern how many horses and servants a man could maintain with seemliness; how funerals should be conducted, and how weddings; what public amusements might be countenanced and what not. And while he slaved at concerns so alarming and dear to him, there went unanswered pleas from his ambassadors overseas and viceroys desperate for Crown policies ("Tell him it will take a year"), and groaning supplications from fiscal officers who expected mutinies unless the armies were paid.

How could a man's goodness be so crushing?

Those who saw him come to the throne saw his father's son, in the tall forehead, the vivid black-and-white eyes, the lower lip permanently outthrust. Even then, as a young man, there was no mark of humor in his face, which was furrowed beside the nose and under the cheekbone. Yet it was a head of grace and distinction, lean above the ruffed collar of Brabant linen, and the puffed doublet worked in gold. His beard and hair, which had a little wave in it, were a golden brown. And then those who saw him long later saw a heavy face, with sallow color, and sacs about the eyes, now smaller and heavier-lidded. His dress was different, he wore a tall black cap and black garments relieved only by the starch-white of his collar. His spirit was heavy, too, and sallow, if souls had color. The feature most unchanged in his face was the deep cleft between his eyes, which made a scowl of abnegation natural to him in youth when he first renounced so much for himself, and which cut deeper in age, when he renounced so much in their own lives for others.

An image of his quality was the palace of the Escorial which he built on the sweeping plain outside Madrid, below the mountains. It was as big as a palisaded mesa. The plain was as barren as a desert. In New Spain and New Mexico was much country of which that was the miniature. The palace rose in a great square of ochreous gray walls. It was so vast that human silence seemed a very part of its design. What no man could see but which the profuse flocks of little martins and swallows could see as they circled over it was that within the great square stood inner walls, crisscrossing one another in the form of a gridiron or grill. It was believed that this was built in imitation and endless reminder of the grill upon which St. Lawrence met his death. Thus Philip could have constant point for contemplation. Within the palace the long corridors that followed the lines of the grill were low and narrow, showing the bare granite of their walls. The floors were of unfinished stone. Coming in from even a hot summer's day the courtier met indoors the chill of the tomb. The palace was so made that a great portion of its internal volume was taken by a dark church whose dome and towers rose above the enclosing walls. The King's own bedroom, a cell, was placed so that he could look out from it through an indoor window and see the Mass at the high altar, which was just below. Church, monastery, palace, and tomb, that tenebrous heart of the Empire expressed in all its purposes the sacred and profane obsessions of the King its builder.

And if the monarch had his palatial rack designed after a saint's, the soldiers, the traders, the shopmen, the scholars, the voyagers of Spain each had his Escorial of the soul, where to endure the joys and the pains of his spiritual exercises he entered alone and in humility.

Perhaps the deeper a man's humility in the privacy of his soul, the more florid his pride in public. All Spaniards, high or low, could use a spacious manner. Its principal medium was the Spanish language. Not many could read; but all could speak like lords or poets. The poorest soldier in the farthest outlandish expedition of New Mexico might be a chip floating beyond his will on the stream of history, but still he could make an opinion, state it with grace and energy, and even, in cases, make up a rhyme for it. He spoke his mind through a common language that was as plain and clear as water, yet able to be as sharp as a knife, or soft as the moon, or as full of clatter as heels dancing on tile. Like Latin, from which it came, it needed little to say what it meant. It called less upon image and fancy than other tongues, but made its point concretely and called forth feelings in response to universal commonplaces rather than to flights of invention. With that plain strength, the language yet could show much elegance, and such a combination—strength with elegance—spoke truly for the Spaniards and of them. The Emperor once said that to speak to horses, the best tongue to use was German; to talk with statesmen, French; to make love, Italian; to call the birds, English; and to address princes, kings, and God, Spanish. In the time of Cicero the Spanish town of Córdoba was famous for two things, its poetry and its olive oil. He said the poetry sounded as though it were mixed with the oil.

SOUL AND BODY

Both within the Spaniard and without him lay the country which Lope de Vega called "sad, spacious Spain." If Spaniards enacted their literature, it was because, like all people, they both created literature and were created by it. So it was with memories and visions in the colony of the river wilderness. Their hopes of what to be were no less full of meanings than their certainties of what they had done, and both found their center of energy in a moral sense that gave a sort of secret poetry to the hard shape of life. The Spaniard was cruel but he loved life, and his melancholy brutality seemed to issue forth almost involuntarily through the humanitarian laws and codes with which he surrounded himself. If his nature was weak his conscience was strong, and if he sinned his first act of recovery must be to recognize his guilt. When one of the most brutal of the conquerors of the New World was dying of wounds given to him by Indians he was asked where he ached, and he replied, "In my soul."

So the baggage of personality brought by the colonists told of their origin, their faith, the source of their power, the human types by which they perpetuated their tradition; and forecast much about how they would live along the river.

But in that very summer of 1598 when the newest colony of the Spanish Empire was settling on the Rio del Norte in northern New Mexico, the Empire was already ailing. Its life stream carried human tributaries to the river, but already at its source, in Madrid, the springs of Spanish energy were starting to go low. It was an irony of history that just as the American continent was being comprehended, the first great power that sought it began to lose the force to possess it. It would take two more centuries for the flow to become a trickle that barely moved and then altogether stopped. But the Spanish effectiveness in government, society, and commerce began to lose power in the New World with the failure of life in the last of the kings of the Golden Age.

Laboring inhumanly to govern his worldwide kingdoms for goodness and prosperity, Philip II left them a complicated legacy of financial ruin, bureaucratic corruption, and social inertia. After a dazzling conjugation of *to do*, the destiny of Spain seemed to turn toward a simple respiration of *to be*. One was as true of the Spanish temperament as the other.

If Philip left to his peoples anything in the way of a true inheritance, one that expressed both him and them, and that would pass on through generations, it was his example in adversity, his patience facing a hideous death, and his submission to the will of God.

He lay through the summer of 1598 in the Escorial holding the crucifix that his father the Emperor had held on his own deathbed. The son in an agony of suppurating tumors repeatedly gnawed upon the wood of the cross to stifle his groans. His truckle bed was run close to the indoor window through which he could look down upon the big altar of the Escorial church. In the early mornings he could hear the choir singing in the dark stalls and watch the Holy Sacrifice of the Mass performed for the repose of his soul whose liberation was nearing. But it came slowly. On August 16 he received the pontifical blessing from Rome. A fortnight later he took the last sacraments, and afterward spoke alone to his son and heir on the subject of how reigns ended and crowns passed and how instead came shrouds and coarse cinctures of rope in which to be buried. For days and nights the offices of the dying were chanted by priests in his cell. If momentarily they paused, he whispered, "Fathers, continue, the nearer I come to the fountain, the greater my thirst." Before four in the morning on September 13 he asked for a blessed candle to hold. Its calm light revealed a smile on his face. His father's crucifix was on his breast; and when he gasped faintly three times, and died, and was enclosed in a coffin made of timbers from the *Cinco Chagas*, a galleon that had sailed the seas for him, the crucifix was still there. By his will the blood-crusted flail left to him by his father now passed to the new ruler, King Philip III. In the austere grandeurs of such a scene the deathly luxuries of the Spanish temperament, as well as the dying fall of the Empire, found expression. At San Juan de los Caballeros, in the valley of the Rio del Norte, near the junction with the Chama, where willows and cottonwoods along bench terraces of pale earth all imaged the end of summer, the Crown's new colony was at work on a matter of enduring importance to their settlement. By order of Governor de Oñate they were already building their church.

HACIENDA AND VILLAGE

PROVINCIALS

Three times during the eighteenth century the successive Bishops of Durango travelled from their cathedral city in New Spain to Santa Fe, the most outlandish town in their province. Each moved by heavy carriage, accompanied by baggage carts, a mounted guard, and various clergy. The Bishop made use of the hospitality of the great river houses. The chapel was thrown open, decorated and lavishly lighted. His miter, crozier, and cope were taken from their leather hampers, he was vested, he gave Benediction at the altar, and touring the premises, he blessed the house. Children were told off to be prepared for confirmation, which he would administer on his return from Santa Fe. The kitchen buzzed like a hive and steamed like a hot spring. The whole house sparkled and shone. It was like receiving royalty to have the Bishop and his train. Every last finery from the great cities to the south and over the seas was brought out, and every local grace was displayed with anxiety. The Lord Bishop was gratified, and weighed homage for its true value, which was the pleasure it brought the giver, not the receiver. When he entered his carriage again in his worn black with edges of purple, he looked only like a country priest, and when he drove off on his squealing wheels, he left whirling eddies of thought behind him. According to their temperaments, some members of the household, at this contact of the great world, were more content, others more dissatisfied, with the homely labors, loves, and beauties of family life in the valley.

So in simplicity of spirit, and in direct productive life upon the land, with the most laborious of methods, the life of the hacienda valley took its way far from the great world. Out in the world, revolutions in psychology, and government, and science, were creating new concepts of living. But Spain, the mother country, consciously closed herself to these; and barely a ripple of late-eighteenth-century European movement reached the river kingdom. The machine was being discovered as a power in civilization. Technology was born. Industry entered upon violent growth. But not in Spain, and not in the far valley of the Spanish river of North America. The Spanish had no gift for technology, generally speaking. Though the pure sciences were studied, their application was left to other nations. But even Spain's rich tradition of scholarly education did not reach to the river frontier. There were no schools for the haciendas, and no colleges. Even the Franciscan classes in the pueblo missions were disappearing in the last colonial century, as the teachers were withdrawn. Children of the river families learned what they could from their parents. This meant a sufficient skill at the jobs of working the land, and saving the soul. But it brought little for the life of the mind. There were no printing presses in New Mexico. The only books that came in the trade caravans went to the friars, and were of a professional religious nature, with perhaps a copy or two of the poems of Sister Juana Inés de la Cruz, Mexico's intellectual nun. An occasional youth was taught to read, write, and consider philosophy by a priest who guided him toward a vocation in the religious life and presently sent him to a seminary in Mexico. For the rest, only sons of the richest river families could hope for a formal education. Such young men were sent to Mexico City to college, or to Spain. They were promising scholars. Baron von Humboldt in Mexico found "that the young men who have distinguished themselves by their rapid progress in the exact sciences came for a great part from the northernmost provinces of New Spain," where because of constant guard against wild Indians they had led "a singularly active life, which has to be spent mostly on horseback." When they came home, they might become leaders in local politics, and enjoy the prestige of having seen the world. But the local horizons and ways of the river prevailed over the sons as over the fathers. Now and then a proud daughter of a hacienda was taken south with the autumn wagons to be educated in a convent where she would learn the crafts of ladyship. In due course she would return to her family, ready to marry an eligible young man, and maintain with him the combination of domestic grace and primitive husbandry that characterized all life in the river estates.

For the rest, it was a life that had its arts. If these did not blaze and tremble with the peculiar acrid glory of Spain at her greatest, they yet glowed behind the somber patience of the people like coals dying under ashes. If their spirit longed for poetry, it had to be content with the doggerel rhymes at dances, and in the nomenclature of the land, like the name given to the mountains between Galisteo and the Rio Grande, which were called the Sierra de Dolores. In such a place name the Spaniards met the landscape of their souls. Their theatre was made of the artless plays enacted by amateurs at Christmas and in Holy Week with deep religious meaning. Their music sounded in the simple scratches of violins at parties, funerals, the wail of the flageolet in the Penitential passion, the singing of High Mass, the celebration of love and adventure in ballads. Their painting and sculpture showed in the saints made in the valley. Their architecture rose out of earth forms in the universal style of the adobe house and church. All expression in art was integrated in the occasions and forms of local living in the long valley. It was all unprofessional and traditional, and none of it was produced for its own sake, but always to serve primarily an intimate function of the society. As the ways of life were taken from the local earth, the texture of living more and more showed the face of local tradition with its Indian source. The river house, Indian dress, dyes, articles of trade, seasonal ceremonies like the opening of the ditches in spring, the drying of succulent foods, the kivalike form and secrecy of the morada, the bogeyman who benevolently scared children into goodness—such details stood for the gradual absorption of the Spaniards into the ancient environment where they came to conquer and remained to submit.

Did they see themselves in their long procession through the colonial centuries—thirsty for discovery, but often scornful of what they found; bearers of truth which all too often they bestowed with cruelty; lionhearted and greedy-minded; masters of great wildernesses that yet mastered them in the end?

Those who lived in the haciendas and villages of the river illustrated a last chapter of what it meant to be provincial in the Spanish Empire. Through three centuries the colonials knew first how it was to move farther away from Spain; and then from Cuba, then from Mexico City, then from Culiacán; and from the big monasteries of New Biscay and Coahuila to the Rio Grande. Every stage brought reduced movement, less color, luxury, amenity, worldly importance in all things. In time, remote from their sources, the colonists lived on hearsay instead of communion. Folk artisanship replaced skilled professional craftsmanship. Barter substituted for money. Home-butchered animals instead of prepared commodities sustained life. Custom overshadowed law. It was a civilization falling asleep—remembering instead of creating, and then forgetting; and then learning the barest lessons of the new environment, until their meager knowledge had to serve in place of the grandeurs of the source. As they were native lessons, so were they appropriate, but as their products in objects and ways were primitive, they were matters of marvel at what was produced, not with so much skill, but with so little. A grand energy, a great civilization, having reached heights of expression in the arts of painting, poetry, architecture, faith, and arms, had returned to the culture of the folk. Defeated by distance and time, the Rio Grande Spaniards finally lived as the Pueblo Indians lived —in a fixed, traditional present.

What they preserved were their distinction and grace of person and manner—all that was left of the Golden Age, whose other attributes had once been so glorious, so powerful across the world.

And yet in their daily realities they found content. Escorials and armadas and missions over the seas were all very well, but now there was enough to do just to sustain life. All about them was a land whose forms of mountain, desert, and valley seemed to pre-figure eternity. The brilliant sky called out life on the hacienda by day; and at night, with tasks done, and reviewed in prayer, and promised

for the morrow, all seemed as it should be, with the sound of frogs
and crickets, and the seep and suck of the river going forever by, and
the cool breath of the fields, and the heavy sweet smell of the river
mud, and the voluminous quiet of the cottonwood domes. The haciendas fell asleep under a blessing of nature.

BOOK THREE
The Mexican Rio Grande

A COLONY FOR MEXICO

The distance was great—twelve hundred miles—and overland
travel from the middle Gulf coast of Texas to the Mexican capital
was toilsome and dangerous. The roads were appalling. Robbers
abounded along the way. As the southbound traveller drew closer to
the Rio Grande two dangers became intensified. One was the lack of
support and habitation for him in the countryside, which became a
wilderness of mesquite and chaparral where water and fodder were
hard to find. The other was the roving presence of mounted Indians
from the North American prairies. Beyond the river, provincial
capitals lay on the way to Mexico City, but their comforts were
meager, their garrisons concerned with guarding governors rather
than voyagers, and their societies exiled from great affairs by rocky
and sandy distance. The mails were irregular, and a letter dispatched
from the river crossings at Laredo or St. John Baptist or Reynosa
might well have to be entrusted to a private traveller going its way.
Any such place was "as poor as sand bank, or drought, and indolence
can make it," in the words of a letter that went from Laredo to the
Texas Gulf coast in March 1822. It was the first of a stream of papers
that Stephen Austin wrote to his people while on the mission that
took him to the Mexican capital for the first time.

He had left the early settlers of his colony on the Brazos and
Colorado rivers of coastal Texas. Eight families were there. A hundred fifty-one men were already at work making houses out of what
they could find, and planting fields for the time when they could

send for their families out of Louisiana. They had come in good faith, under permission granted by provincial administrators of the Spanish Crown. But by the time they arrived, Mexico was independent, and the colonial grants made to the Austins were meaningless without confirmation by the nascent Mexican government. It was to obtain this that Stephen F. Austin went to the capital.

There would, he felt certain, be little difficulty over the matter. A few interviews, an exchange of papers, some signatures—and the trick was done. His case was clear. Anyone with the smallest sense should be able to see it. The grand sweeps of Texas could only mean anything to Mexico if they were populated and developed, loyally, ably, and at once. Austin and his people were ready to swear allegiance to the new Emperor Agustín I, and renounce altogether their United States citizenship. There was work in the new homes to be done, and in his dedicated zeal Austin counted on starting for Texas ten or twelve days after his appearance in Mexico City.

But if there were delays, he was patient. The Mexicans, absorbed with the thousand details of making a new government, were preoccupied with the Emperor's accession. Austin wandered observantly about the streets. The city was "magnificent," though most of the population lived in misery. He lived frugally. With him he had brought four hundred dollars in doubloons that had to last him. He was earnest and polite, and Mexicans formed an agreeable impression of him. He studied their language—his own new national tongue. He launched his petition on its way in various offices. There he heard hints of further delays. It appeared that while the government was glad to hear him, his enterprise, great as it might look to him, was but one of a number of applications already received from other colonizers; and all these together were only details of a much greater question—the whole question of Mexico's colonial policy under her new empire. There were indications that the large policy must be framed before any of its parts could be approved. It was encouraging that the Mexican Congress was at work in committee. It was time to be reasonable, and wait in calm for the new fathers of the empire to act. The Emperor was, he felt, "a very good man as well as a great one," who had the happiness of the nation much at heart.

Though how slowly moved the Congress; and what unsettling rivalries began to show plain. The Emperor had enemies who began to be heard. July passed, and the colonial question waited until in

August the old patriot from the Rio Grande, José Antonio Gutiérrez de Lara, spoke in Congress for the colonial bill. He let himself go, saying that, based on North American patterns, the bill with its enlightened provisions would call to settlers who would pour into the new Empire, bringing prosperity and civilization to outlands presently owned by animals and savages. The great isthmus of Mexico, connecting two continents and standing across the path between Europe and Asia, would become the center of the world's commerce. The bill in its details even embraced Austin's humble case, and he had every hope of seeing it passed and himself on his way home within the month, at last free to get on with his foundation, officially confirmed by the law of Mexico.

But the proud new machinery that would make this possible suffered a violent shock toward the end of August when the Emperor's soldiery seized fifteen deputies of the Congress under a charge of treason. The nation was outraged, and the colonial question was lost in tumult over the government's condition. The new Empire was economically prostrate. The Emperor's court style was already a great burden financially. The Congress was paralyzed. A military tyranny was being born under the Crown, and swept along in the current of patriotic opposition to it were other energies less disinterested; for the unrest of the moment released the ambitions of men who strove to turn the new freedom of Mexico to their own advantage. In the largest sense the constitutional crisis was a legacy from Spain. For by centuries of rigid paternalism, the fatherland had denied the colonial Mexicans any fair share in their own government, had failed to educate them in public affairs, and had so deeply bred in them the hunger for freedom that a man's personal fate—human life itself—seemed trifles to spend recklessly if they could buy a share, whether just or not, of Mexico for a Mexican. All governments were ponderous, all were drugged with the petty satisfactions of daily policymaking, all knew inner conflict, and divided opinion, and the centrifugal tendency to fly apart through partisan loyalties to opposed individuals or beliefs. But the Mexican government at its birth knew these tendencies to extremity and faced almost a century of effort to overcome them.

There were sharp differences in form, style, and motive between the Spanish and Mexican concepts of government. The Austins, in founding their colony, were prepared to deal with Spain's colonial government. Tenuous as it may have become, it was yet experienced and established in its own elaborate authority. Its systems could be studied. Its principles were known and plain and rigid. And then Mexico broke free of Spain, and the official relationship of settler to government had to be redefined and newly approved. At first it might seem that the Mexicans, with their new empire, would merely change the actors and keep the old play. There would be a new set of bureaus, titles, insignia, but surely all would otherwise be the same. But what was profoundly different was what determined all—the Mexican character. Under the Castilian forms that the colonial society had for so long been trained to perpetuate, the Mexican character was not the same thing at all as the Spanish character.

For the people of Mexico, when they found themselves in possession of their own nation, brought with them to power all the qualities of temperament and inheritance that for centuries had been subordinate under the Spanish Crown. These were now dominant over the land, and even where refined in a fragment of the population by Spanish training, were greatly modified by the buried Indian past of Mexico. Between two lost disciplines—the ancient Indian and the formal Spanish—the Mexican character given freedom to express itself did so intemperately. The politics of the new nation seemed to care little for the individual human life. Such indifference was deeply rooted in the sacrificial rites of the ancient sun priests, and in pagan identification with pitiless earth deities, and in savage hunting ways, and in untold Indian centuries of inert impersonality for the mass of people, under which the individual was crushed into conformity with nature's pattern that wasted him in order out of decay to perpetuate the type, all heedless of his human capacities of mind and soul. Spain brought the individual to society in the New World, though she did not bring for him even the modest degree of freedom in representative government that Spaniards knew at home. Independent Mexico looked to the United States for a new pattern of government. A new dimension of freedom had come into the world with the creation of the young and amazingly dynamic nation in North America—it was barely fifty years old—whose constitution and laws and westward expansion Mexico's new statesmen examined with mixed longing and alarm.

But constitutional forms were not absolute, and what a citizen of the United States meant by independence and its methods and what a Mexican meant were not altogether the same thing. The difference in understanding that lay there was another of the difficulties that Stephen Austin began to encounter, along with the paralysis of Mexico's congress, and the stalling of the Texan petition in one after another bureau, and the furies that swept the capital at the Emperor's absolutism. Austin could only redouble his patience, and examine his purse.

His four hundred dollars' worth of doubloons was melting away. Unable to abandon his purpose in Mexico, he drew a draft on one of his colonists, and filled his time with sober enterprises that would both demonstrate his serious intention to enter into Mexican national life and, he hoped, prove useful to the struggling government. Writing for hours, he produced memorials to the Congress that proposed organization plans for legislatures and law courts and colonies. He was invariably polite when he called upon officials to invest them with his greater political experience as a former citizen of a free country. His progress in the Spanish language gratified them. Earnestly he exhorted his younger brother John by letter to study, study, and prove progress by writing him back in Spanish, the language, he was certain, of their whole future in Texas.

Stephen Austin was a small, fastidious man, with a head rather large for his body. His clean-shaven face was full, crowned with disarrayed dark curls. Below the intense scowl of his domed brow gazed his great eyes—the right, level and calm; the left, alight and piercing. He had a large nose that inclined a trifle to the left, and a full mouth, sensitively modelled. It was a visionary countenance, with something of the facile good looks of an actor, through which his intensity could flare in calculated animation. In his dress he courted a sober elegance. His skirted dark coat sat on his narrow shoulders and lifted its rolled collar up beside his smooth cheeks, and higher yet rose the white points of his shirt collar, enclosing his chin above his white stock and bow cravat. He wore a light waistcoat and tapering trousers and squared-toed boots. If there was general fashion in all this, there was also much of his nature—modest, decent, and without any touch of personal style that suggested humor or lightness of spirit. For of these traits he showed no sign. In all the thousands of pages of his preserved letters there was hardly a smile, or a revealed love—except for the establishment of the colony that was his life's trouble and necessity. In Mexico, waiting upon the distracted government, he was a bachelor thirty years old.

By November the Emperor's autocratic actions seemed on the way to acceptance, and the general colonies law once again moved in channels. Austin heard that it would soon go to the Emperor for signature, and on the twenty-second, he wrote to Texas that "in less than ten days I shall be dispatched with everything freely arranged." A quill, an inkpot, "Agustín," and a rubric— But suddenly in the ancient coastal city of Veracruz on December 2, 1822, a republic was proclaimed and once again the Emperor turned aside from the colonies bill. It appeared that, as Austin wrote, the Veracruz revolutionary leader was a "General Santana"—a name he was fated to spell, though no more correctly, for years to come in the struggles that would flow back and forth over the Rio Grande between Mexico and Texas.

The uprising at Veracruz was not a mere provincial disturbance. As December passed, the republicans of Veracruz won the ear of other Mexicans; and though the Emperor sent forces against them at Jalapa that defeated Santa Anna there, the nation had heard with eagerness of the uprising, and as fast as they had swept to the support of Iturbide a year ago, they now turned their support to his opponents. A fight for the crown was looming. The Emperor was preoccupied with it. Austin wrote to John on Christmas Day that Agustín had not yet approved the colonies bill, and held out little hope of action for "at least three weeks more." But at the New Year, word came from the Moncada Palace that the Emperor had read the bill, was returning it to the Congress with minor revisions, and by January 4 the bill was law. Austin took pride in the fact. "I am certain," he wrote, "that if I had not remained at the capital to agitate this subject . . . the law would never have been passed." But one heavy task led only to another. The bill provided the legal terms under which Austin's petition might be approved, but the petition itself now must be acted upon separately. Once again all hung upon the Emperor's attention. This was a restless faculty. Abroad in the nation, provinces and garrisons fell to the rebels, whether in terms of armed allegiance or vehement pronouncement. While the empire crumbled, Austin, again delayed, was obliged to sell his watch for one hundred dollars. His clothes were giving out. His privations were honorable, but tiresome. They contrasted soberly with the talk that was going around concerning the imperial court.

The Emperor—it was said—was drunk every day. The cost of his household was unreasonable—the Empress Ana María ordered chocolate in the amount of 480 pesos, and the Emperor spent too much on his wardrobe. There was a matter of a saddle fashioned from bearskin, green velvet, tooled leather, and gold. Debts running to over two millions of pesos were already contracted by the imperial government. There were more officers and bandsmen in the imperial army than there were soldiers. Think of it: the Emperor might destroy his reign in one final burst of folly, such as a "murderous, bacchanalian orgy. . . ." Austin's purpose seemed lost in such confusions surrounding the "very good man as well as a great one" whom he had courted at the beginning with so much hope. Nevertheless, he pressed his petition until with certain revisions it was signed by the Emperor on February 18, 1823. By then the Emperor's dominion had shrunk until he controlled only the capital of Mexico and its environs. What if the government fell? Would its acts in behalf of the colony be valid? Austin saw too clearly what must follow upon Agustín's "violations" and "usurpations" not to know how these would affect his plans for Texas. The inevitable came to pass on March 19, when the Emperor abdicated, and a delegate in the abused Congress cried, "Agustín! Agustín! you gave us independence but deprived us of liberty!"

At once the Congress passed a resolution declaring that "all governmental measures resulting from the coronation were . . . illegal," and orders went to the provinces that henceforth anyone was a traitor who acknowledged Agustín as Emperor of Mexico. The decree went to the outlandish Rio Grande towns, while the central government moved to establish a republic, and Austin wrote to Congress, who must now once more act upon his colonial grant, "I have already witnessed, with the greatest pleasure, the . . . entire change of the government . . ." and asked once again for a ratification of his claim. He was rewarded at last. On April 19, the Congress, though suspending the general colonies law, approved Austin's establishment. The way was open to the settlement of Texas by immigrants from the United States. It was the most fateful single act of the Mexican nation in the nineteenth century, for by it were released forces that must clash in always increasing energy until in the end they would meet in bloody battle along all but the whole course of the Rio Grande.

The deposed Emperor and the provisional government made certain arrangements for the future. He was to be known as Don Agustín de Iturbide, with the style of "Excellency." He was required to agree that he would depart for Italy, where he was to spend the rest of his life. So long as he lived, he was to receive a pension of

25,000 pesos annually. At his death, his widow would receive a pension of 8,000 pesos during her lifetime. In a matter of a few weeks the exiled family sailed from Veracruz on the British armed merchantman *Rawlins*, Captain Quelch. Their luggage indicated both imperial nostalgia and anxiety for the future. It contained paintings by old masters, personal jewels, hampers of silverware—and the ermine and embroidered velvet, the batons, stars, and crosses of the imperial state regalia. In addition to their Excellencies Don Agustín and Doña Ana, the party included their eight children, and a number of chaplains, secretaries, and servants. The *Rawlins* set out under sail to cross the Atlantic for Leghorn (it was not far from Elba), and once ashore, the exiles hoped to make their way to Rome, where— surely?—they would live, looking westward, forever after.

BOOK FOUR
The United States Rio Grande

"*WAY, YOU RIO*"

"Goodbye. Come back a man," said an Indiana father to his son, a volunteer for the Rio Grande in 1846. The young man "gave him a shower of tears" and left for the war. It was the nation asking for fulfillment of the first significant task of its early maturity. The national policy on the river was at the start in the hands of the regular army—Taylor's three brigades, which represented only a small segment of the American people, and even included representatives of foreign populations. But it would not be long until, through expansion of the army by volunteers, the whole people would feel the war that was fought in their name. On town hall and courthouse the recruiting notices would soon be tacked up, and soon gaunt little coaches connected by swaying chains behind stovelike locomotives would haul volunteer companies to concentration points, and regiments would go down the wide tributaries on scroll-sawed steamboats to the Mississippi that led to the Gulf. Out of the eastern harbors already sailed other transports and supply ships under raked masts and tall funnels, to the tune of a capstan song:

Oh, say, were you ever in the Rio Grande?
Way, you Rio.
It's there that the river runs down golden sand.
For we're bound to the Rio Grande.

And away, you Rio!
Way, you Rio!
Sing fare you well,
My pretty young girls,
For we're bound to the Rio Grande!

The electric telegraph did not yet touch across Texas. News by fastest army courier took two weeks to come from the river to Washington, and mails by steamer were even slower, and most newspapers came out only once a week. The families at home could only repose their confidence in what lay behind the whole people who had already turned to the west in so many other enterprises. The move to Mexico was full of anxiety; met with unpopularity in various quarters of the nation; and, from a certain political view, violated international morality. But its general direction seemed natural, for on an official and national scale it was but one more step in the westward march hitherto taken by individuals, and families, and business associates, and private communities. There was no surprise in its sudden call upon the country to go to the West and Southwest with the largest home army assembled since General Washington's. What had William Becknell printed in a Missouri newspaper so long ago as 1821? Calling for men to join him in a plains trading expedition after horses and mules, he had without intending eloquence or a heroic tone simply announced men "destined to the westward." Whether he meant immediate destination or large destiny, the effect was the same, and his countrymen after him showed no more uncertainty than he.

Oh, New York town is no place for me—
Way, you Rio!
I'll pack up my bag and go to sea.
For we're bound to the Rio Grande!

And away, you Rio,
Way, you Rio! . . .

Even if almost nothing was known about far Texas, and Mexico, and the problems waiting in distance, climate, and the Mexican nature, the United States was confident as the war opened that it would be a short one.

> *We'll sell our salt cod for molasses and rum—*
> *Way, you Rio!*
> *And get home again 'fore Thanksgiving has come.*
> *For we're bound to the Rio Grande!*
>
> *And away, you Rio! ...*

General Taylor's army on the north bank of the Rio Grande in March 1846 represented the third of the three great peoples who came to the river. The American soldiers, taken together, were prophets of a time to come. The collective prophecy they carried was not plain to all its carriers, but it stirred in them like their own seed, and sow it they must. Its nature could be read from fragments out of the ancestries of idea, issue, motive, and way of life that had created them in a society new to the world—a society formed around a central passion: the freedom and equality of democratic man. A taste of this—the American theme—had already come near to the river with the Texan settlers in the south, and the trappers and traders in the north; but now once again change, coming with a final sovereignty, was about to make its way along the river with an energy and a complexity unknown in the earlier societies of the Indian, the Spaniard, and the Mexican. . . .

UPSTREAM AND INLAND

On his level, the Commanding General had special problems. Late in June, General Taylor [at his headquarters near the mouth of the Rio Grande] received an infuriating letter. It was from Major General Winfield Scott, at Washington, and if it held any welcome note it lay in the implication that Scott might not after all appear on the Rio Grande, but remain in Washington, content to issue plans for the defeat of Mexico. But what plans! Working with maps, and making grand assumptions about the geography of Mexico, he issued a stupefying command to Taylor on June 12, 1846:

"Take up the line of march beyond the Rio Grande, and press

your operations toward the heart of the enemy's country. . . . The high road to the capital of Mexico will, of course, be one of those lines."

How easy he made it sound. A brisk walk, the cutting of an arterial highway, and Mexico City must fall. But where was any knowledge of the scale of Mexican distance, or understanding of the north Mexican desert, or recollection of what it took to feed, water, and shelter an army?

General Taylor replied at once to the Adjutant General at Washington, determined, *nolens volens,* to describe certain realities. He was already planning to move upriver to Camargo. But "from Camargo to the city of Mexico is little if any short of 1,000 miles in length. The resources of the country are, to say the best, not superabundant, and over long spaces of the route are known to be deficient. . . . I consider it impracticable to keep open so long a line of communication. It is, therefore, my opinion that our operations from this frontier should not look to the city of Mexico, but should be confined to cutting off the northern provinces—an undertaking of comparative facility and assurance of success." His strategy meant to capture Monterrey, Saltillo, and other key cities of the northeast, just as he had been planning all along.

He received another letter from Washington by the middle of July which gave some comfort. It came from Secretary of War Marcy, and, written before the Secretary had seen Taylor's reply to Scott, it indicated that there were some in the War Department who could look at a map and see more than the army's General-in-Chief: ". . . If it should appear that the difficulties and obstacles to conducting a campaign from the Rio Grande . . . for any considerable distance into the interior of Mexico will be very great, the Department will consider whether the main invasion should not ultimately take place from some other point on the coast—say Tampico . . . or Vera Cruz. . . . The distance from Vera Cruz to the city of Mexico is not more than one-third of that from the Rio Grande. . . ."

General Taylor replied, somewhat stiffly making reference to General Scott's design, that he could not determine whether he could win the war alone in his northern frontier campaign. Practice alone would show whether his army could subsist beyond Monterrey. As for Tampico, he felt it was impossible, and about Veracruz he had no views. He was not disposed further to extend his advice. He knew what he could do with his present resources, and he intended to proceed. Did Washington aim to catch him in a trap? Get him to give advice, then take it, and if it went wrong, blame him? He knew what was behind their attitude—Scott, and Polk, and who else: they were trying to kill the sentiment that was building up all over the country—Taylor for President. They were scared by the Whig mass meetings that had been held at which in spontaneous demonstrations he had been acclaimed as the necessary nominee for '48. That was part of it—the other part was the enraging ignorance of politicians in walnut-panelled offices on the Potomac of what actualities governed the Army of the Rio Grande, two thousand miles away. It was, in the face of these, almost an impertinence for the War Department to have an opinion, way back there, on the staff level, when the reality was here, on this muddy ditch, in this heat, with soldiers dying of their bowels. General Taylor told his fellow field-soldiers, speaking of those safe in Washington, "They have an intention . . . to break me down." His army was to be thrown away, and the venture wasted, "for all of which I shall be made the scapegoat."

But the high-pressure steamboats were already on the river, and on July 26 the first detachment had gone upstream on the *I. E. Roberts*. The rains had continued, the river was running almost at flood level, and on August 4 General Taylor boarded the *Hatchee Eagle* with his staff for Camargo. He arrived on the eighth and at once reviewed the troops that had preceded him. The rest of the invasion forces were coming up both by river and by land for the jump-off into Mexico. Like ten thousand others back home, the wife of a young major felt her heart turn westward. "My thoughts," she wrote in a diary kept for her husband's return, "my thoughts have wandered to the Rio Grande."

After the fall of Matamoros, river towns were occupied by small infantry forces without opposition, and as the heavy movement by road began and continued in late July and early August, the troops found their flag already flying over Reynosa and Mier on their way to Camargo. The march was an ordeal that lasted eight days, through rain and mud, or blasting sunlight and dust. The old Escandón towns offered little shelter—they looked deserted but the men soon saw that "there is scarcely an old wall standing that some family does not live behind." In many places the river road was flooded, and the columns had to make detours to the south. Water holes at evening were brackish and some were contaminated by cattle who to escape the extraordinary heat of that summer stood in them for weeks. There were few reliefs for the troops, though now and then they passed little ranches where young girls gladdened them with waves and laughter. After passing a little beyond Mier, they saw their first mountains— faint blue crowns on the southwest horizon. They started up coveys of plover and sent bands of wild horses glaring and plunging away. One regiment met a Mexican driving his cart full of fresh melons to Matamoros, and in a few minutes, to his delight, bought his whole load at high prices. The heat was presently so frightful that the troops were halted to rest after midday. Reveille sounded at midnight, and the march was taken up again by moonlight, while fifers and drummers, "with a perfect *vim*," did their best to inspire their fellows with the tune of "The Girl I Left Behind Me." It was necessary, though dangerous, to rely on Mexican guides: an infantry regiment was taken astray on the road to Linares, which was a Mexican army station, and was saved only when the treachery of their guide was discovered. Finally, after a march of one hundred and thirty miles—the air-line distance was eighty—the columns came up the rise of land that enclosed the San Juan River and saw Camargo lying below on the near bank, a little way above the confluence with the Rio Grande.

As the army made its way down into the valley, one of its officers was moved by the sight of it. The Rio Grande, "seen in stretches, had the appearance of so many lakes embedded in green foliage. The smoke from several ranchos curled gently and lazily upward . . . and a steamboat—a *high-pressure steamboat*—true emblem of an American, lay moored at the bank . . . lazily working off steam. Add to this the long line of covered wagons—the troops, upon whose bayonets the sunbeams glistened, marching on their winding way, and you have a picture unsurpassed. . . ." Entering Camargo they heard that General Canales had just evacuated it, "after inflicting numerous pains and penalties upon the good people," who "hailed with great joy" the new occupation troops.

The steamboat voyage up to Camargo took from four to seven days. By the middle of August there were twenty vessels in service. They were officered by American masters, mates, and engineers from the inland rivers, and manned by hired Mexicans. None of the steamboats drew more than five feet of water, some as little as three and a half loaded, and eighteen inches light. They burned wood, gathered every evening at the banks. The green mesquite was a slow fuel, and many a boat had to pull into the bank during the day to get up steam before resuming her voyage. If the river was free of snags, it presented a channel that shifted among soft sand bars, so that a master had to feel his way on each trip. Even so, ships went aground all too often. One—the *Neva*—sank one night while tied up to the bank, and everyone believed she had been scuttled. The voyage was slow, and men were crowded together amid bales of supplies, but progress was sure, and it was better than the overland march. The Rio Grande was "a noble river at the present stage of water," and the country along its banks "decidedly pleasing," where mesquite thickets alternated with open cornfields and little ranches or villages whose people came down to watch the little steamers puffing amazingly along. When the soldiers took off their hats and kissed their hands to the girls, they would all "shout and laugh and make themselves most merry." In general the upriver inhabitants were friendlier than those at Matamoros, and at Reynosa especially, said an officer, because of two facts: "first, the Texas Rangers have not been let loose on them, and [second], only Canales has . . . committed outrages upon them, which have rather turned the current of their feeling in our favor." The river voyages of that summer had interludes of high spirits and antic pleasure for soldiers who crowded the little steamers. One night a boat tied up near a solitary hut as darkness fell. An old Mexican came out of the hut to see the arrival. A fiddler, he was soon playing for the soldiers. They begged permission of their commander to go ashore so they could hold "a stag dance." This was granted. The men swarmed to the bank, where some built a fire and began to roast a goat. It was almost like a symbolic sacrifice to the pagan deity who soon inspired them all. An American fifer joined the Mexican fiddler in making music. A soldier who heard them play said they "imagined themselves possessed by the spirits of Pan and Paganini." Scratching and squealing away, they seized the troops with their tunes, and soon all the men were dancing. They danced "by couples, but without much regard to time or order. . . . The dancing . . . became stronger in proportion as the wild strains grew louder" and the soldiers "vied with each other in the extent and singularity of their saltations." Every so often something swept over the whole detachment, and to the light of the goat-roasting fire and the banked furnaces of the moored steamer, they all "indulged in a promenade or rather *gallopade* of two or three *heats* around the hut." In a scene of color, smoke, glow, and animation like a lithograph of the period brought to life, the men feasted and danced and galloped on the riverbank— and then suddenly "a heavy rain terminated the sport on a seasonable hour, and the men returned to the boat much amused and refreshed by their exercise. . . ."

The high water lasted all summer between Camargo and the Gulf. Regular navigation was more difficult farther upstream, though later in the year the *Major Brown* arrived at Laredo with supplies for a new army station there; but before she could cast off to go downstream, the river fell, and she was unable to sail for two years.

And now at Camargo the army repeated the spectacle of Matamoros. On a little stone and clay town with its squared streets and central church and plaza and peach-laden trees descended some fifteen thousand soldiers, with all the animal trains and heavy equipment and greedy hangers-on that accompanied them on the river. Before they could make camp the soldiers had to clear dense mesquite off the ground. The summer floods had swelled over town and field, and receding, had left heavy silt that dried as fine dust. When the wind blew, dust sifted everywhere.

And as always, after flooding, the Rio Grande bred disease. The new base of operations in a matter of days was pest-ridden. Thousands of men went down with the cholerina and hundreds died. The epidemic had come upriver with the transport of troops, and conditions at Camargo spread it. Men bathed and animals drank in the San Juan River that was the camp water supply. Sanitation was poorly regulated, and hospital facilities were limited and little was known or understood of germs, or antisepsis, and though in Camargo there was a druggist's shop—it was the only shop in town—it sold only soda water. Once again deaths were so numerous that military funerals became a mere shuffling of wasted bodies into sandy troughs, while the dead march was sounded by fifers and mockingbirds. Camargo was known as the "Yawning Graveyard." Tremendous heat by day and noisome fogs by night and insects persistent in their millions made matters worse; and the army, through appropriate officers, attributed the epidemic to "noxious gases and deadly miasmas."

But still the slow work of supply build-up went on, and until it was done, General Taylor would not budge, though he had sent advance elements toward Monterrey on reconnaissance. He was in an odd mood, as one of his officers recorded. "The general was advancing in a strangely divided frame of mind—had supreme confidence in his men, but he had little confidence in the movement on which he was embarked." Were those people in Washington trying to cornuck him? If he thought so, it might take the starch out of him, until the time came to move into action, and then a man would get back to where he felt like himself again. . . .

The rains went on, and soldiers were so wet all day that whiskey was issued to them. Tent canvas was rotted till it resembled a sieve. Sometimes after a storm the air was cool for hours—a delicious change, and one night there was a brilliant display of meteors over the immense Mexican plain. The camp heard that Comanches were on the loose near Mier—three hundred were said to have killed the mayor, even though an American infantry company was stationed there. Letters came from home. One from his wife so moved an officer that his heart leaped "at the reflection that she does not outdo me in devotion. Never for one moment has my fidelity been tempted to give way." In an atmosphere of pathetic license, he had his own resources: "Have been all afternoon on my bed reading 'King Henry the Fifth,' one of Shakespeare's best plays"—best, even though it trembled with the soldier's lust:

> And the flesh'd soldier, rough and hard of heart,
> In liberty of bloody hand, shall range
> With conscience wide as hell, mowing like grass
> Your fresh fair virgins. . . .
> What is't to me, when you yourselves are cause,
> If your pure maidens fall into the hand
> Of hot and forcing violation?
> . . . Why, in a moment look to see
> The blind and bloody soldier with foul hand
> Defile the locks of your shrill-shrieking daughters. . . .

Many volunteer units had enlisted for stated, short terms of service. Now at Camargo when all the energy of the army was needed for the coming campaign in the interior, hundreds of men said good-bye and returned downriver on the steamboats that were headed for the Gulf to bring up more troops and supplies. Of those going home, "the great majority" were "pretty well disgusted with their service," which for them had meant only heat, and illness, and inaction on the outlandish river. But enough were left with the General to make a great display, and on August 17 he reviewed them, all drawn up in order of battle. Their line was over three-quarters of a mile long—"one of the most magnificent military displays we have had since the last war." With General Taylor four other general officers inspected seven regiments of infantry and two battalions of horse artillery. All were in dress blues, the officers with gold stripes, except the General, who rode the line "in plain undress." He was himself again. He "never looked in better health or spirits," for action was soon to be resumed.

On the following day the first division moved into Mexico, by way of Mier, to be followed by one division a week until all but small holding forces were gone from the Rio Grande. The transport problem over the deserts had been solved—nineteen hundred pack mules with Mexican drivers took the place of most of the horse-drawn wagons. General Scott should have witnessed the difficulties of loading tent poles and canvas and mess chests and sheet-iron kettles and a hundred other articles on the little beasts, which took several hours at the outset of each day's march, so that the first-packed grew tired of standing, and broke and ran, sometimes bucking or rolling till they managed to scatter their burdens. Still, there was no better way to cross the wastes with an army's duffel.

As the movement got under way, the staff at Camargo heard that Mexico was in a state of revolution. President Paredes, who had marched toward the frontier as far as San Luis Potosí with eight thousand troops, was thrown out of office, and a provisional president had sent for the one man who despite his record could unite all Mexicans under his familiar name—Santa Anna. Under a safe-conduct honored by the United States, Santa Anna on his way home from exile in Cuba had landed at Veracruz on August 16, and was proceeding to the capital to take charge. General Taylor now had his principal adversary.

Monterrey lay a hundred and fifty miles southwest of Camargo. The last of the Rio Grande divisions moved out on September 1 and camped that night under a young moon. The General with his staff accompanied the Fourth Infantry on September 5. He was now in such high spirits that his people wondered if perhaps he were overconfident. Mexicans whom they met assured them that there would be "Mucho fandango en Monterrey," and wondering what this meant, the Americans—correctly—translated it to mean that there would be something of a fracas at Monterrey. The country they passed over was dead level, with unending clumps of mesquite. Those who kept up their journals every night had to write by the light of the new moon—there was too much wind to let them light a candle. So under a wide movement of air over the great empty plain the combat forces of the Army of the Rio Grande slowly faded out of sight into Mexico.

COUNTERDANCE

On December 28—the day following Doniphan's entry into El Paso—a majestic arrival occurred twelve hundred miles away at the Arms of St. James on the Gulf, when a steamer put in to deliver, with his staff, a major general six feet four inches tall, of glaring eye, heavy build, and a manner of solemn amplitude, all sumptuously uniformed in blue and gold. It was Winfield Scott, at sixty years of age the General-in-Chief of the United States Army.

His journey had been crammed with inconveniences most unsuitable to the progress of a major general. It was impossible to imagine how so many "cruel uncertainties" could seek to impede him who so loved the splendid comfort of high rank, even with its unending duties of manner, rhetoric, and ceremony. He had left from New York, where he caught a heavy cold. Sailing for New Orleans, he had been delayed almost a week at sea by vexatious head winds. In New Orleans for four days, he held official conversations, and dined with Senator Henry Clay, and—it was astounding and supremely impertinent—the purpose of his journey, which was the highest strategic secret of the war, appeared in print in a Spanish-language newspaper of the city, and was at once copied by other papers, and sent off to the Eastern press as vital news. In a trice a public that grew by hours knew that General Scott was on his way to the Rio Grande to confer with General Taylor, and to lay down the final arrangements for a landing of American troops at Veracruz to invade Mexico from the east coast. It was hard to know which would be worse—the embarrassments or the dangers that might result from the leak.

Where it had come from, nobody could imagine. He had been particularly careful in writing to General Taylor from New York on November 25, announcing his coming, not to identify Veracruz as his objective. To do so would not have been "prudent at this distance." All he had said was that he was "not coming to supersede you in the immediate command on the line of operations rendered illustrious by you and your gallant army. My proposed theatre is different. You may imagine it. . . ." It was awkward that some Mexican had also imagined it, and had printed a story absurd in detail but correct in general. The letter went on to state that the writer would proceed to Camargo in order to be "within easy corresponding distance from you." It said further, "But, my dear general, I shall be obliged to take from you most of the gallant officers and men (regulars and volunteers) whom you have so long and so nobly commanded. I am afraid that I shall, by imperious necessity—the approach of yellow fever on the gulf coast—reduce you, for a time, to stand on the defensive. This will be infinitely painful to you, and for that reason distressing to me. But I rely on your patriotism to submit to the temporary sacrifice with cheerfulness." If the letter had been intercepted—though nobody knew—the yellow fever at the Gulf and the diversion of troops from one to another theatre may also have told too much. Perhaps the leak occurred at Washington, where the plan had been laid down. What would President Polk think?

He had been most cordial to General Scott of late. Certainly the President had no confidence in General Taylor, and spoke out freely against him. "I am now satisfied that anybody would do better than Taylor," he stated even after the victories of Palo Alto, Resaca, and Monterrey. "Taylor is no doubt brave and will fight, but is not fit for a higher command than that of a regiment. I have no prejudice against him, but think he has acted with great weakness and folly. . . ."

General Scott could but concur—though earlier his opinion of General Taylor had been favorable. But now it seemed discreet to agree with the President, with whom he had "many long personal interviews on military matters," and to accept the command of the great expedition to come. In only four days of staff discussions throughout "the great bureaux" of the War Department, the grand campaign had been mapped, and before leaving for the Rio Grande, the General-in-Chief magnificently wrote a circular to the leading Whigs in Congress commending the President and the Secretary of War for their handsome treatment of him in his hour of added responsibility. He left Washington "highly flattered with the confidence and kindness the President has just shown me." At New Orleans on December 20 he wrote again to General Taylor, enlarging upon the campaign plans, and now calling him to a meeting at Camargo. He marked his dispatch "most confidential . . . outside and in," and sent it by officer express to General Taylor at Monterrey, and prepared to sail from New Orleans for the Rio Grande on December 24.

There was one last exasperation at New Orleans before sailing. General Scott was informed that on the heels of his departure from Washington, the President had sent to Congress a bill creating the office of lieutenant general of the army, and proposing its bestowal upon Senator Thomas Hart Benton, who would thus supersede all other general officers. The President had remarked to a legislator that he had been "compelled to send Gen'l Scott to take command of the Army as a choice of evils, he being the only man in the army who by his rank could command Taylor." The news was incredible. General Scott dismissed it with grandeur.

"If the rank were asked for," he stated, "it could only—remembering Mr. Polk's assurance of support and reward—be intended for me on the report of my first success," and left for Port Isabel.

When he arrived, he found no word from Taylor, and resolved to go upriver without delay. He was in a genial mood as he renewed old acquaintances among the officers, even, in a general amnesty, restoring to favor such as had once felt his ire. One, Lieutenant Colonel Ethan Allan Hitchcock, who had served under him in Washington, hardly expected to meet him now, remembering that General Scott had once "found a place for a flare-up and did flare up in the highest sort of style" against him. But now the General sent for him at Port Isabel, rose, offered him his hand, and made him "a very complimentary speech," ending up with an appointment to his staff.

"Are you ready to move forward?" asked the General.

"Perfectly," replied Colonel Hitchcock.

"Got a horse?"

"Two, General."

"Glad! Glad! You will join me tomorrow?"

"With great pleasure."

"Clever! Very clever! Right! Right! We start early."

"I will be ready, General."

They boarded the *Big Hatchee* the next morning and steamed along the wide loops of the Rio Grande through dunes and marshes, coming to Matamoros by nightfall. There was still no word from General Taylor. Nobody knew what was happening at Monterrey. Matamoros was "wild with rumors," one of which spread the word that Taylor's communications had been cut by the enemy. Transferring to the steamer *Corvette*, the staff continued its progress the next day, with observations upon the natives, who seemed the next thing to "Indians in mud huts," who came to sell wood for $2.50 a cord to the captain; and a pause for an exchange of intelligence with a down-bound steamer, whose news was that Mexican troops were massing below Saltillo under the command of Santa Anna; and hours on deck, when the little ship moved slowly between the banks, while General Scott was "particularly civil," lolling immensely and rumbling on in the satisfactions of high-level reminiscence, amid subordinates who could not take away the topic, but who remained content under the tall funnel to breathe of smoke and sparks and greatness.

General Scott explained at length the orders which brought him there. He outlined in detail the "ultimate objects of his movement." He reenacted with relish his many interviews with the President— "what Mr. P. said, what he said," back and forth, back and forth. If there were brief, ever so brief, moments of silence in which the General undertook to "look so wise as the Sphinx," it did seem that he accomplished only "a puzzled, dubious gaze into vacancy." And then, perhaps in "bad French," he would resume his satisfied soliloquy, or sober his hearers with a "flat joke," or treat them to "agonizing pedantries of connoisseurship in wine and cookery." Since his temper was uncertain, all he said was taken with deference, even, in some cases, with fondness, for those who worked closely with him knew his qualities of bravery, skill, and warmheartedness.

The anticipated conference with General Taylor was odd to contemplate. There could be no two men more antithetical. General Scott exploited every massive grace of high position; General Taylor in rumpled overalls shambled about on a yellow mule. Where one condescended, the other fraternized. If one delighted in exercising his mind and displaying its florid contents, the other—but it was General Scott himself who said of General Taylor that "few men ever had a more comfortable, labor-saving contempt for learning of every kind. . . ." Their opposed qualities were never more sharply stated than by the soldiers themselves, who with their timeless knack for truth in caricature, spoke of Scott as Old Fuss and Feathers, and of Taylor as Old Rough and Ready—nicknames joyfully taken up by press and public.

Given such differences, the conference at Camargo, with its delicate issues of command prerogative, the distribution of troops, and the opportunity for victory, seemed likely to be difficult. And there was even one further bone of contention buried under more official matters: each man, with much popular reason to do so, saw himself as the next President of the United States.

But on January 3, 1847, when the *Corvette* arrived at Camargo, General Taylor was not there, and there was still no word from him directly. It was the staff at Camargo who gave General Scott the information that General Taylor, far from coming to meet him at the Rio Grande as ordered, had instead pursued a project of his own, an extended march eastward into Tamaulipas. He was out of reach for the time being. It seemed to the General-in-Chief that—really—he had done all he could to invite General Taylor's participation in the next immediate decisions; and he now acted with firmness. He wrote orders to General Butler, who was in command of the Monterrey–Saltillo line in the absence of Taylor, to abandon Saltillo, hold Monterrey for defense only, and detach and send at once to the Brazos under General Worth's command a whole division of General Taylor's army. Certain others of Taylor's troops were ordered to Tampico. The dispatch included further details of the Veracruz campaign plan, and closed with General Scott's reflection that though Providence might defeat him, he thought the Mexicans could not. Marked *Private and Confidential*, the papers went not only to General Butler, but in duplicate to General Taylor, for his perusal when he could receive them. There was little more to do at Camargo. General Scott and his people looked over the town and camp the rest of the day, and one of the staff remarked it as "one of the most miserable places I ever saw, dirty and dilapidated and but little better than a Seminole village." They returned to the *Corvette* with relief and the next day started downriver. Five days later they were again at the Arms of St. James, where General Scott pushed preparation for the armada he would lead to the Mexican coast.

All his communications to General Taylor so far ran into trouble. The first, from New York, which was delivered, Taylor dismissed saying, "A more contemptible and insidious communication was never written." The second, from New Orleans, was never delivered, because of what Scott later called "gross neglect of the officer who bore it." The third, from Camargo, reached Taylor on January 14 upon his return from the Tamaulipas reconnaissance. On reading it, he was outraged in every personal and professional consideration. General Butler had already acted on the orders it contained. But there was also a dreadful probability that the Mexicans were reacting in their turn, for the copy sent by Scott to Taylor had been intercepted, its officer courier killed, and its contents hurried on to Santa Anna. The copy that eventually reached Taylor was sent to him by Butler.

General Taylor at once saw the implications of the orders, and their effect upon the enemy. If all the best troops of the Army of the Rio Grande were to be pulled out and sent to Scott, then what an opportunity was left for Santa Anna, with his forces massing below Saltillo! It could lead to a disastrous defeat for General Taylor. He saw it all as a wicked affront, with overtones of persecution. Scott's demands for his troops were leaving him with only eight hundred regulars and fewer than seven thousand volunteers without battle experience. Six general officers were also removed from his army, leaving him only two or three, none of whom had had command experience in combat. Once again the bland decisions of the War Department, and the incomprehensible and therefore hateful personality of General Scott, intruded upon the bleak realities of the front lines of the desert war, with all its labors, its experience, and its human stakes. Washington! What could they know there, where everything was reduced to papers in a conference room, "with its long, official, green-covered table and chairs ranged in official order around it," as another public servant saw, "and official stationery in front of each chair. One could not sit there a moment without official sensations of dignity and red-tapery. . . ." General Taylor's responses were lively.

He wrote to Scott declining to report for a discussion, as he would be busy with matters at Victoria and later at Monterrey. He declared that if Scott had relieved him of his whole command, he would have registered "no complaint." But to reduce his forces so radically, and then to leave him to face over twenty thousand men under Santa Anna, this was hard to understand—or perhaps it could be understood only too well. "I feel," he wrote bitterly, "I feel that I have lost the confidence of the government, or it would not have suffered me to remain, up to this time, ignorant of its intentions. . . ." Nevertheless, "however much I may feel personally mortified and outraged . . . I will carry out in good faith . . . the views of the government, though"—his darkest suspicions welled over—"though I may be sacrificed in the effort." To his son-in-law he raged, "It seems to me the great object so far as I am concerned . . . is to keep me as much in the dark . . . as it was possible to do; particularly as far as the authorities at Washington are concerned." And as for Scott's orders to pull back from Saltillo and cool his heels at Monterrey, General Taylor flatly informed the Secretary of War, "I shall do no such thing without orders to that effect from proper authority." So much for his recognition of the powers of the General-in-Chief.

General Scott continued to be "the most urbane of conquerors." Replying to Taylor, he said, "There are some expressions in your letters which, as I wish to forget them, I shall not specify or recall. . . . If I had been within easy reach of you . . . I should . . . have consulted you fully on all points. . . . As it was, I had to act promptly, and, to a considerable extent, in the dark. . . ." Elsewhere, and later, he commented that his orders for the reassignment to him of Taylor's troops "began to sour [Taylor's] mind in proportion as he became more and more prominent as a candidate for the Presidency," and he spoke of "the senseless and ungrateful clamor of Taylor, which, like his other prejudices, abided with him to the end. . . ." But General Scott was not to escape his own sense of betrayal, and to speak of "the perfidy of Mr. Polk," for it turned out to be true that the President had made every effort to appoint Senator Benton to the supreme command and had only been thwarted by Congress; and furthermore, the President had suspected General Scott himself, "from his inordinate vanity or from some other cause," of having given out at New Orleans the story of his coming invasion of Mexico. In the President's view, "the truth is neither Taylor nor Scott are fit for the command of an army in the great operations in progress and which are contemplated."

General Taylor, in another statement to his son-in-law, set the tone on which the formal counterdance of vanities ended. "One of the expectations of those who perpetrated the outrage against me was, that I would at once leave the country . . . in disgust & return to the U States which if I had done so, would have been used by them to my disadvantage. . . . But in this"—his countryman's ire crackled—"in this I shall disappoint them, as I have determined to remain & do my duty no matter under what circumstances until I am withdrawn. . . . I recd an answer from Genl Scott to a communication I wrote him from Victoria, in which I did not disguise my feelings; he is somewhat tart in his reply. . . . He & myself now understand each other perfectly, & there can for the future be none other than official intercourse between us."

The whole scene of the Rio Grande appalled General Scott. He could not forbear writing to the Secretary of War his impressions in which lay a strong if implied rebuke of General Taylor's management of volunteers. He was "agonized" by what he had heard from reliable witnesses. "If a tenth of what is said be true," the volunteers "have committed atrocities—horrors—in Mexico, sufficient to make Heaven weep, & every American of Christian morals *blush* for his country. Murder, robbery & rape on mothers & daughters in the presence of the tied up males of the families, have been common all along the Rio Grande. . . . The respectable volunteers—7 in 10—have been as

much horrified & disgusted as the regulars, with such barbarian conduct. As far as I can learn"—where was Taylor?—"not one of the
felons has been punished, & very few rebuked—the officers, generally,
being as much afraid of their men as the poor suffering Mexicans
themselves are afraid of the miscreants. Most atrocities are always
committed in the absence of regulars, but sometimes in the presence
of acquiescing, trembling volunteer officers."

But at Port Isabel, General Scott's problems were more immediate. At the War Department he had ordered all the complicated
gear for his amphibious invasion—troops, ships, supplies, and equipment, including one hundred and forty-one surfboats for the landings, and casks of drinking water from the Mississippi, and enough
firewood to last sixty days. But all these were slow to arrive. There
would hardly be time for training in the tactics of putting an army
ashore for battle. The weather was foreboding—northers and high
seas. But at last on January 22, 1847, the build-up began. Worth
arrived downriver with his division. His men were jubilant, thinking
they were homeward bound until, at the mouth, they discovered that
they were assigned to the invasion. Inland at Saltillo, they were replaced by Wool's brigade. On the same day the first detachment of
new volunteers arrived at Port Isabel from the East. Presently, out
of New Orleans, the transports began to appear. Their character was
disappointing—they were brigs and schooners of light tonnage that
rode the stormy Gulf with difficulty. On February 4 a steamer
brought the surfboats—not all that had been requisitioned, but only
sixty-five. Five days later General Scott suffered a more severe blow
yet—he heard that the Mexicans had captured his third letter to
General Taylor, and were in possession of his plans for the assault.
It was imperative now to move fast, and he redoubled the efforts of
the army. Even without sufficient ships or all his supplies, he must
move. But one more woe beset him. A furious norther blew in on
February 12. Sand flew, the shipping strained at anchor, the army
shivered amid the dunes, until finally on February 15 General
Scott was able to embark with the advance detachments for rendez-
vous, first at Lobos Island, then at Tampico on the Pánuco, and the
massed descent upon Veracruz. In a few days the site of the invasion
jump-off at the Rio Grande beaches was once again occupied by only
the garrison at the Fort Polk supply depot, and the forgotten regiment on the tide-washed wastes at the river mouth.

All through the weeks of preparations on the coast, Santa Anna, far inland, was moving up with twenty-five thousand troops, from San Luis Potosí to Encarnación, and finally to a mountain-sided plain below Saltillo. General Taylor, having been pressed, had agreed to run for President if nominated in 1848, had taken and abandoned Victoria, and had retired to await Santa Anna at Buena Vista. There on February 22 and 23 the desert armies met; and in a great if costly victory Taylor with his weakened forces won northern Mexico— and the Presidency. Ten days later General Scott's men began their landings near Veracruz. On March 27 the city surrendered, and on April 8 the coastal army began its march inland over the route of Cortés to the heart of Mexico.

1954

II

BIOGRAPHY

Citizen of New Salem

[Abraham Lincoln, a young villager of New Salem, Illinois, prepares himself to go out in the world.]

What if there was no one at New Salem to teach him the law—no one to "read with," as he said? If a man must do it alone, he could do so. The main thing was to get the necessary books and read them, and study their principal features. What did it matter if New Salem was a small town which "never had three hundred people living in it"? All that mattered were the books and his capacity for understanding them. These would be "just the same" wherever he might be. Surely his own resolution to succeed must be "more important than any other one thing"?

The stage fare from New Salem to Springfield was a dollar and a half. The assemblyman rode in a farmer's wagon or walked to Springfield to borrow law books from Attorney Stuart. He went more than once, and one day at an auction he bought a copy of Blackstone's *Commentaries on the Common Law*. Back home it was now the law books—Chitty or Blackstone—which he took everywhere with him. The neighbors saw him and remembered how he studied wherever he could—"in some nook in a store," or at "the foot of a hay-stack," or "sometimes lying on his back, putting his feet up the tree. . . ." They were used to him and let him be, though to an occasional observer he was a sight. Russell Godbey, the farmer, for whom he did odd jobs, found him one day sitting barefoot at the top of a woodpile with a book. It might seem a curious thing for a farmhand to be doing, and the farmer asked, "What are you reading?"

"I am not reading," replied the farmhand, "I am studying."

"Studying what?"

"Law, sir," said the farmhand with emphasis. Russell Godbey said it was really too much for him, as he looked at the law student, "sitting there proud as Cicero." Going on his way, "Great God Almighty!" exploded Mr. Godbey.

During the spring and summer of 1835 New Salem had its own excitements. Samuel Hill built a carder and storehouse for wool. The carding machine was powered from a treadmill walked by oxen on a tilted wooden wheel with cleats—a late marvel of the mechanic arts. A new sound—the friction of moving wood, the muffled knock of hooves on wood—entered the village day. On August 17 at night a tornado came tubing and screaming over the prairie and in its wake Matthew S. Marsh saw fences flat, trees uprooted, and corn beaten down. At daylight he went to put up his fence and saw to his amazement how "two great wolves walked along unconcerned within 50 yards of me." Eight days later at her father's farm northeast of New Salem, after an illness of six weeks, young Anne Rutledge died.

The law student knew her well, as he knew all her family. She was the third of nine children, and as a boarder at her father's New Salem tavern in 1833 he had surely seen her. She was vivacious and pretty, with auburn hair and blue eyes. At quilting bees she was faster than anyone with her needle, and in the other household arts she was accomplished. She would make someone a good wife.

In 1832 she became engaged to a prosperous young farmer and storekeeper who went East to arrange his affairs with a promise to return and marry Miss Rutledge. Time passed while his letters dwindled and finally ceased. She grieved. The law student saw her so, and certain neighbors wondered if he might be ready to fall in love. A few became sure for all their lives that he courted her and that she was prepared to accept him. She hesitated, but at last wrote to break her engagement. No answer came. Torn between desires, she fell ill and within a few weeks was dying of fever. One of her brothers said she kept asking for the law student and at the last she was allowed to be alone with him. A few days later she lost consciousness and on August 25 she died. They buried her in Concord graveyard.

New Salem sorrowed for Anne. Some said long afterward that the law student sorrowed more than anyone—that once again they feared for his reason. Slicky Greene reported that when the snows or rains fell, the law student was filled with "indescribable grief" at the thought of how they fell on her small resting place in the country graveyard. His inclination to occasional low spirits seemed to be increased by her death. She used to sing hymns to him. The last one she ever sang was "Vain Man, thy fond pursuits forbear." Sometimes, even where advantage lay, human pursuits seemed futile. Where of advantage there was none, depression could the more easily enter a man. "Woefully abstracted," said a friend, the law student would range along the river and into the woods. Neighbors kept an eye on him especially on "damp, stormy days, under the belief that dark and gloomy weather might produce such a depression of spirits as to induce him to take his own life."

It was one thing to be given "the hypo," as he called it, by fugitive annoyances; quite another to be lost to the whole daily world. Finally he was persuaded to stay for a few weeks with the jolly justice of the peace, Judge Bowling Green, beyond the little hills north of New Salem. Judge Green loved to laugh with all his three hundred pounds. The shape of his belly earned him the nickname of "Pot." He was good for the law student. The ordinary matters of life proceeded. The law student tended the post office, though someone complained that he neglected his duties at this time. He studied. He surveyed a ten-acre lot of timber. He wrote to the Governor of Illinois to endorse an applicant for the post of public auditor. On December 7, 1835, he was counted present at the opening of a special session of the Assembly in Vandalia. On March 24, 1836, his name was entered on the record of the Sangamon Circuit Court as a man of good moral character. This was the first of three steps leading to the license to practice law. The law student was coming back to himself. Years afterward, Isaac Cogsdale, formerly of New Salem, said he heard him say of Anne Rutledge, "I loved her dearly . . ."

Throughout the spring he was active as deputy surveyor, but in May he lost his other position when the post office of New Salem was discontinued by the government. The village had ceased to grow—had even begun to decline. Families moved away. A number of them founded the town of Petersburg, which the deputy surveyor had laid out in February. Perhaps the future lay elsewhere.

In early summer an old excitement came back in the air, for it was again a campaign year, and the assemblyman announced his stand for reelection on June 13. "All," he said, should share the privileges of the government "who assist in bearing its burthens." He believed all whites who bore arms and paid taxes should vote, not excluding females—though he could not have imagined women in the army. He declared further that he went for "distributing the proceeds of the sales of the public lands to the several states."

From July 4, when the campaign opened at Petersburg, to the thirtieth, when it ended at Springfield two days before the election, the candidate toured the district with his rivals. They came to meetings on horseback, riding into a grove in the forenoon, when the opposing candidates took turns speaking until all were done. If a fight broke out that seemed to depart from fair play, the tall candidate from New Salem stepped in to shake the fighters apart. He spoke in groves and on farms, supporting the Whig position. On July 29 he spoke at the farm of Isaac Spear, six miles southeast of Springfield, where the campaign would wind up.

Moving on, he rode past the new house of old George Forquer, who was running against him. On top of the house—it was regarded as the finest house in Springfield—he saw, for the first time, a lightning rod.

What a contraption. He never saw the like. It led him to speculate about electrical conduction. It gave him thoughts about the owner.

George Forquer had until recently been a Whig himself, but now he was running as a Democrat, and what was more, as a new Democrat who had been given the post of register of the Land Office at a fine salary—three thousand dollars a year. No wonder he could build a new frame house with a lightning rod on top. It was enough to give a man the hypo. The New Salem candidate rode on to Springfield.

There the next day he took his turn and made his speech. He was the last. When he was done, the crowd began to go. Democratic Land Office Register George Forquer rose to detain the crowd and they turned back to listen.

He was sorry, he said, but of his opponent, who had just spoken, he must say that "the young man would have to be taken down."

The Democrat, as an elderly and prominent man, had much to say and he said it at length, and with every air of superiority. The New Salem candidate stood aside, listening intently and with growing excitement. His chance for rebuttal came, and he took the platform again, made another speech, and ended with this:

"Mr. Forquer commenced his speech by announcing that the

young man would have to be taken down. It is for you citizens, not for me to say whether I am up or down. The gentleman has seen fit to allude to my being a young man; but he forgets that I am older in years than I am in the tricks and trades of politicians. I desire to live, and I desire place and distinction; but I would rather die now, than, like the gentleman, live to see the day that I would change my politics for an office worth three thousand dollars a year, and then feel compelled to erect a lightning rod to protect a guilty conscience from an offended God."

"Wonderful," said a witness, the effect of this reply was wonderful, something he would never forget. The public was captivated by it. Two days later, on August 1, the young man from New Salem—he was twenty-seven—was reelected by the highest vote out of the field of seventeen candidates. On December 5, then, he was present when the Tenth General Assembly of Illinois met in Vandalia.

He came there with his desired goal more clearly in sight, for on September 9 he had applied for a license to practice law in all the courts of the state, and this had been granted to him on the same day. It was the second official step which would lead him to the work he wanted. Only one more remained. But before he could take it, he must serve the Assembly in his elected duty. Because of their height, he and the other eight members of the Sangamo delegation were nicknamed the Long Nine.

In his current term, as in his previous one, the assemblyman met with a wide range of affairs in the bills proposed, the debates which resulted, the hearings which were required, and the disposals made. All these reflected the needs and aspirations, the concerns and the natures of the men and women whose lives they sought to govern for the better.

The assemblyman took part in the vote on such matters as the works of human justice and dignity which appeared in bills on the establishment of circuit courts, and on the powers of justices of the peace, and on legislative procedures, and on the delineation of voting districts and precincts. With his fellow members he voted on the election of the United States Senator. He considered as a committee member the problems inseparable from the disposition of public monies, and with scarcely a half-cent piece in his pocket, he voted on questions of taxation, of banking, and of incorporation of insurance companies and railroads. The Assembly was much occupied with the development of travel and the needs of people coming and going. He considered and helped to decide upon proposals dealing with public roads, toll bridges, canals, and river navigation. Education was public business, and the assemblyman worked on schools in general and schools for orphans. Much of the common concern had to do with the homely life of work, household, and sustenance. He was on the record of legislation covering cattle marks and brands, the regulation of mills and millers, the "Little Bull Law," which meant to govern breeding of cattle but which was repealed as inequitable, the killing of wolves and the determination of bounties therefor, and—an act which reflected with intimacy and compassion the poverty, the need, and the terms of the farmer's life—a bill to declare exempt from legal attachment one work horse or a yoke of oxen, so that daily work might continue. The Assembly took account of human trouble, and the assemblyman acted with his associates on bills looking to the relief of debtors, and bills against gaming, and bills regulating the penitentiary.

It was a broad experience of man and man's ways of constantly reshaping himself as a social being. In his first term the assemblyman had been "silent, observant, studious," as a contemporary said. In the new term, he was, of those his own age and length of service, "the smartest parliamentarian and cunningest 'log-roller.' " These knacks of his enlivened his efforts in the second term to secure the removal of the state capital from Vandalia. Many towns were after the prize, but Springfield was the leader. The assemblyman led the fight and on the last day of February 1837 he saw the bill he backed win the approval of the majority. On March 1 he saw another achievement when in the office of the clerk of the Supreme Court of Illinois his name was entered upon the roll of attorneys as a member of the State Bar. It was the third and final qualification toward which he had worked.

Before the term was over on March 6, the assemblyman, with Dan Stone, his fellow townsman, filed dissent from a resolution adopted by the House. The House resolution went on record against the abolition of slavery. The Sangamo assemblyman and his colleague made a joint statement saying that "the institution of slavery is founded on both injustice and bad policy." In the temper of the time, however, they added that "the promulgation of abolition doctrines tends rather to increase than abate its evils." With this moral act, the assemblyman was ready for the adjournment of the House on March 6.

During this term his self-image found words; for he told Joshua Fry Speed of Springfield that he aimed—it could only be the pinnacle of fame—he aimed at the "great distinction" of being known as "the DeWitt Clinton of Illinois." Governor Clinton of New York was dead since 1828, but he was remembered. Six feet tall, of noble proportions, he was known as "Magnus Apollo." Like the assemblyman, he had started his career in the state legislature. He had gone on to become United States Senator, Mayor of New York City, Governor of New York State, father of the Erie Canal, and a champion of public education. Joshua Speed could be excused if he smiled at the hope of anyone to equal such an illustrious record. On March 7 and 8 the assemblyman, in his short claw-hammer coat and his hiked-up pantaloons, made his way home to New Salem.

He had come there the first time on the heels of a hard winter. This, of 1836–1837, was another such, when weeks of rain left puddles and snow melted to slush. Suddenly one day came a violent freeze and the countryside was fixed in ice. Chickens and geese were frozen fast to the ground. Travellers, caught by the shift of wind which brought the freeze, were endangered, and some died. Washington Crowder, riding to Springfield, was overtaken by the storm. Coming to a store he tried to dismount, but—as a local account of the marvel said—"was unable to dismount, his overcoat holding him as firmly as though it had been made of sheet iron." He called for help. Two men heard him and came out of the store. They tried to lift him down, but his clothes were frozen to the saddle. They loosened the girth and "then carried man and saddle to the fire and thawed them asunder."

Home again in New Salem, the assemblyman contained a new resolve. It would not be long until he should make it known.

New Salem had been his school, his academy, his college. There he had learned how to use language correctly and beautifully; how to speak and debate in public; how to study; how to plan towns; how to write laws by reading law; how to live amid people and how to respect their common concerns and forgive their uncommon ones. There it was he had left the forest and the river, which had also taught him much, and had found the world. Like all others, he had to find out where to look for it, but it was there to be seen, if he would look, in a hamlet in a wood above a river. In all his young life he had worked to overcome disadvantages, and as they enlarged, so did he, in spirit, patience, and strength, among his neighbors of

New Salem. They had suffered him when he suffered, and laughed for him when he reached for their funny bones, and allowed him his hopes, and voted for him when he asked them to. As he was, so had New Salem helped to make him.

On April 12 the Springfield paper carried an announcement that the assemblyman—once a flatboatman, a store clerk, a militia captain, a candidate, a postmaster, a deputy surveyor, a law student, and now a full attorney-at-law—would, with J. T. Stuart, "practice conjointly in the courts of this Judicial Circuit Office No. 4 Hoffman's Row upstairs."

The resolve made, it was time to go.

On April 15, 1837, he borrowed from Judge Bowling Green a small pony with a worn-out saddle. In the saddlebags he put his copy of Blackstone, a copy of the compiled laws of Illinois for 1833, three volumes of session laws, two small miscellaneous books, and some underclothes. When he mounted the pony his long legs nearly reached the ground. His fortune consisted of about seven dollars in his pocket. A friend declared that "superficially he seemed like a farm hand in search of employment." So it was he rode off to Springfield, leaving New Salem, which, in two years, like the store he had once owned with William Berry, would "wink out."

Springfield numbered fewer than a thousand people but it was a lively town and promised, as the new state capital, to be livelier, after the State House was built. Business houses defined the public square, which like the streets was all dust in summer and thick with mud in winter. Street crossings consisted of slabs of wood. A few small brick buildings contained stores and offices, which were furnished with the barest conveniences. Six stores, a merchant's mill for custom work, and three country taverns completed the public buildings. Yet residents could show style. Some went richly dressed in fine carriages. Little luxuries were imported, and gave tone to literary evenings and political dinners. If the frontier was just down the street, cultivated life could be found just indoors.

The new attorney and counsellor-at-law from New Salem rode into Springfield on April 15 and went to the only cabinetmaker in town to inquire for a single bedstead. He then saw the store of Joshua Speed. He tied his pony and unsaddled it and went in, hauling the saddlebags, which he threw on the counter. What, he asked, would the mattress and bedding for a single bedstead cost?

Joshua Speed took his slate and pencil and worked out some figures. The total, he stated, would come to seventeen dollars.

"It is probably cheap enough," said the attorney, "but I want to say that, cheap as it is, I have not the money to pay." They looked at each other. "But," he continued, "if you will credit me until Christmas, and my experiment here as a lawyer is a success, I will pay you then." The tone of his voice, thought Speed, was so melancholy that he felt for him. The attorney said, "If I fail in that, I will probably never pay you at all."

Speed looked at him and said to himself that he had never seen so gloomy and melancholy a face in his life. He said to him, "So small a debt seems to affect you so deeply, I think I can suggest a plan by which you will be able to attain your end without incurring any debt. I have a very large room and a very large double bed in it, which you are perfectly willing to share with me if you choose."

"Where is your room?" asked the attorney.

Speed pointed to the stairs leading from the store to his room. "Upstairs," he said.

The attorney said nothing, threw his saddlebags over his arm, went upstairs and set them on the floor, and at once returned. Speed said his face was "beaming with pleasure and smiles."

"Well, Speed," he exclaimed, "I'm moved."

The satisfaction of this youthful attainment of a momentous stage could not last.

But for now—while still lost in the inexorable future were the circuit and the Congress and the White House and Ford's Theatre and a lodging in the world's heart—it was enough for the former citizen of New Salem.

1961

Josiah Gregg and His Vision of the Early West

To Mexico

THE DOCTOR

There was always a scientific cast to Josiah's thought, and there certainly was a scientist's technique of observation in his records. He had tried being a schoolmaster, a lawyer, a prairie trader, a surveyor. All these were not absorbing enough. They did not seem to make him any the more comfortable. There were many things unanswered. One of the hardest things to understand was perhaps oneself. Why this wretched health? Why this uneasiness in any settled society? Why when he comes home are his resources of health and fortitude so heavily taxed?

The early spring of 1845, at Shreveport, was a lovely season. There was much to observe in the country. The town was five miles away (John had moved again and Josiah was visiting him). It was far enough for a determined hermit. "I cannot even endure our village for more than an hour at a time. I frequently send for the weekly mail to get rid of seeing the streets of Shreveport. . . . I see nobody—hearing nothing but the singing of birds, etc." A man always alone by his own choice must spend much time dwelling upon his own situations. That Gregg did so is clear from his letters and diaries. He is preoccupied with his poor health, which of course made it seem all the poorer. The sympathetic and intelligent brother with whom he spent so many interludes between "enterprises" wrote a fine letter after Josiah's death in which we find many clues to a complex temperament, which when it was happy was not happy in an ordinary way. Over and over John records that Josiah would become restless on returning home. Nothing suited his taste or was adapted to his genius. Josiah himself was at a loss to explain this. But that he realized how his state of health was involved there is plenty of evidence. His scientific knack was visible early in his life. John wrote of him that as a child he had often said, "I can't pass by anything I don't understand."

His next important move may have been dictated not only by his scientific tastes but also by a desire to further his understanding of that which had baffled him so when he desisted for a moment from his pursuit of the active physical life to which, on first notice, he appeared so ill adapted. For in the autumn of 1845 he went to Louisville, Kentucky, to enter a medical college to study for the degree of doctor of medicine. He stayed a little over a year, hearing six lectures a day, each an hour long. Evidently he was not enrolled as a regular student—this middle-aged man with so many determining experiences behind him. But he was granted his degree under the honorary convention at the commencement in March 1846. Study for the doctor's degree in medicine was then not so universally standardized as now, and often a doctor was made simply through the serving of an apprenticeship under a practicing physician. But it must have been perfectly plain to the faculty that Josiah was in every way superior as a candidate for the degree, and by his intelligence and application undoubtedly earned it. The idea of practicing was evidently never very important to him. He wrote his brother that he would certainly never use the title doctor unless he *did* practice.

It is interesting, in line with our notice of his unsociable ways, that he elected Louisville as a place for study because he knew nobody there. After he was there for a while, he wrote home that he hated meeting up with someone he knew who introduced him to many acquaintances—including professors. He said it would interfere with his "grand object" in coming here—his studies. But not long after, he seemed much attached to some of his new friends on the faculty. What barriers of constraint and acute self-consciousness must have surrounded him at first, in any new situation.

He did not feel very well throughout that winter. At one point he was about to quit his studies and leave Louisville because he felt so wretched. ("I am now in no condition to study.") Everything around him was colored by his state. ". . . though I have said nothing on the subject, I fancy *que los señores profesores* [that the professorial gentlemen] are becoming a little more distant, as though they thought I might expect favors; I cannot beg of them, that is certain. Beg *honors* of such a corps!" (Through elegance or embarrassment he often used foreign phrases in his letters and attempted a wry jocosity by the liberal salting of his lines with quotation marks. It is the kind of indirection a shy person making an effort would resort to.) But the same professors did give him his honorary degree, and regardless of how he scorned them, he did accept it. "As for my studies, I have got on badly, what between trouble of mind and ill health." —What is significant here is the conjunction. He, in his time, separated health of mind from health of body. To us, in our time, they seem interrelated. "I could never live under my oppression of spirits anywhere in the U.S. where I would be liable to continued annoyance."

ALIEN ABROAD

This refrain is so frequent that we cannot help countering it with the question, Why? Why didn't society enclose him comfortably? He was literate, well acquainted with polite observances; indeed, he was sometimes very stiff about them. To judge from his photographs (of which there are exceedingly few), he was personable, with a look of vitality and keenness about the eyes, which were dark, and deeply porched by fine brows. His face was rather pointed, revealing its bony formation frankly. His hair was dark and abundant. He had a well-shaped mouth, at rest in a reserved expression. Since he habitually bought the best quality of merchandise, it is likely that he was always well groomed. An engraving in the early editions of his book shows a figure of medium height standing on a knoll with an Indian guide, watching, across a deep plain where prairie wagons are encamped, the approach of a great band of Comanche warriors. In the text Gregg says he ascended this knoll with the guide, and the engraved figure is presumably his. He is wearing a plainsman's wide-brimmed hat and a knee-length coat belted close to the waist, hung with huge pockets. He wears his trousers outside his boots. He is gesturing to the Indian guide to signal the approaching warriors with his white blanket. This miniature engraved figure is not a portrait in the ordinary sense; but it is a glimpse of a man in a moment of truth, however conventionalized by the graphical idiom of nineteenth-century illustration. What it confirms somehow is our sense of his dignity.

"I have no desire to be considered an odd fish," he used to say, according to his brother John. It is a touching admission that he was so considered. He never drank, did not like liquor, was temperate in both food and drink; but he "sometimes would take a glass of spirits with a friend, as it would appear, merely not to be considered *odd*." It is a wistful gesture, the complete solitary reaching out to become one with his fellows. In the curious laws of personality, he was made to *feel* eccentric, and so increasingly, protectively, he *acted* eccentrically, and thus became a "type," a sort of wandering intellectual cartoon among the venturesome men of the Westward period. We may smile at the circumstance, but what remains is admiration for the steadfastness of his essential self, which created his satisfactions out of the hardest materials. Often before, and since, that has been the attribute of genius.

And yet it is hard to blame anyone for misunderstanding him, when we reflect upon his vision of propriety and its inflexibility. He had so little humor in his idle jottings and his formal pages alike that it seems fair to decide even this late that he showed none in his personal dealings. For instance, in his great book,* he describes the smoking of the calumet, or peace pipe, with a tribal circle on the prairies; and he behaves as if the act of smoking itself were intrinsically novel—as if it had been unknown to the white races for the previous two and a half centuries. Without humor, then, he says that the pipe passes around the circle of councilmen, which is not necessarily funny—simply interesting. Then he speaks solemnly of the councilmen, "each sending fumid currents upward from the nozzle."

This is no doubt to him an exact description of what happened. But Gregg hated smoking, and the gravity of his description is

* *The Commerce of the Prairies.* New York, 1844.

disdainful, all out of proportion to the familiarity of the act. What a contradictory man; how interesting to catch this dry flavor from the same man who is moved to deep feeling by other acts of prairie life. We begin to detect his curious insulation against human preoccupations, frailties, oddnesses. It is tempting to think up an explanation of this remoteness in him, which often seems like a lack of sympathy. Perhaps it is fair to excuse him by saying that he was harsh in self-judgment, and disciplined a poor body and an unsocial spirit until he felt their human claims reduced to unimportance. His severity upon others might thus have been induced first by the habit of severity with himself.

He was that anomaly in society, the one who appears to betray his kind by standing apart and observing them; and for him they inevitably hold a sort of uneasy derision. He was neither wholly a trader, nor an artist, nor a scientist, nor a physical man, but a thoughtful combination of all these; and on the frontier, where judgments were simple and likenesses were apt to be crudely reckoned, he was a puzzling creature. He was not even an out-and-out fraud, a pretentious "professor" whose intellectual claims could be howled down in good-humored hazing. There is evidence that Gregg's very abilities, however much their use gratified him alone, exposed him to annoyance.

If society does that to him, he may strike back with "critical intelligence" and enjoy the bleak satisfactions of lonesome superiority. Does this explain why he should be so eternally insulted by steamboatmen, soldiers, lady hotelkeepers, frontier travellers on the trail, the thousand and one thoughtless opportunists who were doing their share in the frontier life he was describing so truly and coolly?

He was, among them, alien.

They were doing jobs and butting against obstacles and lending their bodies and their shrewdnesses to the task of conquest, and of surviving it. All this time he was acting in one further dimension of effectiveness—he was analyzing, reasoning, recording. He was observing the conditions of natural life through which other men passed with shorter sight. He was the theorist, the man of mind, in the West-rolling procession of men of action. To him the highest act of a man was *to understand*. But we all know another kind of man who views with contempt and anger the wresting of knowledge from the frontal experience of life, and who tries to punish any other who would do it. This was expressed in the hazing of the frontier.

Gregg would have been at home in New England; he could have talked with Emerson and Thoreau. But he was torn between the freedom of the prairies, where he was accountable only to his thoughts—where, indeed, they had no audience—and the need for sharing these thoughts. His book is the solution of this conflict. Having no sustained contact with society, for whatever reason, he *wrote* to it, and secured himself a posterity, of which he surely never thought except in terms of what later men would think of the trustworthiness of his work.

"*SERVICE TO MY COUNTRY*"

In March 1846, the new Dr. Gregg is on his way home and has stopped in St. Louis to do some shopping—a few polite gifts for the family, an album for Eliza, a volume of poems for Miss Kitty, the works of Hannah More and Mrs. Ellis, a little picture primer for the baby, and a "dozen ordinary primers . . . for Puss and the babe to learn to read in." Having not much money, he got these literary items in exchange for copies of his own work. He bumped into some old friends, J. T. Cleveland and his wife, who were "very kind indeed," although "they want to *casarme con una viuda* [marry me to a widow], an elegant miniature portrait painter, who says she would be 'delighted' with a life on the Prairies—but they 'can't quite come it.'" Eluding the gifted widow, he hurried home to Independence, with thoughts of the prairies in his head, after a whole winter in the doubly constricted society of an American city and an academic institution.

He soon made arrangements to set sail on the plains with his old friend and partner, Colonel Owens, but delays occurred; goods from the East failed to arrive, and scarlet fever broke out in the family of his sister and brother-in-law, the James Lewises. It was a miniature epidemic. Eight of the family finally came down with it. The neighbors were terrified; "few offered help," and Gregg "was compelled to remain sitting up half of the nights till I left."

But life in this inland port of the prairie sea was already exciting. "The emigration this spring to California or Oregon will be immense." He saw it; he recorded something of its stirring significance between the lines of his diary: "—6000 souls, with 1000 wagons, moving Westward across the great Prairies during the present summer from this part of our frontier." It is like an intonation, as well as the statement of a fact. To the west lay the future. To the south lay Mexico. But Mexico had been a far country since 1843, when Santa Anna closed the Mexican trade because Americans were sympathetic and helpful to Texas in her border troubles. News from Mexico came to Independence, Missouri, earlier by way of New York, two thousand miles away, than by way of Santa Fe, eight hundred miles across the plains.

But this was 1846, and the United States was at war with Mexico, and a venture in the Santa Fe trade was likely to be backed up shortly by the United States penetration into the northern Mexican province.

He sent his books, instruments, baggage, and so on, ahead in the wagons of Colonel Owens and set out to overtake them alone a few days later by horse. The whole country was aware of the war. There was a strong sentiment for intervention. A justification was maintained by debates in Congress. When Texas achieved statehood, the nation inherited the border difficulties of its newest state. Gregg observed that he was with President Polk in the matter, and in a Macaulayian sentence of symmetry and elegance remarked, "for though, when the subject was first agitated, I had my misgivings as to the consequences and policy, and also thought the rights of Mexico should be to some degree respected, the discussion of the matter has dissipated the first difficulty, and the deportment of Mexico the second."

Arkansas and Missouri raised volunteers.

It was a time when citizens felt privileged to serve. Gregg was approached by Colonel Yell, Member of Congress from Arkansas, to go along to Texas with the Arkansas Volunteer Regiment as a kind of expeditionary aide, whose knowledge of the country, people, and Mexican language would be useful. But the request was not very specific as to his duties or rank, and since he had already sent his possessions out on the prairies, he left to overtake the wagons on the plains.

Shortly afterward, as the wagon train was moving overland on the trek, it was overtaken by the owner, Colonel Owens, who arrived from Independence, bringing another appeal to Gregg, this time from Senator Sevier, also of Arkansas, urging him to join the Chihuahua army; and he decided to go. This second letter "substantially warranted me an 'honorable and profitable' situation." He took up whatever luggage he could "conveniently carry on a horse, with my sextant, etc.," and turned back to Missouri—yet if his horse had not happened to run away, he says, he "probably should not have returned but for this casualty; though my horse was brought back to me after I got everything ready to start back, and the wagons of Col. Owens had started on." He went home and waited for more definite mail from Washington. Such matters as his exact status, his rank, his pay, had not been discussed. To a precisionist, this was exasperating.

Nothing came in decent season, so he decided to "start south this morning [Monday, June 22, 1846]; for that is the point where I had the greatest hope of making my humble service of some use. The sacrifice I make on this occasion is certainly very great, for I was compelled to permit my baggage, books, and all my preparations of outfit and convenience for the tour, continue across the prairies with Col. Owens. However, I shall feel amply compensated for all my privations and labors, if my present tour turns out to be of any service to my country."

He was out to do his best; but his services would be the cause of irritation on both his side and the army's. He was wasted upon a job that was neither wholly civilian nor wholly military. He was hazed by the soldiers, and his intelligence was affronted by the poor administration of the high command. The war was a tragicomedy, enacted upon a barren stage under the pouring light of the desert sky. Nothing ever seemed to get done; and yet, one day, the forces found themselves arrayed for a vast engagement; and the wasteful, dreary, inconclusive months were forgotten; and the policy of a continent was secured in battle at Buena Vista.

PRELUDE TO BATTLE

"This is a singular warfare we are waging, is it not?" he asked in one of his letters to the editors of the *Louisville Journal* in 1846. From his point of view, the whole thing was an accumulation of irritations, inefficiencies, and humiliations.

Gregg was rarely the man to temper his judgments, either of himself or of others. He had survived the hardships of the plains, during that decade when the Santa Fe trade was the prosaic instrument of the national design. He was forty years old, and felt, and looked, much older, in the robust and thoughtless company of the United States Army in Mexico, whom he was accompanying as what: guide? translator? interpreter? The point of his status was never cleared up, although he was supposed to receive "the pay and perquisites of a Major." If he felt like an outsider, he certainly talked and wrote like one. His experiences with the army invading Mexico left a bitter taste. He was genuinely eager to be of service. He was ready, like a patriotic American, to march with a well-disciplined force under brilliant officers to a rapid and humane and, above all, efficient conclusion of the Mexican adventure. What he met with was altogether different. Everywhere he turned, someone or something served to bring out his most acidulous opinions. The war was to be fought, here, on this map? Then why was it not done exactly so, on the ground itself?—that baked and reptilian desert, where few men have subdued the natural world according to their orderly designs. General John Ellis Wool, first of all, the commanding officer, was unpopular with "at least ninety-nine hundredths of the troops he commanded. Ergo: could all have been right" with the state of affairs? Wool may have been "an amiable gentlemanly man; yet I fear rather crabid and petulant, and perhaps . . . old-womanish—more efficient in minutiae and details than in grand and extensive operations."

That was what was wanted: "grand and extensive operations," and the war would simply not live up to them. Endless sky, the grit of hot sand, an amateur army, the growing pains of the nation, the vanity of men contending with sense. General Wool moved about the town with staff and guard of twenty mounted dragoons with drawn sabers, a spectacle which Gregg did not like. The other officers, too, were "petulant," "out of their element." They quarrelled, they resigned, they wrote lengthy "reports" and justified themselves, they bore themselves haughtily, even Captain Albert Pike, though he deserved "to stand decidedly 'number one' in point of talent and acquirements," even Pike, on the way to Chihuahua, later, was very remiss of his men's comfort, and was sternly caught at it and duly noted in the evening's session with the bound notebooks.

A certain Colonel Hamtramck was even worse than General Wool at pomposity, a quality which was just a disguise: "The fact is, any man with a fair degree of cunning and management, who is abjectly subservient, and will use a sufficiency of flattery, will hardly fail to gain a great influence over the general's weak mind." As for General Shields and General Butler, the one "is a military monomaniac—crazy—his head addled by his elevation . . . one of the veriest *military* simpletons," and the other, "as a military man, though brave as need be, no doubt, he is rather imbecile." Josiah had occasion to smart under "the rudeness of Gen. Lane and more especially his aide . . . who, to make up for his ignorance and want of talent, put on an air of insupportable presumption—at the same time inclining to treat me as his 'orderly' while I was gratuitously interpreting for them. The low grade in which interpreters are held, and the low class of people, in fact, generally engaged as such, is one reason why I have refused to accept this office, even though at a high salary."

He said that he, himself, would never solicit an army commission from the President, it being beneath his dignity. However, he added, with the offhand sort of hint so binding to relative or friend, that his brother John might take steps, if he liked. As to rank, it was now too late to satisfy him with the rank, as well as the perquisites, of a major: "but *Lieut. Colonel* I should be very well pleased with." He underlined it to make it perfectly sure, and saw himself suitably uniformed; but nothing came of this delicate intrigue, even after he left General Wool to join the staff of General W. P. Butler; and when he left Butler, eventually, Josiah refused the pay accrued and due to him, for the very Greggian reason that although yes, he had earned it, he disdained to accept it because he had never been given a definite appointment. A propriety so fierce, so baffling to the very spirits it intended to educate with an austere rebuke, must have appeared merely cranky to them.

He was tempted many times to give up his association with the army and set out as a freelance reporter of the fantastic campaign. His effects—books, instruments, records—had gone on to Santa Fe with Colonel Owens and from there had been taken down to Chihuahua, where they now awaited him. He was spoiling to get to Chihuahua; to be free of this military society in which he was so uneasy; to recover his possessions; to know again the consuming duty of observing the country, accountable to no one. But there were delays. One of them, as it turned out, was worth the bother.

BATTLE PIECE

At last, for a time, all was forgiven that infinitely puzzling army. For when the long time of preparation was somehow done with, and the foes met by the hacienda of Buena Vista at the foot of that mountain which looked so beautiful at times, Gregg was full of fellow feeling and ardent sympathy with the very soldiers whom he had judged with a sniff, and who had hazed him back, in their cruder way. The battle, he wrote to John, was "that glorious but awful affair." It had been coming for days—a Mexican spy in the town kept reporting to Gregg, and there is an innocent sense that the town evidently knew of the battle plans from day to day.

When the day came and the troops were moving to their stations, the wagons rattled so that the Mexicans thought the noise came from artillery fire.

Josiah was there, riding a horse all in and around the battle, maintaining himself "on high and commanding points . . . so as to have a view of all the operations." He was in great danger from musket fire throughout, with his calm, orderly, recording eye in the midst of the confused action. As usual, his factual net took in details which were the prosaic seedlings of poetry, of feeling. He heard the United States soldiers greet a Mexican cannonade with "hearty yells," and the words suddenly resume their original meanings, and in the smoky blue battle air we see again the toiling little figures by the batteries, and we feel the thudding valor of their hearts, which saved a day and swayed a century.

Josiah wrote several accounts of the battle. He described it to John by letter, and he wrote more formal accounts which appeared in the newspapers back home. Even now, his description reads with excitement and awe, ennobled with the emotion which a less embarrassed and cynical age than that following Korea and Vietnam felt free to associate with patriotism. In the hand-to-hand warfare of Gregg's time, pity was still a right of the victor; and he described not only the suffering of the defeated Mexican troops but also the mercies of the United States soldiers to the wounded enemy after the battle was over. He saw his compatriots tending the wounds of the Mexicans on the battlefield, and giving them water, for which they cried. He found and helped to bury his old friend Colonel Yell, of Arkansas, who had persuaded him in the first place to turn back from an expedition out on the plains and join the Arkansas Volunteer Regiment. From the smoke and loss of the battle, a new continent was struggling to arise. Gregg had intimations of it. The active war, in effect, was over, though much yet remained to be concluded with the withdrawal of troops. Patience? Patience was never one of Josiah's virtues. Possibly the analytical intelligence cannot wait, once it has the answer in mind. But when the answer took form and was paid for dearly in flesh and blood, then the long argumentative months, the uncouth maneuvers, the rude manners of campaigning soldiers were forgiven; and at the Battle of Buena Vista, Gregg admired as heroes the officers and men whose other values and purposes had not reached any sympathy in him.

THE MISSOURI INDEPENDENT

After the battle came an opportunity to make the trip to Chihuahua. A Santa Fe trader named Collins, now interpreter to Doniphan's regiment, had come from that city bringing dispatches from Colonel Doniphan, who had marched down from Santa Fe and was now in control of north-central Mexico. Collins was about to return to Doniphan after Buena Vista, and Gregg was eager to attach himself to the party and reclaim his effects in Chihuahua. It would be a suitable arrangement. Collins's party was to be escorted by troops under the command of Captain Pike, "decidedly 'number one.'" There was only one obstacle, and it had to do with vanity: to go with Collins and Pike, Gregg had first to obtain official permission through petition to General Wool. To ask a favor of this miniature Napoleon indeed posed a struggle between pride and utility. Pride lost, but haughtily.

He made his request in a personal interview. The general had been reading the papers, all along. He was smarting under the published criticisms by his irritable guest, and, worse, he even had heard that Gregg "was going to write a book." It was a chilling rumor. The general received Gregg with a sense of injury. Dr. Gregg bore himself with the mien of justice incorruptible. They conversed. Immediately afterward, Gregg wrote down a report of the meeting. It is plain that, for whatever reason—an eye on posterity in the presence of book writers, or whatever—the general tried to make friends. But Gregg was suspicious, declaring that the general was only angling for admiration and approval. In Gregg's report, Wool does most of the talking, borne on by a torrent of words—"that state of irritability in which a man has to talk, talk, talk, merely to convince himself that he is in the right," as Tolstoy said of the original Napoleon. In any case, the interview ended with permission for Gregg to set out with Collins and Pike.

Free of his doubtful army connections at last, he started off on the five-hundred-mile trip through enemy territory to recover his belongings at Chihuahua. He was fully aware of the dangers involved, but he was as lofty toward peril as he was toward ignorance.

Even the Mexicans themselves were in danger from Indians, and the United States troops sometimes had to help. "This is certainly a novel warfare," wrote Gregg, "fighting and defending the same people at the same time, and killing those who would be our allies if we would permit them. True, although at war with the Mexican *nation*, we have never pretended to hostilize the unarmed citizens, and, under no circumstances, could we permit the savages to butcher them before our eyes. This display of a spirit to defend the people against their worst enemies, the Indians, will, I hope, be attended with good effect."

Gregg had some just and sensible remarks to make on the subject of military reprisals against enemy nationals. General Taylor had issued some particularly sharp orders, and Gregg could see, at the time, how cruel and unjust they were. He took justice and reason with him wherever he went, or tried to, despite the unreliability of his health and his resultant capacity for indignation, which was at times boundless. But if he became indignant on his own account more often than was quite dignified, he also spared no wrath upon those who persecuted others. In his accounts of the army in Mexico, and of people on the move generally, we get his ethical flavor at its best. He never felt that the laws of home should be left behind by the traveller, or that character was a *local* matter.

At Chihuahua he gathered together his belongings, and eyed Colonel Doniphan's column, which had marched down from Santa Fe, won the Battle of Chihuahua, and was now prepared to march east to join General Taylor.

Gregg joined the column, but of course in his own fashion. One day, under the blazing sun, the soldiers beheld an apparition, which they hailed with incredulity and finally with roars of laughter. It was Dr. Gregg, bolt upright in his mule's saddle, with various outlandish accoutrements strapped about him, wearing his habitual expression of disdainful interest, and holding over his head a red silk parasol. Rejuvenating their tired spirits at his expense, the soldiers began to release their wit. Catcalls and remarks, at which he was "a little annoyed as well as amused." He was irked, too, at the "impertinence of the volunteers in other regards. Being constantly employed in collecting botanical specimens, etc.," as he said of himself, the soldiers "must needs know every particular about them

. . . often accompanied by taunting and insulting expressions; so that the naturalist has to pass an ordeal in laboring among ignorant people, who are wholly unable to comprehend the utility of his collection."

For Gregg never ceased his scientific labors, and kept making bundles of specimens of Mexican flora to send, fully catalogued, to his friend Dr. George Engelmann, of St. Louis. His work was of genuine value; but everywhere his experience in performing it was the same. Among the cheerful, the lusty, the rascally, occasionally criminal, characters of our frontier century, with its necessarily muscular values, he was often regarded as a crank. He did not have the one quality which might have saved such a judgment. It was humor. Now and then a pleasantry gleamed wanly through his careful writing; but nowhere was there a healing gust of laughter, which would have blown away the clouds of irritation he so often knew among people. If we imagine him, severe, correct, careful, at his scientific observation, with a solemnity which ruder men might take for disdainful superiority, it is not hard for us to understand, though we would not justify, their view of him. After all, he gravely recorded that at Castañuela he not only saw a dwarf but measured him.

At Monterrey, he found old General Taylor, and measured him, too, though in words. The general was all dressed up in uniform ("pants, with stripes") for the first time—he always used to wear an old, civilian coat, and to dispense with the striking insignia of his rank. Now he wore epaulettes and had sentries, for the Presidency was a genuine possibility, and he made these grand gestures, said Gregg, as marks of respect for Doniphan's Missourians, whom he had previously reprimanded, and whose arrival must now be an agreeable occasion for them to recall at the polls in the autumn.

Through with the army, and far removed from his old life on the plains, Gregg was readily receptive when Samuel Magoffin, veteran Santa Fe trader, proposed a partnership in an "enterprise," Gregg's familiar term to mean a trading venture. Gregg was to go, now, to Philadelphia, where Magoffin had established large credits, and buy merchandise, which would be shipped to Mexico. It was a pleasing return to the pioneer trade, and he went East in the late spring of 1847. He had barely arrived in New York when word came that Magoffin considered the "enterprise" too great a risk financially and that the deal was off.

"He has done me great injustice," wrote Josiah with restraint, "and caused me immense inconvenience; for I had left most of my baggage at Saltillo, upon the faith of the engagement to return." It meant that he would have to go back after this useless journey to get all his possessions, books, instruments, data.

In New York he tried to see his old friend Bigelow, who was never in; nor did Bigelow respond to any of the notes and cards which Gregg left upon him. The venture was altogether a nuisance, and it was in an attempt to snatch something from the long and expensive journey that Gregg went (by way of Brandywine Springs) to Washington, "with the idea I might obtain some government employ in Mexico." But he was appalled, as a proper citizen, at the state of government affairs. He had a visit with the President, and was "astonished at the evident weakness of Mr. Polk." Making a hard judgment upon the man, at first contact, as he usually did, Gregg withdrew from Washington with almost an air of ceremonial disdain for Polk, feeling that he "would not accept anything at his hands." It was "remarkable that a man so short of intellect should have been placed in the executive chair." And yet, to a democrat, with a small "d," it was not so surprising when it is remembered that Polk had not been elected by the people, who would never have done it, "but by a caucus at Baltimore who rather desire a 'creature' than talent to leave designing politicians a tool."

Gregg started West again, writing several letters on the way to his friend Dr. George Engelmann, on botanical matters.

THE ''UNACCOMMODATING''

Always plagued by steamboats and their "unaccommodating" officers—it was his eternal word of censure—he started down the Mississippi. He noted "the great self-importance and commanding tone of the 'mate.' Really, these petty steamboat officers exercise their authority with more 'zest' than a general over thousands!" and "Captains and clerks are unfortunately too often . . . perfect despots within their little floating realm." They were aboard the *Martha Washington*. She went aground several times. A day later (August 27, 1847) he was on board the "small steamer 'Ellen'—a wretchedly mean clerk again." Four days later, "in a little stern wheel steamer 'Jim Gilmer.' Another mean clerk!" As for the captain of the S.S. *Telegraph*, "being pretty tipsy, he flew into a great passion."

He had meant to go straight to New Orleans on the great river, and thence direct to Monterrey, but the yellow fever was raging in New Orleans, and he turned aside again to visit the John Greggs at Shreveport. He improved his stay by exploratory wanderings on the Red River and by listening to accounts of the Great Raft which natives had seen, a frontier marvel too extraordinary to omit. Intermittently for some two hundred miles, and continuously for sixty miles, the Red River was once covered with a solid, water-level roofing of logs and vegetation so dense and "so overgrown with timber for many miles, that the traveler might pass over across the river without knowing it." The phenomenon was mentioned by other frontier recorders, including Farnham and Edwin James, though Gregg had "never seen the person who has witnessed such a state of the river." But he declared that Farnham's account was exaggerated. James noted that the water-borne jungle had been blasted out with powder by government agency.

Presently he moved on again, and in New Orleans on September 24 was obliged to glare at "a hotel clerk—Fallon—most surly, un-accommodating and I fear ill-faithed fellow." It was a description, too, of Captain Dubbs of the steamer *Ashland*, on which Gregg sailed for the Brazos from New Orleans in November 1847. It was a preposterous voyage. "This wretched vessel is short and round-bottomed, without keel or cut-water, and therefore would slide over the water sidewise" before the wind. The master was drunk day and night. Unseaworthy, the *Ashland* was almost disabled in the Gulf of Mexico, when the schooner *Miranda*, of New York, was sighted. The miserable passengers of the *Ashland* were joyful at the chance to be taken off; any change would be, they felt, an improvement. The *Miranda* at first refused to take them aboard and sailed away. But before long, she came about and returned, signalling that she would take the passengers, but that the *Ashland*'s boat would have to bring them. This the drunken Captain Dubbs refused to agree to, and the *Miranda*, of New York, resumed her course. Gregg and his fellow victims were in "despair."

It was a really intolerable adventure, taking seventeen days to cover a voyage ordinarily done in four. When at last they dropped anchor off the Brazos, their drunken captain could not make up his mind. First he would, then he wouldn't, put them ashore, pending repairs on the boiler. He finally let them go, and they drew up and signed a bill of complaints against master and vessel, and through its almost spinsterish genius for converting irritation into logical complaint, who wrote it is unmistakable.

Gregg's next embarkation was on the steamer *General Jesup*, with his luggage and a dearborn carriage, up the Rio Grande, and at last, on board the light draft steamer *Oreline*, he found a steamboat captain who passed muster, "a son of the celebrated divine, Rev. Mr. Moffitt," with whom there was no occasion for "a tart repartee," as Josiah sometimes described his own weapon in his endless quarrel with the "unaccommodating" wretches on frontier travel.

At last he was back in Saltillo, after a wearing journey. The United States armies were still in occupation, but everybody was hoping for a signing of the peace treaty before long. When the troops went home, new heroes would go along; and politics would be enlivened by battle cries. He wrote to Bigelow—who had written a "very gratifying letter," so that his apparent indifference in New York was magnanimously forgotten—giving him a cool and balanced view of General Taylor, from whose readiness the home sentiment was roughing out a piece of Presidential timber. Far from the excitements of national politics, Gregg was able to resist the political contagion of the warrior's legend: "—a very clever sort of old fellow, but as to his being a very *great* man—even as a warrior, and much less in every other regard—it is all nonsense to talk about it." However, politics aside, and the enthusiasm of backers discounted, "if the people would let him stand at what he merits, there is no man, whom in his way, I would esteem higher than Gen. Taylor."

"WAYS AND DOINGS"

In the winter and spring of 1847–1848, he stayed in Saltillo as a medical practitioner, the only time in which his studies at Louisville were formally applied. His services were enormously popular. Writing to John, he said that his fees had grown steadily month by month, and that his high of over four hundred dollars for the month of April could actually have been worth over five thousand dollars if he had wanted to charge as unfairly as his competitors in the town.

There is a sense that he was happy in Mexico: it was a new country to be looked at, and recorded about, and when he was doing that, he was really alive. The Mexicans were engaging. Was there a possibility that here he might find a society in which he would be at home? Here is what might have been an arch hint:

"Tell Eliza and Kitty that I got pretty 'high in the paper' at Saltillo among the *señoritas*. At least I became 'De biggest boy in all de town' with the belle of the city. I was even invited on visits with her and gallivanted through the streets, with her trailing on my arm. 'That's some,' you'll say, *pero no habría más*." ["But there was no more."]

The accent of dead slang and the flurry of quotation marks, and his embarrassed complacency, all give us the bachelor unaccustomed to romance. Aside from the artistic widow who painted miniatures and who was not averse to a life on the prairies, this was the only reference to relations with women in all his known writings.

He collected the little grains of interest which go to make up any local scene. Gossip of the time does more for its history than solemn tablets. The mountains near Saltillo he called "decidedly romantic and beautiful," and we get a flavor of his period from that usage. There was a horse thief who escaped by joining in the hue and cry of "Stop thief!" and we note how unbroken a lineage sustains rascals in their ingenuity. As for politics, or intrigue, there was a project (October 1848) to form a new and separate republic out of four Mexican frontier states, Tamaulipas, Nuevo León, Coahuila, and Chihuahua, to be called La República de la Sierra Madre. But since there were private adventurers behind it, Josiah objected and would have none of it.

Gregg's medical partner in Saltillo was a Dr. G. M. Prevost, and in Josiah's cool, scolding account of him, we can still feel the poor human warmth of folly over a hundred years old: "He unfortunately became in love—desperately so—and what was more remarkable for a man of his intellect, with a little girl (13 years old) without any special beauty or merit—and still less talent and intelligence." The young man was "of rather unusually handsome person." He was swept away from his medical responsibilities by "his high empassioned temperament," and when reproached gave himself "airs of haughtiness and self-importance." Nothing was more distressing to his senior partner than "his utter want of system and order . . . everything in the way of medicines topsy-turvy and in perfect confusion. . . ."

To the self-disciplinarian, such an affair could only be exasperating. What a waste of time and attention! He had a better scheme for improving evenings. He got up Spanish classes in Saltillo, to meet in the evenings, to (1) have "social collections"; (2) educate the officers;

(3) "break up . . . card parties." He organized his venture ardently; but only a few came, and it perished. In February 1848, at Saltillo, he was turned out of his house by the army, and a Major Howard and "a family of prostitutes" moved in. But he was busy as a doctor, he was happy, and he seemed satisfied. "If I could make myself as easy in American society," he wrote John, "I would be willing to live in the United States."

He was evidently liked by the people, and it seems clear that at last he liked them, although he was always more or less in hot water with the official world, even in Mexico. On one occasion he was held in Guadalajara by the local governor, and was proceeded against by troops, but he felt outlandishly confident of being able "to defeat them with only his servants." But good sense dissuaded him from amateur warfare, and the affair ended with an apology from the proper quarter.

Again and again we run up against a quality in him which in the cool medium of his own words sounds priggish, and which in the more vital medium of his living presence must have obscured his great virtues and services from less thoughtful men than he. (We must not allow the infirmity and impatience of this period of his life to disguise his great achievement as historian of the prairies, and we must remember that the dignity and courage of his last days were yet to come.) If he served science, it must often have seemed that he served it with such indignation that others—all others—did not see the responsibility, and the priority, of the act.

He rarely felt the human climate so sharply as he did meteorology. And yet—such was the honesty of the man—he reported the wise "lecture" which General Almonte gave him (April 12, 1849) on Mexico's comparative infancy in the modern world, and the impatience of the United States. Still, a masquerade which he described, and which, by his own details, we find charming, he called "brutally absurd."

Since he was not feeling too well during this period, his irascibility was that of the invalid, the man who found his resources of body unequal to the wants of his interests and imagination. In visiting the mines of Real del Monte, he was "too weak" to go down ladders to the bottom of deep ravines. "As usually happens to me, the ride out in the stage so disordered my stomach, that I was greatly debilitated for a day or two after." Had he become clumsy and uncertain in his movements? He lost his keys by dropping them somewhere. Bending over a pool, he lost his Colt revolver out of its holster, and saw it vanish in the water. The same thing happened again, and the party he was with impatiently went on without him while he tarried behind, trying to recover the pistol.

But he had plans for examining new lands and finding new specimens. He wrote to his friends about these ideas. One project was to go from Mexico City down to South America, passing over the Isthmus, to explore the outlines of the great continent, going first down the Atlantic side, around Cape Horn, a fabulous land voyage, and then back on the Pacific side up into California, and across to Santa Fe (which was by now a territorial capital), and thence home to the United States. He was forty-three years old. There seemed much time yet. The California coast alone would repay an attentive traveller with many new specimens of plant and earth. Abandoning the great coastal survey of the southern continent, he finally decided to cross Mexico to the Pacific and travel north overland along the west coast. There were inconveniences . . . a robbery of a hundred dollars from one Richardson, who was his house guest, by two young men whom he had befriended and trusted and who escaped on his mules, which they stole. The thieves were caught and jailed, but the money and the mules had been "made away with."

There was a scandal at Chapultepec, too, where Josiah had gone to inspect the historic castle. Questioned by a guard, he answered with asperity. There followed insults, he was jailed, reviled, released, and he made a protest to the United States minister, demanding punishment of the offending officers. Would anything be done? "Nous verrons," he wrote in gloomy sarcasm. He tried, and failed, to meet President Herrera of Mexico. "Mere curiosity," he shrugged. The toll agents on the road in Mexico, of course, betrayed "ill breeding and rascality." Discovered in a cornfield with his animals and party, Gregg was attacked with excited words by the owner, and only the arrival of the local *alcalde* prevented serious trouble. But Josiah was "unable to believe that the judge was really in good earnest—or it were only a *ruse* to get out of what he considered a bad scrape— Nevertheless, I felt charitable enough to believe the former." Here was Gregg's lack of grace at its worst, or sickest, for his health was gradually leaving him.

On the other hand, his ingenuity and the plains craft taught him so long ago by his frontiersman father were triumphant when his wagon was upset in a wild hinterland, and with nothing but the rude materials at hand, he managed to replace a broken axle, so that the wagon was in even better repair than before. He rolled on toward the west coast of Mexico, full of the idea of Manifest Destiny, in which he "foresaw" Pacific Mexico all occupied by United States citizens down to Mazatlán and even farther south. In this he echoed the popular idea of his time, which seems so foreign to our regard for the independent integrity of the other republics of the hemisphere.

Gregg was of the order of men who create literature out of their most daily preoccupations, that is, without a transfiguring act of the imagination. Romantic inaccuracy may produce masterpieces, but so may the earnest magpies, the gossips of fact, they who sense the marvel in the trivial, the whole from the part, and so translate acts of life for us that we come to know ourselves better for knowing them, since their bustling literary acts imply much of larger life itself.

For Gregg said, by implications and acts, that freedom was as desirable as growth—indeed, possibly that they were the same thing; that the prairies were natural domains for America to grow into; that the life of the prairies was beautiful and instructive; that wisdom can be brought to bear upon new experience if conscious observation is an ally; that intelligence is a better mate for courage than simple enthusiasm; and that if a man is alive to the best opinion of his present and aware of his inheritance from the past, then he may perform work valuable to later times.

When Gregg was born in 1806, there was no organized civil life west of the Mississippi. When he died in 1850, four great paths had reached the Pacific. In his short lifetime, forty-four years, the United States achieved its continental design; and he was among the men who helped this to happen.

He might be called the intellectual frontiersman of the natural world. There is high poetry in the quality of his achievement, though its terms at the time never look so. His story is part of a great conquest, in which his particular weapons were curiosity and a batch of little bound books with blank pages, waiting to be written upon.

No chronicler who sought the truth ever needed more.

1979

Lamy of Santa Fe: His Life and Times

[*Born Jean Baptiste Lamy in the village of Lempdes, Puy-de-Dôme, in the Auvergne, in 1814, he was to become the great civilizer of the American Southwest in the nineteenth century. The inheritance of Archbishop Lamy as a son of Auvergne spoke through his life.*]

HOMEWARD

[*In 1866 Bishop Juan Bautista Lamy goes to Rome to give an accounting of his first eleven years as Bishop of Santa Fe. Pius IX receives him warmly. Despite the difficulty of visualizing in any full sense the hard realities of Lamy's problems and achievements, the Curia is impressed by his report of progress in religion, education, charity, and general social amenity in his vast territories of the American Southwest. Now with a sizable party of religious recruits to go West with him on his return journey, he sails from Le Havre, May 9, 1867, on the "magnificent sail and steam vessel* Europa."*]

The crossing was mild until on May 19 the *Europa* encountered a violent storm off Newfoundland in a "gulf" which the sailors referred to as "The Devil's Place." For a while the ship was in extreme peril, and all on board suffered; but she made port safely on May 23, coming up the Narrows to New York early in the morning. There, before Lamy's new collection of strangers, lay unknown America and their separate fates. Two days later they were at Baltimore, where Lamy left the seminarians, including his nephew Anthony Lamy, who was Marie's brother, for further study with the Sulpicians, and boarded the railroad train to St. Louis for three days of "remarkable" luxuries and comforts. By June 2 they were in St. Louis, where three Loretto nuns and two Christian Brothers joined the party. After four days of shopping and outfitting, the bishop was ready to lead the way West. He had twenty mules, two small wagons, and five "light ambulances," and two saddle horses. "This outfit," he said, "cost us near $5000" (in today's money, at least twenty thousand). June 7 found the party in Leavenworth, as guests of Bishop Miège, who now had a large house where all the men were put up, and where he gave them every comfort. The nuns—two Sisters of Charity and the three Lorettines—stayed at St. Vincent's Academy. Two Jesuits joined the group there—including one of the Italians from Naples—and also going along were a student, Paul Beaubien, from St. Louis University, the bishop's young business agent, Jules Masset, and two Mexican servants, Antonio and Antonito: twenty-six in all.

Lamy considered which trail to follow over the plains. He had hoped to take the northern fork of the Santa Fe Trail, by way of the Smoky Hill River, Bent's Fort, and the Las Animas River in order to meet with Machebeuf in Colorado. But all reports indicated that the warring Indians were more active there than elsewhere. Through that summer, the whole prairie seemed continuously afire with Indian furies; for, after the Civil War, emigrants were again pouring to the West, threatening the Indian's supremacy in his own domain; and the Indian was striking back with ferocity and skill. So continuous was the struggle, so active was the army in newly established forts along the westward trails, that the eastern papers carried every day a regular news report with the running headline of "The Indian War."

Lamy decided it would be prudent to abandon the northern route and to set out directly to the southwest toward the familiar ford of the Arkansas River to the west of Fort Dodge, Kansas, at a place known as Cimarron—one of two crossings a few miles apart, the other being near the later settlement of Ingalls. This was the path most often used by the wagon trains for Santa Fe and Chihuahua; and in the summer of 1867 Lamy heard that there were many such caravans on the plains. In the company of one or another of those westbound his people would be safer than alone.

The party left from Leavenworth on June 14. Four days later they reached a Jesuit mission at St. Mary's of the Pottawatomies, where in good company they rested for six more days. Leaving there on the feast of SS. Peter and Paul—June 29—they moved on across the southern reach of the Smoky Hill River, and there they entered upon the prairies proper bidding "adieu to civilization." That river, said one of the missioners—it was Father J. Brun, who wrote letters based on his diary—"marked the boundary of the Indian territory, a river sadly famous for the piracies and massacres committed by the savages."

Soon after that crossing, while the bishop's party were encamped, four mounted Indians suddenly appeared. They were painted, wore loops of necklaces and feathered headpieces; and at their belts each had a little mirror which he always carried. Asking for tobacco and coffee, they sharply scrutinized the wagons and the people of the caravan, and departed in silence as suddenly as they had come. "They were spies," said Brun.

He had a stranger's eye and word for the disturbing newness of all that the party encountered. After the eastern travel and its comforts, he now saw "the reverse of the medal." The miseries of the sea were replaced now by those of the land, and they were worse than the ocean storms. He had his list: to sleep on the bare earth under open sky; to use your boots for a pillow; to live in the mud (they met with two weeks of almost unceasing torrential rains); to hump along on a horse all day under a burning sun; to be on the alert at every instant for savages; then, to sleep without supper; to rise and depart without breakfast; to suffer torture by mosquito; to go ten or twelve miles looking for a ford at a river before making camp, fighting the currents which might carry away wagon and cargo. And the exhaustion! What would be the worst misery in ordinary life counted for nothing in the most usual events of the journey. "We asked ourselves," he noted, "whether to laugh or cry." But *pleurer?* —No! he declared stoutly.

They had trouble with straying animals, and herders who got lost looking for them and had to be searched for as well. Once, far off, they thought they saw in a great dark mass far ahead of them an army of Indians massed for the attack. Lamy climbed up on a wagon wheel and gazed through his telescope—it was a relief to see that it was a large caravan bound east from Santa Fe whose members had been as frightened and for the same reason as Lamy's party.

Eventually they overtook a large caravan of eighty wagons, including those of Jewish merchants of Santa Fe, with men well armed, going their way; and the two parties joined together. The better to protect Lamy's people and provisions, Captain Francisco Baca, who commanded the traders' train, divided it into two columns, assigning one to each side of the bishop's party.

According to Captain Baca's scouting parties, there were evidences of a great body of Indians—perhaps a thousand strong—coming together for attack. A hollowing sense of increased danger pervaded the caravan.

On Sunday, July 14, Lamy said Mass and preached on two seriously related topics—one was "the necessity of bearing with fortitude the evils of this world," and the other was the absolute requirement that all must give "strict obedience to orders." For now they began to see little detached parties of Indians reconnoitering and retreating, over and over again, "not unlike those wolves which are said to gather far and near to attack strayed sheep in the desert."

But now another trial—one familiar to prairie voyagers—came to afflict the train: cholera was epidemic on the plains—almost all trains were infected, including a few of Lamy's wagoners, and presently the disease was spreading up and down the straggling and slow-going line, chiefly among the Mexican carters. A priest who travelled part-way with Lamy saw how he "was always the same, affable, in good spirits, stout-hearted, passing his courage along to his missioners." Such steadiness was needed in the atmosphere of uncertainty and in the face of obstacles which the party encountered. Lamy had been assured of military escort from Fort Harker. He sent a detachment to notify the commander that the train was approaching; but the rivers were in flood after the weeks of heavy rainfall and Lamy's men never reached Harker. He went on toward Fort Larned. A detail of troops came to meet him, but because of the cholera, their officer imposed a quarantine and sent the train on a detour away from the fort. Once again, without soldiers, the long train resumed the plodding march to the southwest, drawing away into the low undulations of the distance, where the heat of the sky and the reflected heat of the earth met in a glassy waver which absorbed the line of the horizon and which either enlarged any object entering the mirage, or erased it from sight, as if it had never existed.

PRAIRIE NEWS

Readers of the New York *Herald*, on Friday, July 19, 1867, turning to page 4, where the running headline of "The Indian War" appeared as usual, were shocked to read a "Special Telegram to the Herald" announcing

> Capture of a Train near Fort Larned, with a Bishop, Ten Priests and Six Sisters of Charity—The Men killed and Mutilated, and the Women Carried Away.

The dispatch went on to particulars:

> Leavenworth, Kansas, July 18, 1867
> (6 o'clock P.M.)
> A train was captured last Sunday, near Fort Larned, by the Indians. Bishop Lamy, ten priests and six sisters of charity accompanied the train as passengers, en route to Santa Fe. The men were killed, scalped and shockingly mutilated. The females were carried away captives. This information comes through reliable sources.

The news went rapidly across the prairies, and from Topeka Father Defouri wrote to the Society at Lyon what he had heard of the "horrible death of Mgr. Lamy." Reporting the failure of troops to serve as escort, Defouri stated that he had no details beyond the information that the party had been massacred without mercy, but added, "we know that the body of Mgr. Lamy was horribly mutilated, ten priests were staked out and scalped. The rest were taken prisoner. The poor sisters, what horror! to be slaves at the mercy of these savages; dragged from village to village to be subjected to every kind of outrage and probably to die lashed to the post of torture. Let us draw the veil over it all, and pray."

At Trinidad, Colorado, the pastor, Father Vermare, heard the same story at his outpost near the New Mexican border, sorrowed for those who had been slain, and for their families and colleagues in France, and held a Requiem Mass in his mission chapel for the dead bishop and his companions.

THE BATTLE OF THE ARKANSAS CROSSING

The plains were almost level. There was little or no evidence of rock. As they would start out on the trail in the morning, they could see perhaps fifteen miles ahead the actual end of the day's march. The dimension of this limited vision governed their sense of time and space, and commanded their patience in new terms. The south wind prevailed and often threw obliterating dust across the vast spaces and anything that moved across them. Imprisoned in distance itself, the travellers could find escape only through the inner self—faith in their purpose, whether that of layman or priest or nun, even as they were open to every danger of land, sky, and human attack.

As nearly as the trail allowed, they had followed the Arkansas River with its great bends. It was, after the first half of the plains crossing westward, the main source of water, until it must be left behind at the final crossing west of Fort Dodge. The troops at that post were also ordered to quarantine the caravan because of the quick contagion of cholera.

As darkness was falling on July 17, the bishop's train halted for the night. Men began to unharness the draft animals. Others were preparing the camp. It was never clear whether darkness was a blessing or a further danger. Before the picket lines and the temporary corral had been formed, fifty Indians suddenly as if created in that instant appeared from the west and attacked the halted company with showers of bullets and menacing yelps of battle. The surprise was complete, but the Mexican drivers returned the Indian fire, leaped on their mounts and gave chase to the Indians, who in their usual tactics had ridden by to ready themselves for a return attack. The Indians vanished, and the traders returned to their camp. The attack had been a scouting raid. The camp kept extra watch all night and moved out again with daylight.

Farther west, they met trains—one large, one small—coming from Santa Fe with soldier escorts which had been sent out from Dodge. They had been attacked an evening earlier by elements of the same Indian party. There had been casualties—two men killed, three wounded, some of them troopers, and after two hours the Indians had retired. It was now clear that all the approaches, east and west, to the Arkansas River crossings in the Cimarron stretch were under the constantly moving control of the Indian bands. They were like cloud shadows, now seen, now invisible, according to the contours of the open land as they swept across it.

The trail to the river showed many roughly parallel wagon tracks, as everywhere else on the prairie route. A caravan could be expected, by anyone watching, to follow a known course. Lamy knew the path from having used it before. He knew it when they were coming close to the Cimarron crossing. He rode up and down the column giving strict instructions to all his people. By general consent he was acknowledged as a commander of the whole train, and his orders were taken by the merchant traders and the Mexican wagoners alike. He created a common nerve of understanding, and the purpose of it, as everyone understood, was defense. They moved warily along on the morning of July 22. It was a dry day—hot, dusty. The combination of space and unvaried slow movement over seemingly empty land was often hallucinatory, especially as travellers strained to see, on all sides, that which remained expertly hidden.

At mid-morning—they said it was about ten o'clock—word came to Lamy, and the sisters in their wagon, that young Jules Masset was suddenly writhing with abdominal cramps. He was sweating. His fever rose. It was cholera. One or two of the Santa Fe merchants went to his wagon to do what they could for him. Massaging his belly to ease his cramps, they could only watch him sicken rapidly as the morning went by and the train made no halt for the nooning. Toward two o'clock they came to the low rises beyond which lay the Arkansas River. They soon saw the river and its opposite bank.

The water ran, heavy with silt, in a channel which was part of a much wider dry bed. The approach from the left bank, where the wagons came, was wide and sloping gradually to the ford. The whole crossing was perhaps fifty yards wide. The opposite bank was more abrupt and the trail led from the river and past a grove of cottonwood trees. Tall fox-colored brush grew on both sides, and short, tawny grass, and prickly bushes with black stems and branches and parched leafage. The water was pale, reflecting the hot white sky, and the white salts of alkali showed along the brink. In the far distance ahead were low, pale blue ridges. If the hot south wind blew, it lifted heavy dust—almost sand—from the banks and threw it over everything, so that the general effect was a monotone of pale earth color.

At two o'clock the train broke the line and formed a semicircular camp, with its long side based as closely as possible on the northern bank of the river. The passenger wagons and animals were in the center, surrounded by a stockade of cargo carts close together. Sentries were posted at once to watch in all directions. One Mexican wagon forded the river without incident—though there were sinkholes and quicksand, and the current was more vagrant than it looked. The wagon, which included in its cargo kegs of brandy, rose to the crest of the opposite bank near the trees where the low grass grew. The drivers left it there and returned to camp without seeing what the sentinels saw—two Indians lying "on their breasts in the weeds, like snakes," watching the wagon as it crossed. When enough more had crossed, leaving a divided defense, they evidently meant to make a signal for attack and take the rest of the train before it could move.

A detail of fifteen men was sent out to scout the land behind the low rises above the camp. In almost no time the scouts came tearing back to camp pursued by hundreds of Indians. Two of the scouts were almost taken, but escaped by riding in a wide circle back to the river. The camp was still settling into its routine for the usual brief nightly halt. Lamy's preliminary orders now took hold. There were about ninety armed men in the train; they were at once ready at their stations, with loaded rifles, and on order, they fired at the Indian pursuit.

The battle was formed.

The Indians withdrew to range themselves seven or eight hundred yards away on the low crests. From that main body two small bands rode off, one to the river above the camp, the other below. They crossed the river and met at the stranded wagon. Breaking into it, they found the brandy, smashed a keg, and drank.

From the rear, the main body of the Indians charged down upon the camp and were met with a great salvo from the American rifles, which were effective at long range. The attack drew back. A few fallen Indians were surrounded and carried away in the retreat, as Indians always retrieved their dead or wounded. Once again in order, the Indian phalanx flowed down the low slope but again was forced back. Their arms had less range than those in the caravan —they carried bows and arrows, rifles, and, said the bishop, "*pistoles à six coups*"—six-shooters. They were splendidly mounted and rode wonderfully, concealing themselves all but for feet and hands behind their horses' bodies as they galloped past the riflemen in the wagons. When they fired, their bullets fell "like hail" but without taking serious effect.

As the battle flowed back and forth in fury, confusion, outcry, sweat, and dust, Jules Masset, knowing that he was dying, began to call out for his mother. Lamy was told of his state. The word went also to one of the Sisters of Charity—it was Sister Mary Augustine—

who said she would go to the suffering young man. Told which was his wagon, she began to thread her way along the ground between other wagons. She said the arrows flying all about her sounded like "a disturbed beehive." She reached him and gave him what comfort she could, and before he died, one of the priests came to attend him, while the battle went on outside. (In all, ten persons died of cholera on the journey, and were buried on the plains.)

Now the attackers resorted to a variety of ruses to bring the defenders out of their wagon-fortress. John Geatley, an armed wagoner, said, "The situation was appalling—it appeared we were to contend with all the savages south of the Platte River." The Indians drove up from behind the northward ridge a large herd of cattle they had stolen from the train which had been attacked the day before. They hoped the traders would venture out to capture the cattle. But no one went. Again, a file of Indians rode past the camp, with "incredible agility," to invite a foray into combat. Lamy harshly ordered no one to budge from his post within the stockade. They fired from their places, and he fired with them. The Indians retreated again, only to return in force time and again.

The din was appalling. Those huddling within the wagons, seeing nothing of what went on, but hearing the impact of bullets and arrows on the wagon wheels, the fusillades, and the war cries from one side and the shouted orders from the other, saw in their minds a struggle even worse than the actual one. One of the nuns—the youngest, Sister Mary Alphonse, a Lorettine eighteen years old—was in an extremity of terror. They heard the drumming hooves advance and retreat, hoping that every retreat would be the last; but the sustained onslaught continued for almost three hours. How much longer could it be resisted?

Finally, the main body of the warriors drew away, leaving behind a few small bands who rode back and forth in challenge. But the defenders knew that the surest trick of the Indians was to simulate a retreat, wait for lowered caution, or even emergence of a beleaguered force, and then to resume the attack in new ferocity, often victoriously. But presently there was no Indian in sight.

In the lull about thirty men ventured out of the wagons on to the open space between the camp and the ridge to inspect the battlefield with its scattered trophies—wounded or dead horses and their saddles, bridles, moccasins stitched with dyed quills, necklaces of shells and wampum, arrows, rawhide quivers. In a flash, a line of Indians rode down upon them from nowhere, and the traders barely made it safely back to the wagons.

During one of the charges, a warrior among the Indians was— so a man in the wagons thought—a young white man whom he identified as Charley Bent, the son of the onetime Governor Bent of New Mexico. It was a curious discovery, for young Bent had been educated in Catholic school and college of the Middle West and the East, but had chosen to join the raiding Indians in their plains life.

Toward evening, the Indian groups crossed the river to assemble near the stranded Mexican wagon, which they plundered, cracking open more brandy, and set about getting drunk. One Indian dashed back and forth across the river crying toward the camp, *"Amigos! Amigos!"* but no one responded; and far into the darkness, the traders continued to fire at the Indian bivouac on the far bank. After dark, the caravan animals had to be fed, and were cautiously taken to graze along the river's edge outside the camp. Indians observed this, and some swam over under darkness and in as much quiet as possible tried to stampede the herd. But Lamy's sentinels, whom he kept strictly at their posts, heard them coming, drove them back with rifle fire, and the animals were brought back into the corral. It seemed almost a signal that the battle was over when the Indians set the lone wagon on fire.

Presently all was quiet.

It had been a "terrible day," said Father Brun, "these seven hours of combat." The pious Mexicans of the train considered that they had been saved by the presence of a bishop and his priests, as ministers of grace. Beyond that, it was Lamy's skill and example which had most acted to save the expedition, in support of Baca's command.

Early the next morning, in all caution, the crossing of the river by the entire train began, and took most of the day. They marched until late. There was no sign of the enemy. As they came to their slow halt and the making of camp, the young Sister Alphonse lost all her strength. The bishop was called by the other nuns who attended her. She was dying. Lamy "assisted her for death." She lived during the night, and at the assembling of the train for the next day's march, she begged that her body not be left by the train but be taken on to Santa Fe for burial, for she was mortally afraid that the Indians would desecrate her grave if they found it. She died at ten o'clock on the morning of July 24. Lamy wrote of her that "she was a girl beautifully educated, and a true model of piety and of all the virtues . . . she died of terror" endured in the battle. Her last wish could not be observed—there was always the chance of contamination by the cholera; and toward evening, with Lamy assisting one of the priests, she was buried by the trail, in a rude coffin fashioned out of some planks taken from a wagon. A wooden cross was put at the head of her grave. In a few years this disappeared; but someone found her grave anyhow, near the still-visible ruts of the trail, and not far from the tracks being newly laid for the westward advance of the railroad; for where she was buried, the prairie grass grew higher than that all around.

The train moved on, presently crossed the Cimarron River, and days later came to Trinidad, where they read in the Denver *Gazette* how the bishop and the other men had all been massacred, and the religious led away as captives; and where Father Vermare told them he had sung a Requiem Mass for them all. "It is thus," wrote Father Gasparri, one of the Jesuits in the party, "that history is written." Actually, the massacre report had been denied within a few days by the New York *Tribune*, and Defouri and Vermare had written hastily to Europe to relieve those who grieved for Lamy and his people. The Secretary of War, General U. S. Grant, issued a statement confirming the falsity of the report, and a Washington dispatch stated that it had been the work of "wretches who manufacture lying dispatches and send them broadcast over the country with cold-blooded malice"—the purpose being to inflame public feeling against the Indians the better to have the war of extermination against them intensified and, presumably, the western lands opened more readily to settlers. "The object in view has been too well accomplished. The indignation of the public mind against the poor Indians has been fired."

Lamy and his people came into Santa Fe during the evening of Assumption Day, August 15. Despite a heavy rainstorm, people began to assemble to ride out "on the States road" to meet him, and as he entered the city he was greeted by all the bells of Santa Fe, and a *Te Deum* in the cathedral sung by Vicar General Eguillon. The bishop had been absent for almost a year, and his plains voyage, with all its storms, had taken sixty-two days. "His whole caravan was saved through his foresight, nerve, and kindness," Defouri told Paris. Lamy himself wrote the Society that in a few days he would send the details of the "long, laborious, and dangerous voyage across the prairies," but now he would merely report his arrival, as, at the moment, he felt "a little tired."

[*After three and a half decades of "purgatorial work," the old Archbishop Juan Bautista Lamy cultivates his garden at Santa Fe until "the end of a fine day."*]

THE GARDENER

More spare than before; taller than average, he was still muscular. Callers—according to the season he saw many in his garden—saw his dark eyes somewhat sunken, though still quick to sparkle when he was amused or interested. His jaws and cheekbones and chin now jutted out like the granite outcroppings of his old country of Auvergne. His mouth was folded inward—he had lost teeth. If he had always moved deliberately, now perhaps he went more slowly than before. He had few personal indulgences; and the one he loved best, gave most to, received most from, was the garden behind the cathedral. There his adobe house, with its small chapel, stood at one edge of the five-acre tract; and there through the years he had made a haven away from the parched distances of his far-flung work. It was a silent and living model of what could be done with the desert; and lying all about it, the city of Santa Fe also bore out his belief in planting and cultivating what would take root and grow. Mid-century daguerreotypes of the city showed almost no trees; but in photographs of the 1880s, the plaza and other streets had bountiful shade. From many a plains voyage Lamy had brought cuttings of fruit and shade trees and grapevines all the way in buckets of water, scarce as it was, to be planted on his arrival home.

The garden was walled with adobe by his first French architects, who had crafted its main entrance out of native granite. There was a sparkling fountain, and a sundial stood on a pedestal of polished Santa Fe marble. Aisles of trees, plants, and arbors led to it from all quarters of the enclosure. Formal walks reached from one end of the garden to the other, with little bypaths turning aside among the flower beds and leading to benches cunningly placed in the shade from which Lamy and his visitors could see, on the high ground to the north and east, the old earthen battlements of Fort Marcy, and "the only brick and modern residence in the city, and a windmill, probably the only one in the territory." To the west through the branches of his trees he could make out the long blue sweep of the Jemez Mountains. At the south end of the garden on its highest ground was a spring which fed a pond covering half an acre. From the pond flowed little graded waterways to all parts of the garden. In the pond were two small islands, on one of which stood a miniature chalet with a thatched roof. Little bridges led to the islands. Flowers edged the shores, and water lilies floated on the still surface, and trout lived in the pond and came to take crumbs which the archbishop threw to them. Now and then he would send a mess of trout over to St. Michael's College to be cooked for the scholars.

There was always color in the garden through the warm season, for he chose varieties of plants which would in turn keep new blooms coming. He loved to bring wild flowers in from the country—some said he "tamed" them in his cultivated beds. There was a plot for vegetables. Many of the trees bore fruit, and he worked season by season to improve their size and flavor. From cuttings of California vines he grew Malaga grapes whose bunches finally measured fifteen inches long. His cabbages and beets were huge, and he once showed three turnips which together weighed twenty-five pounds. His strawberries were so spectacular that he was able to sell them for a dollar a box, giving the proceeds to charity. When he came to live in New Mexico there were almost no fruit trees, for the fruit culture of the Spanish and Mexican colonists had vanished. Bringing in new orchard stocks, he encouraged others to do the same. For each tree he spent ten or fifteen dollars; and for freight—when the trees came by stage—ten dollars a pound. One of his pear trees yielded one hundred and fifteen pears in a season, and his prize cherry tree, which he called the Belle of Santa Fe, bore two crops a year of black oxheart cherries. For a visitor he could pick a peach of five and a half ounces, a pear of eleven, or an apple of sixteen. When he gave a caller one of his prize peaches, it was always with the earnest request that the pit be kept—and planted.

Among his shade trees he cultivated elm, maple, cottonwood, locust, and both weeping and osier willows. There were red and white currants, plums as large as hen's eggs, and flawless Catawba grapes. Every vine leaf, every shrub, was sound, and so were the trees —apple, peach, pear (he espaliered the pears with the help of Louis, his gardener, who was remembered as a "wonderful gardener, a little man"). They said that much of Lamy's original garden stock came from Auvergne. When the yield was bountiful, he would thin out his growths for transplanting.

Within his garden walls, he delighted to receive visitors. The garden was a famous sight in Santa Fe—the other, which he could see at the eastern end of his retreat, was the unfinished cathedral, one of whose towers was rising toward its belfry. He would walk the raked aisles with his callers, or sitting by the pond throw crumbs to the trout. A correspondent who signed himself D.T.W. in an Eastern paper had a fine day with the archbishop, who opened for him "a bottle of the best wine I have yet tasted in Santa Fe . . . it would have passed for a very fine Burgundy."

They sit by the trout pond, in which Lamy most "delights his soul." In one corner of the lake, partitioned off from the rest, "is the nursery, where the baby trout are—little fellows, but as spry as can be." Lamy has his favorite seat by the main pond. As they talk, the archbishop commences "throwing bread into the water." The lake, which is as smooth as glass, now looks as though a thunder shower has suddenly dropped upon it. Its whole surface is agitated at once. For every crumb of bread that fell, "I should judge that forty fish rose at once."

So they sat by the lakeside, "the archbishop talking all the time and abstractedly throwing in his bread, while the beautiful creatures swarmed from all quarters, even up to our very feet. . . . He kindly offered a day's fishing, but it would have been murder—as bad as shooting quails on the ground. . . ." The visitor spends two hours with this "excellent man, and a more pleasant, cultivated gentleman I have rarely met."

Everyone saw that Lamy loved the work of gardens; but it was plain that he did not follow it for his pleasure alone. Sweeping the long shady vista and its bright colors of fruit and flower with a gesture, he would say that the purpose of it all was to demonstrate what could be done to bring the graces and comforts of the earth to a land largely barren, rocky, and dry. To help his fellow citizens follow his example, he made them many gifts. On one of his westward journeys over the plains he brought horse-chestnut seeds in a pail of water all the way from Ohio, and a hundred sapling elms besides. He gave these to be planted in Santa Fe, and one day his old friend Mrs. Flora Spiegelberg glanced out of her front window in Palace Avenue and saw the archbishop planting with his own hands a pair of willow saplings at her front gate. When he was done with his spading, he blessed the young trees. In another year he saw English walnut trees planted in the city from his seeds. In another, a thousand fruit trees were set out in Santa Fe where there were so few.

If the garden was his principal joy, he did not see it as his exclusively. The pleasure it gave to visitors rewarded him, and what it had to offer in other ways was at the disposal of those who needed it. One day Sister Blandina, from the hospital nearby, looked over the wall. She saw beds of cabbages, turnips, carrots. In the hospital there were seventy-two patients, thirty-five orphans, and sixteen nuns who had not "a handful of vegetables" in their kitchen. The garden was quiet—nobody there. Blandina "made one athletic spring," with heavy skirts and rosary flying, vaulted over the wall and landed near the cabbage patch. There in haste she threw over the wall at least two dozen cabbages, and many more of the smaller vegetables. A little later, she went to Lamy's house in the garden and knocked.

"Come in."

She went in and said, "I have come to make a confession out of the confessional."

He gazed at her with "that benevolent expression which once seen" could never be forgotten. He saw that she was covered with dust.

"My little sister," he said, "what have you been doing?"

"Stealing, Your Grace. With never a thought of restitution, I dug up enough vegetables from your garden to last us three days."

"And then?"

"Whatever you say," she replied.

"Tell Louis to give you all there are."

She could only say, "Thank you very much." All she ever heard further about the raid was that in a little while he sent sacks of coffee and sugar to the hospital.

Among the occasional visitors was the Swiss-born anthropologist Adolph Bandelier, who brought Lamy news, now and then, of his discoveries. Antiquity was evident everywhere in New Mexico, either exposed and waiting to be recognized, or waiting to be dug up and opened to knowledge. It was not, as in European cultures, continuously assimilated, adopted, modified, and brought along into daily use. Now the newly arrived industrial age seemed swiftly to bypass whole epochs. Bandelier appealed to Lamy's sense of tradition. It was believed that Bandelier became a Catholic. People saw him wearing a clerical collar. When there was a progressive movement launched to raze the old Governor's Palace and replace it with an up-to-date new capitol, Lamy powerfully opposed the idea. Bandelier spent nine months living in a pueblo, slowly becoming a friend and accepted there. His purpose was to discover whether it was true that the Indians had a cult for worshipping snakes. He came away having seen the cult in action, and had his drawings to show in proof. If the snake was a deity, he was also a natural inhabitant, and a priest one day at his altar in San Juan was not prepared for what he saw there near his feet—a huge diamondback rattlesnake coiled in wariness.

So much to talk about with a congenial caller (though sometimes Lamy did not admit all comers, but courteously and briefly stayed them at his door). Somehow an absurd rumor went about in 1881 that he was the owner of a newly discovered and immensely rich gold mine; and he was at some pains to assure Paris and Lyon that there was no truth to it; for such a story could seriously disturb the modest flow of revenue which provided the chief support of his labors. He was prompt and careful in accounting for financial matters—unlike Machebeuf, whose methods were diffuse and impetuous. Month by month, year by year, Lamy made his reports, and gave his hearty thanks for the help which sustained him. When in residence, he worked steadily at his desk. After he drafted his pastoral letters, Mother Francesca copied them for the printer.

One of the Loretto Sisters served as the chapel sacristan. It was her duty to summon the archbishop for early Mass. When she rang the rising bell, she would see his light instantly come on, but he was often late appearing in the sacristy, where she waited to serve his Mass. At the altar, he was never hurried; every motion was exact, careful, devout.

The nuns saw how he kept as much time as possible for prayer and spiritual reading. His library gave evidence of much use. Many of the volumes were water-stained from the shipwreck—how long ago? thirty years—was it possible? They were theological works in French, Latin, Spanish, many of them published in the seventeenth and eighteenth centuries, retaining their original bindings of leather and gold, or vellum with quill lettering. The collection included a seven-volume edition of the *Mystica Ciudad de Diós* (Madrid, 1758), that "Divine History of the Virgin Mother of Christ" by the extraordinary nun María de Agreda. She was famous among the faithful for her gift of bilocation by which, in the 1620s, she was able to

appear to countless Indians of the Southwest to whom she introduced
the cross, though at the same time she visibly remained in Spain at
her post as Mother Superior María de Jesús of the Discalced Sisters
of St. Francis at Agreda, on the border of Aragon and Castile, where
she also had time to write. Among his other books, Lamy had his
own Thomas Aquinas in several editions of the *Summa*—Latin
volumes published variously in 1570, 1790, and 1798. There was a
copy in vellum of *Commentaria in Duodecim Prophetas* (Venice,
1704); a *Virgini Deiparae* (Rome, 1633); a *Theologia Moralis (La
Croix)* (Venice, 1753); a *Commentarius in Esdram, Nehemiam*
(Antwerp, 1645), the wooden cover of which had been cracked in
drying after immersion; and a *Commentaria in Proverbia* (Brussels,
1739). All these bore marks of the sea, some permanently warped by
the waters of Matagorda Bay. To think—so they marvelled in the
convents—of all the bishop's voyages and travels since then! One
journey overland added up to three thousand five hundred miles,
and if all his days of camping out "under the stars" were reckoned
together, they came to more than a thousand. . . .

He liked to share what he had—perhaps most of all the freeing
outlook and closeness to nature of his little ranch in the Tesuque
Cañon. Now and then he would go to St. Michael's College in the
piercing early-morning air of Santa Fe and collect a straggle of boys
and walk them out to the Villa Pintoresca, where they could hear
his Mass, and a couple could serve it for him. He had made a fish
pond there too, and they could fish for German carp which he had
had shipped to him; and when he brought the nuns and other friends
to the country for a picnic, they were told to pick at will among the
peach trees—but to exhaust one place before they raided another.
He once called one of the nuns to come to look at a certain flower
with him. She thought he might be about to pick it; but instead, he
knelt, inhaled its fragrance, and brought her to her knees to do the
same. The scattered families who lived in the cañon saw Lamy as he
went on foot from the villa to the chancery in the mornings. When
he was alone in his lodge, he spent much time reading, and he used
his own caravan telescope to sweep the sky, and the unchanging fan-
tasies of the earth forms, near and far, and the constantly changing
marvels of light and color at sunrise, in daytime storm and cloud
passage and in the fiery fall of evening before the starry dark.

In November 1881, General Charles Ewing—the same who had
been unable to further Lamy's plan for the Pueblo agency schools—

had put up at the Exchange Hotel in Santa Fe and had gone at once to call at the archbishop's "*palacio*." It was a reunion which bound the early days in Ohio to the decades which followed in the West, for Ewing and his parents had belonged to Lamy's parish in Lancaster [Ohio], and Purcell had married Charles Ewing and his wife, all of which Lamy recalled. They toured the garden where snow had fallen, and the general picked a flower out of a snowbank to send his wife.

Lamy invited him to see the Villa Pintoresca, and took him there in a buggy. "The Archbishop drove me himself, and he drove like a Jehu [*and the driving is like the driving of Jehu the son of Nimshi; for he driveth furiously*—2 Kings 9:20]. We had lunch at the ranch —a wild beautiful place from which you can see Mountain Peakes covered with snow that are 120 miles away." Lamy took him to the chapel and showed him a chalice set with jewels, "very old probably over 300 years that he found there thirty years ago when he came here first as Bishop of Santa Fe. The old gentleman was very kind and fatherly—talked of my old home when he was a young Priest where he was often kindly cared for, when I was a child only six years old . . . and his visits there as bright places in his missionary life that never grew dim, but to which he turns with pleasure and loves to talk. . . ." In his life's fabric there seemed to be no broken thread.

CHANGEOVER

In November 1884, Lamy went to Baltimore—by rail, now, all the way—to sit with his fellow American bishops in the Plenary Council presided over by Archbishop Gibbons. Each delegate was to bring two theologians with him. Lamy had none to call upon, or perhaps to spare, from Santa Fe. He asked that two be assigned him by the cardinal. His voice was heard in the debates. It was not so strong as many remembered it. He was more than gaunt—almost emaciated now. His robes hung loosely upon him, and the great size of his skull was accentuated by the outlines of bones and the hollows of his cheeks sculptured by age. His bulky biretta sat high upon his head. His eyes were entirely recessed in shadow, and his face was wholly pale. The long Mexican ordeal, coming after his illnesses and beyond these the lifetime of extraordinary exertion demanded of his so often vulnerable health, had hurried the reckoning which he was ready to meet.

On his return to Santa Fe, he wrote to Leo XIII in December submitting his resignation, with explanations which were sufficient. Now that the succession was insured and vested in Salpointe, Lamy asked again in January 1885 that Simeoni press for the Pope's acceptance of his petition. The request was not yet known to Santa Fe.

Salpointe, after nineteen years in Arizona, returned to Santa Fe in February, now as an archbishop. Lamy at once began to divide his tasks with him. One of his gravest wishes was still to obtain governmental help to establish Pueblo schools; and after discussing the matter with him, Salpointe went to visit the ten nearest pueblos, to examine the state of affairs, and to determine whether such schools would be welcomed by the Indians. Their decision, he found, was unanimously in favor of them. He would now be able to present their case if it fell to him to do so.

Father Peter Bourgade of Silver City had been appointed to succeed Salpointe at Tucson, and in April he was summoned to Santa Fe to be consecrated by Lamy. Inviting Machebeuf to the ceremony, Salpointe wrote, "Do not forget to bring your mitre, crozier, and pontifical vestments. You know we aren't rich here, and have here only what is needed in our rituals." He told Machebeuf also that Lamy was well enough, but now that he had a coadjutor, he wanted to do nothing. "I can't blame him—he worked long for the right to rest. . . ." The old archbishop assisted by Salpointe and Machebeuf endured the four-hour ritual of raising Bourgade to the episcopate on May 1, in the half-new, half-old cathedral; and daylong celebrations followed, with a great dinner, fireworks, and artillery salutes, for it was the first ceremony of its kind ever to have been performed in Santa Fe.

Six months after he had offered it, Lamy's resignation was laid before Leo XIII during the papal audience of June 28, 1885. "His Holiness diligently examined the reasons presented by Archbishop Lamy." On July 18, the Vatican wrote to Lamy that "the Holy Father, with saddened heart, saw the Archdiocese of Santa Fe being widowed by the departure of its good and most worthy Pastor. However, after a close examination of the reasons revealed by Your Excellency, His Holiness has accepted your resignation. Certainly, it seems right and just that Y.E., after all those years of such great and excellent labors in the vineyard of our Lord, should deserve to spend the rest of your life in peace and tranquility. . . . Under your guidance and administration the cause of our faith has made great strides in remarkable growth. . . ."

On the same day, Cardinal Simeoni sent instructions to Salpointe to succeed Lamy immediately, advised him that between them they should arrive at suitable financial arrangements for a pension which would provide a "decent living" for Lamy, and assured Salpointe that at the next papal consistory the pallium would be requested for him.

All formalities accomplished, Lamy was now in a position to take a tablet of faintly blue-lined paper and in the enlarged, deliberate, but still firm handwriting of his seventy-second year, set down the "Resignation of Abp. Lamy and his farewell to the clergy and faithful of the Diocese of Santa Fe," reading:

> For some years past we had asked of the Holy See a coadjutor in order to be relieved of the great responsibility that rested on our shoulders since the year 1850, when the supreme authority of the Church saw fit to establish a new diocese in New Mexico, and in spite of our limited capacity we were appointed its first Bishop. Now our petition has been heard and our resignation accepted. We are glad, then, to have as a successor the illustrious Mons. Salpointe, who is well known in this bishopric, and worthy of administering it, for the good of the souls and the greatest glory of God.
>
> What has prompted this determination is our advanced age, that often deprives us of the necessary strength in the fulfillment of our sacred ministry, though our health may apparently look robust. We shall profit by the days left to us to prepare ourselves the better to appear before the tribunal of God, in tranquility and solitude.
>
> We commend ourselves to the prayers of all, and particularly those of our priests who, together with us, have borne and still bear the burden of the day, which is the great responsibility of directing the souls in the road of salvation. Let the latter remember that, in order that their holy ministry be of any benefit, their example must accompany their instructions. It is with pleasure that we congratulate the most of the clergy of this diocese for their zeal and labors; and we desire those who might

have failed in their sacred duties may give, henceforth, better proofs of being the worthy ministers of God.

We also commend ourselves to the prayers of the faithful, whose lively faith has edified us on many occasions. We exhort them to persevere in this same faith, in their obedience to the Church, in their faithfulness to their daily obligations, in the religious frequence of the Sacraments, and in the devotion to the Blessed Virgin Mary, which is one of the most efficacious means of sanctification.

Finally, we hope that the few religious communities we have had the happiness to establish in this new diocese will offer some memento in their prayers for our spiritual benefit.

We ask of all to forgive us the faults we may have committed in the exercise of our sacred ministry, and, on our part, we will not forget to offer to God our humble prayers for all the souls that the Lord has entrusted to us for so many years.

J. B. Lamy, Archbishop

Given at Santa Fe, N.M., on the 26th day of August, 1885.

The letter was read, in Spanish, in all the churches on Sunday, September 6. In due course, Lamy, no longer entitled Archbishop of Santa Fe, was granted by the Vatican the courtesy title of Archbishop of Cyzicus.

The end of his term of duty was, like each year of diocesan administration, the occasion for a statistical report to the Society for of the expenses of the mission districts the world over. For the end of 1885, the annual report from Santa Fe recorded two hundred thirty-eight churches and chapels where Lamy, in 1851, had found sixty-six; fifty-four priests instead of twelve (which was reduced to nine); two colleges, eight schools, many parish schools, Indian schools, a hospital, and an orphanage, where there had been none of these, thirty-four years ago. This was merely the skeleton of his work. The body of his accomplishment stood forth in the whole character of those people to whom he had given himself, and in the gradual effect of their lives upon the society as it changed—the move toward the Propagation of the Faith in France, which bore so great a share amenity, through respect for three cultures, and ultimately their civilized union.

So as long as he was able, the archbishop had pursued his share of this task with a sort of grave passion, extending the graces of education, charity, and civil progress for all citizens, and the blessings of religion for those of his faith, across his domain of responsibility, which at its greatest had measured about one-tenth of the total area of the United States. As he gave over his task, he wrote to the Society at Lyon: "In the future, kindly address your letters to Mgr. Salpointe, who is taking my place, the Holy See having accepted my resignation. . . . For some years I have felt myself incapable of managing my diocese any longer," and in the same letter, he said fervently, "I take this opportunity to thank you for all you have done for my diocese during the 35 years I have managed it, without which help my mission would not be as it is now. . . . I hope to end my days in the midst of the faithful I have tried to direct into the way of virtue."

Lamy was at peace at the Villa Pintoresca. He had his books, and his telescope, and his far view of the Rio Grande Valley and the blue Jemez beyond the pale orange hills of Tesuque. Salpointe kept an eye on the old man's health and reported often to Machebeuf—Lamy had brought him "some magnificent peaches" from the *ranchito*, Lamy was "habitually well."

He had visitors, who saw in him still what an army captain saw when he had called at the residence in town: "a venerable gentleman, whose finely shaped head, clean-cut features, clear, bright eyes, discover him to be a man of acute intellect and whose gentle smile and modest, courteous manners conceal the great scholar and man of wonderful executive ability he is known to be." Another caller found him "earnestly studying a folio edition of the Holy Gospels, making himself sensitive to the tones of that language which was so soon to be his proper idiom. . . ." Collegians from St. Michael's liked to go to see him at the Villa Pintoresca; and when they came, they were, he said firmly, to walk all the way out from Santa Fe, just as he used to do for so many years. (He now had to ride to town and back.) Yes, Archbishop, they would say, yes, Archbishop—but as often as not they rode, until they came to the hill immediately to the south of the ranch; and there they would dismount, tether their horses out of sight, and climb over the hill to the lodge, puffing with contrived virtue.

Sometimes he would go into town, to take his pleasure of the day by greeting people in the plaza, where there were benches under the trees within the white picket fence along the four sides of the little park. If he stayed overnight, he said Mass at six o'clock the next morning, either in the convent chapel, or at St. Michael's, or in the chapel at St. Vincent's Hospital.

On October 4, 1887, he appeared in Santa Fe to keep the feast of St. Francis of Assisi. There was a procession that evening. The traditional stacks of piñon wood burned along the streets, throwing firelight like banners across adobe buildings. The marchers carried lighted candles through the sharp autumn air. In the procession walked the retired archbishop, and it was a wonder to see him again —so thin and white, so frail and faithful—passing through his streets to the cathedral for vespers at the end of the feast.

He was back again on December 12 to dedicate the chapel of Our Lady of Light at the Loretto convent, now at last completed. The unfinished cathedral was in continuous use, and the choir of St. Michael's College sang the Midnight Mass there at Christmas.

A few weeks later, on February 7, 1888, a message came from the Villa Pintoresca. The old archbishop had been taken sick in the country, and asked to be brought into town, where his cold—he said he had a cold—could be treated properly. A carriage was sent at once.

DAY'S END AT SANTA FE

He was brought to his old, high, square room in Archbishop's House where the white walls were finished at the ceiling with plaster cherubim. Doctors were called—Santa Fe's leading medical men, Symington and Lindell. They diagnosed pneumonia. Lamy's condition gave reason for encouragement. There was some improvement— no call for serious fears. But a few days passed, the pneumonia grew worse, and his strength did not seem to return.

After the first days, then, Lamy, knowing better than anyone what drew near, sent for Salpointe and asked him to administer the last sacraments; and asked him further to give him the indulgence *in articulo mortis*. Lamy said to Salpointe, later, "Thank you. I was able to follow every word of the prayers you came to say for me. Keep praying for me, for I feel that I am going."

Twice in the following week, Salpointe brought him the viaticum. Two nuns kept watch day and night—one of them was his niece Marie, Mother Francesca. When her hours of vigil were over each time, and she returned to the convent for a little sleep, the students, looking out the windows at Loretto, saw her coming from the bishop's house with her veil dropped over her face.

Early on the night of February 12 Lamy seemed to fall into a restorative sleep, and Salpointe, who had urgent matters to attend to in Las Vegas, felt it safe to go there by the train which left Santa Fe at two in the morning.

But Lamy coughed "considerably" during the night, and toward morning he was restless. At half past five, Mother Francesca called the gardener, Louis Mora, who slept in the adjoining room in case of need. He came and together they turned the archbishop in his bed, for he could not do this for himself, nor even make his wants known. They did what they could to make him comfortable.

At seven o'clock, Louis suddenly said to Mother Francesca that he thought it would be well to send for a priest. Archbishop Salpointe was away, all the other priests nearby were saying their Masses. But a quarter of an hour later, one of them came, and saw what must be done at once, and began to recite the prayers for the dying. Within the half hour, the archbishop came to himself, saw them all, and his niece said he smiled as though he saw a heavenly sight, and died without pain or distress. It was February 13, 1888. In a little while all the bells of Santa Fe began to toll, and soon everyone in the old mountain capital knew for whom.

Humble proprieties followed. Lamy's nephew and namesake, and Father Jouvenceau of the cathedral, and other priests, washed the corpse. The undertaker came to take it away for embalming. At six in the evening the archbishop was brought to the Loretto chapel to lie on a bier in the sanctuary while the members of the community kept vigil all night. He was robed in red dalmatic and chasuble and on his hands were purple gloves. The pallium lay upon his shoulders and breast. A white miter emblazoned with the Holy Ghost in gold was on his head. His hands held a crucifix. His large amethyst ring gleamed on his right hand. His feet were encased in purple slippers. The altar was fronted in black and silver. Thirty candlesticks were wrapped in black cloth and their candles flickered in the sanctuary. His face was diminished to the size of the skull, but its integument, so close to the bone, held an expression of peace in mortal sleep.

In the morning Lamy was carried on his bier by six priests, led by Salpointe, through the city and its throngs of witnesses. The procession moved from the chapel in College Street to Cathedral Place, then across to Palace Avenue, around the plaza, and back up San Francisco Street to enter the cathedral which Lamy was never to leave again. He lay in state there for twenty-four hours, and they said six thousand people came by to see him, and many kissed his purple slipper. Machebeuf had hurried by train from Denver, Salpointe from Las Vegas. Each of them, and Monsignor Eguillon, the Vicar General, said a Mass during the morning. It was Ash Wednesday. All day delegations of priests and religious and laity arrived from the outlying diocese.

On Thursday, February 16, at nine o'clock, the obsequies began in a Solemn Pontifical Mass, with Salpointe, Machebeuf, and Eguillon at the high altar before which lay the dead archbishop. The Collect was intoned:

Grant us, Lord, that the soul of thy servant Bishop Juan whom Thou hast withdrawn from earthly toil and strife, may be admitted into the company of thy saints. . . .

And at the Secret:

Grant, we entreat thee, Lord, that the soul of thy Bishop Juan, may profit by this sacrifice, the offering of which, under thy ordinance, earns pardon for the sins of all mankind. . . .

It was the last occasion to draw together the two friends who together had made their escape into their lives half a century ago. At a certain moment, Machebeuf limped forward to speak—"if speaking it could be called," said the rector of the Denver cathedral, who was present; for Machebeuf was all but inarticulate through tears and sobs. His face was runnelled like that of an ancient of days. He remembered what they had passed through together, the two seminarians, the two curates, the two missioners, "these two vicars"; and what together they had transformed in the immense land which they had loved for its very hardness, where they had spent themselves for the lives, mortal and immortal, of others. Of the two friends, the younger was now gone. Over his corpse the older said that his time would come next, and soon.

Presently the tremendous liturgy of the dead was resumed which by its impersonality brought a sense of triumph over death. After communion, Eguillon, the celebrant, sang:

Almighty God, we pray that the soul of thy servant Bishop Juan may be cleansed by this sacrifice, and that in all time to come he may deserve the remission of sins and respite for his soul. . . .

When Mass was over, Salpointe spoke a eulogy in English, Eguillon one in Spanish. At noon the congregation was dismissed. The ring and the crucifix were taken from Lamy's hands, the one to be kept by his niece and eventually to go down through his family, the other to be given to a friend. On the evening of the funeral, the corpse was enclosed in a plain wooden coffin, four days later it was removed to a metallic casket, and then lowered into the narrow crypt before the high altar of the church which the generations have made into the monument over his grave. Dead in his seventy-fifth year, he had been a priest for fifty years, a bishop for thirty-eight.

The next day, when in his memory, his niece, as was her duty, began to lead her people in the *De Profundis* at the end of a meal in the refectory, she began to cry and could not proceed. At St. Michael's, his collegians in a resolution described him as "a second Saint Paul" and decreed the wearing of mourning bands for thirty days. Writing to Europe, Salpointe told how Lamy had lived so long, and was so identified with the desert and the mountain West, that all its people, regardless of their religious beliefs, were attached to him, and prided themselves on belonging to him.

Affirmation was the theme of his life. Who knew how much spiritual energy was thoughtlessly inherited, absorbed, and reactivated in later inheritors? Lamy's unquestioning manner of spiritual commitment could seem as natural to him as all the other simply accepted aspects of his daily life and time. What John Henry Newman wrote of St. John Chrysostom could be as true of Lamy—"his intimate sympathy and compassionateness for the whole world, not only in its strength, but in its weakness; in the lively regard with which he views everything that comes before him, taken in the concrete, whether as made after its own kind or as gifted with a nature higher than its own. I speak," Cardinal Newman said, "of the discriminating affectionateness with which he accepts every one for what is personal in him and unlike others. I speak of his versatile recognition of men, one by one, for the sake of that portion of good, be it more or less, of a lower order or a higher, which has severally been lodged in them. . . . I speak of the kindly spirit and the genial temper with which he looks around at all things which this wonderful world contains. . . ."

Not a philosopher, not a sophisticate, Lamy was an unquestioning perpetuator of the values of almost two thousand years of faith, set forth in every august expression of liturgy, as well as in the daily simplicities of the peasant village life into which he was born like any other local child—except that upon him were visited a form of energy and a need to express it which other children of Lempdes did not receive. The mystery abides. At Clermont it was recorded, *"Sa mort a été la fin d'un beau jour"*—his death was the end of a fine day.

In the next summertime the archbishop's garden yielded fifteen hundred quarts of strawberries, forty gallons of cherries, one thousand of currants, and two hundred of raspberries; while five thousand shrubs, vines, and young trees which were ready for transplanting from the garden were auctioned for charity in the plaza of Santa Fe.

FIDES ET OPERA

1975

Encounters with Stravinsky

CONCERTS IN HOUSTON

[Igor and Vera Stravinsky] arrived in Houston late in the afternoon of January 3, [1958], were duly photographed at the airport, and came to the Rice Hotel, where Mirandi and I awaited them. Embraces. Mirandi kissed the top of Stravinsky's head with the greeting, "Pussycat!" at which he beamed. We arranged to dine together when everyone was settled in and rested, with the airplane out of their ears. I said, "May I take you to the Petroleum Club for dinner?"

"Petroleum?" asked Stravinsky. "In Texas one even dines on oil?"

"No, it is a club in this hotel which is for oil millionaires."

"Aha. That is better. We shall dine with millionaires."

"But the point is, one has to be a member in order to order a drink in Texas."

"But we are members?"

I explained about the guest card [arranged for by John Jones, a young Houston friend].

"My God, what if there was no guest card!"

"No Chivas Regal, then," I said.

"No, my God!"

For I had already assumed the pleasurable duty of seeing that wherever I was in attendance, as it were, his favorite Scotch was at hand.

So it was that at eight o'clock we met in the top-floor club, and our guest card was put to full use. The Scotch arrived, and very presently there was a congenial atmosphere. Like any city seen at night from a height, Houston was a great fancy of lovely lights. The Petroleum Club was almost empty, which was how we all preferred communal places. After a lingering draught of his second glass, the Maestro said in his best comedian voice, thickened not by liquor but by gaiety and drollery, "My God, so much I like to drink Scotch that sometimes I think my name is Igor Stra-whiskey."

All punctually, we met in the lobby after breakfast the following morning. Stravinsky was carrying a great folio of scores, of which I relieved him.

"Did you sleep well?" I asked generally, and Madame replied, "No, he is not well."

Her beautiful voice fell on the last word, and I recognized her habit of meeting distress with unqualified realism combined with objective devotion to her husband.

"No! Maestro!" I said, "what is the trouble? Do you need a doctor?"

"But I must rehearse," he replied, dismissing the doctor, and then with a smile as winning as though he was conveying good news, made a circular motion over his midriff, and said, "C'est *le bul-bul-bul*."

"Digestive?"

"Oui. Up and down all night."

"Oh! *Le bul-bul-bul!*" cried Mirandi. "We call it the Santa Fe summer complaint."

"Have you medicine?"

"Not for this. I need paregoric."

"Then I must telephone a doctor and have a prescription sent," I said.

"There is no time," said Stravinsky. "The orchestra is waiting. The car?"

"The car is out front. —We must do something. Let me try. We must wait just a minute."

He nodded and they took a sofa in the lobby.

"You know?" I heard Mirandi say in her best foreboding voice, as I hurried away. "Travel almost always does this to some people. Sick as *dogs*."

There was a drugstore nearby. I went to the pharmacist and

made a formal speech. The greatest living composer, I said, was the guest of the city of Houston and its symphony society. He was to give two concerts, his first rehearsal was this morning, the orchestra was at that moment waiting on the stage of Houston's Music Hall for him, and he was stricken with a sudden and most weakening dysentery. There was not a minute to lose, no time for a doctor's consultation, or even to telephone for a prescription. The situation was plain and surely understandable, and it was inconceivable that the pharmacist would fail to provide immediately the vital paregoric and bismuth.

He shook his head. Other remedies were available without prescription.

"Not strong enough," I said, for I knew that Stravinsky meant exactly what he said when he specified paregoric, as he was famous for his medicinal expertise.

"Is it chronic?" asked the druggist.

"It comes on when least expected."

"Who is he?"

"Igor Stravinsky."

"Oh." Impressed, the pharmacist looked at me levelly for a long moment. He was a mild and conscientious man and though music was not his passion he could feel urgent need on the part of others, and my will was pressing him in silence and anxiety. The moment was like a stop-camera suspension of life.

Then he said, "Where is he?"

"In the lobby of the Rice waiting to go. But he is weak. He is also elderly. His wife is with him and another friend. We are all going to be with him. He absolutely must give these concerts."

"You realize you are asking me to break the law and traffic in opium?"

"I do, and I apologize very sincerely."

"Well, I'll give you an eight-ounce bottle and ask you to give me your name and how I can reach you if anything comes up. I'll try"—he was mixing the anti-*bul-bul-bul* specific—"to get a doctor to cover this with a prescription by phone. I'll have it issued in your name."

"Yes, yes, thank you, anything, fine, fine. I cannot thank you enough."

In a moment with the life-saving bottle wrapped in a twist of blue paper in my clutch, I paid him and returned to the Rice lobby. The tableau at the lobby sofa had not changed. Stravinsky in his pinched gray felt hat which resembled F. D. Roosevelt's was withdrawn like a small bird in winter into the fluffed-out warmth of his large topcoat. Mirandi and Madame were conversing quietly. I rapidly approached.

"You have?" he asked when he saw me.

I held up the bottle.

His vitality returned instantly. With a surge of strength he stood, took my free arm, and we walked in the tempo of his limp— the right leg and his black walking stick—to the waiting limousine. Merely the presence of the remedy was enough to return his confidence to him. We all entered the car and as we moved off to the rehearsals, he tipped his head back and took a grand swig of the medicine, and like a connoisseur, wiped his lips, and smacked them as if to say, "This is clearly a paregoric of the best year," and put the bottle into his pocket. So far as I know he did not use it again, nor did he inquire how I managed to obtain it. He was often interested in—even fascinated by—idle information; but not when there was work to be done.

All traces of bleakness vanished from our party. At seventy-five he was again the source of strength for us all.

"Pol: you have the scores?" he asked, though he could see them where I held them on my lap as I sat on the *strapontin*. I showed them to him. "Good!" He smiled with closed lips and spread his nostrils. It was the signal for a drollery on the way. "How very tactful," he said, "of Stokowski to leave town for me."

He said a word to his wife in Russian and she replied in kind. I understood later that they were confirming plans for the day. While he rehearsed, she was going to the Cushman Gallery to examine the hanging of her show, and she would return in the car to take us all to lunch. Mirandi was going with her, I with the Maestro.

"Tomorrow night," she said to me, "is to be private view. We must all go. It is black tie. There will be c-r-rowd, ter-rible." She smiled, delicately shrugging her brows, and lifting her furs to her chin, looking calm and delicious.

The hall manager received Stravinsky and led us backstage to a plaster-lined dressing room with metal make-up desk and a mirror, a black leatherette sofa, a chair, and a small bathroom. Stravinsky asked me to give over the scores to the manager, who left to place them on the conductor's stand.

"How do you feel, Maestro?"

"For the moment, that is a needless question. Ask me after the rehearsal. I will now get ready"—this politely dismissive.

"I will be out front if you need me."

"Thank you"—with a little bow.

I went to the auditorium. The orchestra under the work lights tuned and retuned their instruments, playing the Shah of Persia's music. There was a stack of programs in the first row aisle. I took one and retreated to a third row seat. This was the program for the pair of concerts:

BACH-STRAVINSKY	Variations on "Vom Himmel Hoch"
STRAVINSKY	"Orpheus"
	Intermission
STRAVINSKY	"Scènes de Ballet"
STRAVINSKY	"The Firebird" Suite

Behind the orchestra were ranged on a bank of steps the members of a local choral society who had been prepared in the Bach variations by their own conductor. The rehearsal evidently was to proceed in the order of the concert program.

There was an invigorating air of tension over the stage, waiting for Stravinsky. Many looks were directed at the stage side from which he would enter. The Persian cacophony continued and then, as suddenly as though a baton had wiped it out, it ceased, as Stravinsky, hobbling as little as possible with his stick, wearing a gray cardigan, with a towel folded about his neck like an ascot tie, and his left arm aloft in almost a papal gesture of benediction and greeting, appeared in the harsh and stimulating light of a symphony rehearsal. The players rose and applauded. He made his way to the central stand, faced them, and bowed deeply to left, to center, and to right. His rehearsal etiquette was thus immediately established, to the visible pleasure of the orchestra. Then promptly to work.

In an habitual gesture, he licked the thumb and first finger of his left hand and turned the cover of the score on his desk. In a lifted voice, colored by comradely humor, he said, making a pun on the title of the Bach chorale, "Ladies and gentlemen, we will begin by coming down from heaven to earth."

There was a ripple of appreciative amusement over the stage, and then, abruptly serious, he spread his arms, and with his strong square hands furled for the up-down beat, he created the new sort of silence required of the moment, and then broke it clearly and gravely.

His rehearsal manners were an effective mixture of strict professionalism and sympathetic courtesy. He was vigorous in his beat and in his cues, and he swiftly alternated his gaze between the pages of his score and the players. There was never in his conducting a flourish for its own sake. His score indications had of course long been familiar to him and he built his fabric of sound out of the original auditory concept. His better-known works had for decades acquired a sort of "public" sound—that patina of temperament overlaid upon them by the versions of different conductors in recordings and in concerts. All such was swept away when he conducted his own works, and the result was that their anatomy emerged in their primal purity. Total logic was what he sought, never the momentary fragmental effect.

In the Bach variations, the local choral conductor had taken full advantage of the grandeur and beauty of the melody and all its aethereal changes; and he had taught his chorus to sing out in full voice. Had they been alone, this might have been musically acceptable as well as "beautiful." But in this instance, their voices dominated the orchestral fabric, which was a spare webbing of instrumental counterpoint; and the singers were intended to contribute an almost abstract other element*—to become in effect additional instruments in the same register of dynamic values as those in the instrumental writing. At their first young, full-throated entry, in the exuberance of hearing their fine attack, they submerged all else. Stravinsky stopped them.

"No, no, ladies and gentlemen, much less tone. *Mezzo-piano.* Beautiful ensemble you are giving us but too much sound. Please, again."

---

* *Beautifully realized in a recording of the work brought to me from Paris in December 1958 by the Stravinskys when I met them on their arrival in New York. It was conducted by Craft for the series of Les Concerts du Domaine Musicale, and it bore the magisterial statement "Enregistré en présence d'Igor Stravinsky."*

Again; and they were still too loud. It required several tries, but at last there was the balance he required; and the exuberant young Texans found their proportion in a lovely performance entirely different from their first conception of the work. Their response to him was interesting. At first they seemed impressed by the public man, awed, but disregardful of the artist. He was celebrated, he was old, he was small and so "foreign"-looking, he talked funny, he made no dramas of emotion in his face or gestures, he never "lost" himself, he didn't pretend that the musicians were a collective instrument upon which he was playing. Curiosity and puzzlement seemed to hold the earnest singers as they regarded him. But gradually they seemed to forget their preconceptions, their previous lessons about what a conductor was, and entered into serious respect for the task in hand for its own sake, not their, or his, egotistic demonstrations; and I thought I saw affection begin to mingle with their musical concentration as this found its propriety. When they finally began to sing not like choristers but as integral elements of the overall sound he had brought to page in his auditory imagination, their satisfaction was of a new and greater sort than that which they had first revealed. If he was exasperated by the slowness of their learning his requirements, he never showed it; but by his many demands for repetitions of their vocal lines, it was evident that he was for a long part of the rehearsal not pleased. When in the end he was satisfied, he radiated pleasure, and dismissed the singers with a long expressive shrug of thanks, lifting his arms, and showing his palms upward as if to say his gratitude in a silence more eloquent than words.

His deportment with the players was equally direct; professional, respectful. When he moved on to rehearse *Orpheus*—again, who can forget the immediate captivity of ominous pathos, beyond the pure musicality of it, in the descending harp figure which introduces both the beginning and the end of the work—he had a number of occasions to halt the orchestra and instruct an individual player. Invariably, he spoke then in the warm voice of a fellow participant in a task of realization by them both, and he would say, "No, my de-ar," and indicate corrections in beat with his arm and sound with his voice, using his rehearsal syllables which sounded like "ta-rrr-*ahhhh*," in various phrasings. I had never in countless rehearsals I had listened to heard a player addressed as "my de-ar" by the maestro of the occasion; and it was clear that the Houston players, used to more majestic demeanor, were for the moment in love with their guest.

There were several other interruptions which gave everyone concern.

Twice during the *Orpheus* study and again in working on later pieces, Stravinsky halted the playing, and said with disarming candor, "I must ask you to excuse me for a moment. I am in some pain"—a rustle of distress from the desks—"and I must go to the dressing room for a moment." He saw the question on everyone's face, and stated with a sort of sweet dignity which, like many of his most ordinary remarks, reflected a recognition of the human state with all its bothersome miseries, "It is my 'ernia which is hurting me." I had never known he suffered from hernia. "There is an instrument of medical science which is calculated to confine this affliction; but sometimes when it loses its adjustment it becomes a torture worse than the disease. Excuse me." He waved a smile at the orchestra. "I must go rearrange my trüss."

He left the stage. In the silence the concern of everybody was felt. I wondered if I should go to the dressing room, but thought not, since he had preferred to be alone earlier, even while merely changing to rehearsal clothes. Soon enough he returned, acknowledging with a smiling nod the relief on the faces all about. He resumed the rehearsal until the next interruption, required for the same reason. One could only think of the courage of so old and ailing a man to persist in his public work while suffering constant discomfort if not outright pain. I do not think it was simple illusion which made me feel that the musicians responded emotionally to him now, where before they had worked with him in purely professional gratification. Now his little habit of often clenching his left hand near his groin, or on his left hip, took on the meaning of an attempt to ease pain. But nothing caused him to restrain the austere athleticism of his bodily movement as he worked.

He expressed rhythm in every part of his frame. In his music the rhythms were so strongly marked, so frequently altered, not merely, as in so much music, a scheme of on-running pattern, that they required of him powerful and strict muscular movement. This was often—it seemed to me—reminiscent of the most elementary human use of the body; and I was often, sometimes with hilarity, otherwise with wonder at the great play and control of all common instincts in his creations, put in mind of those absently erotic and repeated self-levitations which you so often see in babies or very young children, and which bring to the adult mind reminders of copulative movements which associate pleasure and the making of life in our human/animal nature. I remembered an early statement of his to Paul Rosenfeld about the general place of rhythm in the scheme of compositional values: "It is like this. It is like making love to a woman. . . ." Rosenfeld had also observed Stravinsky's fine politeness with players at an orchestra rehearsal of the New York Symphony Orchestra in the 1920s. Stravinsky, he said, on his arrival onstage, "was an electric shock." Giving his instructions "in very correct English," he was "abrupt, impatient, energetic, but never ironic either of himself or of his interlocutors; most exemplary in his relations with the players. . . . A kind of interest radiated from him to the musicians, who began entering into the spirit of the animal comedy, and kindling him in return."

At the end of the morning's work I went to the dressing room. I expressed concern for the 'ernia. He slapped the bothersome thing away with a gesture, explaining that while an operation would dispose of it, his doctors thought that at his age the risks of any sort of surgery were increased, and that he would do better with a truss—a word which made him smile with distaste.

"And the *bul-bul-bul?*" I asked.

"There is now no occasion for it," he said, and then admitted that before conducting, he often felt the same symptoms of intestinal flow—had in fact since his early youth been subject to the flux. If it was a matter of over half a century, then, I said, he made me think of Voltaire, whose ill health began at nineteen and when his life ended at eighty-four it was not from illness but from exhaustion brought on by glory. In this there was the sort of encouragement which hypochondriacs live on, and Stravinsky, roughly wiping his face with his ascot towel—he was always very locker-room at rehearsals—made one of his affable silent bows of acknowledgment that one had said something worth hearing.

On the evening of that day I dined with local friends and met the Stravinskys and Mirandi for lunch on the following day—Sunday—when there would be an afternoon rehearsal, followed by Madame's private view at the Gallery. Stravinsky was always interested in the track ahead.

"So what is for tomorrow?" he asked.

"I am going to make a little cruise on the Houston ship channel"

—and I explained about John Jones's further benefactions, this time involving the municipal tug, the harbor, the shipping, and the rest.

"No!" he cried. "I must do this too!"

"But you have a rehearsal in the morning," said Madame.

"Aha. You are correct, my de-ar. Could the amiable tugboat wait till the following morning, when there is no rehearsal"—for the first concert was to be given Monday night, and the next day would be free, with the second concert Tuesday evening.

"I should think so," I said. "I will ask."

The tug expedition was rearranged by John Jones, and when I reported this to Stravinsky, he was as gratified as a child at a promise of a feast. In even so small a matter, the future interested him devouringly; his capacity for life always reached ahead; there was interest in the present, too, of course, and usefulness in the past; but in all that was not yet accomplished was expressed, if it did not actually give him, his vital hold on existence. The final act of man's fate threatened him many a time in his life, and in his last years, the threats were again and again almost mortal, but repeatedly he turned them back with astonishing recuperative powers, for more work, more life.

At six o'clock Sunday evening, we proceeded to the Cushman Gallery for Madame's *vernissage*. "All Houston"—the expensively cultured sector—was there. Madame looked elegantly radiant. Her naturalness was as appealing as her unselfconsciously aristocratic bearing was full of grace. I often noted how on her entrance into any gathering her effulgence and style, her unhurried progression among people, her smiling luminosity, the pale light of her dark-lashed eyes under their blue-shadowed lids, seemed to bring responsive repose into the assembly; and I said to myself, She is like a moon-goddess. Tonight she was grandly clothed—pale furs, a softly folded dress of a dark color and severe cut. She wore many rather miscellaneous jewels and these reminded me of an anecdote she told me of how once on tour with her husband she had met an old friend from Paris in a box at the Colón Theatre in Buenos Aires, who exclaimed, "Vera! what wonderful jewels you are wearing. They are real?" to which Madame with simplicity, indicating one after another of her ornaments, replied, "This one is real, that is fake, these are real, and that one, and that one are fake, the earrings are real—" and so on, through the whole catalogue.

Her exhibition looked good, and though the rooms were not large, there was no undue sense of crowding. Drinks were at hand. While Madame received introductions, standing in the center, Stravinsky, after shaking a few hands, looked about for a chair in a corner, went to it, with me trailing, and took his place in the most inconspicuous possible place. The occasion was Madame's event, and he wanted only to sustain her by his presence, and draw none of the usual attention to himself. I brought him a glass of Scotch and he said, without having to explain why, "Pol, let us talk here," so that seeing him engaged, people who might otherwise have made a circle about him, detracting from the exhibition and its artist, hesitated to invade his limited territory. Mirandi knew people at the party, and made a fine jangle with her gold wristlets, and we heard her social laugh, the husky jump from a low note to an octave above, over the increasing clamor as more guests arrived, more drinks were served, and more thermal conviviality of conjunctive bodies grew out of the occasion.

Madame's paintings were highly original—abstractions yet with elusive reminders of familiar forms. Her application of pigment was technically exquisite—some areas of the surface barely brushed, others richly impregnated with dense color as though a wing had dragged paint into natural imprints in some manifestation of anonymous nature—ripples in sand, or striations in long-seasoned stones, or the ghosts of leaves in somberly glowing humus on a forest floor. The guests seemed impressed by her work, and the event had every mark of a distinguished and successful opening, including the rapid warming of the rooms, so that after about an hour, both Madame and the Maestro had had enough; and by a signal to Mirandi, Madame indicated that it was time to go.

The affability of their departure was even more flattering than the high style of their manner on arrival: they left each guest with the feeling that life was operated by an inexorable calendar far beyond their power to revise; that they were as subject to its exigencies as anything in astronomy; and that in taking leave, they regretted more than anyone what must seem like early deprivation. It was all so courtly and final that nobody suspected what must have been the Stravinskys' fact the world over—that casual encounters with strangers however attractive and worth knowing could not lead to anything, and that if fortune dictated that eminence should belong to one and not another, then there was hardly any personal responsibility involved, and once good manners had been exercised, there was little need to protract any occasion.

In brief, we left, went to a pleasant dinner in the splendid emptiness of the Petroleum Club, with more cocktails, and wine later, while over us all, for Madame's sake, remained a warming glow at the enthusiasm which her work had brought forth in the interested people of Houston.

In the morning there was another rehearsal, much like those of Saturday and Sunday. Monday afternoon was given over to rest before the first concert. I went anonymously to bookstores. The day seemed at moments to approach the evening concert with unsettling swiftness, and at others, to drag along at an exasperating and ominous pace, both conditions producing hollow nervousness even in myself, who had but to carry scores and extra towels, and a small bag containing perhaps an extra shirt, and, surely, associated medicaments whose presence in the dressing room would be a comfort, even should no dosages be required.

The management had provided a box for Madame, Mirandi, and myself. I went backstage with Stravinsky while Madame and Mirandi remained in the auditorium. He was somewhat abstracted, his concentration already forming for the work ahead. His movements as he adjusted his professional possessions on the make-up counter, his neatness in all things, were executed as slowly as in a dream. It was no time for small talk, but tension is contagious, and I relieved mine by remarking on the fine cut and fit of his tailcoat.

"Thirty-five years ago or more," he said, smiling broadly. "I had it made in London"—the same tailcoat, surely!

He wore a soft white shirt with collar turned down, and a white tie. Dimly away was the sound of the orchestra already on the stage, tuning and riffling.

"Pol:" he said, "please, come back in the intermission to keep the door. Not to see anyone during the intermission."

Yes, of course, I said to myself. At the interval, he must lie down and rest on the couch, and perhaps change his shirt. I promised to return during his curtain calls, and as I made to go and join Madame and Mirandi out front, he divined my emotion for him, and he took my shoulder and pulled me toward him, and silently and lightly kissed me Russian-fashion on first one cheek, then the other. I felt on my face a mist of cold perspiration among the barely visible crystalline points of his beard, not shaved since morning. I felt remote compunction, betrayal, in leaving him to await alone yet another call into the concert lights.

It was always interesting to listen to one of his performances in the company of Madame. She responded to the enthusiasm aroused by his very first visibility—everybody applauded fame; but something about his frail, determined manner as he would enter the stage (until the very last concerts, without his stick, though he needed it for real confidence at every step) immediately touched the feeling of the audience; and when he turned to bow to the applause, his concentrated gravity brought surges of another sort of response. Everyone moved from the anticipation of the concertgoer merely expecting entertainment to the awe which accompanied attendance at a rite of high consequence. Madame did not applaud, but at the reception he received, she smiled sideways with calm pride. When he began to conduct, I could feel her acute attention for any sign of fatigue, strain, or discomfort. There was always present an element of risk in his public appearances in his last decade, for the two strokes he had suffered during the fifties, one in Berlin, the other in Bologna, left him, he once told me, with no sensation at all in his right leg, foot, arm, or hand—though amazingly he did retain muscular control. It was astounding to me that he could continue with his public engagements under these conditions, and when I wondered—I think to Craft—whether the strain on him might not be too great, I was assured that the doctors encouraged Stravinsky to give concerts, as the exercise was good for his muscles and his circulation. Still, strokes sometimes occurred in sequence, and I myself felt uneasy as I was lofted in spirit by his music brought into the air by his own vision and hand.

His workmanlike rehearsals had produced excellent results. The Bach variations proceeded in the stately balance he had labored for, and the ceremony between orchestra and chorus was beautiful to see as well as hear. The meeting of two masters in the work was a lesson out of *The Poetics of Music*, when in our very presence, we heard how "tradition . . . appears as an heirloom, a heritage that one receives before passing it on to one's descendants," for if Bach was there, so, too, and unmistakably, was Stravinsky.

He left the stage and it seemed to us he was gone a fairly long time, and Madame gave me an inquiring look. I was about to go to the dressing room for news when he reappeared, and it later turned out that he had needed to rearrange his hernia appliance, which had slipped—a tedious process, as it meant undressing and dressing almost entirely. But when he lifted his arm for *Orpheus*, his power was all present, and for the duration of that score I was concerned with nothing but the work itself.

He received so many calls that I was in the dressing room for many minutes before he returned. He came in, seized a towel, and began patting his face with it, while in pantomime he instructed me to lock the door. White with perspiration, he was catching his breath in long draughts through his nose. His little chest rose and fell like the top half of a pair of bellows. I believed he should lie down. I offered him a fresh towel, which he took. Someone knocked and I opened the door a slit and said that Maestro Stravinsky asked to be excused from seeing anyone, and then I locked us in again. He was rapidly coming down to ordinary respiration and I suppose heartbeat.

I felt it suitable to say, now, "Well, Maestro, when I hear you conduct, I feel that not only do most conductors do things that are quite unnecessary, but are often actually harmful."

He threw down the towel. He took my shoulders and declared in a voice of high glee, "Pol! I h-h-ate interpretation!"

I delighted in his vehemence. I laughed—I had not before heard him actually state this famous position. In the context of that dressing room, I could not fail to have a fleeting thought of its absent resident.

"The concert is wonderful," I said, "and the *Orpheus!*"

He had no need to hear superlatives from me, but he saw my excitement, and pulling me to the dressing table where duplicates of the evening's scores lay, he opened to certain pages of *Orpheus*, and began to explain to me the musical anatomy of certain passages. This inversion. That progression. Variation of a phrase prominently heard earlier in a different scoring. To the grasp of these abstract niceties I was inadequate but this did not lessen my fascination with the fact of his demonstration. His animation was as fresh as if the work had just been composed, and despite my inadequacy in technical matters, I received a direct and powerful demonstration of the primacy of form among all the elements of creation in any art. At the same time, in my hinterthought, I was nagged by other questions—the couch; a quick shower or sponging; a fresh shirt; at least attention to the 'ernia and its retainer. But before there was time for anything else, even for finishing the elucidation of the *Orpheus* score, there was a tap at the door, and the call boy said, "Ready, Mr. Stravinsky, please," and the intermission was spent. It had been spent for me, for my interest, in response to my great elation at the performance.

"Is there anything I may do for you before I go out front again?"

"No, thank you, my de-ar," he said, "but come back immediately, we will all escape."

After an early lunch the next day, Tuesday, January 7, we came to the municipal wharf. There was the tug, awaiting us. It was a gray-painted wooden vessel, with its bow up-sloping, its pilothouse and mast and rudimentary funnel leaning back, its afterdeck open, and a comfortable cabin with padded benches. The *Chronicle* ship news reporter was awaiting us. He was a friendly young man who saw us aboard, introduced us to the pilot and the engineer, who comprised the whole crew, and held himself ready to "explain things" on our voyage.

In clear weather but with a slow cold wind, we began edging out into constricted waterways lined with moored freighters from around the world. Houston industry crowded the waterfront on both sides of the harbor, which soon gave way to a winding channel. Our progress was slow until we entered a clear straight path. Though we were all warmly dressed, we felt the cold; but the interest of our various separate observations made it a happy trip.

Stravinsky standing on the narrow starboard deckway, wearing his fur coat and the Roosevelt felt hat, overwhelmed the ship news reporter—who came to instruct and remained to listen—with aptly technical discussions of such appropriate topics as the shipping industry's relation to the balance of trade, the economic implications of an inland harbor rising to the status of the nation's third greatest seaport, the optimum in tonnage likely to be adopted as the most profitable in seagoing cargo vessels, the relative dangers of an oil cargo which might ignite, a metal cargo which might shift, and a grain cargo which might expand and burst bulkheads if not hulls, and such.

Madame was occupied in taking photographs of ships that were tied to the shore, and an occasional one we might pass. She was as interested as her husband but her feeling for the events was visual, and she remained alone in the afterdeck. She had a capacity for silent absorption of anything which interested her; and now she was taking mental impressions with a painter's eye of the whole scene— the flat land almost at the level of the water, the long winter striations of the Texas sky, the black, rust, white, and wooden colors of the dozens of ships with their fluttering house flags, the pale flesh color of the earth where it was exposed at the water line, the obsidian dark gray-green of the channel water, the far hang of industrial smokes over and beyond Houston.

Mirandi was in the pilothouse animatedly conversing with the pilot, and I was in the bow, making rapid pen-scratch drawings of some of the ships and fittings along the shore. Presently I felt cold and went to the cabin, and Mirandi called me to say that the best view was from the wheelhouse. I joined her there. The pilot, a cheerful middle-aged Texan, when I asked him if there might be any chance that I might steer the tug, said, "Sure enough."

We had turned around by then and were heading back to Houston—an hour and a half down the channel, and so back. At our speed, it would have taken three hours to reach the open Gulf of Mexico. There was not time for this—or, actually, interest. We had all seen enough, and though it was interesting, the voyage became in the end monotonous. For me the high moment was to take the wheel and feel the response of the rudder. We were glad enough to disembark, with handshakes all around. Once in the car, we admitted that we were frozen, and Stravinsky said, "Whiskey!"

We were soon settled around a large uncovered table in the hotel bar-club with drinks before us. In the early moments of recovering from its chill, we said that the little voyage had been fun, and I was charged to relay thanks to John Jones, which I did later in the afternoon. In the comfortable silence which followed, I was amused to think of the variety of our characters, and I said, feeling a little uneasily like a gamesmaster on a cruise ship, "Everyone has a single word which is most characteristic of him. One he either uses frequently, and so gives us his most consistent view, or one that others use about him. —Mirandi, do you know what yours is?"

"Tell me."

"You say '*marvellous*' all the time."

"I do? How marvellous."

For if Mirandi said "marvellous" habitually it was because she really saw almost everything as a marvel, whether trifling or great, and so announced it in the italics of her speech.

"So, what is mine?" asked Madame, indulging our nonsense.

"Your word is '*terrible*,' " cried Mirandi with gaiety.

Madame thought about it, and then smiled judicially as if to say that her use of the word was if habitual entirely accurate.

That left Stravinsky. I turned to him and said, "Maestro, I don't think anyone but yourself can settle on any one word which will do for you. Have you a word? What is your word?"

He diminished himself toward the table edge with an expression of abstruse mischief. The gleam of a Cagliostro came into his eyes. He made a mysterious glance around the table and said, "Ha! A vord. I have a vord. I vill give you my vord."

With that he moved everything aside that was on the table— glasses, a dish of pretzels, Madame's scarf, Mirandi's gold cigarette box; and once he had a clear plateau, whose dimensions under his spell seemed to grow into a great plain, he slowly began to build something invisible which, so great was his power of magic, rose before our eyes. He reached far out on every side of the tabletop and with selective care scooped and patted unseen particles of matter toward the center, scowling like an adept in the performance of an arcanum. He kept muttering, "Vord, aha, I have a vord, *ja*," and he worked the unseen substance until we saw a pyramid take shape in our persuaded imaginations. One great hand after the other raised the tabletop to an imaginary peak in its center. It was like seeing the volcano Paricutín emerge before our eyes. His power as a magus was as great as all his other powers. "Vord, *ja*," and his modelling of the structure became grave and elegant as he completed his task—critical adjustments here, a smoothing there. "My vord, aha, I have my vord," an incantation, and when he had stretched our suspense to the utmost, he made a breathy chord of his voice and cried, "*Here is my vord*," and he began now in gleeful haste to tear away and scatter to the floor the invisible stuff he had so convincingly built up, "my vord is *merde!*" and so broke our spell. He joined in our laughter, but so fastidious was his power of illusion that he himself was subject to it, and not until he had swept away every imaginary grain of the *merde* from the tabletop did he stop his work.

Then, with comic exactitude, he restored Madame's scarf, the various glasses, and Mirandi's gold box to their proper order, with a little bow, and the game was over.

The second concert was another success. The Stravinskys never discussed how things went in performance—he had another way of admitting to feeling about that as I later discovered. We again had to fight our way out of the Music Hall, for by word of mouth the first night had brought out even greater enthusiasts for the second, and the Maestro would have been detained for an hour or more if he had not with brief self-deprecating bows insisted on making his way to freedom. The next morning, with triumphs secure over the liquor laws of Texas, the *bul-bul-bul*, the always unpredictable problems attending work with unfamiliar orchestras, the gallery-going public of Houston, and the ennui attending endless unpacking and packing, the concert troupe—for so I regarded the four of us—scattered variously homeward.

PROMISE KEPT

I think often of Stravinsky's last earthly delight—the bird Madame had waiting for him on his final return home [from the hospital], the bird whose song had so startled me on my first visit to that home. For him, she said, it sang and sang and gave him much joy. His own words, given in 1939, come to mind from the chapter under the heading "The Phenomenon of Music," in the *Poetics*. He spoke of "the most banal example . . . including the song of a bird. All this pleases us, diverts us, delights us. We may even say, 'What lovely music!' But all such are of course merely promises of music; it takes a human being to keep them. . . ."

The last scene of *Le Rossignol* might speak for anyone coming to the end of Stravinsky's life, though not of his music.

Death stands in the Emperor's bedchamber . . . Torn by his aching conscience, the dying ruler calls in vain for his musicians to make him forget. But the nightingale returns and so charms Death with its songs that he agrees to allow the Emperor his life. The Emperor revives and offers his saviour a place at court, but the bird refuses and returns to its woodland haunts with the promise that it will sing each evening. Now the courtiers enter, prepared to find the Emperor dead. They are astounded when he sits up in bed and bids them "Good morning!"

The nightingale, death, and the Emperor bring before us music in nature, and the mortal change of all things, and man's insistence on immortality—themes which belong within Stravinsky's vision, even as the magician's wit of the Emperor's true words. Every artist is committed in his own degree to that which never dies.

1972

III

NOTEBOOK PAGES
AND AN ESSAY

Approaches to Writing

Notebook Pages

OF THE MODE

Contemporary taste—the sum of the successes of a period—has great energy and much power to influence the writer and other workers in the arts. By this very fact it should be viewed with caution, and its elements should be examined one by one by the writer to determine whether they tempt him with more than fugitive conformity and the finally vulgar pleasures of being "with-it," to use a current expression generally bestowed as a compliment.

The following section of notes reflects my interest in the artist's own vision, the inexhaustible legacy of the past, and the perils of fashion.

•

No one can say which of the productions of his own time are certain to survive as verities in future history and which, even those once widely admired, will vanish. What one can do, and the artist is wise to do, is to find for his own purposes the conjunction of those elements of the past which have formed him with those of the present which seem to express his nature, while he gives no thought to direct imitation of either. Contemporary subject matter is not in question; only the manner of treating it.

•

Only by knowing a tradition well can one meaningfully rebel against it; and even then, more of it will survive than what has been added to it in the way of counterstatement.

·

What never works: the novel which is more at the mercy of a social thesis than an impulse of art. Tolstoy was great enough as an artist to survive in his work the social theories he came to think so important.

·

Nobody can imagine tomorrow; but anyone can be faithful to all that he truly knows of today through his own uninfluenced discoveries, no matter what organized attitudes may be brought to bear on everything around him.

·

Important problem: how to be truly of one's time as a writer without following its fashions. A solution: to be true first of all to one's own vision, which to know requires much meditation, and then to resist the current cant, and the imperative, and often profitable, chic, of any controlling, if short-lived, theory.

·

There is no essential difference between running after fashionable persons and running after fashionable ideas. Both are harmless diversions, and either may even feed satire.

·

It may be dangerous to echo only the accents of the past—but even more so to replace them with only those of the present.

·

Existentialism imprisons its followers in an eternity of the present tense. For them the past is lost or wasted, the vision of the future is blinded.

·

To be self-conscious about conforming to the "modern" is to be oblivious to the timeless, i.e., the sense of the self and its perceptions, no matter what these may keep alive of the past.

·

Memorandum to a colleague whose manuscript I read: I must note the mistake of falling into the argot of the genre you are criticizing, such as the modish permissiveness which is a present imperative. Vulgar neologisms are certain to lose their meaning, precision, and edge in a very short time, and the more currency given to the hitherto unprintable expressions of obscenity, the less historical respect we can grant to them. We are now in a moment of taste which sanctions—no, requires in the dubious mode—the use of low slang or the vocabulary of latrine graffiti in "serious" writing. The trouble with all such "chic" is that it can never achieve any continuing vitality because the "timely" in expression is never fixed in meaning, style, or relevance. Your work is essentially serious. Your intention is elegant, but too often your manner is raw, and so your thought appears raw also. Its texture, therefore, seems to shrink away from importance and seriousness the more it is made to conform to the highly doubtful modishness of popular mannerism or references derived from the latest vulgate. Everything you mean to say is worth meaning and saying; I would plead for it that it be relieved of the built-in disadvantages of style and idiom more appropriate to the impoverished, sticky self-indulgences of pop-obscenity authors than to the rich, inherited speculative style of your own true thought and concern. In other words, your thinking, so far as I can discern it through its present beclouding texture, deserves better vesture than the cheap pop-folk style which renders it trivial and ephemeral. You are too important a critic and philosopher to have to be nervous about being "with-it." I do not speak out of merely sniffish fastidiousness, but hope to make a case for the aesthetically appropriate. Language and occasion must meet in harmony, or all deeper meanings are dissipated. All "trade" words are useless in the end, and as damaging as the jargon of the academy to anything but commercial communication.

.

In any art, in any style, there can be only one great innovator at a time. Imitations thereafter merely contribute to a body of journalism, or period reference.

.

Those who think only of destroying the present imagine they are creating a future, when all they are doing is repeating the cage rattlings of the past. In this case, motive is all.

.

It is now considered clever to say that the "man of letters" is no more. What we have instead are journeyman specialists in the various separate forms of literature. Many are gifted at single purpose; but how much more gifted they would be if they wrote in many genres, and evoked the several sensibilities necessary to do so, so that each would benefit all.

.

Any art which sets out to be in fashion is sure to end up like yesterday's newspaper.

.

The mass age, with its mechanized commodities, including its visions, has forced many an artist—most individual of creatures—to turn to the wholly subjective to find his expression. What he finds is often intelligible to no one else. Art, then, seems in danger of abandoning its search to communicate in common terms illuminated by an individual vision.

.

The novel, for the moment, is a social statement before it is a work of art. It must "have something to say" to satisfy critics who are scholars of systems—Marxist, Freudian, Existentialist, Black, Absurdist, Sexist, or whatever—before they are responsive to the aesthetic. If a novel fulfills its natural genius to give an effect of life in large traits and intimate details, there will be plenty left over to discuss in terms of "systems"—but "systems" will never motivate a real work of imaginative literature. Let the reader supply his own "statement" in response.

.

Originality for its own sake is always dishonest and thus irrelevant.

.

Every generation does battle for its own enthusiasms; but there are always a few who rise above these in the vision of their own separate sensibilities, which need not necessarily have anything to do with the contemporary vision.

.

The true artist is never afraid of anything—including the glories of the past.

.

To be self-conscious about the "modern" is to be oblivious to the timeless, i.e., the sense of the self and its perceptions, no matter how these may relate to either the past or the present.

.

A reason that the past is so hated by the young is that there is no way to be entirely free of it.

•

A true innovator in the arts cannot be imitated, nor will he have any significant artistic influence. He is useful only to himself—and the public.

•

Fashion makes cowards of second-rate artists. Stylish conformity is their vice.

•

It is a curious tendency which judges books of the past generation according, not to their intrinsic literary value, but to their "relevance" or "non-likeness" to the social conditions and the tone of writing which prevail today. Recently a compendium of work by a brilliant English writer of the Edwardian and subsequent Georgian periods was dismissed by many reviewers as hopelessly old-fashioned and therefore meaningless in its moral and social values. It was as if Jane Austen, say, were to be dismissed for similar reasons. The work was not weighed for its literary achievements.

•

He who fears to be out of the mode does not deserve to belong to himself.

•

It is not always of significance whether an artist derives from a tradition or invents his own; all that matters is that he be an artist. Critics and teachers almost always pay attention to the peripheral matters of external "placement" and miss the essential core.

•

The public hazard, but private gain, when one's new book is most unlike one's last previous one.

•

Those who would now dismiss the *story* as a useful element of the novel are the victims of critical "chic" which turns up every ten years, only to disappear. There is hardly a person alive who does not want to know "what happened next," in any context.

•

To be deliberately contemporary is as fatuous as to be deliberately old-fashioned.

•

For the drug-afflicted social behavior of many young people today, dreams have disastrously escaped from their proper domain, which is the unconscious. Freud offered certain postulates which resulted in confusion—none more than his attempt to identify recognizable reality through dreams. This has too often resulted in efforts to create systematic interpretations of essentially inconsistent subject matter. If there should be clinical usefulness in this process, it has nothing to contribute to an artist's realization of his aesthetic impulse. Was Freud himself more of an artist than therapist? Were his insights more like those of poetry than of science?

•

A reason that the avant-garde never lasts is that it is self-conscious, and another is that time does not stand still, and still another is that the avant-garde's gestures were all agitated two generations before and, being forgotten by those who despise history, are presented once again as new.

•

There are two kinds of artist. One says, "I am greater than art." The other says, "Art is greater than I."

•

It cannot be said often enough: language is the writer's beginning and end, obvious as this must seem. *In principio erat verbum.* Yet present reputations in literature are more often made by notions, fads, current and mindless vulgarisms, what is said, than by how these are expressed. The public speech has declined into indifference to nicety, precision, and structural form. Show business has more effect on expression than the academy, or even the news media. Rhetoric is abominably taught if at all. Young writers grow up to echo what they hear—at the moment the vocabulary is limited largely to "wow" and its popular synonyms—and not to what they read, if they read anything but the work of their styleless near-contemporaries. The *ear* is the good writer's best guide to good style. A writer with no ear is hopelessly disadvantaged. Style is first of all clear and explicit, and then, because there are many choices among ways of expression, fastidious. There are many synonyms for "wow," most of them more durable and exploratory.

•

In many joyfully admired recent novels, love appears as little more than sex-manual instruction, even to the commercial identification of coital lubricants.

•

"Black humor" is a sophomoric attempt to disguise self-hatred.

•

Let a professor of English, history, or social studies invent a striking paradox in his theory of any aspect of his subject, and he can make an entire career out of this single pedagogic commodity. If he can think of a catchword to express it which enters the jargon of the academy, he will attract a generation of disciples.

•

Modishness as against style all too often prevails in academic literature and discourse. There is an always-changing recognition code for persons who can accept the word "intellectual" as a noun. In their jargon they take comfort from such words, recalled at random, as archetype, apocalypse, extrapolate, charisma, *élan vital* (now old-fashioned), paradigm, "black" (as in humor), "absurd" (in relation to a systematic view of life), viable, "radical," explicate, and the rest.

•

We live in the age of the put-on. All periods have had put-ons—but when have they ever become models for success?

•

The absurdity of teaching contemporary literature to its contemporaries.

•

It takes only one great man to create a renaissance.

•

The novelist who sets out consciously to be "of his period" will die with it. If he sets out to be himself, his own times will inevitably be present, and survive with him, if he survives.

•

The present is only the cumulated past, with moment by moment additions.

•

It is difficult if not impossible to find analogies between the virtues of technology and the values of the originating (as against the performing) artist. Our contemporary respect for "systems" seems to urge the artist toward technological (i.e., material) values, yet that which inspires him relates to the life within.

•

Every period has its predominant popular tone, widely influential and pervasive. The writer must select from within this—his contemporaneous tone—as fastidiously as he selects from among those long-established conventions of the past which hold validity for his work.

·

The unquestioned present is of no more value than the unquestioned past.

·

In writing, there are two levels of professionalism: one—the lower—is based on ambition driven by competitiveness; the other is based solely on fulfilling a vision in word and overall design, without regard to what anyone else is writing or publishing.

·

Taste has many conditions and elements. The one certain to be ruinous is that which tries to please others rather than the writer.

·

An editorial or critical cult is usually the extension of the temperament and the bias of one person, or at most, of a very few. In such resides the power to make or break reputations—and all on the basis of necessarily limited views. How, then, can they be taken seriously? But they are, because the energy of the egos behind them is strong enough to require public expression. It is one of the most essentially frivolous and wasting forms of power in culture; and of course as it is subject to fashion or fad, it is eventually superseded by a new critical cult with perhaps directly opposing views. How then can the artist hope for discussion of his work in *his* terms, not theirs?

·

The writer who keeps one eye on the public is sure to be blind in the other.

·

A tiresome current tendency: the deliberate, bad-boy illiteracy which one encounters in novels by youngish persons or others who think all manners of expression equally good. The way for the novelist to refresh the language is not to revert to its worst habits, but to expand temperamentally upon its best.

·

It is one thing to create a fashion; it is another to conform to one; and still another to have no interest in doing either.

·

This may sound fatuous, but in the present climate of the arts, it is pertinent: in themselves, all words are not literature, all sounds are not music, all drops of paint are not painting, all shapes are not sculpture.

•

There is coarseness which passes for vitality in the tone of assumptive knowingness in the writing of certain novelists of the present, who must seem at all costs to be "with-it" in all comment, styles, theories, cult beliefs.

•

The public taste in the United States is frequently so offensive (Muzak, commercial architecture, comic strips-and-books, rock "music," most TV, radio, movies, all pop-pornography, and the rest) that it is enough to raise serious doubts about the stylistic trustworthiness of democracy, which had led to the ascendancy of such expressions. The tyranny of it all is what is off-putting. There is no escape for the individuals who detest these invasions. Worse, there is an inverted snobbery of acceptance of these by some people of cultivated taste, so that it is a disillusioning spectacle to see them go on sprees of aesthetic slumming into the climate of the prevalent cultural pollution. The popular taste will usually seek its comforts in the lowest common aesthetic denominator.

•

For the moment [1969] communication is not regarded in certain influential circles as a principal purpose of the arts. We are to be amazed not at what the artist tells us, or how he tells it, and not even at what he seems to be telling himself, but at the mere fact that he agitates the raw materials or flourishes the instruments of the communicative process.

•

The true artist of the contemporary is not the one who merely tries to fix the scene around him but he who finds in his own sensibility the evidences of the world which made him. If he is true, this is an inescapable process, and as a record it tells us the essentials, while the other vision ends as journalism.

•

Experiments in form, new vessels for each generation, renewed insights, must always be hoped for. The novel at its best is no more static and fixed in a mold than any expressive procedure. But what must never be mistaken for true discovery and new illumination is the formless indulgence of an individual ego, throwing itself about in exhibition of an arrogant self-exploitation, which is rarely more than a public purgation by personal excesses of behavior. A performer with no more of a model than his own anatomy and its often exclusively dubious exercises very soon becomes a bore like a drunk at a party who is self-persuaded that he and his views are the most interesting elements of the gathering.

·

Every period has its projections of ideal figures. This alone is enough to insure the continuing life of the novel, for it is the adventures—mental or physical—of such ideal figures which everyone craves to see objectively in order to feel experience subjectively.

·

The most valuable writers are those in whom we find not themselves, or ourselves, or the fugitive era of their lifetimes, but the common vision of all times.

·

In subtly influenced ways, the novel changes with each generation, even when based on traditional models of earlier times. Nobody in the twentieth century can possibly write a Victorian novel which will be a work of art. It may be a fair imitation, or a hilarious pastiche—but never if the intention of the novelist is serious will it bear stylistic relation to any time but his own.

·

For historical glimpses of the insensitive collectivity of the *populus*, the popular arts are valuable. They rarely carry aesthetic value. It is therefore to a degree maddening that there is a cult which champions them as of artistic importance. If taken seriously at all, the cult really proclaims only an inverted snobbery.

·

The true artist is his own contemporary only.

1973

Preface to
an Unwritten Book*

Because of its mere citations instead of examinations in depth of aspects of our popular culture, I must think of this essay as a sort of preface to an unwritten book. Given time and extent, the book might turn out to be a study of how local character, sectionalism, in various parts of our country, once valid if often naïve culturally, had to give way under machine technics to a certain commonality of attitude, taste, and character. It happens that my lifetime overlaid the final phases of this change from the many regional or sectional styles to a nationalism whose advent we can attribute to new devices of immediate communication. Here we can scarcely describe them, let alone offer a richly furnished judgment of their effect. But I have observed whereof I speak, and so inevitably my preface takes on at times an autobiographical character—that of a witness.

Ever since the immense event of the rapid overtaking of the great West by the established Atlantic society, there was deep response in feeling that more than a geographical triumph was accomplished. Distance and the unknown carried mystery, as always; but there was in addition an element of projected imagination which made "West" as an idea quite as important as "West" as territory and material opportunity. "West" was adventure, was romance, was independence, was a new dimension of selfhood; but it was more—it was health. The prairies, the Rockies, the ultimate Pacific shore, all carried connotations of cure of one or another sort.

*From The Yale Review, Vol. LXV, March 1976, No. 3.

Josiah Gregg, nearly dead in Missouri in his finicky and depressed youth, was sent to the prairies with a Santa Fe trading caravan in 1831 by his family physician, for a last chance to come back to life. When the wagons started west from Independence, Kansas, he had to be lifted into one of them on a litter. Within two weeks he was riding a horse, and by the time he reached Santa Fe after six weeks, he was entirely well. In time, he became a kind of Humboldt of the prairies and desert West, and his book, *Commerce of the Prairies*, published in 1844, the first to describe the Westward experience in full detail and finished form, remains a classic. Forty years later a gifted but debilitated, bereaved young New Yorker went West as a tenderfoot and returned as a man two-fisted enough to become a police commissioner and a President of the United States. In the 1880s the Vicar General of the Archdiocese of Santa Fe reported to the Vatican that "this territory will be, in time, when better known, the great sanitarium of the United States . . . weak persons will find here security to life, and undoubted benefit for the health."

And indeed the Western tradition entered another phase when the climate of the high plains and lower Rockies was medically adjudged beneficial for tubercular invalids. Because my father was one of these, he took his family from New York State to New Mexico in 1915, to settle at Albuquerque. My second view of an American style came into focus there, after a first vision of the world had come to me on the shores of Lake Erie.

New Mexico presented the most clear picture of the laminated history of the Southwest, with its first components the Pueblo Indians, its second the Mexican Americans, and its third the Anglo-Americans—alike those who survived from pioneer settlement and those new immigrants who, like my family, came for climate, and those others who followed the railroad across the continent and for whatever reason stopped to help with the formation of a town somewhere along the line.

Along the line—what a different matter from remaining to live at a fixed point of origin like New York or Chicago or Los Angeles, where the great railroad system both started from and returned to. It was an eloquent statement of the difference when you recognized that the most interesting event of every day in Albuquerque was going to the railroad station to see the California Limited of the Santa Fe line arrive, pause for thirty minutes while travelling celebrities strolled (I remember Douglas Fairbanks and Mary Pickford), and then depart into the perspective, which was both diagrammed and activated by the parallel tracks. Gazing after the train filled the mind with thoughts and images of far away, before a return to the local reality. This reality was like nothing else, and what dominated all was the splendor of the landscape in its vast scale, its earth features, its colors, its immensity of sky, its rarefied air, and its spacious light.

It was impossible not to collect contrasts between East and West.

In the urban East, landscape seemed to withdraw, you could not see it without going to some effort. In every Western town of that time the open country in its vastness could be seen at the end of every street—the desert was there, the mountain in its degree of blue which measured its distance away, the huge encompassing sky. Eastern winters were gray and sometimes as dark as ink over hillocks of snow which lasted for months in city streets. Western desert winters were matters of gold light on yellow sweeps, with occasional blizzards whose evidence often vanished within hours under the sun. In the East, all marvels were manmade, on a scale intimate enough to be bought or rented, visited or inhabited, in man's dimension. In the desert West, all marvels were natural ones on a scale so grand as to make man's survival there an historical triumph. If the East was largely industrial, the West was a kingdom of raw materials, animal husbandry on a broad range, and organized pursuit of health. Sizable fortunes were made out of such concerns, and various amenities survived importation from the East and beyond. Even as the frontier was in its last phase, it was considered desirable for gentlemen of means, or pretensions, or both, to have their shirts sent from New Mexico to Chicago to be properly starched and ironed, and with the railroad came the certainty of Chesapeake Bay oysters on beds of ice.

But in general, as life thinned out going Westward, the manner of it grew less formal, until time and riches brought into being at the extreme of the continent the California patio habits of the heliophile, his relaxed cult of the body accompanied at large by a kindly incuriosity of mind.

The sophisticated East was represented by an audience society. In the West, for a great length of time, members of the society had to perform for themselves what their own experiences could celebrate locally. Amenity and the cultural wealth, in the East, came together in complement. In the West, neither was notably prevalent so long as the local character preserved itself. In one aspect of the culture, sports in the East early became those of the machine—motorcar gymkhanas, motorboat races (the fragile little shells of the boats were called hydroplanes), airplane regattas with the first double-winged Curtiss flying machines unconsciously being rehearsed for military use; while in the West, sports stayed close to the animals of the open country—cattle, and the horses of the cowboys who rode herd on them. The Eastern style of life had old foreign cultural roots; the Western, a condition curiously echoed in many ways which recalled the earliest human terms of survival on the land anywhere.

The contrast seemed to suggest to many a condition of exile, and so did the resettlement of phthisical invalids. The theme was poignantly, indeed, angrily, dealt with by an American artist of beautiful gifts, Miss Willa Cather, of whom I first heard from her sister Elsie, who taught me freshman English in the Albuquerque High School. In a number of early works, Willa Cather posed the pathos, the tragedy, of the higher culture, in the person of a great artist, against the uncomprehending society of the frontier West and its philistine mentality. If Miss Cather's portraits of her exiles seemed to lack full sympathy for helpless states of uninformed life, and to risk seeming overfastidious, the fact remains that great contrasts in cultural ways naturally call forth personal choices—or at least, should afford the opportunity to choose.

In Miss Cather's story *The Sculptor's Funeral*, a distinguished artist's body is brought home for burial in the poor town of his origin—Sand City, somewhere in the West. He had risen from its gritty life to eminence in Boston of a sort which brings to mind such an American sculptor as Augustus Saint-Gaudens. The young pupil who brings his body home to the bereaved family in "this borderland between ruffianism and civilisation," that "bitter, dead little western town"—the young pupil shudders at the complacent ignorance, even the mockery, which underlie the local view of Sand City's only eminent son. In another story, *A Death in the Desert*, Miss Cather has an exquisite singer who also has gone to fame in the great world now dying of her lungs back home "like a rat in a hole, out of her own world, and she can't fall back into ours"—though she had come in a last hope for a cure. The same story contains seeds for the later novel *The Song of the Lark*, about a wondrously gifted girl who rises from a little Colorado railroad town (marvellously described) to the opera houses of the world, an escapee from her birthright of exile. Bitterest of all, the story *A Wagner Matinee* gives us the visit home to Boston of a once-cultivated woman who has married a Westerner and has moved from Boston to exile and hardship—physical and spiritual—on a little ranch out West. How she has starved during all those years on the ranch for what she hears once again, now, in her withered middle age, when the great Boston Orchestra plays a Wagner program in Symphony Hall! When the concert is over, she remains in a daze in her chair while the hall and stage go empty. The narrator, her nephew, speaks to her. ". . . She burst into tears and sobbed pleadingly. 'I don't want to go, Clark, I don't want to go!' " The nephew understands. For her, he reflects, "Just outside the door of the concert hall lay the black pond with the cattle-tracked bluffs; naked as a tower, the crook-backed ash seedlings where the dishcloths hung to dry; the gaunt, molting turkeys picking up refuse about the kitchen door." In such early fiction, Miss Cather touched on three determining themes of the West (though, of course, there were others of a more inspiriting nature)—the cultural exile, the all-powerful railroads, the act of going West to get well, or die.

As these pervaded her early work, they may have reflected her own sense of deracination after the removal of her family from Virginia, with its old traditions, to a raw Nebraska, in her girlhood. Later, to be sure, she fell in love with the open land, wrote fondly of those (usually European immigrants) who made their lives there, and in many a lyric passage she described the Western earth through nostalgic vision. Rude limitations became humble beauties, and behind these lay something more wonderful. This was the prehistoric life of the cave and mesa Indians whose civilization left such noble monuments as the cliff dwellings of the Southwest with their superb artifacts. But if Miss Cather's view softened as she attained her own great eminence far beyond the West, there were still to be seen various evidences of a culturally deprived population striving to fulfill for itself various impulses toward aesthetic expression and enjoyment and self-celebration common to all men at whatever level of taste.

I remember some of these at their most primitive in the Southwest of my boyhood. The art of painting, before the migration of artists of talent to Santa Fe and Taos, was represented locally by store-window artists who painted to order, by formula, on pieces of shirt cardboard, at brilliant speed, and in slickest pigment, lurid landscapes for parlor and kitchen. A gifted few of these itinerant artists could paint with both hands at one time, while sidewalk locals watched and marvelled. Their works could be had for an average of fifty cents each.

Lacking museums, the earlier outlands people flocked to see, in a local undertaking parlor, a huge painting of Christ at Gethsemane which was shown in surroundings hushed not only by the subject (one which all knew and understood well) but also by dense black velvet hangings which extended the night of agony into the room, while soft light was focused on the Bible scene. Most wonderful of all, an electric star glimmered in the sky through a pinhole made in the canvas. For a fee, lines of viewers could advance to enter a reverent and aesthetic experience, until the painting—it was on tour—moved on to its next engagement. Music and theatre were most accessibly available through travelling revival meetings, which set up their tents on vacant lots and filled the lust-laden summer nights with percussive hymns and the drama of visible conversion, under the acid glare of Coleman lanterns. Yet music of fame occasionally stepped off the sumptuous transcontinental Limited trains for a single concert, and Miss Cather's exiles could once again hear such artists as Paderewski, Tetrazzini, Schumann-Heink, Lillian Nordica, Jan Kubelik. Too, dramatic troupes came through with their tent shows and their primitive plays whose predominant theme was the triumph of the red-wigged small-town hick over the fast-talking city slicker. Literature was often the duty of the local editor, who had read Mark Twain and saw himself as a similar wag, or a tubercular invalid from the East with a gasping talent for sardonic remarks in his own occasional little half column on the editorial page. One such whom I remember used the pseudonym "T. B. Crabb." As for architecture, dwellings were mostly humble frame houses, while public buildings reflected aspirations, much diluted, in reference to either the beaux arts or the Richardsonian style.

It is easy, and not illuminating, to see all such primitive manifestations only in comic terms. Their real point is that, as they were characteristic of any removed society, they were allied to unselfconscious folk traditions. Perhaps there was an expectation that, if ever superseded by a national style, their degree of cultural sophistication might rise. We suspend the point for the moment.

Of the indigenous arts, it was the rodeo which spoke for the population at large, when hardy and skillful men showed at great danger and chance their mastery of the animals which supported their living and gave their culture its predominant tone.

Though, to be sure, widely scattered, there were a few islands of sophisticated taste and even elegance. An occasional great house stood isolated on the plains at the center of a vast ranch; and in it might be seen a collection of master paintings, and an impressive library in English and French bindings, and pieces of sculpture by such as Canova and Thorvaldsen, and important visitors who arrived by private railroad car on the nearest rail line. Such exoticism would persist for perhaps one generation only, and then the great possessions would be dispersed, the unlikely mansion worn down by the hot light of the sky and sandstorms stretching across entire states.

But if the intensely local was suggested by all such expressions, it was not for the most part self-conscious in any conspicuous way. Then, however, came the force of the great depression in the 1930s which brought a self-awareness to the various distinct parts of the nation through a study of each state by writers and artists in need of employment—an assignment asked of them by a wise and compassionate government through the Works Progress Administration. One of its great results was the series of WPA American Guide Books which in both the making and the later reading gave each state and region of the nation a clearer idea of itself than it had ever known before.

The effect of this, and of the immediacy of grave human suffering, was to bring to intensified consciousness, discussion, and criticism, both social and aesthetic, the idea of regionalism—a word which suddenly came into wide usage.

My sketchy citation of those aspects of regionalism which I knew by accident—those of the Southwest—could be correspondingly itemized for any other of the distinct regions of the country—the Northeast, the South, the Middle West, the Pacific Coast. Each originally had its localism, which was unselfconsciously evolved out of natural conditions. This is not to claim that the naïve, just because it was regional, had to be preserved for its own sake. But it is to say that a living expression of a sectional character, or local folkism, had an honest character which met its doom when it began to be meretriciously exploited.

Because the impulse of art is universal, artists in all forms of work have always recorded their homage to where they lived. Where they lived was largely determined by accident. One always deals with what one knows through natural association in whatever degree of honest response.

In this there is a kernel of the notion that to elevate regionalism per se into an artistic virtue is somewhat beside the point, and even the more so, when the vogue for organized regionalism, wherever in the land, became pervasive. For then the idea of the corporate regional self became self-conscious, and what followed was all too often a burlesque of the original style, as a common nostalgia promised to become convertible into commercial advantage. Tourism must follow.

Traffic-borne tourism helped to show the way to intellectual tourism, or at least to an organized exploitation of the study of the "folk." Stereotypes were set in entertainment. The local flavor was exploited, and soon enough the question must be asked, How long can a social or historical frontier last? It is innocent enough for people to organize celebrations of their collective character, however crudely, but what won't be of much use is to set up systems of classification of interpreters possessing genuine gifts as artists or scholars by lumping them as regionalists, as though some inherent virtue accompanied the designation. The point is that the true artist always rises above "region"—that is to say, his material. I have never seen a statement by a truly gifted artist which admitted to his being a "regionalist," no matter how firmly he has been assigned the classification by those who make their livings by detecting patterns in accidents and symbols in intuitions, which is to say the sort of critic whose vocation requires certain conveniences. Perhaps all one can finally say on the subject is that the minute regionalism "sees" itself it disappears, and a counterfeit takes its place, with every likelihood of a long and commercially profitable run.

Oddly commingled, the American nineteenth-century tradition of gentility which persisted for so long, and the eager awakening to the regional as matter for exploitation, both in the end succumbed to a force greater than either. Folkways when corrupted by commerce lose first their validity. Gentility when faced with a vast increase in the means of transmitting culture loses first its tradition of high style. Where commerce and wealth are great enough, and population dense enough, and mechanical ingenuity lively enough, the communal behavior and perception are delegated to surrogate means. With the passing of American gentility went the European models on which it was generally based and which American Puritanism sterilized morally.

When, during the 1914 war, America discovered the world four and a half centuries after the world discovered America, many restraints of convention and even law vanished, evidently forever; and very soon afterward, the powerful energy of the established material motive, combined with the fast and often brilliant development of technology, started the headlong trend toward the dishuman in cultural regard and scale.

The authentically regional was engulfed by the national, and the genteel by the unlimited vulgarism which gave public instead of private employment to the extreme vernacular. Technical means of communication were of course the vehicle by which this came about, in a cultural revolution of astonishing power and velocity. As had happened before, historical coincidence brought together at the same moment a change of style and the means of widely distributing it. This one began with the movie film, went on to radio, which caught on very fast, and these started to create a national standard—a substandard—of taste which for commercial purposes seemed to impose a character on the population instead of draw one from it.

Sound recording played an immense part in the process, as did motor travel on a transcontinental scale, and the climax arrived with television in its instantaneous and simultaneous transmission of vision and sound across any boundaries which once might have preserved local character, manners, values, for whatever they were once worth.

Yet previously, too, there had always been a need for the American art to rise above the homely, to let the emerging nation ennoble its ideals visibly and intellectually. America's early architecture, its Greek Revival houses, all the references to the classical established in barely cleared forest lands, and even the machine vernacular (as John Kouwenhoven has so beautifully demonstrated), with its cast-iron business façades and ornamented industrial engines, reached for the high aesthetic. But this was the work of a cultivated few. How in an age of machine popularism could the native cultural habits come to expression en masse, in the broadly pervasive forms?

Was the life-material itself too spiritually meager? Are its current exploiters too ignorant of, or indifferent to, all cultural heritage? Is America now really without a past? But the act and meaning of human life anywhere are always illimitably potential for the artist who remains indifferent to any vision not his own. Was the American creative consciousness too strangled by the national popular speech, which confused democracy with the sort of illiteracy assumed for fear of giving offense through noticeably educated idiom?

Before an American aesthetic revolution could arrive at an orderly realization, in which diversity could be sought in the highest cultural terms, the question became irrelevant; for the finally democratic common denominator was forced into being by technology wedded to commerce. Given two or three more generations, the United States maker of taste might have found heroic forms beyond those demanded by the material imperative of our defined national motive of commercial ambition, before which, in deference to individualism unrestrained by a tradition of style, all has given way, including political probity. The great leveller brought swiftly and too soon the commercial necessity of new forms, from the grotesquely attention-getting advertisement to the short-lived skyscrapers which were built to accommodate crowds in narrow and therefore tall space, and were always being outgrown, torn down, and replaced taller still. Perhaps through the machine a levelling of the arts to a national new folkism is in process, as against the old local vision free of demands of mass comprehension and commercial expediency. No tyranny is more powerful than that of common taste when it has two things to make it pervasive—a commercial purpose, and a mechanical means of transmission to an entire public.

In means of communication, then, and in physical forms alike, and consequently in habits of behavior, common reference, and opinion, centralization seems to have come to govern the American popular expression. For the better? Here is our suspended point of some pages ago: not better in general quality, only more sophisticated in technical means.

Industrial or commercial convenience, not individual human choice, always now decides. Metropolitan increase requires in cities that people live in hives. We now have an imposed neighborliness. It is one distributed to us by engineering means in infinite replication without regard to individual interest or preference among the general population drawn to it by the pathetic tyrannies of gainful employment. And even in non-metropolitan areas, where the older order of separate houses still prevails, what now enters the house, by way of information, idea, and consequent belief, comes through a vastly syndicated electronic or graphic means created by technics. The imposed culture leaves no one alone.

To be commercially successful, most forms of expression now gratify not the highest, or even the average, but the lowest standard of emotional, intellectual, and aesthetic adventure. The central sin of the aggressive society is competitiveness, with its indignities and vulgarities meanly motivated by material ends. On a private scale, this leads to the cheapening of ethical and aesthetic standards not only of the present but of the future, through its inescapable influence on children, who have appetite but no critical judgment. In the national character, it leads to schematic expediency in domestic politics, with a huge part of the electorate, as now, shamefully indifferent to the exercise of the franchise; and conceivably, in foreign policy, it leads to war.

Man's view of himself is all-revealing, as he strives to achieve the ends of survival along with comfort and a position of esteem. It is impossible to overestimate the lowering effect upon this view of two particularly pervasive modern cultural forces, in their degree peculiarly American.

The first of these is the deforming of the human aspect by the general comic-cartoon style, either to entertain or to sell: by representing persons as grotesque or revoltingly whimsical or subhuman, the cartoon, animated or still, cajoles the viewer into feeling superior. It is a visual vulgate which reassures him. Made to feel superior, he is an easier mark for whatever persuasive idea is thus offered to him. The comic strip, the movie cartoon, the canned greeting card, the social exhortation, the flattery of distortion, violence as a joke, provide image and sentiment so impersonal that they even suggest a hidden desperation at the state of man's condition. We have lately seen millions of little round lapel buttons with a smile painted on them in three childish strokes. Why must we be incessantly reminded to smile? Are we inherently so savage that this precaution is nervously needed? Perhaps man's discontent is all too clear to him today, and perhaps he must do his utmost to conceal it, in order to live with it.

The second of the two powerful forces of persuasion and education today is the craft of advertising, which all too often goes beyond its only legitimate purpose, and that is to meet, rather than create, a need. Advertising, with bland contempt for common intelligence, sees truth as a merely relative and adjustable value. A current television commercial has a sternly reassuring man on camera, dressed like a financier, a character which he represents, who is trying to convince us for his own commercial purposes. Hear what he says:

"This is not just an *ad*—it is a *fact*."

There is a sort of wild innocence, if not a bloodless cynicism, in this tacit admission that advertising is not factual, even as it pretends to be. The ethical squalor of this, so widely unrecognized, may tell us much by analogy about why a vast malaise has come over our country. The young people almost alone have recognized it—though in their repudiations of it they have sometimes resorted to measures hurtful to themselves and others. The cheerful acquiescence of the public in the organized dishonesty of most advertising—and its purposeful offspring, "public relations," with all too few honorable exceptions—is a symptom of the ethically unsatisfying nature of much of our technological life. To be sure, in earlier generations, it was not unknown for a gullible public to be cozened by sharpers. The medicine show, with its spielers, its snake oil, its guttering torches, its "free entertainment"—played upon susceptibilities as old as the art of bartering. But the reach was limited and the swindle did not create manners.

If we view today's equivalent nationally, and dismiss it by saying that it is all passing nonsense, lasting only a half minute or so on TV or in an eye-flicked printed sales pitch, and thus without enduring effect, we delude ourselves. For the aggregate of those minutes makes a formidable total, especially through incessant repetition. As a result, without our conscious consent, we become used to it as a style is formed, or a habit of thought is formed, and consequently, behavior is affected, and with it, the future.

So persuaded are we of the authority of technology, and its ability to make mechanical miracles, that we see the whole future in its terms. The future is now a fad instead of a responsibility.

I suppose, as of now, that the best we can do is to say, if technology means the ultimate expression of the material motive in cultural terms essentially undifferentiated anywhere in the land, that our escape may come only through a direct reversal of our material imperative in human affairs. Perhaps the escape from the blandly synthetic—the imposed culture—may lie only in the re-newed pursuit of a higher humanism by which to celebrate the individual body and soul of man among his like-constituted fellows, each of whom is unique. This implies a spiritual rehabilitation which once might have been secured by a common comprehension of the divine. Lacking a general agreement nowadays on the terms of that, perhaps we have to command the technics to perform only their proper function, that is, service, instead of delegating to them that mastery of human life in even its *im*material aspects to which we have been more and more subjected. It is a purpose worth pursuing for the sake of all the positive splendors of our land, and of our founding principles, and of our best institutions, and of the respect owed to the best in our people.

There may be a ray of hope in some recent words of Sir Peter Medawar, who as a medical scientist does not incriminate technology, but only its misuse. "Insofar," he says, "as any weapon can be blamed for any crime, science and technology *are* responsible for our present predicament. But they offer the only possible means of escaping the misfortunes for which they are responsible . . . an entirely new technology is required, one founded on ecology in much the same way as medicine is founded on physiology. If this new technology is accepted, I shall be completely confident of our ability to put and keep our house in order."

Dr. Medawar was referring to the physical environment. Is it apposite at this point to report that the optimistic Santa Fe Vicar General of 1883 could now see a tawny envelope of polluted air over Albuquerque, and more layers of the same at the desert junction of his state with three others? Still: may we hope that the other—the non-physical aspects of our environment—may be reclaimed through a long-term proper use of the very technology which made pervasive an imposed culture—one which falls below the best nature of our people?

We have come a long way around from the idea of local American popular cultures and the often naïve but genuine expressions of their many different styles. But the contrasts which once existed in concrete regional circumstance have been succeeded by others. Serious contrasts now exist between the abstract early idealism of the nation and its erosion in our time through an unworthy exploitation of the technology. It was an idealism resting upon a hope for a people to be enlightened through common control of their own character and condition. How much of this can be recovered? That issue itself, now, is what transcends our present practice in any sense whatever.

1976

I V

SHORT STORY

The Peach Stone:
Stories from Four Decades

National Honeymoon

Somewhere an electric organ began to play the trumpet notes of the Mendelssohn wedding march. The audience began to applaud, for at the same moment a sunburned, heavy man in a flowing gray flannel suit came out of the darkness beyond the stage into a spotlight. He came to the microphone with his head bent, his hands crossed before him in mock solemnity. Footlights caught a sparkle in his eye which flashed over the full studio with suggestive hilarity. He stood for a long moment, creating suspense for the whole throng, mostly women. Behind him on the stage was an orchestra. A sign in scarlet electric letters overhead read ON THE AIR.

Out of sight backstage, standing in the darkness, a young man and a young woman faced each other, trembling.

"I don't know why you had to go and do it," the young man said.

"Please, darling, I didn't dare to tell you before."

"I don't know why not. We've always talked about everything."

"It means so much to us," she said urgently, "and you wouldn't have agreed if I had told you before."

It was his habit to try to be fair, and he thought this over. She studied his face, guessing at his thoughts. In the light that faded over him from the stage she saw that he was honestly troubled now, lost in a little struggle between authority and love. Finally he acknowledged with a grudging smile how well she knew him.

"No," he said, "I don't suppose I would have agreed."

She shook her head at him, and tears threatened to come to her eyes. "It was my surprise for you," she said.

He knew this was not an entirely sincere claim, and he whispered, "Here I get you to Hollywood for our honeymoon, and the first thing I know you drag me to a radio show and the next thing I know we have to be in it. How did you get it all fixed up, anyway?"

"Get what fixed up? What, darling?"

"Now listen. They met us at the plane. They brought us here. They took our picture, and you kept telling me to be quiet and smile."

"Well, you hate to be conspicuous, you know that. It would all have been much more conspicuous if we'd refused and made a scene."

"You didn't answer me. How did you arrange it all?"

"Oh. Why—the radio station at home did everything. So when our plane landed here this afternoon they were ready for us."

"I wish I'd known it before this morning."

"You mean before we were married? Do you mean to stand there and suggest that if you'd known, you'd have— Don't you love me that much? And us married just a few hours ago?"

He made a helpless gesture, conceding all that she wanted to know. She put her hand on his arm.

"Darling. Listen, oh, please be nice."

She motioned toward the brightly lighted stage, where the man at the microphone was changing his personality.

"Dearly beloved, we are gathered together," he said reverently, and then brightened, "for *another* excursion of *romance* and *happiness* on National Honeymoon, and this is your favorite father-in-law, Gail Burke Himself, broadcasting to you from *Hollywood, California*, the honeymooners' *dream* city, over USA, the United Stations Association, with another *brand-new bride and groom* to present to *all* America, a fine young *man* and a beautiful young *girl*, who are going to tell us *their story*, and share their happiness with *every*one, and when *they* are *through*, we have some *surprises* for them that will take their *breath* away, and *yours too!*"

Backstage, the bride smiled brightly at her husband to make him accept such promises of good fortune. "See, darling?" she whispered; and then she clung to him for safety, for their time was about to come, and excitement, stage fright, and strangeness overwhelmed them.

The orchestra began to build up to their entrance with brassy chords and flying runs on violins. At the microphone, Gail Burke Himself enriched his voice, and cried, ". . . ladies and gentlemen of America's favorite wedding party, *our honeymoon couple!*"

He pointed to the wings. Someone came up behind the bride and groom, gave them a pressing caress at their waists and sent them walking out into the glare.

Burke advanced to meet them, leading the applause. Low cries of pleasure arose amid the clapping when everyone saw how beautiful today's honeymooners were. The young man's hair shone like polished white gold when he turned his head under the stage lights. He stood with physical pride, in the new suit whose lines showed how comely he was and strong. He held his wife's arm, which was trembling. She wore a small flowery hat way back on her silky brown hair. There was an orchid on the shoulder of her smoky-blue suit. Her eyes were blue. Her hands gloved in white held her huge, black leather purse with her initials—the new ones—in silver. She kept close to him, looking up at him for safety and forgiveness. Her face, lifted so, was an imploring mask of sweetness.

Burke observed this. He sliced the audience noise into silence with a sharp cut of his hand, and said as though confidentially to the packed rows of seats, "She can't take her eyes off him for a minute!"

The audience roared.

"She hasn't had him long enough," added Burke, and they roared again. "Aren't they sweeties?" he asked, pressing home the aching spectacle.

"Now let's see who they are, shall we, people?"

The crowd cried, "Yes!"

Burke turned.

"First, our groom. My, what a fine-looking young fellow, about six feet two, a hundred and eighty pounds—am I right?" The young man nodded. "Blond hair, good-looking suit. All right, what's your name?"

"G. A. Earickson."

"Aha! What does the G stand for, Mr. Earickson?"

"Gustavus."

"Gustavus!" cried Burke at the audience. "Get that? And what's the A stand for?"

"Adolphus."

"No! Gustavus Adolphus, Gadolphus Astovus," chanted Burke in delight. *"People, do you love it?"* he cried to the audience, and his listeners responded with applause. When he could, he resumed. "What do people call you?"

"Gus."

"Adda-boy, Gus; mind if I call you Gus? I never would get around that Gavvovvus Gusdolphus routine. Say, you must be a Swede. Are you a Swede?"

"No. My grandfather was."

"He was? *Vas a Svaydish yantle-mann* from *Svayden?*"

"Yes."

"And what're you, Gus?"

"I'm an American."

"People, get that? He's an *American!*"

The people cheered back at him.

"Oall right, Gus, what do you do for a living?"

"I travel in wholesale produce."

"Wholesale produce, you mean groceries?"

"That's right."

"How do you travel?"

"By car. I use a company truck."

"Where do you go?"

"I make all the valley towns."

"Aha! That's fine, simply fine," murmured Burke. "I suppose you have to be away overnight sometimes?"

"Sure."

Burke whirled on Roberta May and called over her head at the crowd, "She'll have to watch that, won't she, people? Hubby off by himself, who knows what he might get into, hey?"

This brought a kind of innocently cynical laughter.

Turning back to Gus, Burke said, "Wonderful, wonderful? Now tell us, Gus, how long you been married."

"Today."

"*Today?*" said Burke with sudden quietness. "You mean you have been married only a matter of hours?"

"That's right."

"And how have you spent the time between getting married and now, Gus—would you tell us that?"

Gus, seeing the import of the question, began to blush.

"Say, people, he's *blushing*," cried Burke, making a magician's pass over Gus's head. "What could he have to blush about? Shall I ask him?"

Roar.

"Oall right, *oall* right. Gus, what are you blushing for—is there anything you can't tell us?"

"No. I'm not blushing."

"Oh, he's not blushing, eh? Very well. Oho, *that's fine*. Then just tell us, Mr. Earickson, how you have spent the day."

"In an airplane."

"Getting here?"

"Getting here."

"I see. And what did you do?"

"Nothing."

"*Nuth*-thing?"

"That's right."

There was a dry edge to Gus's voice. Burke got it. He decided it was time to switch.

"Thank you very much, Mr. G. A. Earickson; we'll ask you some more questions later. But now, to this lovely, lovely girl standing before me, holding on so tightly to her new husband's arm—let us ask you your name; will you tell us that?"

"Mrs. Gustavus Adolphus Earickson," she said with great clarity and pride, to reject any mockery that might linger about Gus's name.

Laughing, bested, Burke struggled to recover in the face of his audience.

"Well, I didn't think you were Mrs. Joe Palooka," he said. "I mean, your own given name. I can't go on all day calling you Mrs. Garruphus Astovvus Earickson. What do they call you, honey?"

"Roberta May."

"Roberta May!" Burke pointed straight at the audience. "*Isn't that wonderful?* Let's give her a hand on that!" And they did, to her dismay. But they made her a heroine, and she felt her heart pound more easily, and she looked up at Gus as if to tell him, You see? This isn't so bad—it's sort of fun, and happens to not many boys and girls in the United States!

"Now, Roberta May," continued Burke, "where did you two meet? Tell us that."

"At home. We grew up together."

"You did! Did Gus carry your schoolbooks back and forth for you?"

"No."

"Did he put your pigtails in the ink bottle of his desk in the schoolroom?"

"No. We didn't go to the same school, at first."

"Where *did* you see him, then?"

"Down the street. His house and my house were only a couple of blocks apart."

"I see. And did he ride by on his bike and take you for a spin?"

"No. He just rode by."

"Didn't stop?"

"No, he didn't."

Burke faced the crowd with dismay.

"Say, how're we ever going to get these two together?" he asked, and then turned back to his work. The audience was touched by the simple pride and dignity of the bride and groom, who just stood up there and said what they knew.

"Did he have other girl friends?"

"I guess so."

"Did you, Gus?"

There was a little pause, and then Gus decided to answer, and said, "Yes, when I got to high school."

"Now we're getting somewhere," said Burke. "And did Roberta May go to high school at the same time?"

"Yes, a class behind me."

"Did you fall in love with her then?"

Gus looked at him and kept silent. Burke shifted to her.

"Did you fall in love with him then? In high school, Roberta May? Want to tell us that?"

"Why, yes, I'll tell you. No, I didn't fall in love with him in high school."

"But you saw each other every day?"

"Oh, yes."

Burke turned in comic silence to the audience. They laughed in sudden friendliness; there was a sense that a silent wing of life itself was brushing through the big red-and-gold plaster room, and they stirred unconsciously in response to it.

"Well, when—did—you—fall—in love with him?" chanted Burke. "Can you remember that?"

"Yes, I can remember," said Roberta May. "It was when I heard he was reported missing in action, overseas."

The beat of the wing grew heavier. There was a second of absolute stillness. Presently Burke asked in quiet masterly calm and false respect, "Would you consent to tell us a little more about that, Mrs. Earickson?"

She looked at Gus, who lifted his chin a trifle, as though to say, "Go ahead and tell him." Her heart thumped at his loyal wish that she do well, now that she was there.

"All right," she said. "Why, I was home from the office that day; it was a Saturday—"

"Pardon me, Roberta May," interrupted Burke, whose duty it was to bring out all possible facts in his interview, "did you have a job?"

"Oh, yes."

"What was it?"

"I worked as a secretary at the Building and Loan."

"And do you still?"

"Oh, no. I wanted to keep on, but Mr. Earickson wouldn't let me."

"Wouldn't let you!"

"That's right," said Gus levelly.

"Why, Gus? Would you tell us why?"

"I can support both of us."

At Burke's gesture, applause exploded.

"Thank you. Now go ahead, Roberta May."

"Well, we didn't stay open on Saturday afternoon, and so I was home that afternoon, and the phone rang, and I thought Mother would answer it, and it rang and rang, but she didn't answer, so I went and it was Mrs. Earickson."

"Gus's mother?"

"Yes. Well, she wanted to talk to Mother, and I said she wasn't home, and she didn't say anything for a while, and I said, Is there anything wrong, Mrs. Earickson? And then she said, Oh, Roberta May, and then I heard her voice sort of close up. So I said I would be right over. Well, I hung up, and I went right over, and she was waiting for me on the front porch, sort of hiding behind one of the fern baskets out front there and crying. She had this telegram in her hand and she just shoved it at me, and that was how I found out."

"What did you find out?"

"It said he was missing in action over Germany, and it said they would send more news as it was available."

"Then what did you do?"

"I kissed Mrs. Earickson and took her inside and we sat down and we talked and we talked—she needed to have somebody to talk to. There was a picture of Gus in uniform on the piano, and she pointed at it and said she couldn't bear to look at it. I asked her if she wanted me to turn it around and she said, No, let it alone. But I looked at it, and thought about things, and I knew I was in love with him. I thought it was too late. But I just couldn't get used to the idea of there not being any Gus, anywhere, any more. It left a hole."

She paused. Burke kept quiet, and the audience leaned forward, rapt. She resumed.

"So then I decided Mrs. Earickson needed a daughter—she didn't have anybody else. I was there day and night, and we never gave up believing he was safe and would get back to us. But the funny thing—Mrs. Earickson was worried about *me*, too."

"Why, Roberta May?"

"Why, you see, she found out I was in love with him, and she tried to make me think what would happen if he got back and wasn't in love with me. We just knew each other as kids before, you see, and his mother didn't want me to be let down. So she worried and she worried. But I didn't worry."

"You didn't?"

"No. I didn't."

"Why not?"

"Why, I said to myself, If he comes back, and he doesn't—*you know*—why, I'll just be sensible and look around elsewhere."

It was a relief to crash with laughter and applause at the innocent realism and strength of this statement, which now struck Roberta May as faithless so that she rode above the applause saying loudly, "But the real reason I didn't worry is because I just knew he would feel the way I did when he got back."

"How did you know that?"

"I don't know. I just did."

"And did he?"

"Even before he got back."

"He did? Tell us!"

"Why, when he escaped back through France and got back to his outfit, he wrote to Mrs. Earickson, and at the end of the letter he said, Give my love to everybody, and especially Roberta May when you see her. So I knew then."

"So what did you do?"

"So I began writing to him regularly, and he began answering, and that was all there was to it."

"Isn't—that—wonderful! *Come on, everybody!*" The audience obliged with deafening applause. Burke added, "And when he got home, what did he do?"

She was puzzled a little, and smiled with diffidence. Burke coaxed her.

"Come on, Bridey, what did he do when he saw you?"

"Oh," she said. "Why, he shook hands."

A short laugh.

"Didn't he kiss you?"

"Not right away."

"He *didn't?* When *did* he?"

"It took him two weeks, about."

"Two weeks to make up your mind to kiss a honey chile like this one! What are we coming to?"

"Oh, no," said Roberta May with reproof, "he was serious. He wanted to be sure."

"Serious—wanted to be sure. *People, do you love it?*" demanded Burke, and they did. "Wonderful, wonderful," he continued. "And then did he pop the question?"

"Oh, no, not then. We went together, but we got engaged just last year."

"You waited all that time? Why'd you wait?"

She looked down as though in utmost modesty over something which she could confess, if at all, in the most refined way.

"Why," she finally said, "we couldn't afford to get married at first."

Oddly, there was an instant of fixed silence, and everyone seemed to feel ashamed. Burke was equal to this failure, and said reassuringly, "But you finally made it, didn't you, and got engaged? Will you tell us how you announced it?"

She brightened at once, happy and proud of what she could remember and tell.

"Oh, why, yes—we had a party at my house for all my girl friends. It was cute."

"Cute, so're you," said Burke, imitating a cartoon convention of a bashful boy who scrapes his bare toe in the dirt and twists from side to side. "What'd you do?"

"Why, Mother helped me fix it up, and we had all the drapes drawn, and candles, and refreshments, and—this was the cutest part —we had the mantelpiece in the living room fixed up with a wide white satin ribbon painted with gold paint, and it said, Gus and Roberta May, June 22. And on the mantelpiece there was a toy white kitten just like it was just getting out of a bag—we had a brown paper bag tipped over, and that was our idea to tell the news."

Burke clutched his brow. "You mean *the cat was out of the bag?* Is that what it meant?"

"Yes."

Burke whirled on the audience.

"D'you get it, people?" They did. "Isn't it wonderful? Thank you, Roberta May, thank you. And now—" He turned to Gus. "Now, Gus, can you tell us a little something about how you courted this lovely, lovely bride of yours? Could you tell us a little about that, h'm?"

"We just had dates, I guess."

"Aha, dates. And what did you do on your dates?"

"Oh, ride out in the country, mostly."

"Use a little moonlight, and play the radio, is that right? Park under some trees and thissa and thatta, like all the boys and girls, h'm?"

Gus murmured something. Nobody could hear it.

"What was that? A little louder, please—right here, right into the microphone, please."

"I said, yes, I suppose so."

"Thank you. And what else did you do on your dates? Go to the movies?"

"Yes."

"Fine. Fine. Tell me, Gus, did you ever have a fight over anything? You know, little lovers' quarrels, disagreements?"

How hungry the listeners were to taste the experience of that pair of lives.

"Well, sure, I guess so, yes."

"Oh, you did, eh? What about?"

"Oh, little things—they didn't mean anything."

"Like what, though, son? Tell us."

"I told you they didn't mean anything," said Gus.

"Oh, so you won't talk, eh?" snarled Burke in a burlesque of severity, because what he and his national instrument feared most was a moment's silence.

He was saved by a flushed inspiration from another quarter. Roberta May, swept along by the contagion of the moment, broke in, saying, "We had quite a row over that job question. I was really worried, there, for a while."

"*Sweet-heart!*" cried Burke. "Tell us!"

She felt lightheaded, but even so, she knew now that she was betraying her husband in public. Trembling for what she did, she could not, under the lights, the power, the applause, the national hookup, help doing it.

"Why, he sprang it on me without warning," she said, "that when we got married I would have to quit my job. So I said I didn't want to, he'd be gone all day, what would I do all day, and I said I could help with payments on the house, and our things, and besides, I liked my job, it brings you in touch with lots of people and everything. So I said no."

"What did he do?"

"Nothing. He just didn't come around, or call up or anything."

"Why, Gus, you old *meanie*," said Burke, trying to make him laugh. Sick for her betrayal, Gus decided to share in it for her sake. He laughed.

"Go on, go on, I can hardly stand it," Burke said to her. "Did you ever marry the guy?"

Smiling, she went on, enjoying the occasion now to the fullest.

"So I went and I asked Mrs. Earickson what to do. She said to wait a few days, and if he didn't really mean it, he would get over it by then. But if he did mean it, then he wouldn't get over it, and I would have to make up my mind which meant more to me—keeping my job, or getting married to him.''

The outcome was already known, and Burke turned out front with his familiar, *"People, do you love it?"* and when they answered him as he wanted, he took it as love for himself, and made a cozy face and hugged himself.

But Roberta May could not quit. She said, bright and charming, as though talking on the telephone to an intimate friend, instead of over a microphone to the nation, "So I finally said, all right if that's the way you feel about it, I'll give up my job, but I hope we have a lot of babies right away, I said, just to give me something to do, I said.''

There was a shock of silence, and then the crowd took a meaning that she had not meant. They shrilled hysterically.

Burke began to sweat. The thing could get out of hand. They could get put off the air. He yelled above the storm.

"Wonderful, wonderful! A *wonderful* little girl, here, all right, and a fine boy. We wish them *all* happiness and success, and in a minute we will prove just how much we mean it, but in the meantime an important message from our sponsor.''

No chains held the Earicksons there. No guards restrained them. There was free passage off the stage, and out to the alley, across the parking lot, to a bus line. But they stood there under the light waiting to be told what to do next.

After the sponsor, the orchestra played again, then faded down, while Gail Burke Himself returned to the microphone. The stage lights slowly darkened, and white spotlights came up on the bride and groom and Burke. The auditorium was hushed to a panting stillness, for everyone knew what was coming.

Gus and Roberta May could see dim movement off the far side of the stage. More people were gathering out there in the shadows beyond the silver velvet curtains.

From the audience came an almost visible wave of emotion. More than a thousand eyes glittered with material desires.

"And now," cried Gail Burke Himself, "we want to do our part to make *today's* National Honeymoon the *greatest* one *ever yet*, and I feel humbly grateful that it falls to me to speak for all America's families and families-to-be, in presenting today's wedding presents to

our guests of honor, Mr. and Mrs. Gustavus Adolphus Earickson—
got it that time, eh, boy? So let's move on to the wedding presents
and see what we've got for you!"

The orchestra played a smashing chord.

"*First,* placed at the free disposal of the bride and groom during
their entire stay in Hollywood, a super-deluxe convertible sports
coupe with all expenses maintained by the proprietors, the Wil-Bev
Motoria!"

A young man with hair like gold leaf over scrolled carving,
dressed in a page's scarlet uniform, stepped out from the far wings
holding a large colored picture of such a convertible coupe. A spotlight hit him like lightning. There was applause; he stepped back
and disappeared.

Each item, heralded by a blast from the stage band, was exhibited
in fact or effigy by the uniformed pages.

"*Next, for the groom,*" chanted Burke, "two complete changes
of sports clothes, presented by The Male, Incorporated, of Hollywood!" The garments made their appearance while the audience
avidly imagined Gus as he would look in his new clothes.

"*And now for our lovely bride. Wait* till we put her eyes out
with this, a lovely, lovely half-carat solitaire diamond ring from
Lydia Lennox, Limited, Fine Jewels, of New York, Miami, and
Hollywood!" And as the gray velvet box was thrust into Roberta
May's hands, sighs rose like a prayer.

They rose higher and higher, sometimes with applause, as the
catalogue continued: fresh corsages, for day and evening, every day,
for the bride; a honeymoon patio suite for two weeks at the Beverly–
Westwood Hotel; a conducted tour of the motion-picture studios,
with autographs guaranteed and lunch with favorite stars; a chest of
flat silver specially monogrammed; one dozen silk sheets with lace
trimming and embroidered initials; and more; and more.

"And now, Roberta May, you must have something in your heart
you want more than anything else. What is it? Tell us on National
Honeymoon, and if we can possibly give it to you, we will! Can you
tell us?"

She licked her lips. She looked at Gus where he stood beside her
with his head bent, his legs spread, as though to be strong under
assault. They were beaten and stunned with munificence. He shook
his head to tell her that he was out of this.

"Why, yes," she said. "Someday, when we can afford it, I want a special kind of room in my house—we have the *room*, I mean, but there's a certain way I want it done. There's this extra room, and I want two sides of it paneled in knotty pine, and the other two sides of it papered in something bright, and the ceiling the same way. I want a fireplace in it, and a solid-color carpet all over, and drapes just like the wallpaper so the wall where the windows are would all look alike."

"What, no furniture?" asked Burke.

"Why, yes, we would get some red-leather furniture, because my husband would like that."

"What would you do in this room, Roberta May, tell us that?"

"Oh, why, *everything*, I—"

The audience laughed. She flushed.

"Oh, I don't mean *everything*, I—"

They laughed again, harder than ever.

She tried to rise with her voice over the crowd.

"I mean play cards, and have buffet suppers, and read, and just talk."

"Oh, I see, just talk, eh? You and Gus have a lot to talk about?"

"We just love to just sit and talk."

She confessed so much in this, so quietly, that for a moment the snickering in the big hall was hushed. When the thought and its meaning came home to everyone, a wave of applause began with some sensible woman's hard, virtuous, single handclap, and spread in a roar through the house. Burke, after a glance at the clock, let it ride for a few seconds, and then he stopped it with his hands.

"Well, Roberta May, I'll tell you what National Honeymoon is going to do for you. We are going to see that that room is decorated and furnished just the way you have described, and just the way you want it done! *Would you like that?*"

She brought her hands together and seemed to pray. Her eyes misted. Her voice quivered.

"Oh, yes, Mr. Burke—"

"Fine, fine," Burke said, with a look at the clock, whose hand was falling toward the end of time. "And now to wind up, we have a lovely, lovely gift for our guests of honor on National Honeymoon today, Mr. and Mrs. Gustavus Earickson of New Mexico—two sets of special trousseau garments exquisitely handmade. Here they are— *think how they'll look in these!*"

He pointed dramatically and the pages came to center stage, one bearing a long transparent black silk nightgown with much lace and embroidery, and a flesh-colored silk negligee; the other bearing a pair of red silk pajamas and a blue silk robe.

The garments swam in midair, fantastically animated by the pages as they walked; an illusion of life filled the nuptial vestments and erotic images began to glow in the heads of Burke's public, while all eyes were fixed on Gus and Roberta May. The young couple bowed their heads in confusion. Applause rolled over them in unnecessary sanction. Until the end of the program, the pages stood in sight, holding the symbolic garments.

"And now, Gus and Roberta May, and ladies and gentlemen of National Honeymoon, here in the Hollywood studios of the United Stations Association, and all across America, I see that our time on today's Honeymoon is just about over. But before we play our Grand Recessional, we have one more little remembrance for our happy couple here today, and here it is—"

Burke pointed to the last page, who, to the sound of tiny, tinkling musical bells playing a nursery tune, wheeled a baby carriage out on the stage and over to the group in the center, while in climax, a storm of cries and laughs and beating of palms arose.

"— a brand-new Storkmaster Baby Coach, *big enough for twins,* if our happy couple *should* have occasion to use it, God bless them! *How about it, people, do you love it?* Goodbye, goodbye, and until tomorrow's National Honeymoon, this is Gail Burke Himself saying —Goodbye-Now."

The music rolled up with organ and orchestra, and the crowd whistled and called and clapped in exhaustion and fulfillment, and at thirty seconds before four o'clock National Honeymoon went off the air.

Late, late that night, Gus and Roberta May lay sleeping in a patch of light from the waning moon which shone through the window of the hotel suite whose daily rate was equal to a week's pay at home.

The moonlight moved slowly and came to rest on their faces. In his sleep, Gus passed his hand across his eyes against the quiet brightness, and the act awakened him. He found that he was gazing at Roberta May, who was sleeping with her cheek on her hand, with tears going slowly down her face in the moonlight.

He wanted to touch her tears with his fingers, softly so as not to awaken her. But he was clumsier than he knew, and his touch awoke her. She threw her arm upon him and fell to his shoulder sobbing like a child.

He asked her what was the matter.

She pressed her face against his breast and shook her head. He knew that in a few minutes she would try to tell him; and she did.

She said she was sorry with all her heart for what they had given away that day.

It was theirs alone, and smilingly they had let it be given to everybody else—their very own love story.

"I want it to belong just to ourselves," she sobbed. "And it's too late now."

"Hush. Hush."

"It was all my fault. I started it all. And I told out loud all the things that meant so much to us, just us. Talk, talk, talk. I just kept on talking. And some of the things I said!" She choked with grief and pity for what was gone. "The way everyone laughed at them!"

"Ro, honey."

"Why did you let me?"

He would have thought that this would make him angry; but not at all; a wave of choking tenderness went through him.

"Never mind," he said softly, "never mind, never mind, never mind, never mind."

"If we could only get it back!" she sobbed.

He thought for a moment.

"Do you want me to?" he asked against her cheek.

"You can't."

"Yes I can. Most of it. The important part of it."

She stopped crying and rose to look at him in the moonlight. "You're crazy," she said.

"Will you leave it all to me? No matter what?"

She leaned down to him again and rested her head on his heart in aching humility.

"Forever and ever, in everything," she said.

She fell asleep again before he did. He now knew that things could happen to two people together which nobody else would understand, and that yesterday's experience was one of them; for if to marry each other did not mean to marry the very world, in its terms as well as theirs, what did it mean? Now everything took its proper place in the good knowledge that among the great things that had come to them were the power and the desire to forgive each other and be forgiven, for all of their lives.

At four o'clock the next afternoon Gus and Roberta May were waiting at the stage door. Presently the musicians, the attendants, and the star of National Honeymoon came through the stage door after their day's work, talking it over.

"How *was* I?" asked Burke.

"But wonderful, Gail," one of the attendants assured him wearily.

"I don't know—yesterday was *tougher*, but it was somehow better. Say, look who's here!"

Gus came forward.

"Mr. Burke," he said, while Roberta May, proud of what he had made her understand, nodded yes, yes, yes, "we've come to return all the things. Here." Gus put the jeweler's velvet box into Burke's hand.

"Return—the boy is *but mad!*" cried Burke, consulting his fellow showmen with a comic look. They stared back at him impassively. Something in them began to rejoice.

"Yes," said Gus, "we left all the other presents at the hotel when we checked out, and the car is back at the garage, and you needn't send the things to us at home. If you do, we'll send them back."

"You can't do this to me!" snapped Burke. "In all my *years* on National Honeymoon a thing like this has *never* happened to me. Think if it ever got *around*. You people here"—he swept the other members of the show with a fierce look—"you people just keep this quiet, hear?"

But someone laughed, "Ha!" and one or two in the little throng whistled approval at Gus.

"And the room," insisted Burke, "and the furniture. You said you *wanted* all that!" He was almost pleading.

"Well, if we do," said Gus, "I'll buy what we need, and if we can't afford it yet, we'll wait till we can."

Burke stared at everyone, his heavy, tanned face sagging tragically.

Roberta May felt a pang for him. "Never mind, Mr. Burke,"

she said with sweetness. At that final punishment, everyone else laughed out loud.

"All right, Ro," said Gus. "Come on." He took her away.

They kept in touch with everybody back home by postcard every few days, and had a glorious time on their own for the rest of their honeymoon.

1967

The Peach Stone

As they all knew, the drive would take them about four hours, all the way to Weed, where *she* came from. They knew the way from travelling it so often, first in the old car, and now in the new one; new to them, that is, for they'd bought it secondhand, last year, when they were down in Roswell to celebrate their tenth wedding anniversary. They still thought of themselves as a young couple, and *he* certainly did crazy things now and then, and always laughed her out of it when she was cross at the money going where it did, instead of where it ought to go. But there was so much droll orneriness in him when he did things like that that she couldn't stay mad, hadn't the heart, and the harder up they got, the more she loved him, and the little ranch he'd taken her to in the rolling plains just below the mountains.

This was a day in spring, rather hot, and the mountain was that melting blue that reminded you of something you could touch, like a china bowl. Over the sandy brown of the earth there was coming a green shadow. The air struck cool and deep in their breasts. *He* came from Texas, as a boy, and had lived here in New Mexico ever since. The word "home" always gave *her* a picture of unpainted, mouse-brown wooden houses in a little cluster by the rocky edge of the last mountain step—the town of Weed, where Jodey Powers met and married her ten years ago.

They were heading back that way today.

Jodey was driving, squinting at the light. It never seemed so

bright as now, before noon, as they went up the valley. He had a
rangy look at the wheel of the light blue Chevy—a bony man, but
still fuzzed over with some look of a cub about him, perhaps the
way he moved his limbs, a slight appealing clumsiness, that drew on
thoughtless strength. On a rough road, he flopped and swayed at the
wheel as if he were on a bony horse that galloped a little sidewise.
His skin was red-brown from the sun. He had pale blue eyes, edged
with dark lashes. *She* used to say he "turned them on" her, as if they
were lights. He was wearing his suit, brown-striped, and a fresh
blue shirt, too big at the neck. But he looked well dressed. But he
would have looked that way naked, too, for he communicated his
physical essence through any covering. It was what spoke out from
him to anyone who encountered him. Until Cleotha married him,
it had given him a time, all right, he used to reflect.

Next to him in the front seat of the sedan was Buddy, their nine-
year-old boy, who turned his head to stare at them both, his father
and mother.

She was in back.

On the seat beside her was a wooden box, sandpapered, but not
painted. Over it lay a baby's coverlet of pale yellow flannel with
cross-stitched flowers down the middle in a band of bright colors.
The mother didn't touch the box except when the car lurched or the
tires danced over corrugated places in the gravel highway. Then she
steadied it, and kept it from creeping on the seat cushions. In the
box was coffined the body of their dead child, a two-year-old girl.
They were on their way to Weed to bury it there.

In the other corner of the back seat sat Miss Thatcher, the
teacher. They rode in silence, and Miss Thatcher breathed deeply
of the spring day, as they all did, and she kept summoning to her
aid the fruits of her learning. She felt this was a time to be intelligent, and not to give way to feelings.

The child was burned to death yesterday, playing behind the
adobe chickenhouse at the edge of the arroyo out back, where the
fence always caught the tumbleweeds. Yesterday, in a twist of wind,
a few sparks from the kitchen chimney fell in the dry tumbleweeds
and set them ablaze. Jodey had always meant to clear the weeds out:
never seemed to get to it: told Cleotha he'd get to it next Saturday
morning, before going down to Roswell: but Saturdays went by,
and the wind and the sand drove the weeds into a barrier at the
fence, and they would look at it every day without noticing, so

habitual had the sight become. And so for many a spring morning the little girl had played out there, behind the gray stucco house, whose adobe bricks showed through in one or two places.

The car had something loose; they believed it was the left rear fender: it chattered and wrangled over the gravel road.

Last night Cleotha stopped her weeping.

Today something happened; it came over her as they started out of the ranch lane, which curved up toward the highway. She looked as if she were trying to see something beyond the edge of Jodey's head and past the windshield.

Of course, she had sight in her eyes; she could not refuse to look at the world. As the car drove up the valley that morning, she saw in two ways—one, as she remembered the familiar sights of this region where she lived; the other, as if for the first time she were really seeing, and not simply looking. Her heart began to beat faster as they drove. It seemed to knock at her breast as if to come forth and hurry ahead of her along the sunlighted lanes of the life after today. She remembered thinking that her head might be a little giddy, what with the sorrow in her eyes so bright and slowly shining. But it didn't matter what did it. Ready never to look at anyone or anything again, she kept still; and through the window, which had a meandering crack in it like a river on a map, all that she looked upon seemed dear to her . . .

Jodey could only drive. He watched the road as if he expected it to rise up and smite them all over into the canyon, where the trees twinkled and flashed with bright drops of light on their new varnished leaves. Jodey watched the road and said to himself that if it thought it could turn him over or make him scrape the rocks along the near side of the hill they were going around, if it thought for one minute that he was not master of this car, this road, this journey, why, it was just crazy. The wheels spraying the gravel across the surface of the road travelled on outward from his legs; his muscles were tight and felt tired as if he were running instead of riding. He tried to *think*, but he could not; that is, nothing came about that he would speak to her of, and he believed that she sat there, leaning forward, waiting for him to say something to her.

But this he could not do, and he speeded up a little, and his jaw made hard knots where he bit on his own rage; and he saw a lump of something coming in the road, and it aroused a positive passion in him. He aimed directly for it, and charged it fast, and hit it. The car shuddered and skidded, jolting them. Miss Thatcher took a sharp breath inward, and put out her hand to touch someone, but did not reach anyone. Jodey looked for a second into the rear-view mirror above him, expecting something; but his wife was looking out of the window beside her, and if he could believe his eyes, she was smiling, holding her mouth with her fingers pinched up in a little claw.

The blood came up from under his shirt, he turned dark, and a sting came across his eyes.

He couldn't explain why he had done a thing like that to her, as if it were she he was enraged with, instead of himself.

He wanted to stop the car and go around to the back door on the other side, and open it, and take her hands, bringing her out to stand before him in the road, and hang his arms around her until she would be locked upon him. This made a picture that he indulged like a dream, while the car ran on, and he made no change, but drove as before . . .

The little boy, Buddy, regarded their faces, again, and again, as if to see in their eyes what had happened to them.

He felt the separateness of the three.

He was frightened by their appearance of indifference to each other. His father had a hot and drowsy look, as if he had just come out of bed. There was something in his father's face which made it impossible for Buddy to say anything. He turned around and looked at his mother, but she was gazing out the window, and did not see him; and until she should see him, he had no way of speaking to her, if not with his words, then with his eyes, but if she should happen to look at him, why, he would wait to see what she looked *like*, and if she *did*, why, then he would smile at her, because he loved her, but he would have to know first if she was still his mother, and if everything was all right, and things weren't blown to smithereens—bla-a-ash! wh-o-o-m!—the way the dynamite did when the highway came past their ranch house, and the men worked out there for months, and whole hillsides came down at a time. All summer long, that was, always something to see. The world, the family, he, between his father and mother, had been safe.

He silently begged her to face toward him. There was no security until she should do so.

"Mumma?"

But he said it to himself, and she did not hear him this time, and it seemed intelligent to him to turn around, make a game of it (the way things often were worked out), and face the front, watch the road, delay as long as he possibly could bear to, and *then* turn around again, and *this* time, why, she would probably be looking at him all the time, and it would *be*: it simply would *be*.

So he obediently watched the road, the white gravel ribbon passing under their wheels as steadily as time.

He was a sturdy little boy, and there was a silver nap of child's dust on his face, over his plum-red cheeks. He smelled rather like a raw potato that has just been pared. The sun crowned him with a ring of light on his dark hair . . .

What Cleotha was afraid to do was break the spell by saying anything or looking at any of them. This was *vision*, it was all she could think; never had anything looked so in all her life; everything made her heart lift, when she had believed this morning, after the night, that it would never lift again. There wasn't anything to compare her grief to. She couldn't think of anything to answer the death of her tiny child with. In her first hours of hardly believing what had happened, she had felt her own flesh and tried to imagine how it would have been if she could have borne the fire instead of the child. But all she got out of that was a longing avowal to herself of how gladly she would have borne it. Jodey had lain beside her, and she clung to his hand until she heard how he breathed off to sleep. Then she had let him go, and had wept at what seemed faithless in him. She had wanted his mind beside her then. It seemed to her that the last degree of her grief was the compassion she had had to bestow upon him while he slept.

But she had found this resource within her, and from that time on, her weeping had stopped.

It was like a wedding of pride and duty within her. There was nothing she could not find within herself, if she had to, now, she believed.

And so this morning, getting on toward noon, as they rode up the valley, climbing all the way, until they would find the road to turn off on, which would take them higher and higher before they dropped down toward Weed on the other side, she welcomed the sights of that dusty trip. Even if she had spoken her vision aloud, it would not have made sense to the others.

Look at that orchard of peach trees, she thought. I never saw such color as this year; the trees are like lamps, with the light coming from within. It must be the sunlight shining from the other side, and, of course, the petals are very thin, like the loveliest silk; so any light that shines upon them will pierce right through them and glow on this side. But they are so bright! When I was a girl at home, up to Weed, I remember we had an orchard of peach trees, but the blossoms were always a deeper pink than down here in the valley.

My! I used to catch them up by the handful, and I believed when I was a girl that if I crushed them and tied them in a handkerchief and carried the handkerchief in my bosom, I would come to smell like peach blossoms and have the same high pink in my face, and the girls I knew said that if I took a peach *stone* and held it *long enough* in my hand, it would *sprout*; and I dreamed of this one time, though, of course, I knew it was nonsense; but that was how children thought and talked in those days—we all used to pretend that *nothing* was impossible, if you simply did it hard enough and long enough.

But nobody wanted to hold a peach stone in their hand until it *sprouted*, to find out, and we used to laugh about it, but I think we believed it. I think I believed it.

It seemed to me, in between my *sensible* thoughts, a thing that any woman could probably do. It seemed to me like a parable in the Bible. I could preach you a sermon about it this day.

I believe I see a tree down there in that next orchard which is dead; it has old black sprigs, and it looks twisted by rheumatism. There is one little shoot of leaves up on the top branch, and that is all. No, it is not dead, it is aged, it can no longer put forth blossoms in a swarm like pink butterflies; but there is that one little swarm of green leaves—it is just about the prettiest thing I've seen all day, and I thank God for it, for if there's anything I love, it is to see something growing . . .

Miss Thatcher had on her cloth gloves now, which she had taken from her blue cloth bag a little while back. The little winds that tracked through the moving car sought her out and chilled her nose, and the tips of her ears, and her long fingers, about which she had several times gone to visit various doctors. They had always told her not to worry if her fingers seemed cold, and her hands moist. It was just a nervous condition, nothing to take very seriously; a good hand lotion might help the sensation, and in any case, some kind of digital exercise was a good thing—did she perhaps play the piano. It always seemed to her that doctors never *paid any attention* to her.

Her first name was Arleen, and she always considered this a very pretty name, prettier than Cleotha; and she believed that there was such a thing as an *Arleen look,* and if you wanted to know what it was, simply look at her. She had a long face, and pale hair; her skin was white, and her eyes were light blue. She was wonderfully clean, and used no cosmetics. She was a girl from "around here," but she had gone away to college, to study for her career, and what she had known as a child was displaced by what she had heard in classrooms. And she had to admit it: people *here* and *away* were not much alike. The men were different. She couldn't imagine marrying a rancher and "sacrificing" everything she had learned in college.

This poor little thing in the other corner of the car, for instance: she seemed dazed by what had happened to her—all she could do evidently was sit and stare out the window. And that man in front, simply driving, without a word. What did they have? What was their life like? They hardly had good clothes to drive to Roswell in, when they had to go to the doctor, or on some social errand.

But I must not think uncharitably, she reflected, and sat in an attitude of sustained sympathy, with her face composed in Arleenish interest and tact. The assumption of a proper aspect of grief and feeling produced the most curious effect within her, and by her attitude of concern she was suddenly reminded of the thing that always made her feel like weeping, though of course she never did, but when she stopped and *thought*—

Like that painting at college, in the long hallway leading from the Physical Education lecture hall to the stairway down to the girls' gym: an enormous picture depicting the Agony of the Christian Martyrs, in ancient Rome. There were some days when she simply couldn't look at it; and there were others when she would pause and see those maidens with their tearful faces raised in calm prowess, and in them, she would find herself—they were all Arleens; and after she would leave the picture she would proceed in her imagination to the arena, and there she would know with exquisite sorrow and pain the ordeals of two thousand years ago, instead of those of her own lifetime. She thought of the picture now, and traded its remote sorrows for those of today until she had sincerely forgotten the mother and the father and the little brother of the dead child with whom she was riding up the spring-turning valley, where noon was warming the dust that arose from the graveled highway. It was white dust, and it settled over them in an enriching film, ever so finely . . .

Jodey Powers had a fantastic scheme that he used to think about for taking and baling tumbleweed and make a salable fuel out of it. First, you'd compress it—probably down at the cotton compress in Roswell—where a loose bale was wheeled in under the great power drop, and when the Negro at the handle gave her a yank, down came the weight, and packed the bale into a little thing, and then they let the steam exhaust go, and the press sighed once or twice, and just seemed to *lie* there, while the men ran wires through the gratings of the press and tied them tight. Then up came the weight, and out came the bale.

If he did that to enough bales of tumbleweed, he believed he'd get rich. Burn? It burned like a house afire. It had oil in it, somehow, and the thing to do was to get it in shape for use as a fuel. Imagine all the tumbleweed that blew around the state of New Mexico in the fall, and sometimes all winter. In the winter, the weeds were black and brittle. They cracked when they blew against fence posts, and if one lodged there, then another one caught at its thorny lace; and next time it blew, and the sand came trailing, and the tumbleweeds rolled, they'd pile up at the same fence and build out, locked together against the wires. The wind drew through them, and the sand dropped around them. Soon there was a solid-looking but airy bank of tumbleweeds built right to the top of the fence, in a long windward slope; and the next time the wind blew, and the weeds came, they would roll up the little hill of brittle twigs and leap off the other side of the fence, for all the world like horses taking a jump, and go galloping ahead of the wind across the next pasture on the plains, a black and witchy procession.

If there was an arroyo, they gathered there. They backed up in the miniature canyons of dirt-walled watercourses, which were dry except when it rained hard up in the hills. Out behind the house, the arroyo had filled up with tumbleweeds; and in November, when it blew so hard and so cold, but without bringing any snow, some of the tumbleweeds had climbed out and scattered, and a few had tangled at the back fence, looking like rusted barbed wire. Then there came a few more; all winter the bank grew. Many times he'd planned to get out back there and clear them away, just e-e-ease them off away from the fence posts, so's not to catch the wood up, and then set a match to the whole thing, and in five minutes, have it all cleared off. If he did like one thing, it was a neat place.

How Cleotha laughed at him sometimes when he said that, because she knew that as likely as not he would forget to clear the weeds away. And if he'd said it once he'd said it a thousand times, that he was going to gather up that pile of scrap iron from the front yard, and haul it to Roswell, and sell it—old car parts, and the fenders off a truck that had turned over up on the highway, which he'd salvaged with the aid of the driver.

But the rusting iron was still there, and he had actually come to have a feeling of fondness for it. If someone were to appear one night and silently make off with it, he'd be aroused the next day, and demand to know who had robbed him: for it was dear junk, just through lying around and belonging to him. What was his was part of him, even that heap of fenders that rubbed off on your clothes with a rusty powder, like caterpillar fur.

But even by thinking hard about all such matters, treading upon the fringe of what had happened yesterday, he was unable to make it all seem long ago, and a matter of custom and even of indifference. There was no getting away from it—if anybody was to blame for the terrible moments of yesterday afternoon, when the wind scattered a few sparks from the chimney of the kitchen stove, why, he was.

Jodey Powers never claimed to himself or anybody else that he was any *better* man than another. But everything he knew and hoped for, every reassurance his body had had from other people, and the children he had begotten, had made him know that he was *as good* a man as any.

And of this knowledge he was now bereft.

If he had been alone in his barrenness, he could have solaced himself with heroic stupidities. He could have produced out of himself abominations, with the amplitude of biblical despair. But he wasn't alone; there they sat, there was Buddy beside him, and Clee in back, even the teacher, Arleen—even to her he owed some return of courage.

All he could do was drive the damned car, and keep *thinking* about it.

He wished he could think of something to say, or else that Clee would.

But they continued in silence, and he believed that it was one of his making . . .

The reverie of Arleen Thatcher made her almost ill, from the sad, sweet experiences she had entered into with those people so long ago. How wonderful it was to have such a rich life, just looking up things! —And the most wonderful thing of all was that even if they were beautiful, and wore semi-transparent garments that fell to the ground in graceful folds, the maidens were all pure. It made her eyes swim to think how innocent they went to their death. Could anything be more beautiful, and reassuring, than this? Far, far better. Far better those hungry lions, than the touch of lustful men. Her breath left her for a moment, and she closed her eyes, and what threatened her with real feeling—the presence of the Powers family in the faded blue sedan climbing through the valley sunlight toward the turnoff that led to the mountain road—was gone. Life's breath on her cheek was not so close. Oh, others had suffered. She could suffer.

"All that pass by clap their hands at thee: they hiss and wag their heads at the daughter of Jerusalem—"

This image made her wince, as if she herself had been hissed and wagged at. Everything she knew made it possible for her to see herself as a proud and threatened virgin of Bible times, which were more real to her than many of the years she had lived through. Yet must not Jerusalem have sat in country like this with its sandy hills, the frosty stars that were so bright at night, the simple Mexicans riding their burros as if to the Holy Gates? We often do not see our very selves, she would reflect, gazing ardently at the unreal creature which the name Arleen brought to life in her mind.

On her cheeks there had appeared two islands of color, as if she had a fever. What she strove to save by her anguished retreats into the memories of the last days of the Roman Empire was surely crumbling away from her. She said to herself that she must not give way to it, and that she was just wrought up; the fact that she really *didn't* feel anything—in fact, it was a pity that she *couldn't* take that little Mrs. Powers in her arms, and comfort her, just *let* her go ahead and cry, and see if it wouldn't probably help some. But Miss Thatcher was aware that she felt nothing that related to the Powers family and their trouble.

Anxiously she searched her heart again, and wooed back the

sacrifice of the tribe of heavenly Arleens marching so certainly toward the lions. But they did not answer her call to mind, and she folded her cloth-gloved hands and pressed them together, and begged of herself that she might think of some way to comfort Mrs. Powers; for if she could do that, it might fill her own empty heart until it became a cup that would run over . . .

Cleotha knew Buddy wanted her to see him; but though her heart turned toward him, as it always must, no matter what he asked of her, she was this time afraid to do it because if she ever lost the serenity of her sight now she might never recover it this day; and the heaviest trouble was still before her.

So she contented herself with Buddy's look as it reached her from the side of her eye. She glimpsed his head and neck, like a young cat's, the wide bones behind the ears, and the smooth but visible cords of his nape, a sight of him that always made her want to laugh because it was so pathetic. When she caressed him she often fondled those strenuous hollows behind his ears. Heaven only knew, she would think, what went on within the shell of that topknot! She would pray between her words and feelings that those unseen thoughts in the boy's head were ones that would never trouble him. She was often amazed at things in him which she recognized as being like herself; and at those of Buddy's qualities which came from some alien source, she suffered pangs of doubt and fear. He was so young to be a stranger to her!

The car went around the curve that hugged the rocky fall of a hill; and on the other side of it, a green quilt of alfalfa lay sparkling darkly in the light. Beyond that, to the right of the road, the land levelled out, and on a sort of platform of swept earth stood a two-room hut of adobe. It had a few stones cemented against the near corner, to give it strength. Clee had seen it a hundred times—the place where that old man Melendez lived, and where his wife had died a few years ago. He was said to be simple-minded and claimed he was a hundred years old. In the past, riding by here, she had more or less delicately made a point of looking the other way. It often distressed her to think of such a helpless old man, too feeble to do anything but crawl out when the sun was bright and the wall was warm, and sit there, with his milky gaze resting on the hills he had known since he was born, and had never left. Somebody came to feed him once a day, and see if he was clean enough to keep his health. As long as she could remember, there'd been some kind of dog at the house. The old man had sons and grandsons and great-grandsons—you might say a whole orchard of them, sprung from this one tree that was dying, but that still held a handful of green days in its ancient veins.

Before the car had quite gone by, she had seen him. The sun was bright, and the wall must have been warm, warm enough to give his shoulders and back a reflection of the heat which was all he could feel. He sat there on his weathered board bench, his hands on his branch of apple tree that was smooth and shiny from use as a cane. His house door was open, and a deep tunnel of shade lay within the sagged box of the opening. Cleotha leaned forward to see him, as if to look at him were one of her duties today. She saw his jaw moving up and down, not chewing, but just opening and closing. In the wind and flash of the car going by, she could not hear him; but from his closed eyes, and his moving mouth, and the way his head was raised, she wouldn't have been surprised if she had heard him singing. He was singing some thread of song, and it made her smile to imagine what kind of noise it made, a wisp of voice.

She was perplexed by a feeling of joyful fullness in her breast, at the sight of the very same old witless sire from whom in the past she had turned away her eyes out of delicacy and disgust.

The last thing she saw as they went by was his dog, who came around the corner of the house with a caracole. He was a mongrel puppy, partly hound—a comedian by nature. He came prancing outrageously up to the old man's knees, and invited his response, which he did not get. But as if his master were as great a wag as he, he hurled himself backward, pretending to throw himself recklessly into pieces. Everything on him flopped and was flung by his idiotic energy. It was easy to imagine, watching the puppy-fool, that the sunlight had entered him as it had entered the old man. Cleotha was reached by the hilarity of the hound, and when he tripped over himself and plowed the ground with his flapping jowls, she wanted to laugh out loud.

But they were past the place, and she winked back the merriment in her eyes, and she knew that it was something she could never have told the others about. What it stood for, in her, they would come to know in other ways, as she loved them . . .

Jodey was glad of one thing. He had telephoned from Hondo last night, and everything was to be ready at Weed. They would drive right up the hill to the family burial ground. They wouldn't have to wait for anything. He was glad, too, that the wind wasn't blowing. It always made his heart sink when the wind rose on the plains and began to change the sky with the color of dust.

Yesterday: it was all he could see, however hard he was *thinking* about everything else.

He'd been on his horse, coming back down the pasture that rose up behind the house across the arroyo, nothing particular in mind— except to make a joke with himself about how far along the peaches would get before the frost killed them all, *snap*, in a single night, like that—when he saw the column of smoke rising from the tumble-weeds by the fence. Now who could've lighted them, he reflected, following the black smoke up on its billows into the sky. There was just enough wind idling across the long front of the hill to bend the smoke and trail it away at an angle, toward the blue.

The hillside, the fire, the wind, the column of smoke.

Oh, my God! And the next minute he was tearing down the hill as fast as his horse could take him, and the fire—he could see the flames now—the fire was like a bank of yellow rags blowing violently and torn in the air, rag after rag tearing up from the ground. Cleotha was there, and in a moment, so was he, but they were too late. The baby was unconscious. They took her up and hurried to the house, the back way where the screen door was standing open with its spring trailing on the ground. When they got inside where it seemed so dark and cool, they held the child between them, fearing to lay her down. They called for Buddy, but he was still at school up the road, and would not be home until the orange school bus stopped by their mailbox out front at the highway after four o'clock. The fire poured in cracking tumult through the weeds. In ten minutes they were only little airy lifts of ash off the ground. Everything was black. There were three fence posts still afire; their wires were hot. The child was dead. They let her down on their large bed.

He could remember every word Clee had said to him. They were not many, and they shamed him, in his heart, because he couldn't say a thing. He comforted her, and held her while she wept. But if he had spoken then, or now, riding in the car, all he could have talked about was the image of the blowing rags of yellow fire, and blue, blue, plaster blue sky above and beyond the mountains. But he believed that she knew why he seemed so short with her. He hoped earnestly that she knew. He might just be wrong. She might be blaming him, and keeping so still because it was more proper, now, to *be* still than full of reproaches.

But of the future he was entirely uncertain; and he drove, and came to the turnoff, and they started winding in back among the sandhills that lifted them toward the rocky slopes of the mountains. Up and up they went; the air was so clear and thin that they felt transported, and across the valleys that dropped between the grand shoulders of the pine-haired slopes, the air looked as if it were blue breath from the trees . . .

Cleotha was blinded by a dazzling light in the distance, ahead of them, on the road.

It was a ball of diamond-brilliant light.

It danced, and shook, and quivered above the road far, far ahead. It seemed to be travelling between the pine trees on either side of the road, and somewhat above the road, and it was like nothing she had ever seen before. It was the most magic and exquisite thing she had ever seen, and wildly, even hopefully as a child is hopeful when there is a chance and a need for something miraculous to happen, she tried to explain it to herself. It could be a star in the daytime, shaking and quivering and travelling ahead of them, as if to lead them. It was their guide. It was shaped like a small cloud, but it was made of shine, and dazzle, and quiver. She held her breath for fear it should vanish, but it did not, and she wondered if the others in the car were smitten with the glory of it as she was.

It was brighter than the sun, whiter; it challenged the daytime, and obscured everything near it by its blaze of flashing and dancing light.

It was almost as if she had approached perfect innocence through her misery, and were enabled to receive portents that might not be visible to anyone else. She closed her eyes for a moment.

But the road curved, and everything travelling on it took the curve too, and the trembling pool of diamond-light ahead lost its liquid splendor, and turned into the tin signs on the back of a huge oil truck which was toiling over the mountain, trailing its links of chain behind.

When Clee looked again, the star above the road was gone. The road and the angle of the sun to the mountaintop and the two cars climbing upward had lost their harmony to produce the miracle. She saw the red oil truck, and simply saw it, and said to herself that the sun might have reflected off the big tin signs on the back of it. But she didn't believe it, for she was not thinking, but rather dreaming; fearful of awakening . . .

The high climb up this drive always made Miss Thatcher's ears pop, and she had discovered once that to swallow often prevented the disagreeable sensation. So she swallowed. Nothing happened to her ears. But she continued to swallow, and feel her ears with her cloth-covered fingers, but what really troubled her now would not be downed, and it came into her mouth as a taste; she felt giddy— that was the altitude, of course—when they got down the other side, she would be all right.

What it was was perfectly clear to her, for that was part of having an education and a trained mind—the processes of thought often went right on once you started them going.

Below the facts of this small family, in the worst trouble it had ever known, lay the fact of envy in Arleen's breast.

It made her head swim to realize this. But she envied them their entanglement with one another, and the dues they paid each other in the humility of the duty they were performing on this ride, to the family burial ground at Weed. Here she sat riding with them, to come along and be of help to them, and she was no help. She was unable to swallow the lump of desire that rose in her throat, for life's uses, even such bitter ones as that of the Powers family today. It had been filling her gradually, all the way over on the trip, this feeling of jealousy and degradation.

Now it choked her and she knew she had tried too hard to put from her the thing that threatened her, which was the touch of life through anybody else. She said to herself that she must keep control of herself.

But Buddy turned around again, just then, slowly, as if he were a young male cat who just happened to be turning around to see what he could see, and he looked at his mother with his large eyes, so like his father's: pale petal-blue, with drops of light like the centers of cats' eyes, and dark lashes. He had a solemn look, when he saw his mother's face, and he prayed her silently to acknowledge him. If she didn't, why, he was still alone. He would never again feel safe about running off to the highway to watch the scrapers work, or the huge Diesel oil tankers go by, or the cars with strange license plates—of which he had already counted thirty-two different kinds, his collection, as he called it. So if she didn't see him, why, what might he find when he came back home at times like those, when he went off for a little while just to play?

They were climbing down the other side of the ridge now. In a few minutes they would be riding into Weed. The sights as they approached were like images of awakening to Cleotha. Her heart began to hurt when she saw them. She recognized the tall iron smokestack of the sawmill. It showed above the trees down on the slope ahead of them. There was a stone house which had been abandoned even when she was a girl at home here, and its windows and doors standing open always seemed to her to depict a face with an expression of dismay. The car dropped farther down—they were making that last long curve of the road to the left—and now the town stood visible, with the sunlight resting on so many of the un-painted houses and turning their weathered gray to a dark silver. Surely they must be ready for them, these houses: all had been talked over by now. They could all mention that they knew Cleotha as a little girl.

She lifted her head.

There were claims upon her.

Buddy was looking at her soberly, trying to predict to himself how she would *be*. He was ready to echo with his own small face whatever her face would show him.

Miss Thatcher was watching the two of them. Her heart was racing in her breast.

The car slowed up. Now Cleotha could not look out the windows at the wandering earthen street, and the places alongside it. They would have to drive right through town, to the gently rising hill on the other side.

"Mumma?" asked the boy softly.

Cleotha winked both her eyes at him, and smiled, and leaned toward him a trifle.

And then he blushed, his eyes swam with happiness, and he smiled back at her, and his face poured forth such radiance that Miss Thatcher took one look at him, and with a choke, burst into tears.

She wept into her hands, her gloves were moistened, her square shoulders rose to her ears, and she was overwhelmed by what the mother had been able to do for the boy. She shook her head and made long gasping sobs. Her sense of betrayal was not lessened by the awareness that she was weeping for herself.

Cleotha leaned across to her, and took her hand, and murmured to her. She comforted her, gently.

"Hush, honey, you'll be all right. Don't you cry, now. Don't you think about us. We're almost there, and it'll soon be over. God knows you were mighty sweet to come along and be with us. Hush, now, Arleen, you'll have Buddy crying too."

But the boy was simply watching the teacher, in whom the person he knew so well every day in school had broken up, leaving an unfamiliar likeness. It was like seeing a reflection in a pond, and then throwing a stone in. The reflection disappeared in ripples of something else.

Arleen could not stop.

The sound of her 'ooping made Jodey furious. He looked into the rear-view mirror and saw his wife patting her and comforting her. Cleotha looked so white and strained that he was frightened, and he said out, without turning around: "Arleen, you cut that out, you shut up, now. I won't have you wearin' down Clee, God damn it, you quit it!"

But this rage, which arose from a sense of justice, made Arleen feel guiltier than ever; and she laid her head against the car window, and her sobs drummed her brow bitterly on the glass.

"Hush," whispered Cleotha, but she could do no more, for they were arriving at the hillside, and the car was coming to a stop. They must awaken from his journey, and come out on to the ground, and begin to toil their way up the yellow hill, where the people were waiting. Over the ground grew yellow grass that was turning to green. It was like velvet, showing dark or light, according to the breeze and the golden afternoon sunlight. It was a generous hill, curving easily and gradually as it rose. Beyond it was only the sky, for the mountains faced it from behind the road. It was called Schoolhouse Hill, and at one time, the whole thing had belonged to Cleotha's father; and even before there was any schoolhouse crowning its noble swell of earth, the departed members of his family had been buried halfway up the gentle climb.

Jodey helped her out of the car, and he tried to talk to her with his holding fingers. He felt her trembling, and she shook her head at him. Then she began to walk up there, slowly. He leaned into the car and took the covered box in his arms, and followed her. Miss Thatcher was out of the car on her side, hiding from them, her back turned, while she used her handkerchief and positively clenched herself back into control of her thoughts and sobs. When she saw that they weren't waiting for her, she hurried, and in humility, reached for Buddy's hand to hold it for him as they walked. He let her have it, and he marched, watching his father, whose hair was blowing in the wind and sunshine. From behind, Jodey looked like just a kid . . .

And now for Cleotha her visions on the journey appeared to have some value, and for a little while longer, when she needed it most, the sense of being in blind communion with life was granted her, at the little graveside where all those kind friends were gathered on the slow slope up of the hill on the summit of which was the schoolhouse of her girlhood.

It was afternoon, and they were all kneeling toward the upward rise, and Judge Crittenden was reading the prayer book.

Everything left them but a sense of their worship, in the present.

And a boy, a late scholar, is coming down the hill from the school, the sunlight edging him; and his wonder at what the people kneeling there are doing is, to Cleotha, the most memorable thing she is to look upon today; for she has resumed the life of her infant daughter, whom they are burying, and on whose behalf something rejoices in life anyway, as if to ask the mother whether love itself is not ever-living. And she watches the boy come discreetly down the hill, trying to keep away from them, but large-eyed with a hunger *to know* which claims all acts of life, for him, and for those who will be with him later; and his respectful curiosity about those kneeling mourners, the edge of sunlight along him as he walks away from the sun and down the hill, is of all those things she saw and rejoiced in, the most beautiful; and at that, her breast is full, with the heaviness of a baby at it, and not for grief alone, but for praise.

"I believe, I believe!" her heart cries out in her, as if she were holding the peach stone of her eager girlhood in her woman's hand.

She puts her face into her hands, and weeps, and they all move closer to her. Familiar as it is, the spirit has had a new discovery . . .

Jodey then felt that she had returned to them all; and he stopped seeing, and just remembered, what happened yesterday; and his love for his wife was confirmed as something he would never be able to measure for himself or prove to her in words.

1967

V

NOVEL

No Quarter Given

THE ROSE ARBOR

[Edmund Abbey, young American composer, is obliged to look for work in a Broadway producer's forthcoming 1930s musical. At the same time his symphonic aspirations are recognized.]

I

Before noon the next day, Peter came upstairs and said he had a taxi waiting in the street; and that there was an appointment with Mr. Brinker for twelve o'clock at the Goldman Theatre. While I dressed, Peter walked around my room in excitement, talking.

"Last night I went and looked up Jerry King. I went back to see him after his show. He's in that revue of Roy Goldman's that's playing at the Selwyn Theatre. I caught him in his dressing room, receiving dozens of people. He likes to sit in his skin, with nothing on but a pair of white pants. You watch him take his make-up off, and he gives a performance of how to do it. I managed to get him away about twelve o'clock, and we went to a lunchroom for something to eat. I steered him off the hotels and night clubs, because he loves to be recognized. But we couldn't have talked in a place like that. Well, the upshot is that Roy Goldman is getting an operetta ready, and Brinker wants to shoot the works and make it a distinguished musical success. Jerry says Brinker is fed up with jazz. He says it's a Viennese score, with some adaptations, and there's a good chance that you could get some coaching to do, and so on. —We're going to pick

Jerry up first, and then go up to the Goldman Theatre. It might work out."

I took up my coat, which was one of my few purchases in Austria, and we went down to the taxi. It was a November day that had some strange melting sweetness in the sky, as if spring were waiting nearby. We drove up to an apartment hotel on Fifty-eighth Street near the Plaza. In the small lobby, dimly lighted with amber glass torchères, we were told by the clerk that Mr. King was out. Explanations: we had an appointment. The clerk telephoned up. A voice said, "Who?" when he gave our names. A doubtful pause; then the atmosphere cleared, and we were told to go up.

A Japanese houseboy let us into the apartment. Peter walked through the living room, which was painted pale green and clothed in yellow silk, and called, "Jerry!"

A voice as old as a vulture's answered from the bedroom. It cracked and sighed. There were in it all grades of despair and collapse and humor.

"Owh! Come hyah, my dyah!" it said.

We went in. Lying in a huge circular bed one half of whose rim was sloping with pillows, Jerry King lay blinking and heaped in all the traditional moods and anxieties of a hangover.

"This is Edmund Abbey," said Peter.

"You must forgive me, Abbey. I'm depraved this morning. I can't get up. —Such a night! Oh, boy!"

He hove up to his pillows and threw off his covers. He wore silk pajamas. His face was dark tan, his hair was black, his eyes were pale gray. Their whites were very vivid. With a trembling and bony hand—he was very thin—he reached for a cigarette and dizzily inhaled and coughed. The Jap came in and put up shades. The light gave King a sheet of pain over his brain. He rolled on the pillows and kicked his long legs like a child. In the light, the pillows showed rubbings of dark tan make-up from his face and neck.

"We've got to go and see Brinker, so get up," said Peter.

"To hell with the old bitch," groaned Jerry, dragging himself to kneeling in the bed. He looked around with genuinely tragic eyes for some dimly imagined relief from the throbs of last night and the engagements of today. The Jap came out of the bathroom with a foaming drink in a tall yellow glass. Jerry drank it with elbowed gestures of chic distaste, and rolled his eyes over the rim of the glass. Then he drank a jigger of whiskey which the Jap handed him, and stood with sudden enthusiasm and burlesqued determination. He dropped off his silk sleeping clothes and stretched, rising on his toes. The Jap hung a bath towel eight feet square over him. He wrapped himself in it; with instinct he made a towel a costume; swaying vaguely, he nevertheless created his toga and went to his bath as to the senate. He cried and howled as the water hit him; he swore now like a brakeman, and now like a debutante. At last he emerged, shaven and violet-jowled, sleeked and brown, trembling crazily, but filled with genial impulse and ready for the day whose realities, ten minutes ago, had made him shudder. In his clothes, he looked older. The shoulders and waist and hips and knees of his suit proclaimed an actor in British fashion. He put on a narrow hat, and took a stick and some yellow gloves, and went, with the smiling secret of fame that so many New York faces wore, to the street with Peter and me. He decided to walk down to the theatre. He inhaled great breaths that shocked his gut and made him cough. He walked in long loose strides, sideways, with a shoulder raised, and his stick pressed high under his arm. People knew him now and then, and with more false humility, he'd duck his head and walk faster. He had collected somehow between the rising and the sally forth a great vitality, which made him remarkably handsome, though powdered with dark powder; and gave his movements, beyond mince, a rangy grace. At the height of his popularity as a musical-comedy dancer, with a huge salary, he now and then had a flash of the American high-school boy in him, in a laugh, a funny dirty curse, a nervous lift of his chin, or a blank naïveté at something he didn't understand.

"After you left last night," he said to Peter, "I went on to Baba's. She was having the damnedest party; and I got so-so-so tight. And Sis traced me there by telephone, and said he had one of his headaches and for me to come up and see how he was. I told him to go physic himself, the old cluck, and hung up. He called right back, and said he would forgive me. God! was I drunk! —Hello! Swell to see you! Come around back some time after the show! —"

He lighted up at the genial duty of touching the public as it passed him on the street.

"What's the show Brinker has in mind," I said.

Jerry turned and looked at me as we walked. His eyes blankened. He pursed his mouth in consideration. He became hard and remote; he even seemed a little offended.

"I don't know a thing about it," he said. "My friend Mr.

Brinker can answer your questions. It's not the sort of thing that int'rests me, rilly."

"No, I suppose not."

"What?" he said suspiciously.

We reached the office entrance of the Goldman Theatre. Jerry resumed his handsome and winning demeanor as he entered, greeting people, employees and actors and applicants in the hall, the elevator, the upstairs corridor, with all the gestures that belonged to each recipient: a tug at the elbow, a wink, a finger in the ribs, a pat on the cheek, a lascivious purse of the mouth, "Hi, boy!" "—darling!" "My dyah girl, he*llo*," and the rest . . . all varieties of small social coinage, from that of the barbershop to that of the imitation British accent he had learned from the comedies of Basil Lunting, which were so popular.

Upstairs, we left the elevator and entered a long room with dirty walls. It was packed with actors and actresses waiting for interviews. Each one was displaying that sad little banner of personality that best became charm, or modesty, or serene assurance, or friendly indifference, or synthetic desperation. Down through those hopeful ranks, Jerry led us with the unquestioning right of entry. He spoke to a few of those waiting. An office boy with a voice like a duck call said Mr. Brinker was busy right now, and then winked; and said, "But you c'n go on in."

Jerry paused to light a cigarette, after which he offered his case to Peter and me. I thought what a curious and yet what a typical approach we were making to authority in New York. A friend knows the "friend" of the director, and is so conducted to the presence at once, while dozens with as urgent needs are told to wait for the turn that most often never comes. A party to corruption, I followed Jerry and Peter through the battered door beyond the phone desk, and came into a sunlighted office that looked like an upstairs drawing room in a Long Island country house. There was a lively wallpaper and the furniture was plumply upholstered in flowered cloth. There were bookcases, painted white. In the sunniest corner stood a long black Steinway grand piano. Sitting in a swivel chair lined with cloth cushions was Mr. Maurice Brinker. Jerry King went up to the desk where Brinker sat, and flung his long legs along the edge of it, and blew cigarette smoke languidly into the sunlight around Brinker's head.

"How d'you feel:" Jerry asked.

"Too dreadful. Who is that:" replied Brinker, in an old parrot voice, waving at me and Peter. He gazed petulantly at us and inserted a cigarette into a long ivory holder. He was a small man, with a large head sitting on his thick shoulders in a regal sort of angle. His eyes were pale and their lids had many folds of weariness and skepticism. His nose was small and thick and indefinite in shape, above a mouth whose corners drooped in dejection, letting sweeping lines of cheek down to his neck in heavy sorrowful collops. He moved his hands delicately. A square diamond in heavy platinum flashed from his fastidious movement. He looked like Queen Victoria . . . prim, humorless, and irritated even by his own authority.

"This is Peter Fremont, and this is Edmund Abbey. Mr. Abbey wants to approach you about getting something to do in that new musical you're putting on."

"What does he do?" Mr. Brinker asked, looking at Jerry, and ignoring me, where I stood near the desk. "Does he act? Surely not, in those clothes. He probably cannot sing. I can't see anyone. Tell Mr. Abbey I can't see him this morning."

He leaned across the desk for Jerry to light his cigarette, and as he puffed, his terrapin eyes shifted and stared washily at me.

"Well, there he is," said Jerry, waving, and humming a bored tune.

There was a disagreeable silence, while Peter made an almost soundless music inside his nose, and I watched Brinker, and Brinker looked at me, head to toe, holding his cigarette with both hands arched and drooping at his chest. His air of deep sadness grew heavier, as if he had to go into this after all.

At last he said, "Did you say your name was Abbey? What have you done: where? What do you want to do here? What: oh my God, I get so tired of these people who think the show business is simply *waiting* for them . . ."

I told him who I was, and what I had done. I told him what I could be expected to do in his theatrical enterprises.

"Conduct?" he said. "You think you could conduct my new play? Well, perhaps you could. I suppose this is a concession for you to be making. You are a serious musician," he said with a pursing of his mouth into a little leer. "You have made concert tours, and studied in Vienna with that modernist."

He touched his cravat elegantly. His face flushed a little, and the spanked and desperate barbering suggested by his skin was now supplanted by an old man's temper . . . eyes watering and bulging, cheeks mottling, and neck filling out over the too-tight collar.

"And as a matter of fact," he continued, "I heard you play for Lily Remusat once or twice. That's where I heard you."

He swung around in his chintz swivel chair and stared over the roofs of theatres nearby. The light fell directly over his cheek now, and I could see a surface powder over rouge, or so I thought. Perhaps it was the impression I'd had of him before this interview that colored his likeness.

"Well, what about it?" said Jerry King, winking in my direction then with a sudden friendliness.

"I'll give him an audition," said Brinker. "I do need a conductor. Sammy wants to handle the musical end of the show. But this one is different. There's no jazz in this. D'you understand that?"

He whirled back to us.

"I am producing a musical show that has the loveliest and most delicate music, and I am going to have real singers, and an augmented orchestra. It is a Viennese operetta I've had my eye on for a long time."

He stood and went to the piano and indicated a score lying there. Standing, he looked smaller than I expected. His shoulders and head were large, and his chest was squablike; but his hips were almost ludicrously narrow, though his buttocks lifted his coat round and far in back. He walked with a short-stepped rapidity, leaning forward, with his head on the side.

"You see? My regular musical chief, Sammy Weinman, is perfectly ma'velous in a revue or a musical comedy. For this, I *must* have musicianship. Not *just* showmanship, d'you see? Because I want something *really* artistic:"

He sounded enthusiastic. He came over to me, and emphasized his words by pushing my arm.

"It sounds very interesting."

"I've got a superb cast in mind. —You come back here this afternoon, come alone, I can't have people around when I give auditions. I'll hear you play, and we'll see. Jerry? You stay to lunch. Have lunch with me, I've so *much* to talk t'you about . . . Goodbye, Mr. Abbey, goodbye, you other man, Mr. —— never mind. Come at half past four, Mr. Abbey. I can give you some tea. Goodbye, just a minute, Jerry; I want you to stay."

Peter and I went out. In the anteroom, the office boy was receiving a phone message and refusing to connect it with Mr. Brinker's office. The actors and actresses were still waiting.

"You'll probably have one hell of a time getting in there again this afternoon," said Peter. "Everyone who comes here says they have an appointment. It's the first thing to say, always. —How about the old cluck?"

"It's like calling on a minor German royalty. I have a cousin in Vienna who is just like that, the old Prince Ertz und Leuchtwitz. He lived like an old whore until after the war; and then, without a penny, and all the rest of it, he suddenly got good sense and found a job in a music publisher's office and has lived ever since with much enthusiasm."

"The thing is, Jerry King got into a Goldman show a few years ago through this Brinker, and Brinker is a damned shrewd man, and he knows talent the minute he sees it. Now he thinks Jerry is ungrateful for all the opportunities he's given him, and in that new show Jerry is starred with two others. Brinker did all that. He always has to get sentimental over his protégés. They never do over him. He's no fool. He always picks people who are really gifted. They call him Sis because he goes to pieces at rehearsal now and then . . . rather often. And he weeps and raves, like an hysterical woman."

We turned into Times Square, where the noon hour was moving crowded and sunlighted through traffic and gray pavement, with background of electric signs, lavish and bleak in daylight. The character of the crowd always seemed the same in that square, though all sorts of people came and went, as different as possible from one another. What stood out were the two aims of the crowd: one large faction coming here to get pleasure, the other to sell it. The gold-studded canopies over theatre doorways rippled and snaked as the light went down the lines of bulbs. I heard a certain kind of taxi horn that always reached clearly above the woven sound of the streets . . . a high note that throbbed with electric impulse. It always made me shiver, in its strange solo flight over the confusion of sound in the city.

In the afternoon I returned to Mr. Brinker's office. For two hours we stayed at the piano, he leaning on it and gazing at me with his draped eyes, which would water with enthusiasm and simple pleasure when I played something from his operetta score which touched his emotions . . . the main waltz, which he conducted as I played, giving a dying value to the lines of melody that ran uphill, and paused at a brink, and then desiring all, with a catch of the breath, swooped down into the violins. It was a competently composed score, in the popular Viennese idiom. I played it with all the humorous and sad juiciness which a memory of Tante Charlotte could evoke . . . cake-icing grandeur, and moonlight on Hapsburg fountains, and surrender to the dance, the waltz, with melting one-two-threes making love and deriding it drolly at the same time.

The afternoon darkened. Times Square brightened beyond the window curtains. Mr. Brinker rang a bell and a servant in a white coat came in with a wheel table bearing champagne in an ice bucket. He said he would give me a contract to conduct the show, *The Rose Arbor*, tomorrow morning. He would assign rehearsal schedules at once. I would have the prima donna to coach, and the choruses, which were "ma'velous, and very important." He poured the wine and handed me a glass, shaking his mottled, flushed head sideways in little wags of satisfaction. He clinked my glass, and we drank. Presently he sat down at the piano, and taking off his diamond ring and placing it beside his champagne glass on the piano shelf, he began to play florid scales and arpeggi. He hunched his shoulders; he shut his eyes, and distended his nostrils, and leaned sideways. Then, with an unannounced attack upon the bass, he thundered into a fragment from Beethoven's C Minor Variations. He played with the last shreds of style. His fingers trotted thickly and woefully on the keys. There was a sickening tone and desire somewhere in the music he made, a loss of edge, a projection of emptiness, if that were possible. Over all that, his bodily dramatics made a caricature of him as a musician. Yet it was clear that some time he had not only possessed music, but had been able to share it with others.

I watched the silver sheets of light fan farther and farther up on the smoky sky that darkened into the color of metallic dust. The theatres and the electric ads pulsed waves of light skyward. It was the second wakening of the city for that day.

Brinker at last stood up, and put his ring on again, turning it speculatively on his finger, and eyeing me.

"Come back in the morning," he said. "Study the score tonight."

He handed me the printed book. Then he took my hand, and shook it, walking with me to the door. There he paused, and said, "Wouldn't you like to dine with me? I can cancel what I'd planned, and we could have it anywhere you like."

He watched my eyes the way movie actors watch the eyes of

their partners in close-ups, shifting his gaze from my eye to eye in a longing expression of search and understanding.

". . . No, I see it," he said. "You have other things to do. Always. Good night, Mr. Abbey. I'll see you in the morning."

He dropped my hand, and put his hands against his round waist and hips. He tapped his toe in calculation, and saw me out of the door. It was late, but the office boy and a few despairing men and women still sat in the anteroom. Mr. Brinker surveyed them from his doorway a moment and in the pale, blood-robbing light of the single china fixture on the ceiling they came alive and alert on their chairs, leaning forward, or drooping "easily," each beginning to act his own little drama of personality and appeal. One woman near the inner door started forward with both hands out, palms down, making a theatrical scene of recognition, with furpiece flying and voice husky with delight:

"My dear Maurice Brinker, it's you at last," she began, walking at him. He said, "Oh . . ." and shuddered, and clapped his ringed hand to his forehead in exhaustion and stepped back, slamming his door shut on the impulsive actress and her chances and the chances she had lost for everyone else. In a moment the phone desk buzzed, and the boy took a message.

"Yes sir. Yes, Mr. Brinker. Every one of them, Mr. Brinker. Good night. —Mr. Brinker says no more today. He won't see anybody else today. I'm closing gup the office now. Come on, let's get going."

They arose, and folded their prides or their furies around themselves, and went, each the axis upon which a world spun.

I I

There followed many weeks of furious work in preparing *The Rose Arbor* for the opening. Through that time went a rhythm like the movies, in which events unfolded with naïve propriety, and in which people either stood distinct, or were submerged, forgotten, and in which places had the same insubstantial yet familiar look of movie sets, the merest surface of likeness.

The star of the show was Marcella Cadeen, a small woman with a plump throat and fat little arms, but a slender waist and pretty legs. Her hair was pale red, very silky, and her gray eyes were always very wide open in a sort of questioning wonder. She acted an innocence that her profuse furs, her pearls, her drink-husky voice and her body thrust forward all belied. She was married to a very rich manufacturer, and came to the Goldman Theatre for rehearsals in a foreign limousine. She had had some experience in serious opera, singing in provincial Italian theatres as Madame Marcella Cadini. But on her return to America, her auditions for the two great opera companies had been failures; and Broadway had known her ever since as a light-opera prima donna. She was now about thirty-three years old.

Her attitudes were good on the stage, and she made the most of costume. She could sweep into song with the orchestra and produce over and over, with an almost dull dependability, those high tones that audiences loved to hear as the curtain came down and the kettledrums trolled and the footlights dazzled the descending fringe.

I rehearsed privately with her for ten days, teaching her the score. She was hard-minded and soft-souled. Between numbers, she liked to lean on the piano, smoking, and wetting her lips before smiling, so they'd shine; tell dirty jokes, widening her eyes with a negative innocence; and at last laughing with her husky voice that cleared so strangely the moment it was lifted in song. When she spoke, she always sounded as if she had a cold or a hangover. By her doll-like insistence upon the frailty of all women, their helplessness, their need for orchids, furs, pearls, kisses, beds, husbands, and lovers, she had managed for great wealth, a popular career, and complete independence. Nothing meant much to her that didn't augment her comfort. But she wasn't wry in her spirit, and could take simple pleasures as humbly as anyone, with the exception that they didn't create in her any habitual desire or custom.

All through the rehearsals on the stage, when the orchestra had been gathered, and the stage manager had the choruses ready in routine, and Mr. Brinker sat in a box and watched, sometimes eating lunch and drinking champagne from a table sent in with two waiters from a restaurant around the corner, we could all see that Miss Cadeen, in a pink enthusiasm which she scarcely troubled to conceal, was falling lightly in love with the actor who played opposite her, a baritone named Richard Duncan, and was singing to him with a ladybird pipe in her treble, curving to him in embraces and closing her eyes while she kissed him. She always came out smiling and vigorous from such betrayals, and the whole company felt secretly the current that ran between those two, and everyone could feel Brinker's gloomy displeasure at the situation, which could so easily brighten into something very detrimental to the show as a whole.

Richard Duncan was tall, and dark-haired, and his voice rolled out with a rich but incomplete quality. He was handsome, and in the military costumes he wore he was a figure of romantic style. In his stage lovemaking with Marcella, he had at first been merely proficient in gesture; but when she besought of him more than that, he had blushed, grinning like a boy discovered in erotic glee, and taken her offerings.

In the latter weeks of preparation, Marcella's husband, who was named Shelden, came to watch rehearsal. Marcella would come to the footlights, during pauses, and shade her eyes from the lights with her arms held at her breast, and call in her husky chirp, "Oh-ho? Darling? D'you like it? Don't you think it's a perfectly darling show?"

He'd clear his throat and stir in his chair, delighted and embarrassed before the theatre people, and call back some inaudible enthusiasm. Then the signal would be given, and I'd bring up the orchestra, and the scene would resume, with Marcella laughing through her eyes at Richard Duncan, waltzing against his body while they sang together, and Mr. Shelden, watching, got no sympathy because it was clear that he was grateful for as much of her as she was willing to let him have.

But no one expected him to insist upon coming along on the tryout tour. Marcella made an issue of it in her dressing room at the Goldman Theatre after our last rehearsal in New York. Before her husky good-humor was restored, Mr. Shelden had promised to take her on the tour in a private car. On hearing this, Mr. Brinker made many wry and scornful remarks, at the same time ordering the publicity department to be sure to mention Miss Cadeen's private car in all advance copy about the Goldman Theatres Corporation's forthcoming Viennese waltz triumph, *The Rose Arbor*, staged and directed by Maurice Brinker.

Pictures from the out-of-town tryouts:

The opening night in Buffalo at the Teck Theatre was the night when a blizzard rose off the lakes and struck inland, crying levelly down the blue pavements and streaming veils of snow and ice past every lamppost. Whatever cars were abroad that night proceeded more obliquely than straight, from the thin ice that froze layer on layer and the gale that blew anything moving off its path. Miss Cadeen chose to live on board her private car with her husband, and Mr. Brinker and I dined there with her early on that evening. The windows were frosted, except where steam brushed upward from open pipes under the car. Through steamed patches of window, then, we could see the railroad yards where we were anchored, and see the great engines breasting into the city through the storm, their smoke torn and scattered as it left the stacks, their bosoms and their long hoods caked with ice. We ate in that stretched atmosphere of false gaiety that showed each of us the other's nervousness. Mr. Brinker constantly rolled his eyes upward, as if to belch, and took deep breaths. He smoked constantly, twisting his long holder. He patted Marcella's hand and kept asking, "How do you feel?" to which she would reply in her wheezy little voice, "Don't you worry, darling. I'm glorious." Mr. Shelden smiled complacently at this, and she stared at him impersonally, hardening toward him quite as openly as she softened toward Richard Duncan. The dinner was profuse, and much food came and went; we ate very little, though we made great clatter about it. At last the steward was asked to phone into the station for a car, and we stood up, putting on coats and furs. Mr. Brinker wrapped himself in a great cloaklike coat of sables and held it together with his arms in a fat chic. When we stepped into the vestibule, and felt the wind tearing through the train door, it took our breaths. Marcella made high birdy noises of dismay and unbelief. Brinker screamed with a vast petulance, "Nobody'll come to a show on a night like this." At the theatre after a long and crawling ride over ice, we were glad to hear the old steam pipes shrilling and clanking, and to smell the musty warmth backstage, and to see familiar activity going on in a sort of snugness. Ten minutes before the curtain we heard screams and a florid line of curses. It was Marcella Cadeen shrieking at Mr. Shelden to for Jesus Christ's sakes get to hell out of her dressing room, couldn't she be *alone* for a *second*? He left her and stood in the wings watching the stagehands finishing their first-act job. Someone saw Richard Duncan knock softly and bend, listen, and enter the star's dressing room. When she emerged later, just before I went down to the orchestra pit, she was excited but happy, and later in the floods of light and in Duncan's arms, she sang with a laughing sort of gaiety that captivated the rest of us, and created, as just such a thing can, one of those moods in the theatre in which everything takes on a fresh glitter, some quality beyond routine that is precious and immediate, and full of emotion that touches each person in the audience as if no one else were there to receive this most beautiful and romantic message. The orchestra strove without trouble, and sounded like a full-strength group, though for the tour we were using a reduced crew, and would augment it only for the

New York run. The audience was very small, but at the first-act curtain they forgot blizzards and inconvenience, and clapped like fools.
As the curtain rose and dropped for calls, I could see Brinker standing in the wings biting his nails like a hungry dog biting a bone, and
blurting brief pouts of laughter in relief, as Marcella and Richard
Duncan together were courtly at each other and the audience. After
the show, which everyone said was a sure hit, there was a party at the
Statler Hotel and the company began to feel the currents of professional life moving and reassuring: phone calls from local admirers of
certain actors, the papers, the society editors, the frank travelling
stares of other guests, the fraternal bellboys. Mr. Shelden ordered a
case of liquor through devious channels. Long after, Mr. Brinker felt
drunken and wrapped in grandeur, and responding to calls, added
a bedspread to his grandeur, and gave his famous imitation of Melba
giving an encore with frigid distaste. Miss Cadeen and Duncan were
nowhere to be seen. Almost desperately, yet with slangy cleverness,
two of the other women in the cast kept giving Mr. Shelden drinks
of his Canadian liquor, and breaking down his mature formality into
strange echoes of boyhood with recitations of all the dirty jokes they
could remember, until he himself was laughing weakly, and remembering all he could of the popular obscenities of the era when he had
worked his way through Purdue University, long, long ago, when he
was as earnest as ever, and confident of the happiness he sought in
these days by grasping at the elusive woman who was upstairs in
Duncan's bed at that very moment. . . .

Leaving Buffalo on Saturday night, in the special train which
the company used, we headed for Philadelphia, to reopen on Monday. Mr. Brinker was going on to New York after our Monday show,
and we would come into town a week later, ready for the opening at
the Goldman Theatre. Richard Duncan was now spending a large
part of his time in the sitting room of the private car which was attached to the end of the train. Mr. Shelden sat there too, listening
to the shop talk and the dull vanities of Marcella and Richard,
amazed at himself for supporting this sort of indignity, and humble
every time he rehearsed in his mind what he should be doing at the
very moment: rising with the dignity that made him an ideal board
chairman; clearing his throat and nipping his pince-nez off his nose;
and inviting Mr. Duncan to leave the room in such starched and
excellent words that the handsome actor would feel cheap, and would
suddenly realize what a fool he'd been acting, and take his leave of

Marcella with apology, and of Mr. Shelden with gratitude for such civilized treatment. It was a comforting private picture; meantime, Duncan lay frank and happy in the plush armchairs, reciting daily the same autobiography, which Marcella never heard. She simply lolled and liked him with her eyes and her memory. She was well-fed by the circumstances of her life now. After years of trials in stock companies and memories of the red brick upstage walls of so many theatres all over the country, and years of struggles to stay pretty and well dressed, and years of desperate delusions about becoming an opera star, she now had a private car, a handsome lover who wasn't too much bother because he thought mostly about himself, a husband who accepted both these commodities, and she had her career. She felt it in her bones that the show would be a great success, though Brinker wasn't yet satisfied with it. But her flowered sense of well-being enclosed her like a garment. She was friendly with everyone in the company. She'd go forward in the train and sit on the arms of Pullman sections, smiling with her wetted lips, and chatting with the girls of the chorus. A little farther forward was a compartment car. Richard Duncan occupied, alone, Compartment C. Just before Mr. Brinker put on his face cream and tied his muslin chin-form under his jaws, he thought he heard a shout. Then he knew he heard a scream, and he opened his door, looking down the narrow metal mahogany corridor. A door was open and in a second Marcella came out, weeping furiously, and pinning her hair up in angry jabs. Mr. Shelden appeared a moment later, and Marcella kicked his shanks ineffectually but bitterly. He gently turned her shoulder and pushed her along toward the exit door. Duncan then showed his head. He was in pajamas. Mr. Shelden turned and said something to him, and Duncan with a sniff of sudden hot outrage, drove his fist to the older man's head, and knocked it grotesquely sideways. Marcella turned just in time to see it. Her eyes cleared instantly. This was promising to be too inconvenient. Duncan, yes, but after all: she came back and with brisk realism she walked up to Duncan and slapped his face with one hand, while with the other she slapped down into passivity the fists that Mr. Shelden was sparring toward the actor in a pathetic middle-aged imitation of a man defending himself. Brinker walked down the aisle. The whole scene was now common property, all doors were open, and the details were soon passed up and down the whole train. The retirement of Mr. Shelden and his wife to their private car was very soon admitted to be a sensible solution of the

whole mess. Brinker didn't sleep a wink, he said, perfectly sure that
the prima donna and the baritone would now ruin their stage rap-
port. But on Monday night she was as melting as ever, and from my
desk in the orchestra pit I could see that they murmured and laughed
secretly, in full view of the audience; and in the entr'acte, Brinker
was seen backstage with his arms around Marcella and Richard,
squeezing them for being so attractive together, and murmuring like
an old madam, suggesting in attitude what he failed to put into words.
Mr. Shelden was again elevated to official unawareness of the thing he
had impulsively discovered on the Philadelphia train. Whatever
happened between then and now, everyone credited Marcella with
being a perfectly grand manager, and according to her world, her
standards were after all of the most virtuous, for, public property,
like any other actress, she had to organize her life into its depart-
ments and see that they interlocked with her private desires. Her
best moments were when we arrived in a new city, and she came
into the view of the cameras, waiting with flashbulbs. At such times,
with her arm through Mr. Shelden's, her lips shining and her eyes
swimming with modesty and voluptuousness, she would pose with
him on the steps of the private car and adjust her orchids, her furs,
and her squeeze all for his sake, and speak of him to reporters as
"My Shelly," and in all ways of busy possession, show herself to the
public as his wife and his leman. In those press photographs, his
likeness would appear, smiling in almost foolish gratification, standing beside her and accepting her imitation of respectability as the
token of something he had wanted all his life. That it sufficed was,
after all, enough to justify anything Marcella chose to do. It was both
his success and his failure. He never would know it, though in half-
moments of clairvoyance he would wonder what was eluding him.
But the mind to find that out would never be the mind to make him
a business success. He was satisfied with symbols. There are many
such. They are generally happy, in a vague way. With her instinct,
Marcella knew all this, and led her life accordingly. The flashbulbs
powdered and lightninged. She stood on the stones of Philadelphia
smiling up at her husband. She already knew the number of the room
reserved at the Bellevue–Stratford for Richard Duncan.

The Philadelphia run was somewhat less exciting than the earlier stands of the tour. The audiences were never capacity, and the
press was something short of lyrical. But we did more than average
business, and everyone was confident of a successful engagement in

New York. The company had settled down to a communal relationship, subdivided into the usual intimacies, frank scandals, sentimental
hatreds, and the like. Mr. Shelden went back and forth to New York,
and Miss Cadeen's temper toward him gradually improved, even
when they were presumably alone with each other. They had moved
into the Bellevue–Stratford, at her insistence. The private car stood
for two days abandoned in the yards and at last Mr. Shelden paid his
Pullman bill, dismissed the car, and said they could go back to New
York with the others. Even this didn't annoy Marcella, and riding up
and down in the hotel elevators made of brass lace, she could be seen
prattling with him very pleasantly. When he was out of town, she ate
with Duncan. . . .

I I I

On Sunday, we moved on to New York. A rehearsal call had
been posted for Monday morning. I returned to Mrs. Yafko's, where
I had left my belongings, and knocked at Peter's door; but he was
out. I found letters waiting for me, including one from Sally, wishing
me success on the opening of the show. It was almost impersonal
in tone.

At the rehearsal the next morning, the augmented orchestra
gathered for the first time. I had instructions to drill them until the
company gathered at ten-thirty. We were opening that night. The
house was all taken, according to the gossip, and over everyone there
hovered again that atmosphere of special gaiety and dread they all
knew so well.

My rehearsal was halted by Mr. Brinker when he came out on
the bare stage, and clapped his hands, and held up his right one,
turning slowly from side to side for attention. In his light-gray tight
suit, he looked like a sleekly furred little animal. When he had perfect silence from the whole cast, facing him, and the orchestra, down
behind him in the pit, he began to speak.

"People, we have some final brushing up to do before tonight.
Mr. Goldman and I are just so sure you're going to give us the performance of your *lives* tonight. We're just sure of it. But my stars! if
you could have seen yourselves Thursday night in Philly! Sammy
Weinman and I went down and saw the show. We didn't wantchou
to know we were there. But it certainly was a shock and it certainly
was a surprise to see how you could let the *pull* drop out of your
work like that! Like you did on Thursday night!"

He paused, and had his fat little hands on his hips; turning with a hurt attitude in his figure, he used the silence as rebuke. His voice, in the empty theatre, made a dry, flat sound, like some marsh bird heard from a distance in still weather. His face, with the prominent eyes and the small fat nose curving down, and the mouth that opened like a parrot's mouth, supported the bird likeness. Everyone was uncomfortable, shocked at having been spied upon, though they had no right to be.

"Now, people:" resumed Brinker, punching his fist into his palm with inadequate force in the gesture, "we're going right through the whole thing, and I am going to make suggestions, and Mr. Weinman is going to help us, and Mr. Goldman may be here himself. So give me the very best in you, people. And remember tonight! You can't let me down. I am trying a new kind of musical production in this, and if it succeeds, why, we'll all be very happy, I'm sure. All right, Ike."

He turned to the wings. The stage manager came out, and called for act one, scene one: no scenery, or costumes; just positions. The curtain was dropped, the house lights went down, and from the third row, which he had reached by the side doors behind the boxes, Brinker called out, "Go ahead, Abbey."

I began with the orchestra.

For several minutes I heard low talking behind me. Then, "No, no, no!" and Brinker clapped his hands, his usual signal for a halt. The actors turned. I tapped my stick. Sammy Weinman came down the aisle, making a sign for "no, no, no," with his hands. He climbed over the curtained rail into the pit, and took my stick, and pushed me aside. He gave some orders to the men, backed them up several bars, and began to conduct. I was too surprised to wonder. I sat down on a backless chair beside the first violins, and watched him. He was short and slender. His head stuck forward with the force of conviction. He had knife-sharp features, and hair in black brilliantined ripples close to his skull. With fists of energy, shouted directions, and scowls of "rage" on his pale, beard-pocked face, he whipped the orchestra and led the singers into new tempi by whacking his stick on the score. His neck was the most expressive organ he owned. It seemed to concentrate its expression at the back, between hair and collar. He bobbed his head in accent, tight muscular movements, like those of a leering boxer.

And the music, the singing, the waltzes, underwent the process of showmanship. Every rest was exaggerated; every climax was pushed to bursting; every rhythm was kicked into the boxed beating of jazz. Under his revision, the stage became more animated. The singers understood the idiom. He brightened everything by making the brasses louder, and putting the double basses in for string-plucking even where they had rests. In his first pause, he put down the stick, and mopped his gray face with a handkerchief, and bobbed his head forward at me.

"D'ya get it?" he said, half smiling, but frowning with the immense conviction of his terrible skill. "More of that. Give me no highbrow business. The public always like the most a'tistic thing after all. They'll eat it up if you give them what I am giving now. More pep! More hot! Make 'em sing out over you with all they've got, not expect you to support them. We've got a nice property here in this show, but we can't affawd to let it die out! —Ready! Let's hit it: ta-*da* . . ."

Once I turned around and looked at Brinker. He closed his eyes and shuddered his face at me, and shrugged. Then he waved his hand, as if to say, "I know, but what can I do? The man is right . . ."

After more demonstration from Sammy, he gave the orchestra back to me and said, "Aw right. Now take it on, *like that.*"

I gave as good an imitation as I could of his style, and got much the same results, though of course, with conviction lacking, some triumphant and vulgar success was lacking too. He felt it, and walked up and down just behind me, humming and beating, necking his head forward and up and down, and making exasperated comments, unable to relinquish the direction wholly.

This indecision at the last moment was very typical of how shows got to Broadway. It unsettled everyone in the cast, and it reflected the news that had seeped around like drainage through sand that the new Goldman opus was only fair; did a good open in B'fo, cracked house in Dorchester, but slowed up in Philly with nut far exceeding Met pay-off now likely, though star personally popular and show good clean lattice-and-roses yarn, with some songs soupy as classic hits of the past, like *Sari* and *Merry Widow.* Changing anything at the last minute wasn't technically hard, for the actors were all professionals and could remember. But it disheartened them, and for the first time, the pouting doubt on Brinker's face, his dissatisfaction, was understood, and the whole company began to feel, though they'd never confess it, that they were about to open in a dud.

We worked through the lunch hour, and had a brief recess, which ended in a notice posted on the backstage board that the company was dismissed until tonight, for the opening. I stayed and reworked the augmented orchestra all afternoon. Sammy Weinman finally left, buttoning himself into his tight black overcoat with the velvet collar over his white silk scarf, and half whistling with an open sense of virtue at having saved the show from a disastrously artistic performance.

The curtain went up that night half an hour late; but the house was full, and over it hung the network of sound, buzzing conversation that suggested a whole audience made up of people who knew each other. They called across aisles in greeting, and they waved, turning. The women gave a general impression of shop-window smartness . . . enamelled and arranged, all in the same New York manner, with bobbed hair in blazing waves, and diamond bracelets from wrist to elbow, and powdered knees showing silky and plain below the short skirts that were hiked up when they sat down, revealing the long shanks of that time. The men . . . many of whom were, and many others of whom desired to be, famous first-nighters . . . ranged from banker to bootlegger; but all were correctly dressed, whether of blue jowl or pink. As I came in, the lights were still up, and I saw the uneasy triumvirate of Goldman, Brinker, and Weinman standing in dinner jackets behind the barrier of the last row. They had just phoned from the box office to start the show. As I came down from the stage to the orchestra door, I passed Marcella Cadeen. She was standing in her first-act costume, holding a cigarette and a glass of gin, and she was shuddering over her smile. She called me in her husky voice.

"Well, good luck, dear," she said. "Here's to us."

We kissed and she offered her gin. Seen up close, she looked like a little kitten, with gray eyes framed in beaded lashes, and her small mouth made smaller with an inner outline of dark rouge. Her chin had a soft little roll of flesh above her throat. It quivered when she sang, like a canary bird's throat.

"Oh, Christ, I hate this sort of thing," she said, gesturing toward the auditorium, where the talk rose and the people gathered. I went on.

Nothing went wrong. Marcella's voice cleared, as always, when she began to sing, and her little plump arms rose and fell in appealing gesture. Duncan was dark and romantic. The waltzes besought and whispered, and after each act there were plenty of calls. But nothing went particularly right, either, as it had when the first performance came off in Buffalo. The electric line between the stage and the house was simply not there. To make up for it, we all were overenthusiastic in the intermissions, hugging and kissing, and assuring everyone that it was going marvellously, and that we had a hit: listen to that out there? A hit.

Duncan had a solo in the last act, and he sang it better than he ever had before. It stopped the show. Marcella had to sit smiling on him in character for an embarrassingly long pause while he modestly bowed over the heads of the audience at the ceiling, to avoid the stigma of having come out of character, but at the same time to thank his good friends the public. When the act was resumed, there was a curious, minute but significant change in the mood between the two of them. No one had foreseen a personal hit for Duncan. Marcella left the stage at the last curtain and was sent back for her calls by the stage manager only after a short, hot argument. What she, and any other actor, lived on had lost intensity that night; and though on the surface she was sparkling and moist-eyed with excitement, the alert eyes and ears of the company knew exactly what was up; and she knew they did, for the theatre of all places is the place whose workers look at everything quite clearly, with an almost malicious realism, no matter how much they might disguise their bland awareness with sentimental protests and softheartedness, which could be quite as genuine as the severer knack of admitting it when things went to hell.

The crowds streamed backstage, and Brinker brought Mr. Goldman, who spoke to the star and the leading man, and other principals, and then stood in his tilted top hat, staring around like a white rat at the others, without expression. The lesser actors, passing him, greeted him with assumptive elegance, and Brinker went to Marcella and kissed her without saying anything. She thumbed her little double chin, and looked at him with fatalistic calm. He went over to Duncan, standing tall and rich-voiced, smiling and bowing to people. Brinker watched and waited till Duncan saw him, then he waved his hand, and said, "My dear boy, it was too stunning."

Miss Cadeen suddenly became animated with friends who stood with her. Mr. Shelden came up, and she cried out his name, and held her hands to him.

"Shelly pets, how was I!"

He could hardly speak, for the sincere and marvelling devotion he felt surge up in him. She felt it, and it was welcome to her to-night. They both looked slightly embarrassed, to be the victims of simple and honest feeling here in this backstage clatter of smart talk and praise that meant nothing.

I turned around and saw Peter and Sally coming down behind the setting which the stagehands were striking. They were in evening clothes.

"We've come to take you out to supper," said Sally. We shook hands, and exchanged high nonsense about my being now a maestro, and a waltz king, and so on.

"Wouldn't you like to meet Miss Cadeen?" I asked them. She heard me, and called out, "Bring them over, Eddie. I'd *love* to meet your friends."

It was more important to her than gold, of which Mr. Shelden had plenty. Peter and Sally made their salaams with the proper blend of sophistication and reverence, and Miss Cadeen smiled up at them with wistful pussycat eyes, as if to say, "How kind people are! And how much, much they see in me that really isn't there . . ."

We started across the stage to go. Mr. Brinker stopped me.

"Whatever it was, I don't think it was your fault," he said. "We'd better rehearse in the morning. Sammy is planning some cuts. The orchestra really sounded tonight. We may put back those two inter-ludes we took out."

"I'm sorry the spirit was taken out of the company this morning, Mr. Brinker. I think that was as much the trouble as anything."

"Of course I'm so-so-so sorry," he said with veiled looks and a slight lisp for sophistication, "that the first fine frenzy of Cadeen and Duncan is over. That was an asset. It made her feel young, and made him feel like a big shot. Oh, well . . . I suppose *that* end of it'll be more difficult than ever, after Duncan's hit tonight. Cadeen's no fool; but she's an actress. I never saw one who wasn't jealous. It'll probably ruin Duncan, too."

IV

The Rose Arbor settled into a fairly prosperous run, and Rich-ard Duncan's name went up on the marquee in lights with Marcella Cadeen's, and he began to be seen in shadowy backstage moments talking to one of the chorus girls, gently reaching toward her from his splendid heights, and earning in return her huge-eyed glances of invitation and skepticism. Miss Cadeen and Duncan were still much together; but this from habit now rather than excitement and happiness.

I grew to enjoy the routine at the Goldman Theatre, and to like the theatrical atmosphere of that old playhouse, with its archaic boxes, its green velvet curtains and seats, its many-branched silver chandeliers holding electric candles that were shaded by little hoods of yellow silk, the deep spaces backstage, and the smell that hovered there, a smell that suggested water sprinkled on old wooden floors, the heating of glue in the property room, the acid sting of hot electric wires and lamps, and the dusty cumulus of old stretched muslin and canvas: the scenery and the curtains that hung in the black loft above the stage.

Now that *The Rose Arbor* was launched, I saw less of the Goldman executives. Mr. Brinker was busy casting and projecting a musical comedy, and though he used the stage of the Goldman mornings for group tryouts, I was never there then. Now and then I'd see him in the streets, riding in his long-hooded English car, a touring car, with the top down, and a liveried man at the wheel. In the rear seat, Brinker sat in a hunch of petulant composure, dressed in his sable coat and jaeger hat. Beside him on the seat was always a great colloped bulldog. Neither of them saw anybody, as the car flashed its way through traffic. They both looked straight ahead, with drooping lids and jaws, resembling each other. Crossing Times Square, this equipage always made a stir, for everyone knew the owner, and many bowed and waved, but never got any notice.

But Brinker, with all his disdain, remoteness, and activity, found time to know everything that went on in any of the Goldman enterprises, and also to follow the orchestra concerts, the important art shows, the interesting revivals at the opera, and to appear at all the parties organized by famous people for each other. He was highly thought of as an intelligence, I soon discovered, and often laughed at as a personality. The combination was entirely feasible in Manhattan, and to tell the truth, there was a suggestion in Maurice Brinker's pursuit of his orbit that he enjoyed the kinds of eminence he owned. It was satisfying to him to be an instantly recognizable figure in the great world of New York notoriety. He also knew that at his profession, he was reinforced by great experience and good judgment. He was said to be the only man who could alter the strangely derived opinions of Mr. Goldman.

One afternoon just before one of our matinees of *The Rose Arbor*, I met Brinker in the stage manager's office of the theatre. He was smoking through his long holder. His furs were draped over his shoulders like a cape. After greeting me, he stared in a pout for several minutes, while I looked through a copy of *Variety* that lay on the desk.

"What are you working on," he said, at last, in his driest and most parrotlike tone, a compound of unwilling effort and detachment.

"What d'you mean, Mr. Brinker."

"The music. I'm told you are composing. What are you doing?"

"—Oh. Yes, I am. I'm at work on a symphony. I've been busy with it for over a year. I made my design while I was in Vienna. I've been trying all year here in town to get a chance to work on it."

His expression hardly changed. Perhaps his cheeks grew a little puffier. "What are you going to do with it?"

"I hardly know, except to send my score around to conductors, who will return it unopened."

"Of course," said Brinker, shrugging his lavish furs that smelled of faint snow and musk sachet. "I suppose I know every musician of any consequence. —Well, why don't you bring your thing around and play it for me? Perhaps I could do something for you. For instance, if I liked it, I could send it to Katchelsky. I know him intimately."

"You mean the Boston conductor?"

"Certainly. *In*timately. He's a very intelligent man. He always wants new works. Come up to my place Sunday afternoon. There will be nobody there. Just Jerry King, perhaps. No one else. I don't very often make an offer like this. I— There are so-so-so *many* dull frauds around . . . Of course, I know music, Abbey. You may not think so:" He gathered his furs in a jewelled clutch with his posed hands, and bridled a little. "You many think anyone in the show business, like me, must be very insensitive to the really great things. I could have had a great career. Some time I'll tell you about that."

I told him I thought his musical taste and knowledge very impressive.

"Your sympathy is instinctively fine," I told him.

"Well, you come on up Sunday. You will?"

"I'll be delighted."

"I can do a lot for you with Serge Katchelsky. He has real respect for my opinion. I knew him for years in Paris."

v

Sunday at half past three I arrived at Brinker's apartment on upper Fifth Avenue, facing the Park.

He lived in an iron-grilled white marble house that had been converted into four apartments. A manservant opened the front door and led me up a flat-stepped stairway in white marble that curved to right and left from a landing. We turned to the left and through a heavy door entered a drawing room that had a billowed window aspect on the Park. The iron grilles curved with the windowpanes. It was a long room, panelled in white wood. A long piano stood against one wall, and opposite to it was a fireplace, in which a lazy Sunday-afternoon sort of fire sent up a thin smoke to the sky. The rugs were rich and complicated in color and design. The end of the room opposite the windows was filled almost entirely with glass doors whose panes were mirrored, so that the sky over the Park, and the trees, showed back from the deep end of the room. There were chairs cushioned in dull, heavy green silk, and marble tables holding white-shaded lamps. It was a formal room, without the appearance of having been lived in. Everything was too spotlessly arranged. Even the fireplace ashes were brushed and combed into neat little hills under the logs.

The servant went to the mirrored doors and opened them.

"Who is that? Is that Mr. Abbey?" said Brinker, out of sight. He called me and then walked into view, trailing a napkin. "Come in here, we're just finishing lunch. Have some pie with me. D'licious lemon tart. My cook is a genius."

He led me to his dining room. He was alone. The delicate restrained light of Sunday afternoon came through the windows and somehow exposed the arid atmosphere in which my host lived and thought. The whole house protested its owner's wealth and sound taste; and just as clearly showed his aimlessness. He struck me today as a very sad and lonely man. Where was Jerry King? Mr. Brinker was lively with a sort of early gaiety that would fade as the day advanced, and as he wore out the good which sleep had done him.

We sat together and ate lemon tart.

"Did you bring your notes?"

"Yes. They're with my hat in the living room."

"You're too modest. You shouldn't leave your symphonies lying around like that . . . I shall never forget the day I lunched with Debussy at Serge Katchelsky's flat in Paris. Debussy had some music with him, and Serge kept trying and trying to get him to play it. Finally he asked if I was trustworthy. Dear Serge said, why, certainly, of course; and so Claude Debussy went to the piano and played what he had there, and it was a scandalous burlesque of Saint-Saëns, and all French official music. —Killing? Debussy thinking it was anything to be dis*creet* about?"

He rang for some coffee, and we returned to the drawing room. He looked around with an habitual estimate of his surroundings, and seemed vaguely satisfied but restless. At last he went to the long green silk couch before the fireplace and, stirring his coffee delicately, waved me to the piano. I felt a little stage fright, which surprised and annoyed me.

It was in a fading daylight that I finished my performance, said goodbye and thank you, and went away. Brinker's response was so curious and yet so sincere that I couldn't stop speculating about it all the way down to my house. I played; he sat now nodding, and now staring stonily into the fireplace. He was always silent except for little mouth noises when he was particularly struck by some passage. When I started, his face, flushed with food, and powdery with his complexion, was merry and expectant and cordial. But as I went on, he became more and more depressed, and his hands moved nervously when I would look up from the pages for a second; and he'd hold his head, or push his cheek against his eye, and sigh; I could only conclude that what I was doing made him nervous and saddened him. As the light got paler, and the formal shadows in that lifeless room grew deeper, so his mood went from generosity to resentment, and when I stood up at last, he buried his face in his hands and took a deep breath as if to reestablish his petulance and his social imperturbability. Then he stood up, and came to the piano. He took up the pages and glanced over them. He said he would send the symphony to Katchelsky. He said it with a grim sort of sadness. I could only think that he was impressed by my work, and sure of its excellence. I had to think further and say to myself that its very excellence filled him with grief and melancholy, showing him pictures of what young artists were doing, and reminding him of how much in the past he had himself looked forward to at one time, such things as artistic integrity, a career founded on severe ideals, and nourished by a genius whose well would surely never dry up. He looked at me with glistening tragic eyes, and snatched my pages almost angrily. He said a few things that were conventionally kind, but behind his words was a much more eloquent opinion, and I felt it, and I was grateful for it, though more than ever I was touched by his innate sadness and his recognition of defeat. Finally, he turned me rather irritably out of his apartment, saying he had an engagement for tea, and would have to be getting ready. We shook hands very formally, and he watched me down the white marble stairs that had a pale ghostly polish in the reticent light that seeped in from Fifth Avenue. A last word he called down to me,

"You needn't think I won't do it, because I shall do it. Whatever there is about me, I always keep a promise. They'll admit that even on Broadway. Never you mind what I think of this work. I know what I think. —Katchelsky will pay some attention to me."

V I

I didn't see him for days afterward. They said around the theatre that he had had one of his nervous breakdowns, and had gone to Florida for ten days. But the show kept on, and the audiences gradually grew larger, though never extraordinary. No one was surprised when Duncan frankly forsook Miss Cadeen for the chorus girl, who quite as frankly took him on. To see her waiting backstage for his exits was a cruel trial for Marcella. But she came through it with a lump in her throat and a smile on her mouth. It was more difficult on the stage to simulate the abandon which in the early days of the tour had been so laughingly real between the two principals. Duncan continued to win the larger part of the applause every evening, and it gave him an authority and a dash during his scenes that must have cut her to the heart. He would pursue her in the waltzes, and simulate his adoration for her with a zeal larger than life. He would embrace her until she would need breath, and make his great blue-shadowed eyes at her, destroying the last resentment against him in the audience, and reminding Marcella of how meaningful all this had once been. Her voice became a little hard in its edges, losing the sweet pulse she had first sung with. But she made all the traditional signs for romantic love in *The Rose Arbor,* and caused the women in the house to murmur that she was a sweet little thing, and to wonder how old she was, and if that leading man meant anything to her.

He meant enough so that she forgot herself one Saturday night. She had been drinking gin before the show and during her offstage moments, and by the time the intermission came along, she was flushed and panting with accumulated resentment. Her dressing-room door was open, letting light and sound out on the steel deck that supported the rooms of the other principals, one low story above the stage floor. Maurice Brinker was in town again and made his customary visit backstage during the intermission, simply to stand around and let his eyes record details that might need attention. A door above on the steel tier opened, and then he was grieved to hear Marcella Cadeen's voice, husky and choked, gasp out a series of obscenities. He looked up. The violet-eyed chorus girl had just come out of Duncan's dressing room, down the deck from Marcella's, and Marcella was slapping the girl on the cheeks with flailing hands. Duncan came and pushed Marcella back. He made rumbling noises of reproof and hushed her sternly, grasping her upper arms and squeezing masterfully. It was too much; she slapped his face, and shrieked at him. Maurice Brinker gathered up his long thick coat and almost ran to the steel stairs and went up, puffing like an out-raged she-bear. The chorine was weeping and making refined re-marks to herself.

"Stop this!" commanded Brinker, bearing down on the three lovers, spanking his hands like a teacher who has taken all that could be expected in the way of naughtiness. "Let her go, d'you hear? Duncan! Marcella, be quiet. Shut up! Shut your trap!" he said to the girl, who was, for his benefit, telling Marcella what a hellcat she was.

"Keep your dirty little mouth out of this," said Marcella to Brinker, sobbing on her palms and reeking with the breath of drink. "I'm just about fed up! The God-damned cheap bastard, run-ning after a little bitch like her, and stealing all the spots in the show!"

"Marcella, you're hysterical," said Duncan, rolling his heavily made-up eyes at Brinker, in sympathy.

"I'm sure I've never been talked to like that in my li—" said the chorus girl to Mr. Brinker, and Marcella continued, "Who're you to say anything, Sis Brinker! You God-damned"—catalogue of his habits; he blanched and sucked in his breath against the back of his hand. She was in a frenzy, her eyes flashing through tears, and her hands trembling and rubbing her shoulders where Duncan had grasped her. Her breath was spasmodic. Duncan folded his arms and said, like a clergyman, "Oh, come, come." Brinker let the tears blurt to his eyes and down his powdered face.

"Why, you filthy little ingrate," he said. "How dare you talk to me that way: after all I've done for you: and for you, Duncan: this is a perfectly disgraceful scene! Now stop it! *Stop* it! D'you hear?"

His voice rose. He shrieked hysterically himself. Marcella was shocked into silence. Her sobs died. Duncan was horrified by the weeping and passionate Brinker. The chorus girl began to weep again, in sympathy. They all became suddenly very sober except Brinker, who was trying to control himself. The other actors and actresses looked up from down on the stage, and along the steel deck, watching, treasuring every word and attitude; yet trying to look as if they were just incidentally glancing around.

Marcella now stood, white and sick, recognizing the public finish of her love. Duncan was fatuously regretful of the whole scene. But it was Brinker who with a valiant fury recovered his calm, and sent them back to their dressing rooms to get ready for the next act, which was already overdue. His face was a streaked and tragic mask. But in his wry, shuddering voice were command and disdain. Miss Cadeen trembled and tried to beg his pardon; he stared her into turning around and running to her maid. With an angry, pathetic majesty, he waddled down the steps to the stage, and ordered me to the orchestra pit, to start the entr'acte without delay.

"If they're not ready in the wings for their cues, it'll be just simply too bad."

He pulled out a handkerchief and raked at his inflamed eyes.

The show went on. Now and then, between phrases of song, I could hear an echo of a sigh or a sob in Miss Cadeen's voice. But she was steadier than I had expected; her voice took on something again of the pulse that had made it seem better than it really was; and I thought that perhaps having spent her emotion and faced its images, she was restored to a certain freedom. In any case, the second act brought her a greater measure of applause than she'd been getting lately; and it pleased me that the calls were so obviously for her, rather than Duncan, that she could afford to take one or two alone, and then graciously hold her hand to him, and invite him to join her out here before these people, in this diamond-yellow spotlight, and look into the velvet atmosphere of the theatre with an actor's grateful heart.

In the next few days, Mr. Shelden came to the theatre with his wife, evidently with her plain consent. She seemed content to be dull and grateful for the new luxuries he was offering her . . . a new coat of ermine, some jewels, a satin couch for her dressing room. At the Wednesday matinee she was again alone, and the tongues began to taste the fact that at the end of the show she waited in her dressing room for a long time, then sent her maid away, and came out to meet Sammy Weinman, who grasped her arm aggressively and led her to her car that was waiting by the alley mouth of the stage entrance. They said Sammy looked around with an expression that hoped he was being seen stepping out with Miss Cadeen, and also hoped he was escaping unnoticed.

VII

One night after the show, the stage manager told me to go up to Mr. Brinker's office in the front of the building. I went through the empty theatre that was fantastically lighted by the spotlights which the charwomen saw to clean by. Their stiff and sagging bodies made great shadows on the walls of the house as they bent to their work in the aisles and the rows. Mr. Brinker was waiting for me on his chintz sofa. He regarded me with brooding eyes and then said,

"I have heard from Serge. You will be amazed and delighted. He has accepted your work, and will try to play it this season. He said he has a concert here in six weeks, and he may try to work it into that program. If not, then he'll play it next season. Aren't you pleased?"

"Well!"

"Well what: can't you say something? I knew Serge Katchelsky would give it real attention. —Do you realize how very fortunate you are? This isn't an everyday occurrence, you know," he said, with an irritable tone that seemed to regret his part in bringing me such news. "There are plenty of very talented boys not getting a hearing of any kind. D'you hear? —Serge Katchelsky wants you to come to Boston to meet him and be there for the rehearsals, if he produces the work this season. You can't go, because this show will run at least two months longer. I'm sorry: it's very unfortunate, but you'll just have to wait and hear your symphony here. I'll get Sammy to take your place that night, so you can go to the concert."

He was short of breath, and his powdered face quivered. His eyes were moist with what looked like envy, and I knew that they were again looking upon himself, desiring again the wasted youth that had never brought him what he had helped to give me.

"—This has been wonderfully generous, Mr. Brinker. I can hardly thank you enough."

"What?"

"—It's the chance of a lifetime. Dr. Katchelsky is a magnificent artist, and his orchestra is one of the great ones of the world . . . You've given me an opportunity of the rarest kind."

"You really think so? You realize this?" He looked hungry for thanks and praise, for some share in the matter. He seemed to be waiting for more from me, some overwhelming proof of my gratitude. I couldn't think what more to say. At last, in the silence, he pulled the letter from Katchelsky out of the sleeve of the kimono he was wearing over his evening dress, and tossed it to me. There was no opinion in the letter; simply Katchelsky's thanks, and a statement that he would produce the work this season or next; that he wanted me to come and see him, attend rehearsals, and check over the copied parts; and a few personal words to Brinker, signed "Votre affectueux Serge."

"You can't possibly go to Boston," said Brinker. "You can write Katchelsky now, and be sure to explain why you can't come. I hope you're glad, after all the trouble I went to."

It was impossible to satisfy him. I sat down and began to talk. We talked for hours. He talked with the eagerness and the intimacy of a man to whom nobody would ever listen. He mixed gossip, triviality, and a grieving wisdom in his words, boasting hopefully of his life, and attempting to rebuild its events into a majestic design of achievement. Nothing lingers of his thought; only a few sketches of his person as I imagined him in various times and places. I could see him (as he prattled woefully) in the Kansas railroad town where he was born, a changeling in that brood of God-struck farmers, trainmen, and sunbonneted women, all of whom were suspicious of him, at fifteen—his plump elegance, his feverish search in the town library for a pathway to something beyond the gorgeous scorched wheatfields that he detested. His salvations (from the point of view of escape) were the music teacher he took piano from and the organist who came in the spring with the famous evangelist, when that showman of God set up his dusty tent in a field by the main-line tracks and there in dim lantern light roared and moaned like the trains that passed shaking the ground from Chicago to Los Angeles. The music teacher was a woman who never understood Maurice, but who gave him all she could of her arid learning in the art he adored. The organist was a man who smelled of perfumed soap, and who, estimating Maurice's personality, told him lavish stories of "life" in the "great world," and suggested that he run away to make his own life. The day the revival caravan moved on, Maurice went home and delivered a passionate farewell to his mother, who used to beat him for being a sissy, and to his father, who dropped his eyes and mumbled sighs every time he thought intensely of the fat, pink, and alien son he had amazingly seeded. There wasn't any life here in this town, Maurice told them, standing on the front porch and weeping with excitement and confused desires. He wanted to go to the opera and drink champagne and see Lillie Langtry in her carriage and become a concert star and dine at the Waldorf-Astoria and smell the lilacs in Paris. They let him go, though a few hours later they were stricken by what people would say; and they sent the sheriff after the runaway. But the organist cleverly convinced him that Maurice had left them to return home away back yonder down the road. He never went back to Kansas, hating it so much that this hatred might really have stood for something very different.

He mentioned Chicago, and flight from the organist who, in the city, behaved disgracefully in public, where nobody paid much attention. He mentioned feats of muscular and tempered strength that sat oddly with his image now . . . riding freight trains, working in a canning factory in a seaport loading cans all day long and sometimes half the night, shovelling coal in a steam laundry, and an enlistment in the navy, which left him in England, at the end of his time. By that time he was nineteen years old, and wiser than happy. He got a job, and enrolled for some courses in the Royal College of Music. Eight years later he was one of the best-known organists in England, and he appeared later with many orchestras, and came to America to make a concert tour, billed as an "English organist," though it soon got around that he was really an American, and he now had ceased to care what they thought of his origin. He declared with a belligerent look that he probably would have been knighted had he stayed in England. "Sir Maurice Brinker," he said, in hopeless rehearsal. With an English poet who lived with him for a while, he composed an operetta which had a good success, and was later produced in New York. Coming here to attend rehearsals, he gradually formed his interest and attachment for the exhausting but essentially easy tasks of the commercial musical theatre, and before long he was in the Goldman organization, where he had come to command in these days.

It was evident from the way his thoughts travelled that somewhere, some time, the heart had gone out of him, for either serious work or idle happiness. I felt sure that no one respected him according to his potential values; for these could be shown only by intimacy, and no one had any relationship with him except that of the theatre.

It was very late when I got up to go, and we shook hands. He was glad he'd had someone to listen to him. I was wondering at his lack of reserve in his narrative. I decided that he must be so sophisticated that he really didn't care what anyone in the world thought of him, and that this might really be the very heart of his loneliness.

"Be sure to write Serge Katchelsky a very nice letter."

I promised to do this; and did so; and in a week received an answer that regretted my inability to come to Boston for rehearsals; but announced that the schedule of programs had been so arranged that performance would occur in the New York concert in March, at which time it would be Dr. Katchelsky's pleasure to make my acquaintance, if I would have the goodness to call between four and six the day of the concert at the Ritz-Carlton Hotel: signed, V. I. Volkonski, secretary.

On that day in March, I gave my name to the clerk at the Ritz-Carlton Hotel, and waited to be received upstairs. In a few moments, a young man with a white face and large doubtful eyes came out of an elevator, and asked the clerk for me. He turned, and bowed.

"Mr. Abbey? Dr. Katchelsky vould like for you to come op. Blease."

"Thanks. Are you Mr. Volkonski?"

"This I am."

We went upshaft and down the hall to a suite which had a pale-walled drawing room furnished with gold-and-white French furniture. The day was still bright outside but all the curtains were drawn, and the lights were on, casting a yellow complexion over everything.

In this artificial atmosphere, occupying chairs behind a low table with cocktails standing on it, were a man and a woman. They watched us enter with friendly interest. The man stood up, walking over to me with short heavy steps, somehow expressive of cordiality. He was not tall, and he was elegantly suited so that his thickening figure seemed full of grace. He was smiling. He spoke with an accent that affected the lift and fall of his words, rather than their pronunciation.

"Misser Abbey? I am Serge Katchelsky. This is very delightful, to see you, and to welcome you, because I want to speak of your beautiful symphony. I am delighted with it. In orchestra, it *sounds*. How curious: that this should come to us in Boston? in this way. Please, come to sit down."

He led me to a chair by the cocktails, and presented me to "Madame Grünstein," who was in middle age, and full of the devices of beauty which would have left her a caricature if she had not also had a strange warmth in her personality: her face was shadowed by a huge black hat; her eyes were kohled; her cheeks were mask-white, and her lips peony red. She was dressed in black with white pearls and white lace at her shoulder and tremendous black furs. We drank a cocktail, after Madame glistened her huge eyes over the toast, "The new symphony." The secretary, V. I. Volkonski, sat with us, but not of us. He turned his pale bird's head in distant thought.

"Are you nervous?" Katchelsky suddenly asked, nodding at me humorously. His eyes were light gray, under heavy black eyebrows that had a sensitive lift to them. His face was sad, even when smiling. He had a curved nose and a sharp mouth, curving down in the center and up to the corners. He was gray-haired, which made his face seem dark. "I have done beautiful things with your music . . . even the cuts you will approve."

Madame Grünstein laughed mysteriously over her raised shoulder at him. "Cuts? You dared? Serge!"

They poured out a certain warmth that was racial, I thought. Their eyes lived in the lively light of intelligence supported by rich spirit. Katchelsky's face in particular was marked by delicate response to living. He had character in his person, and anywhere would have seemed a distinguished, if not a great, man.

Madame Grünstein suddenly stood up, and gathered her furs for departure. She and Katchelsky spoke in Russian for several moments, then she looked at me, and said, with a lavish warmth, "Ach, how beautiful to be with genius and so young! I shall split my gloves applauding tonight! Serge tells me it is very fine. Adieu."

She was conducted out by Volkonski, who didn't come back. Katchelsky and I sat down and I answered questions for almost an hour. Everything he asked was strictly relevant to his attempt at understanding me as a person, now that he knew me as a musician. He very shrewdly asked me if I'd ever studied under Gluckwald, and said he had thought so in one or two passages of the symphony. Like all Jews, he had a genius for making discoveries, and like the truest Jews, he gave out much more warmth than he demanded of others, having that beautiful admixture of generosity and sensitiveness which is especially Hebraic.

The phone kept ringing in the other room, and Volkonski would answer it dimly. We could hear the door buzzers going now and then, and once a maid came in with a great vase of flowers. Katchelsky watched her place the vase on a table, and adjust the ferns, and turn the vessel a trifle; continuing to talk, he watched her with the most intense interest, as if he were studying the technique of what she was doing. When he looked back at me, his small gray eyes were full of satisfaction. It was the way he observed and partook of everything.

Finally, at a little past five, he stood up, and held out his hand.

"Now I must rest. I have arranged for you to be in my box at the concert tonight. They always give me a box. This pleases you? I hope you can bring friends with you. There are six chairs, and only two are already reserved. Come back to see me after the concert. I hope you will be happy."

I thanked him. He turned and called, "Vladimir Ilyitch!"

"Da, da . . . I come, Sergei Pavlovitch."

"Please: take Mr. Abbey down. Goodbye. Au revoir."

I had no dinner. I called up Peter at Mrs. Yafko's and asked him to pick up Sally, and to meet me in the lobby of Carnegie Hall at eight-fifteen. Then I walked up Broadway for a long time, watching the currents quicken for night, the lights, the cars tracking in gold reflection on the polished pavements, the walkers crowding at corners and then, obeying the green-light release, unravelling out across the street. In the movement of cars there were the usual dramatic highlights . . . a fire engine turning out of a side street, the traffic stilled for its thudding and belled rush; and once later an ambulance panning along a parallel street, unseen but loud. At last I turned back to the Goldman Theatre, where my evening clothes were. In my dressing room was Sammy Weinman, getting into his clothes.

"Well, good luck, kid," he said, and halved his lids in hard-boiled doubt.

I dressed quickly and thanked Weinman for taking my place for one night. To this he said nothing, but merely looked steadily and hardly at me, the eye of New York.

Later, in the crowd, I found Sally and Peter. I produced the tickets Volkonski had given me.

"We're to be in Dr. Katchelsky's box," I said.

"Oh, darling!" cried Sally. She was pale and nervous, wearing a bright smile that could have been rubbed off with her rouge. Her eyes seemed feverish. She walked with us prattling to deny excitement. Peter caught her fever, and to overcome it, he was slow and deliberate in his movements. As for me, I had stretched feelings that were physical. I yawned; they thought me unbelievably bored. We entered the box and took the three first seats. Already the fluttering confusion was filling the house, and as people moved and turned, they made a broken pattern like the pattern of sunlight on little waves. When the orchestra began to come out, I felt a little numb. I found that I was dragging painfully at the flesh on my jaw, and that Sally was watching me do it with a look of loving grief on her face. Just then an usher appeared, and brought Maurice Brinker into the box, who turned and placed a chair for Madame Grünstein. We stood, and returned to amenity with introductions. Madame was sleek and her body, wrapped in white velvet, seemed insistently beautiful. Brinker was pinched into a high smart collar. Under his barbered and powdered look, he was excited. He bore himself with an air of responsibility.

The orchestra was ready. Even before I saw him, Madame Grünstein leaned sharply forward and murmured as if she couldn't help it, "Lieber Serge!"

Katchelsky appeared walking rapidly on the apron of the stage. The applause hastened him to his stand. He bowed his head, which looked Roman and noble above his high collar and his squared shoulders. At this distance, he was a strange new version of the man I had sat with in the afternoon. Very quickly, he hushed the audience, and took the orchestra alive into stillness. He was starting the concert with the Istar Variations of D'Indy. Next would come a

Mozart string suite, and a short symphony by Miaskovsky, followed by the intermission. After that came my symphony. He lowered his arm. The orchestra sounded.

In the intermission we went out to smoke, and when we returned to our seats, we were all ready for my work. And now there was a clean impersonality about all of that concert to me, and I felt quite unrelated to the various bits of publicity, Sunday articles, etc., that had been discreetly appearing. As I listened, I watched the audience now and then, and felt suddenly grateful that they should lend their ears to the voice of a stranger. The orchestra dwelled superbly on my work, now coming back to me with the voices I had given it but never heard before. Katchelsky sustained the silence between the movements, and when he was done, he slowly let his arms down after the long hymn for strings that closes the work, and bowed his head, as if waiting to see what would opinion be. They began to clap, and he walked off the stage quickly, acknowledging nothing. The applause surged up as he vanished, and he came back at once, and before he bowed, he turned to the box where we sat, and raised his am, quivering his fingers.

"He wants you to stand, you fool," squawked Brinker into my ear, applauding wildly.

At the same moment, V. I. Volkonski appeared in the door of the box, and said, "Blease, Sergei Pavlovitch wants you to come down."

The people saw me stand and turn to go, and they saw Katchelsky gesture toward me. They smiled and busied themselves with clapping, until I came down the passageway to the stage, and was conducted by Katchelsky to the podium, where he took my hand and beamed first upon me and then upon the audience, congratulating us both. The orchestra men were applauding too, the string players tapping their bows in a little rain of dry sound upon their racks. My legs were trembling, and in my mouth there was a sandy dryness. We went off the stage, and several more times I was sent out to bow. There followed an hour of meetings backstage, in Katchelsky's dressing room, noisy with the bright impersonality of acclaim. Madame Grünstein and Brinker came back with Sally and Peter. Madame glistened and swam through a wave of blissful pleasure. I kept thinking, I have at last had my work produced by a major orchestra, and wondering why I did not feel more convinced than I did of the importance of such an event. I said to myself, while bowing and shaking hands, This is not only something to sustain; it is something to surpass. The goads of labor were already at me in what Brinker called my hour of triumph.

At last Madame Grünstein reminded Dr. Katchelsky that if he was to make the Boston train, they must go at once. "Da, d'da," he said, and came to shake hands with me wordlessly, dramatizing in perfect taste the feelings we had; he raising his brows in a sort of happy suffering, I trying to thank him in phrases that sounded old but meant something new for me. They went, wrapped in furs and circumstance, followed by Volkonski and a body servant. The place was suddenly empty. The librarians were gathering the parts off the racks on the stage, and the great concert lights were off; only a single clear work light showed above the empty stage.

"We must have a party," said Sally. "Just the three of us."

"We shall have a bohemian party," said Peter. "Ach, to be young and famous! —What is the rest?"

"And in love," said Sally. "Never forget that, for vie de Bohème."

To be bohemian consisted in doing something faintly foolish; we therefore took a taxi and crossed to Hoboken on a ferryboat that fanned sedately across the dark current like a peacock whose opened tail drifts sideways in the wind. In Hoboken we entered a saloon much patronized by genuine thugs and newspaper reporters. Peter had been there once with Jerry King.

It stood in a side street in a sinister darkness marked by the faint occasional bloom of weak street lamp on tarnished red brick.

"We shall all be set upon," said Peter, "and murdered, robbed and given to the mother river. Two faultlessly garbed men and one fashionably gowned young woman will disappear because they loved Bohemia and knew it didn't exist. What?"

In the saloon there was a sour murky atmosphere, compounded of fumes and smoke-skeined lights. A nostalgia which was genuine on the part of the proprietor had kept the place unchanged since 1909, and the result was that its appearance was liable now to be called fearfully clever . . . the long mahogany bar, the etched mirrors, the high ceiling plastered with photographs of celebrities and the round tables with single brass supports.

"I cried and cried," said Sally. "When you were standing down there in all that rumpus. I felt so proud! Look here, Peter Fremont, we'd better make the most of this."

"Count on me. —Make the most of what?"

"Of this party right now. We won't have Edmund much longer. He's off, now. We won't have him much longer."

"Nothing is changed."

"You don't appreciate what it is, Edmund. You're really either terribly conceited or very simple."

"He is both," said Peter. He lifted his glass of whiskey. "To the critics!"

We bought some early papers when we got back to Manhattan. Standing together under a lamppost on lower Fifth Avenue, we read what they had to say. Their intentions were for the most part friendly. As for the music, they might not have heard it at all.

1933

A Distant Trumpet

THE ESCAPE OF OLIN RAINEY

[In 188–, a platoon of United States Cavalry commanded by Lieutenant Matthew Hazard is moving across the southern Arizona desert in pursuit of an Apache war party.]

Under his duty as trumpeter, to whom the commander in the field would give commands to be relayed by bugle, Private Rainey rode at the head of the column with the lieutenant. There were long hours of riding when watching the distance the leaders of the column were able also to converse. Trumpeter Rainey was talkative. Matthew listened to him and regarded him now and then sidewise. Rainey was artless. Anything that had ever happened to him was fit matter to tell about. Matthew put down smiles now and then, and now and then he was moved by the vividness of a place or an event which Rainey evoked with unconscious style. A commander never knew, thought Matthew, what went into the making of his men. Every one of them was different in his way from the others, and yet in their official and natural similarities of body and endowment, they were to be counted as exactly alike, for military purposes. It was a rare man who gave himself up so openly out of his past as the trumpeter. He was young, only nineteen. He would no doubt discover reticence as he grew older.

This man; those men; the lieutenant was responsible for them; they were responsible to him, and to each other; community held them. If it made them strong together, it made Matthew stronger than all—or so he prayed in feeling beyond words. Private Rainey's summoning up of the days when he "was young," as he put it, gave Matthew a close sense of identity with his troopers.

The trumpeter was not tall, but he was stoutly made. He gave a generally blunt effect. He often wore a scowl which looked to Matthew like an effort to focus himself—to give detail to his blurred face, with its freckles, and sharpness to his mind, with its youthful vapors. Otherwise he seemed like a boy much younger, afraid for the sake of manliness to seem too good-natured. Matthew had never heard the bugle played so truly as Rainey played it. The same true feeling came free as Rainey talked to his commander.

Olin Rainey's mother, Cleora, said to him one Saturday afternoon when he was bothering her in the kitchen, back home in Galena, Illinois, where he was born,

"Olin Rainey, you'll have me taking a lank fit with all your askings for your doings. Sometimes I wish you'd do instead of ask. No I don't," she added at once. "All right, I'll see what your father says about it."

"Don't ask him!" said Olin. At fifteen he was coming into a blunt-nosed power that made him try everything to have his way. "Don't tell my dad," he insisted.

"Your dad is my husband. I've got to."

"No, you don't. You didn't tell him when you let Bethesda go to the magic-lantern show."

"He wasn't fit to tell, that's all why."

"Maybe he won't be fit to tell about me going to Cedar Rapids, then."

Cleora said, "You should be a lawyer."

"No, Mordell's more likely for lawyer."

"All right," she said, "I won't tell your father. Go along. Come here." She hugged him. "Now go along or I'll think of what you could do for me that'd keep you here, so go on."

She thought he didn't hear her, but he did, when she added under her breath, "And don't come back, ever, my honey, but go on to better people and places and chances for yourself."

He had the permission he needed. It was permission to take the first trip of his life—to go, tomorrow, Sunday, with some slightly older friends of his in a buggy to attend an outing in Cedar Rapids, Iowa. They would leave Galena, Illinois, early in the morning. It was a fine prospect. Olin knew of only one place where he could go to think about it in peace.

His haven was a little open room of willows facing the Mississippi River, which ran by Galena. He spent all possible time there on the bank of the river under the bluff on which the town of Galena rested. He often went alone, though the river was the playground of most other boys he knew.

Galena was a river port where the old side-wheel steamer *Menominee* called. Olin would watch her, and imagine going away on her someday, perhaps next week, maybe next year, to steam downstream (never upstream—why was that?) to another world where nobody knew him. He did not know what he longed to find, but he knew well enough what he wanted to get away from.

His father, Ruben Rainey, worked hard in the lead mines at Galena for little pay to support his large family. They lived in a narrow red brick house on one of the streets high above the center of town. There was not room enough for everybody in comfort; the family had to double up in beds, share every corner, and (so it seemed) apologize for their individual existences to maintain any sort of order in their horizonless world. When he looked ahead, Olin could only see himself coming home at night in his turn from the lead mines, with his face gray and his hands dark with the rubbed-in grease of the velvety mineral which was taken out of the earth in such great quantities and yet earned so little in wages.

He would like to get away from pretending that his father was not a drunkard and a braggart who refought his days in the Civil War every other night, sitting around in Ferguson's store. If he couldn't help his dad, and he didn't know how he could, Olin was ready to get gone.

He would like to get away from sleeping with his brother Mordell, who was a year younger than he and skinnier, and more full of words. Like him, Mordell also wanted to be alone sometimes, but alone in a different way. If Mordell had a book—any old book, it seemed—he could be alone in the middle of everything. Mordell never minded to have the other children around—Jane Mary, next youngest; then Bethesda; then Martha Mary; and then Benjamin, the baby. Knowing all these people better than he did anyone else in the world, Olin still thought they were practically strangers.

He would like to get away from having to come home afternoons wondering "how things were," and then having to see that look on his mother's face sometimes, when she would go white and all but fall. He and Mordell would sometimes manage to catch her.

Once she fainted *sitting down* and that was the worst of all. Dr. Jimson said he didn't know what caused it—she was just "subject" to it. Relieved to be left with only a familiar worry, they thanked him for not finding anything terrible. The doctor surely knew. He had a roomful of books and was always buying more.

Finally, Olin wanted to get away from being Olin Rainey as he knew him, so he could be Olin Rainey as he wanted to be. He could not say just what this was to be, but his dream did not seem entirely hopeless. Somebody else had once lived in Galena and had gone away, and Olin often dawdled past the house of this man, which was two streets lower toward the town than the Rainey house. The man was Ulysses Grant, who in Olin's boyhood was President of the United States. President Grant's house was not much different from Olin's. Years ago it was part of the town lore that Ulysses Grant, as a clerk in his brother's harness store in Galena, would never amount to much, and the fact that he'd proved everyone wrong didn't seem to make them any the less pleased with themselves. If they ever thought of saying the same thing about Olin Rainey, the miner's son, perhaps they'd be wrong there, too.

Everything about going away kept Olin interested. He liked to go to the levee to watch the old *Menominee* come in and tie up, and unload, and load, and then cast off. Cautiously she'd backwater with one big paddle wheel while the other went slow-speed ahead. He cocked his head to hear the bell signals somewhere deep inside her. The dark water by the steamer dock was churned up white. Red brick buildings in the reflection shattered and broke. Birds flipped up from treetops back of the shore.

The *Menominee* let go with her whistle and began to pick up speed, letting the water come back to black glassy stillness. Her twin stacks side by side rose high in the air and ended in iron crowns blackened by smoke. Her windows looked black except where the fancy curtains showed, looped apart. Her deck was only a little way above water. People on deck walked close to the water. If only he were on board, Olin would lean over all day long and watch the water go by under him as he went away. Sometimes he would go to his willow brake to watch the *Menominee* as she trundled herself downstream like a wide duck on the sailing current. He saw the steamer safely receding into the engulfing light until she vanished. He always went there to watch her away as she took some part of him along.

At other times he kept returning to his grove of river willows for another purpose, which at first he did not rightly grasp. He went to listen. He liked to sort out the river sounds. There were all kinds, once he listened for them separately.

The difference between the sound of water close in to the bank, and water far out in the stream.

The kinds of wind, high or low, in branches or in grass.

What a steamer whistle did upwind and downwind.

Best of all, the songs of birds.

Olin would listen with his cheek turned toward a bird singing somewhere, and then he would try to imitate it, whistling. Then he would wait for an answer. It was some time and many visits to the river before he got his first answer, and when it came, he fell down on the little floor of damp river grass and hugged his ribs and rolled over and back, laughing fit to be tied. When he got his breath he stood up and tried again, and again the bird answered him. From that time on, so true and pure was his whistling, he could make birds answer him whenever he wanted to. He did not say so to himself, and nobody else knew, of course, but this was music. He was trying to make music, using the only instrument and the only teachers within his reach.

But there were other tunes, and he practiced these too, and on that Saturday afternoon when he had his permission to make the excursion tomorrow, he went down the river to his place, and after a few exchanges with whatever old birds happened to be around, he set to work practicing his best pieces. He began with "The Brown Eyes Polka," and worked his way through "Tenting Tonight" and "Darling Nellie Gray" to the "Boston Waltz." It seemed possible that tomorrow, on the way, or actually at Cedar Rapids, someone might want to hear him whistle. He meant to be good and ready.

"On Sunday morning four buggy-loads left for Cedar Rapids," said Trumpeter Rainey to Lieutenant Hazard as they rode, "and I filled the last seat."

The young people were all going to attend the band festival which was staged every few years in springtime by members of the Cedar Rapids Bohemian colony. The understanding was that if Olin would help to care for the horses and make himself generally useful, he need not worry over expenses, for his friends would see that he got fed. The rest of them were paired off boy-and-girl. Olin had

never been out with the young people before. They thought it was
high time.

The trip over saw the birth of his social sense.

"Well, let's all do our part," they said to him. "Can you tell us
a story? How about a riddle. Can you sing?"

No, but he could entertain with his whistling.

"Your *what?*"

He showed them. The buggy horse pricked up his ears and so
did they. First he gave them birds. The sweetness and wit of this
made them laugh with delight. Then he tried his real tunes, and on
the inspiration of the moment, he mixed in a few bird sounds with
these, and they all said the effect was way downtown. They applauded.

"Let me show you, Lieutenant," he said to Matthew, and demonstrated how he mixed bird songs with real tunes. The horses in
the column, and the troopers, lifted their heads to listen. Just so, on
the ride over to Cedar Rapids, he had lifted the spirits of the young
people. He also released their real reason for making the trip to
Iowa. Much sparking and daring came out between the young men
and women of the party. Olin caught his first glimpse of courtship.
It made him wonder and then it made him more secret than ever
with his feelings which, under suppression, were dear and bothersome.

One of the girls took a liking to him and pretended to prefer
him to her fellow, just to bring advantageous jealousy into the air.
Olin's head swam. Shucks. He grinned. His features felt as though
they blurred together at what he felt. The others pointed to him
and laughed, but not unkindly. He gripped his hands together between his thighs. He felt far from home.

But the band festival wiped out all his other new excitements.
Several bands competed in the festival. He listened to them all. The
greatest, and the winner, was a band of silver valve cornets—the
John Huss Silver Cornet Choir. He had never imagined, much less
heard, such beautiful sounds. He followed the players around when
they were through, and finally got up enough nerve to ask one of
the younger musicians to let him see his silver cornet.

"Here, you want to hold it?"

Olin took it and pressed the sparkling valves with their inviting
action cushioned on little trapped columns of air. He held it to his
face as if to play it, and then lowered it.

"Go on, try it once," said the young Bohemian.

"I don't know how."

The player showed him how to fix his lips, inflate his cheeks, and make a tone. Olin tried it, making some cracked noises which embarrassed him. The owned nodded with encouragement and he tried and tried again, until he heard himself blow a long, pleasant, if somewhat breathy, tone.

"Good. Good," said the cornetist. "You'll catch on easy!"

The leader of the choir was nearby. He came over and smiled generously at Olin's first trial. Then, taken by what he saw in the boy's face, he asked him if he would like to learn to play the trumpet.

Olin blushed and nodded. He felt like a bump on a log.

"Here, there," said the leader, "you come over here, once," and led him to a grove of trees away from where the festival crowd were eating their picnic. Right then and there the professor gave him a lesson on the cornet, and when they were done, he said that Olin Rainey had a natural talent for music and for the cornet, and added, "When you get home, you tell your pa and ma, you tell them to get you lessons."

"Thank you."

Olin knew the thing was hopeless. Why did *anybody* have to want what they couldn't have?

When he came back to Galena from Cedar Rapids he was somebody else. His mother recognized this at once, for she had known well who he was when he went, and now he could see her wondering what kind of somebody else he was who came home from the outing she had let him have, for which she had had to pay dearly over the weekend.

Olin didn't say anything, but on Tuesday afternoon his mother came into the kitchen and saw him with her china beehive in his hands.

"Olin Rainey! Drop that, no don't drop it, give it here to me, you—oh!"

In the china beehive was the money she had saved. It was the treasure she kept against calamity. He handed it to her and she boxed his ear.

"I was not stealing it," he said. "I was just counting it."

Now over her fright, she saw he told the truth.

"What for?" she asked.

"To see if there was enough for us to get me what I saw down in Mr. Ferguson's store window."

"And just what is that?"

"A secondhand valve cornet."

She folded her hands across the beehive against her bony breast and stared at him. So this was what had happened to him in Cedar Rapids. Music. And all the while she'd figured what else. She nodded and in a few words he told her what he had discovered on the outing. He knew he could speak to her without sounding like a fool, and all his longing became an open secret between them.

"How much is it?" she asked.

"Nine dollars and four bits."

She did not have that much money. It may as well have been thirty-five dollars so far as the beehive was concerned. It angered her and she beat back at injustice.

"I'll certainly not give you any nine dollars and four bits. And what if one of us fell sick? Medicines cost money. And what if Bethesda or Benjamin or the others need clothes to keep warm? Or what if your father gets taken so he can't work for a while and then who buys what I must cook for my hungry mouths? Just so you can have a brass horn to make noises on! You may be the oldest, but that don't fit you to have everything and the rest nothing! Do you know who is always after me to buy him books? Mordell is, that's who. Did I, though I would if I rightly could? No!" She went to the closed shelves and put the beehive back where she always hid it. "I'm not going to hide it in a new place," she said, "for I trust you."

"Yes, you do, yes, and you can."

Her eyes suddenly held a sting. She winked it away.

"Maybe Ferguson don't have to ask that much for it."

"Yes. I asked him."

"He always was *near*."

Like other discussions which skirted crisis in that family, this one ended only in a gradual settling back of silence, and of old familiar troubles.

To Olin these seemed sharper and more hopeless as new discoveries came his way.

The next time a steamer arrived, it was not the old *Menominee* which, they said, was laid up for repairs downriver. It was the United States mail and passenger packet *New St. Paul*, a younger, grander ship. When she came in, Olin was at the levee, for she tied up after school.

The channel was narrow and she lay athwart it at a long angle. Her bow touched the shore, and dockhands first unloaded her from the bow and then took new cargo up along inclined planks. From the side she looked like a two-story store front with wooden galleries. On top was a deckhouse and on this again was the pilothouse, which resembled a miniature bandstand. Just behind it rose her twin stacks tall and black. Her side wheels were encased in great half-drums which carried her name. Somewhere down under breathed her engines, asleep and softly hissing out steam. Olin tilted his head. There was another sound.

He came closer. What would they do to him if he ran up the planks? Perhaps he could find a bundle of some sort to carry which would justify his going aboard. For a moment he hesitated to take the risk; but what he heard pulled at him, and then, scowling forcefully and striding like a man, he simply walked straight across the levee, fell in between two work parties, and marched right up to the foredeck of the *New St. Paul*. Once there, he continued the march until he was inside the main saloon cabin, where he found the source of the sound that called him.

It was the sound of a square pianoforte. Framed by yellow velvet draperies looped with gold ropes and tassels, the piano occupied the center of a shallow little stage at one end of the magnificent steamboat room. An old man who looked like Andrew Jackson in the history book was making long fancy glides on the keys. When he reached the top he would linger and tremble his fingers until Olin was dazzled by the brilliant blur of sound. Then he would swoop downward to the thunder of the other end, and scowl, and make rumbles, and grind his teeth, sinking his narrow, bony, loose-skinned chin inside his stand-up collar. Knowing someone was listening, he played all the grander and harder. Even if he knew it was only a boy, he had to show what he could do, and at one point he rose off his cut-velvet piano stool and flipped out his coattail as if it were part of the music and came down again on the stool and suddenly went limp. He rolled his eyes to heaven and then shut them and made a pursed smile and his fingers played like gentle rain on the keys, and he seemed to show that he could be a poet of all moods. Then suddenly he changed, stopped playing, woke up, and asked Olin, "Well, what can *you* do, now?"

"No, I can't do anything. Except listen. It surely was mighty fine."

The artist shook his head and showed his long, yellow, horse teeth in a sad smile.

"Oh, it was, once upon a time. It was, for certain. These hands have played before crowned heads and they have won gold medals and scrolls at many an international exposition of science, art, and industry. But what are they doing now? Playing storm effects and moonlight mush for passengers who hardly listen on a moth-eaten old Miz'sippi steamboat."

"I don't think she's moth-eaten. I wish I was on her."

"Could you earn your way?"

"I don't know doing what."

"I lost my orchestra at Natchez last month, by which I mean my horn player. Can you play a cornet?"

Olin's heart took a jump. "No, but I surely wish I could learn."

"I can teach you, if you have a cornet."

Olin felt like crying for the first time in many years. "I don't have one. I know where I can get one, but it costs too much."

"What makes you think you could play it, anyway?"

"The bandmaster at Cedar Rapids told me I could learn."

"Well, he probably knows. Can you do anything else with music?"

"Well, it isn't music, just like that, but I can whistle."

"Then whistle."

The pianist turned to his keys and began to make up music that called for birds in the trees. Olin, at first hesitantly, then more confidently, began to do his birds. In a very short while the two performers were one in creating a kind of music that went right along.

"Try this!" cried the pianist without pausing, but switching to a real tune which Olin knew—the "Boston Waltz." Olin whistled the melody, but he kept his birds in too, and the result moved the old man to stand up and clap his hands once or twice.

"You're an entertainer!" he sang out. "What's your name? I am Professor McKlarney. Whistling won't do forever, but if you can learn to do as much on the trumpet, you'll never starve!"

"Olin Moresby Rainey. I can learn it."

"Oh, my gracious, how I need a trumpeter! That's all they'll listen to when they get to really having a good time on board. —Do you drink?"

Olin was both complimented and shocked at this. "No, sir."

"Well, that's a relief. I lost my last one through drink. But what'm I saying. I can't take you. Oh, you could come along and whistle, but that would do only till you learned the cornet. And you haven't a horn and neither have I, nor do you play."

Professor McKlarney knew too much of old disappointments to spend much time on new ones. He shrugged his bony shoulders, swept his long gray hair out of his collar, and sat down as if to resume his study of music.

"If you ever get a horn, speak to me again," he said, and began to exercise his hands in octave scales.

There was a short, shaking blast from the steam whistle of the *New St. Paul.* The professor angled his head at Olin to tell him to get off—they were about to sail. Olin left him, taking along the remarkable knowledge that he was—according to a professional—an entertainer. With him, too, went the sorrowful certainty that nothing could be done about it.

That night at home they all held their breath.

It was past nine and the father had not yet come home. They all knew, even little Benjamin, that when he came, matters would be much worse even than this stretched feeling in the stomach, which everybody got by looking at the mother. Her face was white and when she smiled to ease their fears they could have sobbed dryly.

Olin and Mordell stayed close to Cleora and moved still closer when they heard footsteps on the porch.

They were firm steps, slow, heavy, and important. Ruben Rainey when at his worst acted deliberately. His rages built themselves up out of the depths of his wounded silence. For a long time he would not say a word, but only hang his head forward and stare at them all in turn. His silent accusations were borne along his hot, red-rimmed gaze which looked as if it must hurt him as it left his eyes. Though he was powerfully built, his menace was something beyond body.

He came in this night and spoke to nobody but went and sat at the kitchen table.

"Would you have your supper now?" asked Cleora.

He shagged his great head about to see her and made no reply. His head swayed forward and back slowly, like a heavy weight delicately balanced. Cleora motioned to her sons to go to bed. The younger children were already upstairs, but wide awake, listening for the fury which sooner or later must explode.

"Not him. Him," said Ruben, indicating that Mordell was to leave, but Olin was to stay.

Cleora nodded and Mordell departed, walking backward until he was in the dark of the narrow steep hall. His stomach tasted in his throat. If his father struck his mother tonight, just this once more, he would come flying down the stairs and do his best to kill his father. With this resolve it was possible for him to leave as ordered.

In the kitchen nothing moved but the brass pendulum of the walnut clock on the shelf above the sink.

Olin knew that his father had been aggrieved for days because he had gone to Cedar Rapids. He knew that his mother was still in danger for having let him go. His guilt was unbearable and it moved him to speak.

"It wasn't her fault," he said. "I begged her to let me go and not tell you because I thought you would say no if we asked you."

A look of weary sweetness came over Ruben's work-grimed face and lingered there briefly. At last the excuse had come to him to break the hard thick shell of his own trouble.

"Come here," he said to Olin, almost lightly.

Olin glanced apprehensively at his mother as if to ask whether to obey.

"Don't look at her," said Ruben thickly but in a gentle voice. "Just come here to your father."

Olin went to him. As he went, he watched his father's heavy arm draw back to gather the distance from which it would strike him when he was near enough.

When the arm was as far back as it wanted to be, Ruben's face went broken and wild. His body tensed stiff as iron, braced to destroy. His voice let go with a shout. He smashed Olin to the floor with one strike and picked him up to do it again. His lungs were bellows blasting out the sounds of his humiliation and his hatred before the whole world.

Olin bled. He put his young arms across his head, his face, but still he bled. The house shook the small hearts upstairs.

"Not good enough, are we," bellowed Ruben and struck again.

"Get away whenever you can, hey," and struck. "Go crawling around asking the price of a valve cornet, will you," and slapped his son with an open hand like a hickory board, "when nobody here has enough to eat, hey?"

Olin on the floor assumed protectively the shape of an unborn child. His mother came to cover him.

"You," cried her husband, and sent her across the room with a crashing swing. The air was rank with the breath of the corn whiskey which had brought him home as temporary master of his world.

In the door appeared Mordell. He saw Cleora pulling herself upward by holding to a chair.

"Did he strike you?" he yelled, "for if he did, I will kill him!"

Ruben Rainey heaved himself aback and stared at his second son. Anger went soft and melted into grief. He sank against the table, covered his face, and wept aloud in a hooting voice for the son who would kill his father. Upstairs the little ones clutched each other and hugged with relief. Like Olin, they knew that the nature of the terror below had changed, and that presently peace would descend, after the father had been hauled to his bed as if never to awaken again.

When Ruben was safely lost in sleep, Cleora came to the boys' bed and, as she expected, found Olin awake. She took him quietly away, in the dark, to the kitchen, and lighting no lamp, she bathed his cuts and bruises with cool water, as if to bathe his beaten heart. As she worked, she held a whispered conversation with him.

"We've got to fix it for you to go," she breathed. "I shouldn't have waited for tonight to know it."

"Go where?"

"Anywhere. Can't you think of where to go? I know your father. He's got his mind set now about you. It'll only get worse the longer you stay."

"Why does he hate me."

"He don't hate you sober, son. He just can't stand to know he can't be what he would be to you if he could. He sees you're a man, just about, and it makes him feel less a man. I don't know. I don't know."

She spoke in mysteries, but never had she failed him in her good sense, and he tried to know what she meant.

"Where can you go, Olin?"

"I could have gone today, only I couldn't."

"Where!"

He told her about Professor McKlarney, the want of a valve cornet, and the United States mail and passenger packet *New St. Paul.*

"He said I would never starve if I could learn the horn."

"Do you figure he meant it, or was he just talking for talking?"

"I figure he meant it."

She gasped between a laugh and a catch of her breath and put her cheek to his brow for a moment of hidden leave-taking. Then she got them both to their feet and said, "Go to bed and sleep, my honey. It may take a bit to fix everything, but whatever it'll have to happen afterward, it'll be worth it."

He was so drowsy with assuagement and love that he hardly heard her, and only remembered her words when the *New St. Paul* was reported to be scheduled for Galena again on the following Wednesday.

On that morning, Cleora said to Olin as he was about to leave for school with his lunch in a newspaper packet, "Come home at noon."

He held up his sandwich and gave her his best look of comical puzzlement.

"I know," she said, "you've got your lunch. But you come on home. Alone."

When he came at noon the house had another of its particular stillnesses. This one was created by young children who were told to stay upstairs in the bedroom with the door shut no matter what.

As he came to the house, he heard her start to make busy noises, slamming this and shoving that, like a woman working so hard she don't know which way to turn. So it was that she managed to look cross when he stepped in, and the slapped-at tears on her face might have been beads of honest sweat. She hardly gave him a moment to turn around, but said straight off, "Now, Olin Moresby Rainey, you take this bundle." She reached it out from under the kitchen table. He took it. It was a bundle of a few of his clothes, tied with twine. It was heavy because of something inside it. She went on, "The *New St. Paul* is to be here this afternoon, for I asked and they told me down to the levee. Now you go and keep yourself somewheres out of sight till she comes in. Do you know a place to go?"

"Yes. I have a place by the river."

"Well, wait there till she's ready to go off again, and then you run lickety-split and you climb on, and go find your piano professor, and you just tell him yes: there you are: you have come to work for him. You know what's inside that bundle. First I went to the beehive and took some out. Don't look so, there's some left. Then I got Mr. Ferguson to give the cornet to me to pay the rest on it so much a week and when you're rich and famous you can send me some money to make it up. You stay out of sight, now, hear? And if the *New St. Paul* keeps coming back to Galena, you just lie low till she's gone again. Not that she will, once the *Menominee* is back on the run."

"Mother."

"I know. I know. Now don't you go to saying it. It's hard enough as 'tis." She opened a cupboard. "Now here's some extra sandwiches to tide you over. And here"—she reached in her apron—"is what can be spared out of the beehive to start you off in the world."

He reached for her fisted money and then broke against her in a wild hug. At the moment when she gave him the freedom he longed for, he would not go. She kissed him hard and set him away.

"Go on, my honey. Don't you let me see you till you can come back stronger than all of us."

She took him to the door and put him out. He went down the hill and turned to see if she was watching. She was not. He knew she could not have borne to watch him go. . . .

Trumpeter Rainey fell silent, thinking about something he heard a long time afterward from his family.

"After I left home that day," he said to Matthew, "she waited till she heard the whistle blow on the *New St. Paul* and she knew I was safely gone. Then she fetched out her china beehive again, and took out what was left. It was two dollars. Then she marched down to Dr. Jimson's office, and she said, no, she told him, it's not for me, I'm not sick, she said, but I want you take this two dollars here, she said, and next time you send for books, Doctor, send for a two-dollar book for my son Mordell Rainey, to read and keep, and help *him* on *his* way for the way *he* wants to be, she said, when the time comes. —*That's* the kind of woman she was, sir."

Matthew nodded seriously. It was enough of a tribute for

Trumpeter Rainey, who knew that his lieutenant was moved to hear of a mother like that, and maybe, even, was thinking about his own.

"I told everyone I was twenty," said Rainey, "and nobody believed it, but I felt like it soon enough."

"How did you ever get into the U.S. cavalry from a Mississippi steamer?" asked Matthew.

The trumpeter sighed strenuously.

"Just the way life does you," he said, with every accent of a personally earned philosophy. "I made good money for several years, and then Professor McKlarney took sick and died, and I lost everything I had, waiting to get a new job. I was every kind of a danged fool, sir; I had too much freedom all of a sudden. Gambling and likker and women—one woman specially. Anyhow, I knew it was time for me to straighten up. I enlisted. They sent me to Fort Sheridan, someone heard me blow a cornet, and before I knew it, I was an army trumpeter. And here I am."

1960

The Richard Novels

Things As They Are

M U Z Z A

How do we manage to love at all when there is so much hatred masquerading in love's name? I saw, if I did not understand, how this could be when I lost forever a friend whom I tried to rescue from peril. But a larger peril claimed him.

His name was John Burley. Nobody ever loved him enough to give him a natural nickname. Instead, he was the subject of a mocking refrain.

"John, John, the dog-faced one," sang the other boys our age when they saw John and me playing together in our neighborhood. He was my next-door neighbor, and I didn't know there was anything really different about him until I saw him abused by other children.

Before we were old enough to go to school we owned the whole world all day long except for naptime after lunch. We played in the open grassy yards behind and between our houses, and when John was busy and dreaming with play, he was a good friend to have, and never made trouble. But when people noticed him, he became someone else, and now I know that his parents, and mine, too, out of sympathy, wondered and wondered how things would be for him when the time came for him to go off to school like any other boy and make a place for himself among small strangers who might find his oddness a source of fun and power for themselves.

In the last summer before schooltime, 1909, everyone heard the cry of "John, John, the dog-faced one," and even I, his friend, saw him newly. I would look at him with a blank face, until he would notice this, and then he would say crossly, with one of his impulsive, self-clutching movements, "What's the matter, Richard, what's the matter, why are you looking crazy?"

"I'm not looking crazy. You are the one that's crazy."

For children pointed at him and sang, "Crazy, lazy, John's a daisy," and ran away.

Under their abuse, and my increasing wonderment, John showed a kind of daft good manners which should have induced pity and grace in his tormentors, but did not. He would pretend to be intensely preoccupied by delights and secrets from which the rest of us were excluded. He would count his fingers, nodding at the wrong total, and then put his thumbs against his thick lips and buzz against them with his furry voice, and look up at the sky, smacking his tongue, while other boys hooted and danced at him.

They were pitiably accurate when they called him the dog-faced one. He did look more like a dog than a boy. His pale hair was shaggy and could not be combed. His forehead was low, with a bony scowl that could not be changed. His nose was blunt, with its nostrils showing frontward. Hardly contained by his thick, shapeless lips, his teeth were long, white, and jumbled together. Of stocky build, he seemed always to be wearing a clever made-up costume to put on a monkey or a dog, instead of clothes like anybody else's. His parents bought him the best things to wear, but in a few minutes they were either torn or rubbed with dirt or scattered about somewhere.

"The poor dears," I heard my mother murmur over the Burley family.

"Yes," said my father, not thinking I might hear beyond what they were saying, "we are lucky. I can imagine no greater cross to bear."

"How do you suppose—" began my mother, but suddenly feeling my intent stare, he interrupted, with a glance my way, saying, "Nobody ever knows how these cases happen. Watching them grow must be the hardest part."

What he meant was that it was sorrowful to see an abnormal child grow physically older but no older mentally.

* * *

But Mr. and Mrs. Burley—Gail and Howard, as my parents called them—refused to admit to anyone else that their son John was in any way different from other boys. As the summer was spent, and the time to start school for the first time came around, their problem grew deeply troubling. Their friends wished they could help with advice, mostly in terms of advising that John be spared the ordeal of entering the rigid convention of a school where he would immediately be seen by all as a changeling, like some poor swineherd in a fairy story who once may have been a prince but who would never be released from his spell.

The school—a private school run by an order of Catholic ladies founded in France—stood a few blocks away from our street. The principal, who, like each of her sisters wore a white shirtwaist with a high collar and starched cuffs and a long dark blue skirt, requested particularly that new pupils should come the first day without their parents. Everyone would be well-looked-after. The pupils would be put to tasks which would drive diffidence and homesickness out the window. My mother said to me, as she made me lift my chin so that she could tie my windsor tie properly over the stiff slopes of my Buster Brown collar, while I looked into her deep, clear, blue eyes, and wondered how to say that I would not go to school that day or any other, "Richard, John's mother thinks it would be so nice if you and he walked to school together."

"I don't want to."

I did not mean that I did not want to walk with John, I meant that I did not want to go to school.

"That's not very kind. He's your friend."

"I know it."

"I have told his mother you would go with him."

Childhood was a prison whose bars were decisions made by others. Numbed into submission, I took my mother's goodbye kiss staring at nothing, eaten within by fears of the unknown which awaited us all that day.

"Now skip," said my mother, winking both her eyes rapidly, to disguise the start of tears at losing me to another stage of life. She wore a small gold fleur-de-lis pin on her breast from which depended a tiny enamelled watch. I gazed at this and nodded solemnly but did not move. With wonderful executive tact she felt that I was about to make a fatally rebellious declaration, and so she touched the watch, turning its face around, and said, as though I must be concerned only with promptness, "Yes, yes, Richard, you are right, we must think of the time, you mustn't be late your first day."

I was propelled then to the Burleys' house next door, where John and his mother were waiting for me in their front hall, which was always filled with magic light from the cut-glass panes in bright colors flanking their front door.

Mrs. Burley held me by the shoulders for a moment, trying to tell me something without saying it.

"Richard," she said, and then paused.

She looked deep into my eyes until I dropped my gaze. I looked at the rest of her face, and then at her bosom, wondering what was down there in that shadow where two rounded places of flesh rolled frankly together. Something about her personality led people to use her full name when they referred to her even idly—"Gail Burley"—and even I felt power within her.

Her husband had nothing like her strength. He was a small gray man with thin hair combed flat across his almost bald skull. The way his pince-nez pulled at the skin between his eyes gave him a look of permanent headache. Always hurried and impatient, he seemed to have no notice for children like me, or his own son, and all I ever heard about him was that he "gave Gail Burley anything she asked for," and "worked his fingers to the bone" doing so, as president of a marine engine company with a factory on the lake front of our city of Dorchester in Upstate New York.

Gail Burley—and I cannot say how much of her attitude rose from her sense of disaster in the kind of child she had borne— seemed to exist in a state of general exasperation. A reddish blonde, with skin so pale that it glowed like pearl, she was referred to as a great beauty. Across the bridge of her nose and about her eyelids and just under her eyes there were scatterings of little gold freckles which oddly yet powerfully reinforced her air of being irked by everything.

She often exhaled slowly and with compression, and said "Gosh," a slang word which was just coming in in her circle, which she pronounced "Garsh." Depending on her mood, she could make it into the expression of ultimate disgust or mild amusement. The white skin under her eyes went whiter when she was cross or angry, and then a dry hot light came into her hazel eyes. She seemed a large woman to me, but I don't suppose she was—merely slow, challenging, and annoyed in the way she moved, with a flowing governed grace which was like a comment on all that was intolerable. At any moment she would exhale in audible distaste for the circumstances of her world. Compressing her lips, which she never rouged, she would ray her pale glance upward, across, aside, to express her search for the smallest mitigation, the simplest endurable fact or object, of life. The result of these airs and tones of her habit was that in those rare moments when she was pleased, her expression of happiness came through like one of pain.

"Richard," she said, holding me by the shoulders, and looking into my face to discover what her son John was about to confront in the world of small school children.

"Yes, Mrs. Burley."

She looked at John, who was waiting to go.

He had his red-and-black plaid japanned collapsible tin lunch box all nicely secured with a web strap and he made his buzzing noise of pleasure at the idea of doing something so new as going to school. Because he showed no apprehension over what would seem like an ordeal to another boy, she let forth one of her breaths of disgust. She had dressed him in a starched collar like mine which extended over the smart lapels of his beautiful blue suit, with its Norfolk jacket. His socks were well pulled up and his shoes were shined. She looked at me again, trying to say what she could not. Her white face with its flecks of fixed displeasure slowly took on a pleading smile. She squeezed my shoulders a little, hoping I would understand, even at my age, how John would need someone to look out for him, protect him, suffer him, since he was a child of such condition as she could not bring herself to admit. Her plea was resolved into a miniature of the principle of bribery by which her life was governed—even, I now think, to the terms on which Howard Burley obtained even her smallest favors.

"Richard," she said, "when you and John come home after school"—and she pressed those words to show that I must bring him home— "I will have a nice surprise waiting for you both."

John became agitated at this, jumping about, and demanding, "What is it, Muzza, what is it?"

She gave one of her breaths. "John, John, be quiet. Garsh. I can't even say anything without getting you all excited."

For my benefit she smiled, but the gold flecks under her eyes showed as angry dark spots, and the restrained power of her dislike of John was so great that he was cowed. He put his hands to his groin to comfort himself, and said, using his word for what he always found there, "Peanut."

At this his mother became openly furious at him. "John! Stop that! How many times have I told you that isn't nice. Richard doesn't do it. Dr. Grauer has told you what will happen if you keep doing it. Stop it!"

She bent over to slap at his hands and he lunged back. Losing his balance, he fell, and I heard his head go crack on the hardwood floor of the hall where the morning light made pools of jewel colors through the glass panels. He began to cry in a long, burry, high wail. His mother picked him up and he hung like a rag doll in her outraged grasp. The day was already in ruins, and he had not even gone off to school. The scene was one of hundreds like it which made up the life of that mother and that son. I was swept by shame at seeing it.

"Now stop that ridiculous caterwauling," she said. "Richard is waiting to take you to school. Do you want him to think you are a crybaby?"

John occasionally made startling remarks, which brought a leap of hope that his understanding might not be so deficient as everyone believed.

"I *am* a crybaby," he said, burying his misery-mottled face in the crook of his arm.

A sudden lift of pity in his mother made her kneel down and gently enfold him in her arms. With her eyes shut, she gave her love to the imaginary son, handsome and healthy, whom she longed for, even as she held the real John. It was enough to console him. He flung his arms around her and hugged her like a bear cub, all fur and clumsiness and creature-longing.

"Muzza, Muzza," he said against her cheek.

She set him off.

"*Now* can you go to school?" she asked in a playfully reasonable voice.

John's states of feeling were swift in their changes. He began to smack his lips, softly indicating that he was in a state of pleasure.

"Then go along, both of you," said his mother.

She saw us out the door and down the walk. Curiously enough, the self-sorrowing lump in my throat went away as I watched the scene between John and his mother. Things seemed so much worse with the Burleys than with me and my start in school.

* * *

I led John off at a smart pace, running sometimes, and some-times walking importantly with short busy steps. We paused only once, and that was to look in the window at a little candy and news shop a block from the school, where with warm, damp pennies it was possible to buy sticky rolls of chocolate candy, or—even better—stamp-sized films which when exposed to light darkened in shades of red to reveal such subjects as the battleship *New York,* or the Flatiron Building, or the Washington Monument.

John always had more money than I.

"Let's get some," he proposed.

"No. After school," I replied. "We will be late if we stop and we will catch the dickens."

"Catch the dickens," he said, and began to run away ahead of me. I overtook him and we entered the main door of the school—it was a red brick building with a portico of white pillars veiled in vines—and once in the dark corridors with their wood-ribbed walls, we seemed to lose ourselves, to become small pieces of drifting ma-terial that were carried along to our classrooms by a tide of children. Boys went separate from girls. John and I were finally directed to a room containing twenty boys in the first grade, presided over by Miss Mendtzy.

She met us at the door and, without speaking but sustaining a kindly smile, sent us with a strong thin finger on our shoulders along the aisles where we would find our desks. We gave her wary glances to see what she was like. She had a narrow little face above a bird's body. Her hair was like short gray feathers. Before her large, steady, pale eyes she wore a pair of nose glasses that trembled in response to her quivering nerves and sent a rippling line of light along the gold chain that attached her glasses to a small gold spring spool pinned to her shirtwaist.

John and I were at desks side by side. When all the room was filled, Miss Mendtzy closed the door, and our hearts sank. There we were, in jail. She moved trimly to her platform. Her slim feet in black, high-buttoned shoes looked like feet in a newspaper advertise-ment, because she stood them at such polite angles to each other. On her desk she had placed a vase of flowers with a great silk bow to give a festive air to the opening day. Touching the blossoms with a flourish of artistic delicacy, she launched into a pleasant little speech. Everyone sat quietly out of strangeness while she said, "Now I want all of my new first-graders to come up here one by one, beginning with this aisle on my left"—she showed where in a gesture of blood-less grace—"and shake hands with me, and tell me their names, for we are going to be working together for months and years, as I will be your homeroom teacher until the sixth grade. Think of it! Quite like a family! And so we are going to become great friends, and we must know each other well. Miss Mendtzy is ready to love each and every one of you, and she hopes each and every one of you will learn to love her. We are going to get along splendidly together, if every-body is polite, and works hard, and remembers that he is not the only boy in this world, or in this school, or in this room, but that he is a boy among other boys, to whom he must show respect, even while playing. Now, shall we start here, with this boy, at the front of the first row?"

One by one we went to her platform, stepped up on it, shook hands, spoke our names, received a bright, lens-quivered smile and a deep look into our eyes, and then were sent on across her little stage and down the other side and back to our seats. Some among us swaggered, others went rapidly and shyly, hiding from such a public world, one or two winked on the final trip up the aisles, and all felt some thumping at the heart of dread followed by pride as we went and returned.

There was no incident until John's turn came. When it did, he would not rise and go forward.

"Come?" said Miss Mendtzy, beckoning over her desk and twin-kling with her chained glasses. "We are waiting for the next boy?"

I leaned over to John and whispered, "It's your turn, John. Go on. Go on."

He went lower in his seat and began to buzz his lips against his thumbs, terrified of rising before a crowd of small strangers, who were now beginning to nudge each other and whisper excitedly at the diversion. I heard someone whisper "John, John, the dog-faced one," and I could not tell whether John heard it. But, a professional, Miss Mendtzy heard it. She smartly whacked her ruler on the flat of her desk. It was like a nice pistol shot. Silence fell.

She put on her face a look which we all knew well at home—that look of aloof, pained regret at unseemly behavior.

"I must say I am surprised," she said quietly and deadlily, "that some of us are not polite enough to sit silently when we see someone in a fit of shyness. Some of the finest people I know are shy at times. I have been told that our Bishop, that humble, great man, is shy himself when he has to meet people personally. Now I am going down from my platform and down the aisle and"—she glanced at her seating plan of the classroom—"I am going to bring John Burley up here myself as my guest, and help him over his shyness, and the only way to do that is by helping him to do the same things everybody else has done. So."

She went to John and took his hand and led him to the platform and stood him where each of us had stood, facing her, in profile to the rest of the room. Speaking as though he had just come there by his own will, she said, "Good morning, John. I am Miss Mendtzy. We are pleased that you are with us," first giving us a sidelong glare to command our agreement, and then like a lady holding forth her hand to John, with a slightly arched wrist and drooping fingers.

John put his hands behind him and buzzed his lips and looked out the window.

"John?"

"John, John, the dog-faced one," again said an unplaceable voice in the rear of the classroom, softly but distinctly.

"Who said that!" demanded Miss Mendtzy, going pink, and trembling until her lenses shimmered. The very first day of school, she seemed to say, and already there was an unfortunate incident. "I simply will not have bad manners in my room, and I simply will not have one of my boys treated like this. Whoever said that is to stand up and apologize instantly. I think I know who it was"— but clearly she did not—"and if he apologizes now, and promises never, never to do such a rude thing again, we shall all be friends again as we want to be. Well? I am waiting?"

The silence and the tension grew and grew.

John stood with head hanging. I saw his hands twitching behind his back. He was trying not to clasp them over himself in front.

"One more minute?" declared Miss Mendtzy, "and then I will do something you will all be very sorry for."

Silence, but for a clock ticking on the wall above her blackboard.

John could not bear it. Moving as fast as a cat, he threw himself forward to Miss Mendtzy's desk and swept her vase of flowers to the floor, where it shattered and spilled.

All the boys broke into hoots and pounded their hinged desk

tops upon their desks, making such a clamor that in a moment the door was majestically opened and the Principal, always called Madame de St. Étienne, who came from nobility in France, heavily entered the room. Even as she arrived, someone in the rear of the room, carried on by the momentum of events, called out, "Crazy, lazy, John's a daisy."

The Principal was a monument of authority. Above her heavy pink face with its ice-blue eyes rose a silvery pompadour like a wave breaking back from a headland. Her bosom was immense in her starched shirtwaist. Over it she wore a long gold chain which fell like a maiden waterfall into space below her bust and ended in a loop at her waist, where she tucked a large gold watch. Her dark skirt went straight down in front, for she had to lean continuously forward, we thought, if the vast weight and size behind her were not to topple her over backward.

She now glared at Miss Mendtzy with frigid reproach at the breach of discipline in her classroom loud enough to be heard down the hall, and then faced us all, saying in a voice like pieces of broken glass scraped together at the edges, "Children, you will rise when the Principal enters the classroom."

She clapped her hands once and we rose, scared and ashamed.

"Now, who is this?" she demanded, turning to the tableau at the teacher's platform.

"This is John Burley, Madame," replied Miss Mendtzy, and got no further, for John, seeing the open door, bolted for the hall and freedom.

Madame de St. Étienne gave another queenly, destructive look at Miss Mendtzy, and said, "Pray continue with the exercises, Miss Mendtzy."

She then left the room, moving as though on silent casters, for her skirt swept the floor all about her short, light steps, amazing in a woman so heavy and so enraged.

Burning with mortification, Miss Mendtzy began our first lesson, which was an exercise in neatness—the care of our pencil boxes and schoolbooks. There was a happy material interest in this, for the pencils were all new, and smelled of cedar, and we went in turn to sharpen them at the teacher's desk. Our erasers—promises of fore-ordained smudges of error—showed a tiny diamondlike glisten if we held them in a certain way to the light of the window. If we chewed upon them, little gritty particles deliciously repelled our teeth. Our schoolbooks cracked sweetly when we opened them, and the large, clear, black type on the pages held mystery and invitation. We became absorbed in toys which were suddenly now something more than toys, and our cheeks grew hot, and we were happy, and we forgot to want to go to the bathroom, and I was hardly aware of it when the door opened again before Madame de St. Étienne. Late, but earnestly, we scrambled to our feet, as she said, "Which is Richard—?" giving my full name.

I put my hand up.

"Pray come with me, Richard," she ordered, ignoring Miss Mendtzy entirely. "Bring your boxes and books."

A stutter of conjecture went along the aisles at this, which Madame de St. Étienne, gliding on her way to the door, suppressed by pausing and staring above the heads of everyone as though she could not believe her ears. Quiet fell, and in quiet, with my heart beating, I followed her out to the hallway. She shut the door and turned me with a finger to walk ahead of her to her office at the entrance way inside the pillared portico. I wanted to ask what I had done to be singled out for her notice, which could only, I thought, lead to punishment.

But it appeared that she had enlisted me as an assistant. In her office, John was waiting, under guard of the Principal's secretary. He was sitting on a cane chair holding a glass of water, half full.

"Finish it, John," commanded Madame.

"I don't like it," he said.

"Hot water to drink is the best thing for anyone who is upset," she answered. "It is the remedy we always give. Finish it."

Raising a humble wail, he drank the rest of the hot water, spilling much of it down on his chin, his windsor tie, his starched collar.

"You are John's friend?" she asked me.

"Yes."

"Who are his other friends?"

"I don't know."

"Has he none, then?"

"I don't think so."

John watched my face, then the Principal's, turning his head with jerky interest and rubbing his furry hair with his knuckles in pleasure at being the subject of interest.

"You brought him to school?"

"Yes."

"Yes, *Madame*."

"Yes, Madame."

"And you will take him home?"

"Yes, Madame. After school."

"I have spoken on the telephone with his mother, to arrange for him to go home. She prefers not to have him come home until the end of school after lunch. Until then, I will ask you to stay here in my office with him. You will both eat your lunches here and I will see that you are not disturbed. Tomorrow you will be able to return to your classroom."

"With John?"

"No. John will not be with us after today."

John nodded brightly at this. Evidently the Principal had given an ultimatum to Mrs. Burley over the telephone. I can imagine the terms of it—careful avoidance of the words abnormal, special case, impossible to measure up to the progress of other boys his age, and such. With arctic, polite finality, Madame de St. Étienne would have read John out of the human society where his years put him but where his retarded mind and disordered nerves, so clearly announced by his rough, doglike appearance, must exclude him. Gail Burley's despair can be felt. How could she ever again pretend even to herself that her child, if only thrown into life, would make his way like anyone else? How could she love anything in the world if she could not love the son who was mismade in her womb? What a bitter affront it was to her famous good looks of face and body, her hard brightness of mind, her firm ability to govern everything else that made up her life, if she must be responsible for such a creature as John. How to face a lifetime of exasperated pity for him? How to disguise forever the humiliation which she must feel? The daily effort of disguising it would cost her all her confident beauty in the end.

"Why don't we go home now?" I asked.

"John's mother thinks it would look better if he simply came home like the other children when school is dismissed this afternoon."

Yes, for if they saw him come earlier, people would say once again what she knew they were always saying about John. I knew well enough the kind of thing, from hearing my own father and mother talk kindly and sadly about my playmate.

Let him come home after school, like everyone else, and tomorrow, why then, tomorrow Gail Burley could simply say with a shrug and a speckled smile that she and Howard didn't think it was really just the school for John. There was something about those teachers, neither quite nuns nor quite ordinary women, which was unsettling. The Burleys would look around, and meantime, John could be tutored at home, as Gail herself had been one winter when she had gone as a little girl with her parents to White Sulphur Springs. Leaving the school could be made, with a little languid ingenuity, to seem like a repudiation by her, for reasons she would be too polite to elaborate upon for parents of other children still attending it.

The day passed slowly in the Principal's office. At eleven o'clock there was a fire drill, set off by a great alarm gong which banged slowly and loudly in the hall just above the office door. The door was kept closed upon us, but we could hear the rumble and slide of the classes as they took their appointed ways out of the building to the shaded playground outside.

"I want to go, I want to go!" cried John at the window. "Everybody is there!"

"No," said Madame de St. Étienne, turning like an engine in her swivel chair, "we will remain here. They will presently return."

John began to cry.

The Principal looked to me to manage him and calmly turned back to the work on her desk, placing a pince-nez upon the high bridge of her thin nose with a sweep of her arm which was forced to travel a grand arc to bypass her bosom.

But at last, when the clock in the office showed twenty-five minutes past two, she said, "Now, John, and now, Richard, you may take your things and go home. School is dismissed at half-past two. Perhaps it would be prudent for you to leave a little before the other boys. You will go straight home."

"Yes, Madame."

She gave us each her hand. To John she said, "May God bless you, my poor little one."

Her words and her manner sent a chill down my belly.

But in a moment we were in the open air of the autumn day, where a cold wind off the lake was spinning leaves from the trees along the street. John capered happily along and, when we reached the candy store, he remembered how we would stop there. I wondered if stopping there would violate our orders to go "straight home," but the store was on the way, and we went in.

John enjoyed shopping. He put his stubby finger with its quick-bitten nail on the glass of the candy counter, pointing to first one then another confection, and every time he made up his mind he changed it, until the proprietor, an old man with a bent back in a dirty gray cardigan, sighed and looked over his shoulder at his wife, who sat in the doorway to their back room. His glance and her return of it plainly spoke of John's idiocy.

"There!" said John finally, aiming his finger and his hunger at a candy slice of banana, cut the long way, and tasting, I knew, of cotton mixed with gun oil. The candy banana was white in the center with edges stained orange and yellow.

I moved on to the counter where you could buy the magic photographic plates which showed nothing until you exposed them to the light. I wanted to buy one but I had no money. John came beside me and said, "Richard, I'll get you one."

"Oh, no."

"Oh, yes. I'll get you two."

He put down four pennies to pay for two prints and the storekeeper gave me the box to choose my prints. On the edge of each little plate was the name of its subject. I chose the liner *Mauretania* and Buckingham Palace.

"Here," I said to John, offering him one of them. "You keep one."

He put his hands behind his back and blew his tongue at me between his thick lips.

"All right, then, thanks, we have to go home now. Come on, John," I said.

Eating his banana, John was compliant. We came out of the store and went on to the corner, where we turned into our street. Our houses were a block and a half away. We could just see them. Under the billowing trees and the cool autumn light they looked asleep. They called to me. I wanted suddenly to be home.

"Let's run, John," I said.

We began to run, but we got no further than a large hedge which ran up the driveway of the second house from the corner.

* * *

It was a great house, with a large garage in back, and a deep lawn. I knew the brothers who lived there. Their name was Grandville. They were a year or two older and very self-important because of their family automobiles, and their electric train system, which occupied the whole top floor of their house.

They now jumped out from behind the hedge. With them were three other boys. They had all just come home from school. While we had idled in the candy store, they had gone by to wait for us.

"John, John, the dog-faced one!" they called, and took John, and dragged him up the driveway toward the garage in the windy, empty neighborhood. "Crazy, lazy, John's a daisy," they chanted, and I ran along yelling, "Let us go, let us go!"

"Shut up, or we'll get you too," cried one of the brothers.

"Richie!" moaned John. "Richie!"

The terror in his blurry voice was like that in a nightmare when you must scream and cannot make a sound. His face was belly-white and his eyes were staring at me. I was his protector. I would save him.

"Richie! Richie!"

But I could do nothing against the mob of five, but only run along calling to them to "let go of us"—for I felt just as much captive as John, whom they dragged by arms and legs. He went heavy and limp. They hauled him through the chauffeur's door—a narrow one beside the big car doors, which were closed—and shut the door after us all. The center of the garage was empty, for the big Pierce-Arrow limousine was out, bearing Mrs. Grandville somewhere on a chauffeur-driven errand.

"Put him there!" yelled one of the brothers.

Four boys held John on the cement floor by the drain grille while the other brother went to the wall, uncoiled a hose, and turned the spigot. The hose leaped alive with a thrust of water.

"Now let go and get back, or you'll all get wet," called the Grandville boy. As the others scampered back he turned the powerful blow of the hose water on John. It knocked him down. He shut his eyes and turned his blind face to the roof. His shapeless mouth fell open in a silent cry. Still clutching his candy banana, he brought it to his mouth in delayed memory of what it was for, and what had been a delight was now a sorrowful and profitless hunger for comfort in misery.

"Get up, dog-face," yelled one of the boys.

Obediently John got up, keeping his eyes closed, suffering all that must come to him. The hose column toppled him over again. Striking his face, blows of water knocked his head about until it seemed it must fly apart.

"I know!" cried an excited and joyful young voice, "let's get his clo'es off!"

There was general glee at this idea. The hose was put away for the moment, and everyone seized John and tore at his clothes. He made his soundless wail with open mouth and I thought he shaped my name again.

When he was naked they ordered him to stand again, and he did so, trying to protect his modesty with his thick hands. They hit him with the hose again and buffeted him like a puppet. The hose water made him spin and slide on the oily floor. The noise was doubled by echoes from the peaked high roof of the garage.

Nobody thought of me.

I backed to the door and opened it and ran away. On the concrete driveway was a tricycle belonging to the younger Grandville. I mounted it and rode off as fast as I could. My chest was ready to break open under my hard breathing. My knees rose and fell like pistons. My face was streaming with tears of rage at John's ordeal and the disgrace of my helplessness before it. I rode to John's house and threw myself up the front steps, but before I could attack the door it was opened to me. Gail Burley was watching for us, and when she saw me alone in gasping disorder, she cried, "Why, Richard! What's the matter! Where's John!"

At first I could only point, so I took her hand and tugged at her to come with me. It was proof of the passion and power I felt at the moment that without more questioning she came. I remounted the tricycle and led her up the street to the Grandvilles'. In a little while, as I went, I was able to tell her what was happening.

When she understood, she increased her stride. She became magnificent in outrage. Her hazel eyes darkened to deep topaz and her reddish-golden hair seemed to spring forward into the wind. She was like a famous ship, dividing the elements as she went.

"Oh! Those horrid, cruel little beasts!" she exclaimed. "Oh! What I would do to them—and Richard, you are an absolute *darrling* to get away and come for me. Oh! That poor John!"

We hurried up the driveway. The game was still going on. We

could hear cries and the hiss of the hose. Gail Burley strode to the door and threw it open. She saw her son pinned against the far brick wall by the long pole of the spray. He tried to turn his face from side to side to avoid its impact. It swept down his white soft body and he continually tried to cover himself with his hands. Non-resistant, he accepted all that came to him. His eyes were still closed and his mouth was still open.

Stepping with baleful elegance across the puddles of the floor, Gail Burley threw aside the boys who were dancing at the spectacle, and came to the Grandville brother with the hose. She astounded him. In his ecstatic possession, he had heard no one arrive. She seized the hose and with a gesture commanded him to turn off the water, which he did. She dropped the hose and went to John and took him dripping and blue with cold into her arms. He fell inert against her, letting his hands dangle as she hugged him. But he made a word at last.

"Muzza," he said thickly, "Oh, Muzza, Muzza."

"John-John," she said, holding his wet head against the hollow of her lovely neck and shoulder. "It's all right. It's all right. Muzza is here. Poor John-John."

The boys were now frightened. The oldest said, "We were only trying to have some fun, Mrs. Burley."

"Go to the house," she commanded in the flattest tone, which held promises of punishment for all as soon as she could inform their parents, "and bring a big towel and a blanket. —Richard, you might throw together John's things and bring them along."

She was obeyed soberly and quickly. In a few minutes she and I were taking John home. He was huddled inside a doubled blanket. He was shivering. His teeth chattered.

"Where's my banana?" he managed to say.

"Oh, never mind," said his mother. "We can get you another banana. What were you doing with a banana anyway?"

"It was a candy one," I explained.

"I see."

Her thoughts were falling into order after the disturbance of her feelings by the cruelty she had come to halt.

My perceptions of what followed were at the time necessarily shallow, but they were, I am sure, essentially correct.

"Those wretches!" exclaimed Gail Burley, leading John by the hand while I trotted alongside. "What would we ever have done without Richard? You are a true friend, Richard! —Oh!" she said, at the memory of what she had seen. And then, as John stumbled because she was walking so fast and his blanket folds were so awkward to hold about himself, she jerked his hand and said, "Stop dragging your feet, John! Why can't you walk like anybody else! Here! Pull up and keep up with me!"

At her suddenly cold voice, he went limp and would have fallen softly, like a dropped teddy bear, to the sidewalk. But she dragged him up, and said with her teeth almost closed, "John Burley, do you hear me? Get up and come with me. If you do not, your father will give you the whaling of your life when he comes home tonight!"

"No, Muzza, no, Muzza," muttered John at the memories which this threat called alive. He got to his feet and began half-running along beside her, dragging his borrowed blanket, which looked like the robe of a pygmy king in flight.

I was chilled by the change in Mrs. Burley. Her loving rage was gone and in its place was a fury of exasperation. She blinked away angry tears. With no thought of how fast John could run along with her, she pulled and jerked at him all the way home, while her face told us after all that she was bitterly ashamed of him.

For at last she took the world's view of her son. Represented by his own kind, other children, the world had repudiated him. Much as she hated the cruelty of the Grandvilles and their friends, sore as her heart was at what her son had suffered through them, she knew they were society, even if it was shown at its most savage. It was the determining attitude of the others which mattered. She had seen it clearly. Her heart broke in half. One half was charged with love and pity as it defied the mocking world which allowed no published lapse from its notion of a finally unrealizable norm. The other half was pierced by fragments of her pride. How could it happen to *her* that *her* child could be made sport of as a little animal monster? Gail Burley was to be treated better than that.

"John?" she sang out in warning as John stumbled again, "you heard what I said?"

Her cheeks, usually pale, were now flushed darkly. I was afraid of her. She seemed ready to treat John just as the boys had treated him. Was she on the side of his tormentors? Their judgments persuaded her even as she rescued her child. She longed for him both to live—and to die. Cold desire rose up in her. If only she knew some

way to save this poor child in the future from the abuse and the use-
lessness which were all that life seemed to offer him. How could she
spare John and herself long lifetimes of baffled sorrow? She made
him dance along faster than he could, for being such a creature that
others mocked and tortured him, at the expense of her pride.

When we reached her house, she said, "Richard, you are an
angel. Please drop John's wet things in the butler's pantry. I am
going to take him upstairs to bed. He is having a chill. I'll never be
able to thank you enough. Your after-school surprise is on the hall
table, an almond chocolate bar. Come over and see John later."

But that evening, just before my nursery supper, when I went to
show John the developed prints of the *Mauretania* and Buckingham
Palace, his father met me in the living room and said that John was
ill—his chill had gone worse. His mother was upstairs with him,
and I must not go up.

"Well, Richard," said Howard Burley, "God only knows what
they would have done to John if you hadn't come to get his mother.
They will catch it, never fear. I have talked to their fathers."

I had been feeling all afternoon a mixture of guilt and fright for
having snitched on the boys. Now I was sure they would avenge
themselves on me. Something of this must have shown in my face.

"Never fear," said Mr. Burley. "Their fathers will see to it that
nothing happens to you. Come over and see John tomorrow."

But the next day they said that John was really ill with grippe.

"Did they send for Dr. Grauer?" asked my mother.

"I don't know," I said.

He was our doctor, too, and we would have known his car if he
had come to attend to John. But all day nobody came, and the next
day John was worse, and my mother said to my father, with glances
that recalled my presence to him which must require elliptical conversation, "Grippe sometimes goes into pneumonia, you know."

"Yes, I know," replied my father. "But they know how to treat
these things."

"Yes, I know, but sometimes something is needed beyond just
home remedies."

"Then Grauer has not yet—?"

"No, not today, either."

"That is odd. Perhaps he isn't so sick as we think."

"Oh, I think so. I talked to Gail today. She is frantic."

"Well."

"But she says she knows what to do. They are doing everything, she says. Everything possible."

"I am sure they are. —Sometimes I can't help thinking that it might be better all around if—"

"Yes, I have too," said my mother hastily, indicating me again. "But of course it must only be God's will."

My father sighed.

I knew exactly what they were talking about, though they thought I didn't.

On the third day, John Burley died. My mother told me the news when I reached home after school. She winked both eyes at me as she always did in extremes of feeling. She knelt down and enfolded me. Her lovely heart-shaped face was an image of pity. She knew I knew nothing of death, but some feeling of death came through to me from the intensity of color in her blue eyes. The power of her feeling upset me, and I swallowed as if I were sick when she said, "Richard, my darling, our dear, poor little John died this morning. His chill grew worse and worse and finally turned into pneumonia. They have already taken him away. His mother wanted me to tell you. She loves you for what you tried to do for him."

"Then he's gone?"

"Yes, my dearie, you will never be able to see him again. That is what death means."

I was sobered by these remarks, but I did not weep. I was consumed with wonder, though I was not sure what I wondered about.

There was no funeral. Burial, as they said, was private. I missed John, but I was busy at school, where I was cautious with the Grand-villes and the others until enough days passed after the punishments they had received to assure me that I was safe from their reprisals. Perhaps they wanted to forget that they had given away death in heedless play. Howard Burley went to the office quite as usual. His wife stayed home and saw no one for a while.

"I cannot help wondering," said my mother, "why she never called Dr. Grauer."

"Hush," said my father. "Don't dwell on such things."

But I dwelled on them now and then. They were part of my knowledge on the day when Gail Burley asked my mother to send me to see her after school.

"Mrs. Burley has some things of John's that she wants to give you. You were his best friend."

I knew all his toys. Some of them were glorious. I saw them all in mind again. I went gladly to see his mother.

The housemaid let me in and sent me upstairs to Mrs. Burley's sitting room. She was reclining against many lacy pillows on a chaise longue in the bay window. She was paler than ever, and perhaps thinner, and there was a new note in her voice which made her seem like a stranger—a huskiness which reflected lowered vitality.

She embraced me and said, "Do you miss John?"

"Yes."

"Poor little John."

Her hazel eyes were blurred for a moment and she looked away out the window into the rustling treetops of autumn, as though to conceal both emotion and knowledge from me. "Oh, my God," I heard her say softly. Then she let forth one of her controlled breaths, annoyed at her own weakness as it lay embedded in the general condition of the world, and said with revived strength, "Well, Richard, let's be sensible. Come and pick out the toys you want in John's nursery. What you don't take I am going to send to Father Raker's Orphanage."

She led me along the upstairs hall to John's room. His toys were laid out in rows, some on the window seat, the rest on the floor.

"I suppose I could say that you should just take them all," she said with one of her unwilling smiles, "but I think that would be selfish of us both. Go ahead and pick."

With the swift judgment of the expert, I chose a beautiful set of Pullman cars for my electric train, which had the same track as John's, and a powerboat with mahogany cabin and real glass portholes draped in green velvet curtains, and a battalion of lead soldiers with red coats and black busbys and white cross belts tumbled together in their box who could be set smartly on parade, and a set of watercolor paints, and a blackboard on its own easel with a box of colored chalks. These, and so much else in the room, spoke of attempts to reward John for what he was not—and, for what they were not, the parents, too. I looked up at his mother. She was watching me as if never to let me go.

"Your cheeks are so flushed," she said, "and it is adorable the way the light makes a gold ring on your hair when you bend down. Richard, come here."

She took me in her hungry arms. I felt how she trembled. There was much to make her tremble.

"Do you want anything else?" she asked, again becoming sensible, as she would have said. Her concealed intensity made me lose mine.

"No, thank you, Mrs. Burley."

"Well, you can take your new toys home whenever you like. You can't carry them all at once."

"I'll take the boat now," I said.

"All right. Garsh, it's big, isn't it. John loved to sail it when we went to Narragansett."

She took me downstairs to the door. There she lingered. She wanted to say something. She could have said it to an adult. How could she say it to me? Yet most grown people spoke to me as if I were far older than my years. Leaning her back against the door, with her hands behind her on the doorknob, and with her face turned upward, so that I saw her classical white throat and the curve of her cheek until it was lost in the golden shadows of her eye, she said, "Richard, I wonder if you would ever understand—you knew, didn't you, surely, that our poor little John was not like other children?"

"Sometimes, yes."

"His father and I suffered for him, seeing how hard it was for him with other children; and then we thought of how it would have to be when he grew up—do you know?"

I nodded, though I did not know, really.

"We are heartbroken to lose him, you must know that. He was all we had. But do you know, we sometimes wonder if it is better that God took him, even if we had to lose him. Do you know?"

She looked down at me as if to complete her thought through her golden piercing gaze. When she saw the look of horror on my face, she caught her breath. Conventional, like all children, I was amazed that anyone should be glad of death, if that meant not seeing someone ever again.

"Oh, Richard, don't judge us yet for feeling that way. When you grow up and see more of what life does to those who cannot meet it, you will understand." She was obsessed. Without naming it, she must speak of the weight on her heart, even if only to me, a first-grader in school. In my ignorance, perhaps I might be the only safe one in whom to confide. "Garsh, when you see cripples trying to get along, and sick people who can never get well, you wonder why they can't be spared, and just die."

The appalling truth was gathering in me. I stared at her, while she continued, "John was always frail, and when those horrid boys turned on him, and he caught that chill, and it went into pneumonia, his father and I did everything to save him, but it was not enough. We had to see him go."

Clutching John's beautiful powerboat in both arms, I cowered a little away from her and said, "You never sent for a doctor, though."

A sharp silence cut its way between us. She put one hand on her breast and held herself. At last she said in a dry, bitter voice, "Is that what is being said, then?"

"Dr. Grauer always comes when I am sick."

She put her hand to her mouth. Her eyes were afire like those of a trapped cat.

"Richard?" she whispered against her fingers. "What are you thinking? Don't you believe we loved John?"

I said, inevitably, "Did you have him die?"

At this she flew into a golden, speckled fury. She reached for me to chastise me, but I eluded her. I was excited by her and also frightened. Her eyes blazed with shafted light. I managed to dance away beyond her reach, but I was encumbered by the beautiful power cruiser in my arms. I let it crash to the floor. I heard its glass break. Escape and safety meant more to me just then than possession of the wonderful boat. I knew the house. I ran down the hall to the kitchen and out the back door to my own yard, and home, out of breath, frightened by what I had exposed.

The Burleys never again spoke to my parents or to me. My parents wondered why, and even asked, but received no explanation. All of John's toys went to Father Raker's. In a few weeks the Burleys put up their house for sale, in a few months Howard retired from business, and they went to live in Florida for the rest of their lives.

1964

Everything to Live For

FIREWORKS AND QUARRY

[*Richard in his last school vacation goes to visit rich distant relations at their country estate in a summertime of the early 1920s, and meets his cousin Maximilian Chittenden. There is a traditional Fourth of July party out of doors near the family's great glass aboretum, which is nicknamed the Crystal Palace.*]

Because the household had to be there early to receive, I saw the party from the first. The Crystal Palace was itself like a great firework laid out in the air, arrested to earth, and sparkling with thousands of lights and their reflections. Green depths within the long glass vaults underlay the glitter, and as night deepened, a row of searchlights laid face up at the edge of the terrace below sent a colonnade of beams straight up into the heavy air. Cars coming on all the valley roads made a web of lights converging on us. Where they came to a halt to deliver their passengers, servants took wraps, and the guests came into the Crystal Palace, across the central court where a fountain kept its plume hovering high under tall palm trees, and out to the terrace overlooking the valley. There, in a sort of pavilion made of painted canvas and large flags, the family stood waiting to say how do you do. Farther out on the terrace and reaching both ways along its floor were supper tables dressed in bright colors. At each place, party favors commemorating the Fourth of July were laid out—miniature hatchet with a sprig of cherry attached; eagle and shield with the red, white, and blue worked in shiny silk; a tiny trophy of drum, musket, saber, and laurel; and for everyone to wear, a black tricorn hat made of shiny thin cardboard. On a red-carpeted platform against the wall of the greenhouse an orchestra in Continental Army uniforms and white bag-wigs played popular, polite dance music. In a clear space among the tables a dance floor was waiting for the couples who gradually drifted to their places at the tables, only to leave for a few steps before supper.

No cocktails were served—only wines at table. Uncle Alec did not believe in Prohibition, but he felt that serving mixed drinks before food went too far, and that a law prohibiting this practice would be justified. But no one could ask a handful of friends, as tonight, when he expected a hundred and some guests, without bringing out several dozen each of sherry, Pouilly Fouissé, claret, and champagne. Below me three terraces made great steps down the hill front. The second one supported a row of fountains whose basin waters spilled down to the third, which held an illuminated pool of white stone lined with peacock-blue tiling. The fourth terrace was given to grass and plants, and it was there that the fireworks crew were working at the final arrangements for the pyrotechnic concert to come later. I could see the figures of the men—Frazier and others of the staff, and a few boys from their families, in their white shirts with the sleeves rolled up so that they dramatized the style of free citizens on an outing, however much during the rest of the year they were decorously confined in the guise of servants—and I could detect in their movements the controlled excitement they felt for the occasion and the form of celebration they would presently release into the darkening summer sky.

As people arrived, I kept to shadows, for a number of reasons. I knew nobody, everybody sounded intimate with each other and spoke in loud, calm calls which seemed to me like a foreign tongue, they were all older than I, though many were of Max's age, and all were so self-assured that I believed they would look at me with blank politeness and move on, if I spoke to them. And there was another reason—they were all wearing dinner jackets to go with the evening frocks of their girls, and I was outcast by my clothes, for none of Max's had fitted me, and I ended by putting on my Dorchester blue suit, which in drying out under the iron of Max's valet had shrunk enough for me to feel it, though Max assured me after I was dressed that I looked "spiffy."

"But you," I said, when he came to my room to drive me to the party, "why aren't you dressed?"

For he too was wearing a blue suit with a long dark tie, just as I was.

"I thought we'd *both* be different, and tell them to go to hell if they didn't like it," he said, with a general smile of rebellion which made him my accomplice in bumpkinry.

"You didn't have to do that," I said.

"Don't be proud," he said. "If it suits me to do it, I do it, and vice versa. The funny thing is, they'll pretend not to notice, but they'll all mention it to each other. Let's go."

He was right, for as people came down from the receiving line, I could see them indicating Max with a glance or a wave, and laughing over him. I had a leap of belief that later when they should happen to notice me, the visiting cousin, dressed as outlandishly, they would suddenly decide that it was really quite distinguished of the two of us to set our own style.

I kept watching for Marietta to arrive with her parents. I had been feeling a strange knot of resentment and excitement about her since the afternoon; but now, alone in this loud and alien throng, I longed for her; and so my eye was on the pavilion most of the time. My cousins were now in their public character, and I could only admire it. Uncle Alec, in his old-fashioned tuxedo that was a bit more loose on him with each passing year, looked, from my distance among the tubbed trees on the terrace, whiter and more frail than before, but his smile was flashing, as he made his birdlike lifts and turns, and his glasses winked, his high handshake with his elbow up seemed like an accolade, and now and then a fragment of his welcome came to me in a sort of stylish shriek which made others turn and laugh, and say, "Alexander is really marvellous tonight," so indicating that his general incapacity was well known, but in a sense admirable, if he could work it up to such a party as this, in such idle magnificence, with such dynastic implications.

For his wife standing beside him was, if you watched from a little way away, for all to recognize the perfect consort for a reigning house. She too was pale, but the fall of light from overhead modelled her with such strong relief that her famous beauty came back upon her, and as she felt that it was being seen again by others who had almost forgotten how beautiful she had been, she was given strength to stand so beautifully erect, to offer a smile so general that was yet taken so particularly, to give her hand so fondly that nobody noticed at the time which hand it was. She wore white kid gloves that reached above her elbows. Her right arm was suspended in a sling of black lace and hung heavily at her waist; but in the lace she had twined a long chain of small diamonds—far from attempting to conceal her deformity she called attention to it by this device, and pleased everyone by putting them at ease to notice the sling and its jewels, which as she moved winked like fireflies inside the cloudy lace. Her dress was white, long, and shimmering. She had obeyed her husband to the extent of celebrating the day by wearing a string of rubies, below which was a string of white pearls, which was supported by a string of sapphires. Guests could exclaim at the wit of this, and use their time with her by doing all the talking themselves, which spared her saying much herself, so saving her strength. How wonderful they are together, was what many of them said, seeing with what animation Alexander would relinquish a guest to her, and how she would thank him with a sparkle of her eyes as she accepted her charming duty, and then, how, leaning sweetly to remind Max who it was he must now welcome in his turn, she would make the word "darling," which she meant to be overheard, seem to include playful love as the open secret of motherly pride, and an adult gaiety which took the guest in for tonight as one of the family. It was hard to remember the exhausted and troubled lady whom I had been with at four o'clock that afternoon.

Max in public himself was all she could ask, as he took one after another of the guests in his turn. I was reminded of my first glimpse of him—how he leaned a little forward, his glowing face turned to seek in other faces the nature of their desires, which he would promptly meet—and in certain cases of the old and corrupt or the young and eager who came this evening he would (unspokenly) suggest desires of his own, and invite excesses in their thoughts which if they should ever be revealed he would then laugh at.

While I was observing him from an orderly thicket of tall plants, where spokes of shadow wheeled across the terrace cast by figures that moved in the crowd, a voice said near to my ear, "I don't know how much longer he can stand it."

I turned.

"Marietta. I was watching for you."

"I came around the other way. I never go down the receiving line."

"They are all being splendid, aren't they?"

"Lissy loathes to be seen, and this means she must put herself for all to see. You know what the locals in society call the Chittendens? They call them the Imperial Family."

"You look lovely."

"A junior hag," she said.

"Oh, no."

"Oh, yes. I am exhausted. Always. Don't I look it?"

In the flickering half-light of the party, I regarded her. Her face
was pale, her eyes were deep under her brows, and her face narrowed
about her smiling lips, which quivered in a tiny spasm now and then.
Somehow this suggested wit. She looked ghostly and lovely, in spite
of the remote reminders she again gave me of the look of a skull,
and of consuming appetite the nature of which was ambiguous, except that the working flare of her nostrils suggested the perennial
presence of desire. Unlike the other girls at the party, who wore
modish knee-length frocks weighted with crystal fringes and bangles,
she was dressed in a long close gown of light silk patterned in leaves
and branches of several shades of green, so that her thin, eager, restless figure seemed to be entangled in a thicket of vines. Her hair fell
loose on her bare shoulders. She looked small and vital, and I wanted
to enfold her protectively with my arms, as if she were an exquisite
child escaped from the nursery in her warm, trailing nightgown.
With her knack of catching a thought and talking in refraction, she
said, "You are going to save us all. I am so glad, the telegram has
been sent."

"You mean to my parents?"

"Yes."

"You know all about it."

"All."

"Does Max?"

"No—only that you were going to be asked. Are you pleased?"

"I—"

"You don't know. You rather hate the feeling that someone is
buying you. But you see what is needed and you feel you might do
some good. And we are all strange but interesting, and one can learn
something from any situation. You half hope they will say no at
home, but if they say yes, you won't be sorry. Perhaps this will be a
summer you will think of as memorable. But you cannot help the
notion that there is something a little unwholesome about having so
many odd new friends wanting something they think you can give
them." She shrugged. "Or don't you want to talk about it?"

"No, I don't."

"Oh, Richie, as Max calls you, you are priceless. I adore you
when you look lofty. It means you are puzzled but refuse to admit
it. Do you want to dance? Or be dragged around to meet people?"

"Let's dance."

We moved to the dance floor, where she hung upon me, yet not close to me, stepping shortly in her own rhythm, and not facing me but swaying limply at right angles to me. In an elusive way, she was like a small wild creature under restraint. Friends called to her and she flickered at them with the fingers entwined in my hand. The party was suddenly complete. We saw the Imperial Family come down from their place and move slowly to their tables. It was a signal for the dancing to stop and everyone to be seated. Uncle Alec presided at one round table, Aunt Lissy at another, Max at another where places for myself and Marietta were arranged, with her between us. Three other couples completed the table. I was not introduced to any of them.

"Oh," said a ripe, brunette girl in a throaty voice, "let's all be George Washington," and put on her tricorn hat. Everyone glanced at Max. He nodded and put on his hat, at which everyone else did so. Marietta put her fluttering hand on Max's arm.

"I *know*," she said, "but it can't last forever. They love it. You're being superb."

"Richie, am I?" he said, leaning across her toward me.

"If you are," I said, "I don't know what about."

Max and Marietta sighed in concert at my insensitivity.

"Isn't it all divine?" said another girl, who sat at my right. I turned. She was an enthusiastic blonde with a permanent smile and a clear, lifted voice in which she drawled her remarks, carelessly confident that they would be of interest to everyone. "I mean, the Alexanders really are something, don't you think? I mean, who else gives such divine parties. I have never seen you here before. Who are you?"

"I am a remote cousin of this family. I have never been here before."

"Where are you from?"

"Dorchester."

"Delaware?"

"New York."

"Oh, *there*. Good heavens above. Do you hear?" she said generally, while others turned to hear her. "He's from Dorchester, New York. Can you bear it? We had a girl from Dorchester, New York, at school, for a short while. Nobody could understand a word she said. She was a pretty little thing, too. She had to leave us because she didn't care for horses—or perhaps it was the other way round."

"Gwennie, you're awful," said a boy across the table.

"I know, and you love it," she replied. She turned and pointedly looked at my suit. "Love your suit," she said.

"And Max's?" asked Marietta, suddenly appearing to her. As she stretched to speak, she leaned against me and I could feel her deep quivering energy.

"Oh, and Max's, naturally," said Gwennie. Then she turned away to her partner on the other side.

"Thank you," I said to Marietta.

"She had to be sent packing. Let's us three just make social noises at each other."

Max looked at me with his head lowered. For the benefit of the party he retained his smile. But for me he had a simmering gaze which silently said what he must not say aloud.

"Absolutely *divine*," came at random over the shoulder on my right.

The party was now fully launched.

Max took Marietta to dance. I kept my seat. Presently Gwennie turned to me again. "I'm a dreadful bitch, don't you think?"

"If you think so."

"Oh, come *on*. React."

"There's not much point."

"I suppose not. What do you do, at college, I mean."

"I am in my last year of school. I plan to take a pre-medical course."

"My dear. I took you for a college man. *Now* won't you forgive me?"

"Why do you want me to?"

"Very well. If you won't keep it *social*, I'll tell you. Because you are a cousin of Max's, and that means we really ought to be nice to you, because if Max ever gets mad at anyone they have an awful time making up with him, and I *like* being asked here, and my mother would snatch me *bald* if I ever did anything to make trouble for any of us with the *Alexanders*. So now you know why I took any more trouble with you, and now I suppose you will tell Max anyway, so why should I ever *not* be a bitch?"

I laughed out loud at this, and I remember thinking what a remarkable report I could take home to my friends about how children of the rich behaved at Chittenden Hills.

"No," I said, "I won't tell Max anything."

"Say, you're a real prince of a fellow," she said, burlesquing an innocent air. "—Did you know they're engaged?"

"Who."

"Then you don't. Max and Marietta. My mother—all the old people—have been told quietly this evening. No formal announcement. Just intimate family news. No wedding, of course, until after Harvard."

"I see."

"Do you like her?"

"Oh, yes."

"Yes, I can see you do. You really open up to her, don't you? I mean, it's how you look when you talk to her or she talks to you. I can tell by the back of your head."

"You ought to take it up professionally."

"Now who's a bitch."

I was beginning to like her. She thrust and invited, she was working so hard to put forward her own idea of herself, and her inverted style of offensive attention was in the end flattering, as she meant it to be.

The music was slowing to a pause between dances. Max and Marietta returned. She said, "Gwennie, let him alone. He belongs to us."

I think now of the reflected meanings of this, none of which were consciously intended; but at the time all I felt was a little chill of apprehensiveness at the note of possession, and I dreaded to know how my parents would reply to the telegram which asked for me. Gwennie ignored Marietta and made a kiss through the air to Max and turned back to her other dinner companion.

"Dance with her," said Max, handing Marietta to me.

"You might let him ask," said Marietta.

"No," I said, "I was going to."

As we went to the dance floor Max took his way off between the tables, turning and twisting among them and pausing as arms and smiles went out to him. He had a word for each, and a kiss here and there, and beyond, I had a shuttered impression of his mother's face, watching him fearfully between the heads and bodies whose relation to him, and to her, and to us on the dance floor, changed as he moved, and we. Aunt Lissy's head was held beautifully erect and her throat was stretched in a regal pose so that a casual glance would seem to collect an impression of a reserved but serenely confident and happy lady of great position enjoying with her devoted husband and her handsome, gifted, and adoring son a simple meeting of friends to observe Independence Day. Banking upon their long history, the Chittendens could be pardoned for making something of a proprietary reference to the Revolution, in terms beyond the appropriate privileges and material means of most others.

We danced a little while more or less on the same spot of the dance floor in obedience to Marietta's habit of ignoring the rhythm, the movement, and the idea of dancing. She said, "It is idiotic, isn't it."

"What?"

"The idea of dancing. I mean people on their hind legs going around face to face in couples to noises made by other people to keep them moving all the same way. I never do."

"I've noticed."

"Let's go and be somewhere."

Holding my hand she took me away to the end of the terrace where high stone urns held flowering bushes whose branches showered down to the terrace floor. In the shadow of one of the urns we sat on the wide balustrade looking out over the valley. Fireflies defined a low ceiling over the meadow floor with their little lost and found lights. The dance band was muffled at the small distance where we were. The dense summer night seemed to have its center in my belly. I was choked with anticipation of I knew not what. The air was heavy and sweet. Down in the valley, with the power to hurt which is part of any universal banality, the lights in Mr. Standish's house looked somehow promising and dear, making me wish I had a house with windows lighted at night against the impersonal dark, while inside the house might abide my life with someone I loved.

Marietta took my hand and made her butterfly touch on my upturned wrist. I was flooded with desire and my pulse leaped in my wrist and made me shift my thighs.

"Oh, it is lovely," she said.

"Marietta."

"I mean, to have it respond that way."

I think it was in that moment that I first knew how desire reached outward as well as inward. I took her in my arms. She flinched away into nothing and turned her head away.

"Oh, Richie, let's wait. Nothing is clear."

I held her and then let go. The night was heavy on us again. She breathed in a loud whisper and shook her head and made a groan of longing under her breath.

"What's the matter," I said.

"The same thing. Always."

"Max?"

"Yes. —Richie, what can I do when things engulf him until he has to disappear for a day or a night?"

"What does he do?"

"He says he cannot help it, he does not know what causes it, he does nothing, he just sits somewhere or lies on something, and the tears run down his face. He does not even weep, I mean, with noises and things. But something inside breaks like a dam, or a heart, or something, and he cannot stand anything for a while, but all he can do is be part of some sorrow of the whole world. And so young! Like tonight. You know? When he left us?"

"But he seemed to be having a beautiful time."

"Oh. It was nearly killing him."

"The party?"

"All of it. Everything. And especially his family."

"But they seem happy."

"Oh, Richie. It is just because you are generally happy. Everyone else seems happy to you. I hope you can always stay that way."

"I'm not any way, particularly."

"Oh, yes you are, and I adore it; but I know more about it than you."

"Can't you help Max?"

"I keep thinking so. I used to be able to, at first, but when he began to see that things were not going to be good again, nothing seemed to help him. We've tried lots of things. You're the latest."

"We?"

"Oh, yes. I keep having ideas."

"Did you tell them to keep me?"

"Yes. —D'you mind? Oh, don't, please, mind. I was so—so desperately pleased when I saw how Max took to you. If you knew. He hasn't taken up anybody new in ages. —Oh, but how can I make you see. Even this, now, with you—he is furious at me underneath because he *knows* without being told that I have tried to give you

to him. He hates to be managed, he knows he needs it, and what he
misses most is the joy of discovery. Perhaps I have made a dreadful
mistake."

"About me?"

"Yes. Perhaps he should have been left to make you love him."

"Oh, I never heard so much talk about love."

"But, darling Richie, all this is about that, and nothing else.
In fact, that's all anything is ever about, if you look far enough."

I was so much stirred by this that I must pretend not to be,
and so I said, "It doesn't sound quite decent, to me. Are there no
things you won't talk about?"

She sighed and set her head against my arm, like a wishful
child.

"It is talk or go mad," she said. "If I had one wish for us all
here in the Hills, it would be that we would never want to look past
the surface of things. That is what is killing Max—feeling and knowing things under the grand outsides of the life he comes from."

"What outsides?"

"Oh: surely you know. His non-father, and his crippled mother.
The loss of everything too soon. We are all going to lose everything,
but most of us have a chance to get ready. He didn't. —He has such
doubts. He remembers such happiness."

"I know. He told me about when he and his sister were young,
and his father, and the games they played at the quarry. Uncle Alec
was evidently quite a man in those days."

"Oh, yes. Even I can remember. Alexander was a darling—so
handsome and such imagination and so much fun. The clever thing
to say around here is that Lina murdered him. And when Alicia
needed him, he was dead, and he couldn't"—shrug—"anything.
And Max lost the mother he knew, and so he has to hate her for it,
and of course everybody else, and himself, and everything about his
life, and this party, and those Gwennies and Sonnies and Didis and
Tooties and Poopsies over there dancing. —My father told me all
this. I am too dumb to know it by myself. Aren't you sorry you ever
came?"

"I didn't want to."

"I know. I adore the terrible candor of the provinces."

"That's not very nice."

"We don't have to be nice, do we?"

"Not if you're rich enough, I suppose."

"Oh, Richie, I have made you cross. I am sorry. My father told me years ago to begin by saying half as much as I'd like to. And then to cut what was *left* in half, if I ever wanted to be liked."

"It's all right."

But I was made forlorn by a memory of the city which had shaped my life, Dorchester, of which my father approved so warmly and innocently; and when it was made fun of, as vaudeville comedians always did to raise a sure laugh, I was indignant. I wondered what was so funny about being born in a city in Upstate New York, at the other end of things from New York City, and I would think hotly that people in New York City and Dorchester were both people, and I would ask what could be so different about them? But tonight there were differences to be seen, and these were too new for me to know how I felt about them. That they existed was enough of a shock. I kept silent, watching the lovely net of firefly lights far below. The dance band went silent, too, and in the pause, I heard another sound—drifting under the low clouds from the fold of the hills, it was the whistle, given in long phrases, of the night freight train downbound to Olympia. It had a sort of rainy sound, for the night was humid and the air pressed close.

"Oh, how beautiful," said Marietta. "I love to hear it and feel sad—it is so wonderful to have something *there*, and not *here*, to be sad about."

"Let's stop being sad," I said, happy that we had come together again.

And as if in reply to my words, just then, from the lowest terrace below us, with a hissing chord of fiery power into the sky rose a golden curtain of sparks made by the exhausts of twenty rockets which went up in a long row at the same instant. Startled, the guests all gave out a great chord of their own, crying "Oh-h-h!" in a sustained sigh of enchantment. The curtain rose to a ragged edge across the sky, there was an instant of darkness and silence, and then the rockets burst in a line, throwing firelights of green, red, yellow, and rose, which exploded to release showers of diamond-white needles falling back from the apex like spray of fountains or fronds of willowy trees against the dense summer night. The concert immediately cast a spell against whose dazzle of glory no one who watched could maintain, while it lasted, any visions of his own, especially those which fed on darkness or sorrow. In their act of enchantment supremely innocent, fireworks restored innocence, for the moment, to anyone who watched them.

How suddenly a rocket went out at the end of its glory; and how craftily Uncle Alec's crew timed the elements of the display so that there was hardly a pause between one glory and the next. The concert was to last an hour, and for the time I saw of it the heavens were never dark, and there were few outright repetitions of effects. Salutes exploding on high had their bombardment doubled by the echoing hills, and when these were topped by falling stars of red fire we thought of battles and patriots. Arbors of green arcs were woven in the sky, and in turn these were pierced by hissing comets which streaked aloft and still climbing died in wafts of golden sparks which fell slowly into nothing. Gardens of immense gold chrysanthemums were planted high over the meadow—bursts of curly light all radiating from a sun which burned the dark and then joined it. Pagodas rose crown by crown, and in the little pause before each stage took fire, we chanted "Oh-h-h-h" in chorus, and our voices rose each time a new shaft grew from the last, and we ached with delight at how the splendor was protracted, and when at last the pagoda was finished, we still held our breath, thinking another climb and burst would surely come. But before we could measure disappointment, something else went up, and took us with it.

The greatest rockets were those which on reaching the apex made a great soft sound something like a kiss, and then released their fronds of light in falling traceries which seemed to me like a picture of the very nerve tree within the human body. Having it made visible in fancy was like suddenly feeling everything everywhere at each nerve end, a sensation mercifully brief, for its intensity and wholeness must have been impossible to bear for long. Our very flesh was pierced by those threads of light, and we possessed glory and color as part of our being.

I looked about at the rapt faces and tense positions of the guests. I was struck by a notion which, I am sure, would never have come to me at home at such a moment. I thought of what pathos attended the need and fulfillment of play. Playgrounds and amusement parks, fireworks and games, all seemed pathetic monuments to human desperation. Why must our lot be made bearable by spectacle, and what must it be if the longing to be delivered from it even briefly was so constant? How much better, for the most part, people deserved in the way of relief from their human estate than what they were given, usually at considerable expense.

"Oh-h-h-h!" we said again, as the darkness was made bright by a great rise of whirling discs in every color. They filled the sky and seemed to fly away to infinity, growing smaller and yet brighter, until, mere sparks, they seemed to part an invisible curtain and enter another sky where we could not follow.

We were holding hands as we watched when Max suddenly stood behind us and leaned over between us.

"Let's all get away from here," he said in an urgent whisper.

We turned. In the light of the fireworks he looked to be carved out of marble. Marietta groaned and put her hand on his face.

"What do you mean," she said.

"We've had enough."

"Yes, of course, though it is lovely. But we can't leave."

"Why not."

"It would look dreadful. It would hurt Alicia. This is supposed to be *our* party."

"Yes. I give it away freely."

"I cannot go. If you want to, go. But I must stay and handle things if people ask for you."

"Come along, Richie," he said, disdaining further discussion. Confident that I would follow, he started toward the steps leading down from the terrace away from the tables. I looked at Marietta.

"Oh, go," she said. "If it wasn't this, it might be something worse. Bring him back in an hour or so."

Feeling that my duties had already begun, I followed Max down the steps, around the grassy hump beyond the Crystal Palace, and down the driveway until we came to his car. He drove without lights until we were headed away from the Crystal Palace along the quarry road. I was full of things to ask which Max would hate to answer. Feeling this, he drove in silence, refusing to break the wall of privacy which contained him.

The headlights were now turned on, and he drove fast. We rapidly closed on Mr. Standish's cottage. I saw and was about to exclaim a warning of what Max saw in the same moment. Standing in the middle of the road, watching us bear down on him, was Chief, the Dalmatian.

"God damn them," cried Max, braking hard, "they're not supposed to let him out!"

Before we skidded to a halt, the dog was dancing alongside our right front wheel trying to bite the tire.

"Careful!" I yelled, "you'll run over him!"

"That's all I need!" exclaimed Max. He jumped from his seat and his dog rose to dance his old dance with him, but Max cuffed him down, grasped his collar, and led him through the picket gate to the cottage. There he pounded angrily on the door. I saw a woman's shadow slowly and heavily move on to the frosted-glass door panel, and then the door opened. I could not hear what they said, only the blur of their voices. With irritating calm the woman —it was Mrs. Standish—took the dog by his collar and drew him into the house, a process which he made as awkward as possible by relaxing into a dead lump of weight. Max returned now freed into speech by his encounter with the gardener's wife.

"The silly cow. What horrors that sort of women are. She thinks its vulgar to do what she is paid to do." He started the car and we were off again. He imitated the woman's bridling whine. "It wasn't her fault. It wasn't Standish's fault. There is a hole under the fence of Chief's pen which they'd been meaning to fill up, but what with Mr. Standish, she called him the Mister, being off at all hours in the greenhouse watching for that thing to bloom, and herself so busy around the house, they never—and my! aren't the fireworks just so pretty, she was watching from her bedroom window, and she thought she heard a knock, and so she came to see. —She thinks she will cease to be a lady if she ever admits she's been wrong about anything. Poor Standish. Anyway, she promised to keep Chief in the house till they get the hole filled. My poor dog, living with that sagging slut."

"Max, Max."

" 'Max, Max,' yes, yes. I know."

We came to the ridge and climbed the chattery road. At the top I said, "We'd better walk down."

"Scared?"

"No."

He turned toward me with a calculating grin, moving his jaw slowly. By the light of the instrument panel he could see that I was not scared. He laughed and said, "I believe you. Then we'll walk. I only drove back up once after dark and I actually did run the rear wheel off the edge. They had to come and haul me back onto the road."

He left the car on the ridge. With a flashlight he took from under the seat he showed our way down to the quarry lake. We walked out to the point of the Peninsula and climbed up on the limestone blocks, which looked like architecture. From there, the air was black, the high chiseled walls blacker, and the water blacker still. It took minutes for my eyes to become adjusted to the cup of darkness where we were, and all seemed quiet. But slowly the senses reached for the world outside, and I could see, as though I were pressing upon my eyes with the lids shut, a wavering faint glow in the far sky, a wash of light cast on the low clouds by the fireworks four or five miles away. I watched, hoping to see a rocket reach its dying height above the quarry walls so far above us; but never did. And too, in the quiet I began to hear the faintest reduction of the explosions from the airy salutes at Newstead, and then nearer to us I could hear the murmur of summer creatures, an occasional flap and splash of a fish, and the threading song of distant crickets. A great trembling seemed to hover above the stillness which was made of so many combined live sounds. By the contrasts slowly made manifest in sky and air, the lake seemed to be deeper and darker than ever, a pool of oblivion, a world nowhere and welcoming, to a self lost and searching.

We sat in silence for perhaps a quarter of an hour. Was I supposed to break the quiet? "How peaceful," I might say—but though I could hardly see him, my cousin beside me was held by anything but peace, for if he was silent, he seemed to be using silence as a refuge from powers which menaced him from within and without. How was I supposed to help him? How could I know what he wanted not of me so much as of his life? At last I heard him move—I could hear the small moist sound of his eyes as he rubbed them roughly. When he spoke it was with his familiar air of mockery but his voice was choked.

"When was the last time *you* shed tears?" he asked with almost a dry, professional inflection.

"I would have to remember."

"Tell me why you did, and where. How long ago?"

"It isn't very interesting."

"Never mind. Go on."

"Why, I think it was two years ago when I broke my arm

tobogganing in Commodore Perry Park. The run was icy and I missed a turn and flipped over. It was when they picked me up. It hurt so that I couldn't help it, I felt the tears running down my face and I couldn't stop them for several minutes. But finally I did."

"You are right, it is not very interesting. You were not really *shedding tears* about something. Physical pain is of no importance."

"I suppose not. But you asked me."

"Yes, I asked you. And I have asked others. And nobody can tell me."

"Max?"

"Yes?"

"What is it?"

A pause. Then, "Are you going to stay?"

"Oh. I won't know until I hear from my parents."

"Do you like them?"

"Yes, I do."

"Do you want to stay?"

"Partly yes. Partly no."

"A just reply, most potent, grave, and reverend signior. I could phrase it better, but the substance is surely proper— Do you hate beauty?"

"Good God, of course not."

"Do you hate staying well by keeping busy?"

"God, I don't know."

"Don't be impatient. These are great questions. And so is this one: do we find true happiness only when we live for others without regard for self?"

Mocking the precepts played at him at home in that house of invalids, he was trying to show me something of life which unless it engulf him he must despise, and despising, fight against. He talked on in the darkness. His thoughts were not consecutive, about the nature of which there were many theories but no proofs.

Dr. Osborne had used his privilege of old retainer now and then to advise Max to seek professional help for his "nerves." But Max told him that he felt intelligent enough to find his own cure for what ailed him. Dr. Osborne sighed and disagreed, knowing what he knew, but not risking any direct reference to it, and aside from keeping a keen eye on him, he let Max alone, obviously waiting for the moment when Max would no longer be able to make a show of rationalized resistance. Meanwhile, though he was willing to let Max and his daughter be the closest of companions, he withheld his approval of an official engagement—hence tonight's seepage of romantic information through the medium of matronly gossip. In due course if all went well with Max he would be happy to bless the union. But not yet. Not yet. The idea occurred to Max that Dr. Osborne was entertaining in thoughts to which he denied full daylight the idea that time and mortality would resolve Max's difficulty. When he came into his inheritance, when his parents died, when he need not hate what he loved too well in memory, Max would probably be fully one man instead of a collection of fragments from his own childhood, and from the youth of his parents, and from the bored, fastidious, languid, but brilliant Max of Harvard. People went to such lengths to "understand" him that they ended by misunderstanding him into unreality. The black water in the quarry, whose every rock and ledge and face he knew so well above the water, held depths he could only imagine. Did they only mirror what was above? How would he ever know? When did his life turn into an eternal question, while the lives of other young men seemed arrogantly and joyfully to be certain, however wrongly, only of answers?

I heard a reflection of his voice in that rocky cup. I asked, "Is there an echo here?"

"Ai, God," he said. Then in a deliberately restrained voice he said, "When we were little we talked to it all the time. We never saw it, but we knew it lived here, and we used to think of things to ask it. It always answered. If you want to hear it, I can summon it up for you. —All right." He stood up and drew a deep breath, and then in a tremendous voice he cried out one word four times, lengthening it as far as his breath would let him:

"Howl, howl, howl, howl!" —and the great palatial rocky walls threw it back at us and then echoed their own echo, and I heard "Howl—owl—owl—wl—l . . ." and though I did not then know where his word had come from, it plumbed me with a weight of dread which pressed my heart down, down.

When the echo had returned to the silence where it lived, we said nothing for a moment, and then Max said, "Do you want to try it?"

"No, thanks."

"No, there is little use. All you discover is that every question is finally its own answer."

It was the kind of remark which meant nothing or everything, and I was not at ease with such. Kindly accepting my silence, "Smoke?" he asked, taking his cigarettes and a briquet from his pocket.

"No, thanks."

"You don't ever?"

"No."

He lighted his cigarette. His shapely head bent over the flame, his high color, the tawny marble of his hands carved out by the brief light, gave a picture of such fine health that I was startled, for what he had been trying to say for so long and dark an interval had made a different likeness of him—that of an invalid being drawn help-lessly into the illness all around him, which he had helped to create.

"Why don't you smoke. Do you disapprove?"

"No, I don't disapprove. Years ago, my father promised me a thousand dollars when I reach twenty-one if I promised not to smoke until then. I promised."

"So now," said Max, to whom a thousand dollars was not a fortune, "you don't want to lose a thousand dollars?"

"It isn't the thousand dollars, though I can't sneer at it as you can. But what I don't want to lose is my promise."

My cloddish virtue exasperated him, with its terms of inno-cence and honor. He said, envious of the settled simplicity of my life, "How do you know your father will keep his? Great God, haven't you ever taken a straight look at life? Don't you know even yet that nothing is what it seems to be? When are you going to wake up?"

But under his words something else said: Richie, Richie, don't ever wake up; and I knew long later that the very thing everyone hoped to purchase of me for Max was that part of my father and mother's abiding faith which I carried in me—their faith in what-ever it was which created instead of destroyed.

"If my father is alive when I reach twenty-one, he will keep his promise," I said.

"Ah, God," he said, cast down even further by what he had not credited me with—the ability to contemplate with calm, though surely never to experience without grief, such a catastrophic event as the death of the father. If Max was frantic as we escaped from the fireworks party—"festival for the peasants," he had said—now he seemed deeply depressed by his conversation with me, which was just the opposite of what was supposed to come from our healing contact. He sat and smoked in silence with his head turned away until his cigarette was gone. Then abruptly he stood up and began to haul off his clothes.

"Let's take a swim," he said.

"I'll wait for you."

"You don't want to?"

"Not specially."

"The water is cold."

"Yes. It isn't that. I'd rather just sit here and feel the night."

My flesh threw out goose pimples and my teeth made as if to chatter, but I bit my jaws together. It was a close, hot night. How could I shiver?

"Then a good night to you," he said, and dived off the great limestone cube and vanished into the black. Would he come back? I asked myself, and then I recoiled from the question, asking why anything like that should ever occur to me.

The summer night pulled all the rankness of the countryside into the heavy air. I listened for water sounds but heard nothing. Across the quarry rim the distant lights came and went in the sky but gave no illumination here. It was like seeing the dying flicker of a hearth fire gone so low that its last cast of color was not rosy but wan pale. The fall of another coal or two, a final spark, and all would be dark. I thought of calling out his name, but for fear of seeming foolish if he should answer, I kept silent. I held my breath to hear without the drumming of my pulse. Somewhere an owl spoke —a small one, by the sound. What would they say if I returned without him? First I must find Marietta and if necessary put my hand over her mouth to keep her from crying out when I told her my news. Then we would have to find a stratagem to take Alexander and Alicia away from the terrace party without having anyone notice anything. Could we say that the head gardener wanted them briefly in the Crystal Palace, perhaps because the night-blooming cereus was showing signs of movement in its folded buds? And then beyond the crowd of guests, we would go in a motorcar back to the hilltop house, and there my duty would end with the news I brought. Surely it would be wise to ask Dr. Merriman Osborne to be with us at that moment. Nobody would shed tears but Uncle Alec, who would turn his narrow head aside and, extending his long neck in birdlike thrusts, would then release a series of broken dry sounds which would sound more like illness than grief. A few cars would presently come up the driveway with people who would want to know if anything was wrong. What instinct would have brought them? A word would have to be sent at once to the estate work force to go to the quarry with lights, ropes, a boat, a Pulmotor, perhaps a salute cannon to fire across the water in classical fashion to bring up by its vibrations any burden held by the deep. Such activity would be impossible to conceal. In an instant the entire throng of guests would have the news, and face each other with it in horror and excitement. How could it possibly have happened? He had been such a superb swimmer—so excellent that, because of his prep-school record in the pool, he had been asked at Harvard to join the varsity squad, which he had disdained to do. Someone was sure to say that something like this could have happened all through the years, the quarry lake had long been a menace, and nobody had heeded warnings that it should be drained and dried up for good. Over Newstead and its impregnable evidences of great position the fates would seem to be gathered, as if one success in calamity after another deserved still another. How would it be possible to look into Aunt Lissy's face as she was turned and taken up the long winglike curve of the grand staircase to her room and ultimate solitude? Before daylight the reporters and photographers would be everywhere. The efficient apparatus of disaster would come into play for the satisfaction of all who could read.

I could not be still with my racing thoughts. I clambered down from the blocks and tiptoed—why I tiptoed I did not know—feeling my way to the edge of the Peninsula as if to see and hear better. I felt like a prisoner in a palatial dungeon whose invisible chains were made of darkness itself. But where was the flashlight? I returned to the rocks and felt for it everywhere but could not find it. I did not know whether five minutes had passed or a half hour. I looked across the lake toward the opposite limestone wall. If I called out, my voice would echo strongly, and surely there would be an answer from some quarter of the sheer cavity? Then I saw a long edge of most dim pale light along the top of the wall. It revealed the crest, and as I watched transfixed, it travelled with breathless slowness down the limestone face, throwing into dark relief against the stone the occasional ledges where foliage had rooted and grown in a wonderful persistence of life out of siftings of dust caught in invisible crevices. I turned, and there over the other crest was rising a hazy quarter moon which as it rose sent its light down the far quarry wall and must eventually show it all, and touch the water. How long this would take I could not calculate, but my entire will was bent to join the rising of the moon, as though I could hasten its movement, for if there was light, however remote and confusing, I would not feel buried in mystery and solitude.

"Yes," I said aloud, in an idle tone calculated to sound reassuring, "perhaps it is time to go."

I turned my head to listen for a reply. None came. My body seemed compact of a silent groan which if it could have been heard would have said, "No, no, no, please."

I went to the blocks, climbed up, and lay down on my back to watch the sky and the moon. I was trapped with them in the inexorable design of the passage of the heavenly bodies. Like the heavy air itself, my underthoughts hung under a misting atmosphere of dread into which flickers of reasonableness tried to penetrate. But like the shadows in the summer undergrowth at night, everything conscious within me merged into a single depthless form, which slowly made itself felt as a knot of suspense and desire, hunger and shame—for what, except for life itself, I could not say. Later, I knew how any extreme of feeling—grief, rage, relief—could find expression, however inappropriate it might seem at the moment, in an act of sex.

I suddenly sat erect.

What sound was that—what touched the water with a little slap?

I turned my head. I heard it again. Then I heard the long luxurious indraught of the swimmer lazily rolling aside for his breaths in an Australian crawl of, surely, perfect form. It was my cousin returning. I felt a thump of relief in my chest, immediately followed by a prickling gather of anger. My wild concern, with its ceremonies of the imagination, now seemed childish and idiotic. I was humiliated by it. Before I would let it show to Max, I would perjure myself. I lay back on the rock and rolled to my side and curled myself in a position of sleep, and pretended to be asleep when he climbed up dripping to the edge of the Peninsula and came to the block where he had left his clothes. There was now enough moon for him to see me.

"Richie?" he called.

I slept on, disgusted at having been a fool.

Max laughed gently and began to dress. In his coat he found cigarettes and lighter and began to smoke. The little flame, the smell of tobacco, made a distraction which I could recognize with dignity as a reason to wake up. I awoke.

"Hello," I said sleepily, sitting up.

"Hello. What time is it?"

"I don't know how long I've been sleeping."

"Were you concerned about me?"

"Asleep?"

"I see."

"Did you have a good swim?"

"Mostly underwater. I wanted to see the view from Lethe. I've always believed an underground river ran below the quarry. The upper world would look quite different from there. The quarry is my entrance to the underworld. I went to be washed of my other life."

"And were you?"

"I won't know until I return to it again."

"Then you weren't, if it is still there."

"What are you so irritable about?"

"I hate to be waked up."

"I don't think you were really sleeping."

"You don't?"

"No, and I believe you were beginning to be worried when I stayed away so long, especially before the moon came up. You couldn't find the flashlight, could you."

"I didn't look for it."

"I put it in my shoe so I would be able to find it if I ever wanted to. You wouldn't think of looking there."

Unguardedly, I said, "No, I didn't."

"So you did look."

"What of it."

"You were concerned for me," he asserted calmly.

Was it this he had gone to find out? How many suicides have been aborted by vanity, the curiosity of the self-victim to know the effect of his act? What pleasure remains in punishing someone if you don't know what you have made them feel? It was too much to admit, and moreover, it needed no further admission. He seemed content for the first time that night. To some degree, anyhow, he knew that I thought of him, and with concern. Our bickering annoyed me further, while it give a small lift to his spirits. Suddenly again in his attitude of command, he said energetically, "Let's go back. It must be late."

In silence I followed him up the ragged trail on the side of the ridge. He played his flashlight about with bravado, as if its beam were a rapier. Our return was so much less spectacular than the one I had agonized over in the dark by the quarry lake that I preserved my silence as a measure of dignity and reproof. What could I say to him? I could hardly say that I was glad he had returned safely without confessing below the words that I had thought of the alternative; and no more could I reproach him for not drowning, without admitting that I regretted the loss of the sensational consequences which would have followed. Max, too, said little, only remarking as we drove up toward Newstead, "Richie, I'm beginning to think you are a very complicated individual."

Nor could I protest this without claiming to be simple, and, so, not very interesting.

As we approached the Crystal Palace we saw that its grand illuminations were turned off. A few figures moved here and there in the limited light of ordinary work. The staff were restoring order after the party. Everyone else had gone.

So we must, after all, have been at the quarry for a matter of hours—two or more? The moon was high above the horizon. Its washy light made the countryside insubstantial, and the mists of long after midnight muffled the night creatures in their secret lodgments.

Running on to Newstead, we saw the house dark but for the main portico and lobby. No one was there—or so we thought until we came in. Max's mother was waiting in a huge brocaded armchair near the foot of the stair. When she saw us she rose and we went to her. She had put off her red, white, and blue jewels and had folded about herself a dressing gown as plain as a linen sheet. She wore a ravaged look, and now that she saw that her son was home, whatever effort of self-supporting control she had kept up in her vigil fell away, and cradling her carved hand she seemed to diminish in her bones and sway on her feet. Max moved to steady her but she nodded him away imperiously. We stood before her. She turned to go upstairs, but paused facing me. She looked into my face—to read what? I did not know. But so intense was her look that I was aware only of her eyes—dark coals of burning spirit in the long, blank oval of her face. The anguish and energy of her wondering, all gathered in her gaze, made the powdered skin about her eyes tremble uncontrollably. Max lounged nearby, but she did not look at him. She seemed to indicate that anyone who could abandon his social duty and be rude to a hundred guests, not to mention his parents and his all but fiancée, need not detain the interest of any responsible person. But as for me: who but myself could be interrogated with justice about the matter? Who else had been asked to assume a splendid responsibility? Who else had betrayed it either through compliance or—worse—inspiration? If I was to blame, I must be made to feel blameworthy. Where had he taken me—or I him? Why? Was this what trust came to, always? I could read such notions in her regard, and I felt a spurt of anger at my bondage and the injustice which accompanied the views of the rich. I made to speak, but she closed her eyes in tragic patience, silencing me by her choice of misery. Then disentangling her closed gaze from its mesh of lashes, she looked long into my—I think this was the word she would have me use—my conscience; then she turned and with infinite weariness made her way upstairs.

When I closed my eyes in the dark of my room I still saw the eyes of my cousin Alicia trembling in formless pale light. What made her wonder so, and look so into my heart, to discover what I knew of her son? Why had we vanished during such an important family festival? What had we fled from, what had we fled to? With what faith—broken or reaffirmed—did we return? Had we seen death? Life? Love? Despair? Futility? I could only dissolve her remembered gaze by opening my eyes and when I did so, I was once again the creature of a hostile summer.

The hum of summer was like the fever in my ears and in my bones which summoned me to manhood. Awake and mighty with desire I felt the hot meadows beyond my open window. Their scent, moving heavily on the slowly stirring air, smelled of generation—sap, crushed vegetable pungency, cast seed, snowy bark, dried sea foam, the ozone of wet minerals, the salt of tears and kisses. I begged of the dark to be let go, or granted consummation. The little motors of crickets sounding away in the multitudinous summer night seemed to eat mindlessly into the edges of my conscious mind. To resist such an invasion I must summon thought, any thought, and I remembered that country where I was the ruler, which I entered whenever I took a book to read.

Our house at home (the night began to lift its pressure as I thought of this) was full of the dark red leather volumes of Everyman's Library. My father would often come home with a package of five or six of the volumes and let me unwrap them. They had intricate gold designs on the spines in the manner of the Pre-Raphaelites, vines and leaves intertwined, and it was usually I who had first claim on the new volumes. I was not permitted to take them to my room on the top floor unless I could state that my school-work was all done; but if it was, there was no limit to the time I could spend with Everyman's. —I now was able to shut my eyes with safety, and instead of the stinging night, or Alicia's anguished wondering, I saw the backbones of our books, and I told over all the titles I could remember. I remembered a little scene of one time when my father had brought us some new books of the series, which lay rich and unsullied on the table in the living room. My mother took up one of the volumes and with a gaiety which abandoned her to a piece of the drama in the presence of her husband and her son, while my father stood smiling at her with his arm around me, she read aloud in a lovely pealing tone of intimate belief in life's good things, so that we all had the same heady feeling: "Everyman, I will go with thee, and be thy guide, In thy most need to go by thy side"—the motto printed on the flyleaf of all the volumes, of which we had so many. In this modest cultural possession, which stood for more than itself, we all felt learned and lucky, valorous and faithful.

1968

The Thin Mountain Air

THE ANIMAL CREATION

[*During his early college years, Richard, son of the ailing Lieutenant Governor of New York, takes a summer job on a New Mexico sheep ranch owned by a wealthy old New Mexican, Don Elizario*

Wenzel. The old man is married to a beautiful, very young wife,
Concha, whom he guards with frustrated jealousy. A vagrant ranch
worker, Buz Rennison, has a dangerous eye for her. It is the season
of the shearing and dipping of the sheep.]

I see my own work of that summer of a half century ago as
though the years were a deep physical distance away. Everything
stands in miniature though distinct detail lighted by halations of
memory, watched from a height looking down at the swarming
creatures, men and animals, at their hard tasks; and somewhere in
the midst of it all at my various jobs is my young self.

The figures are tiny, seen from so long ago, but brightly lighted.
I have the feeling of an illicit observer, an eavesdropper, for they do
not know I am looking and listening. Years and distance away, they
seem to create a harmony now out of the confusions of that far time.
Even as I remember those, I taste the foulness of the task they are
doing. Their colors are brilliant, they throw shadows like spilled ink,
for the sun is furious. This little group seems to stand as all humanity
at timeless purpose and act, and they forge again a link in the human
chain reaching from antiquity, so that their commonness becomes a
marvel of discovery about man's enduring habitude. A dimly remembered passage from the third of Vergil's *Georgics* in Dryden's trans-
lation tells me again of the persistence of human ways in the parallels
between the Roman shepherd's husbandry and mine, as a youth:

> *Good shepherds, after shearing, drench their sheep.*
> *And their flock's father (forced from high to leap)*
> *Swims down the stream, and plunges in the deep.*
> *They oint their naked limbs with mothered oil;*
> *Or, from the founts where living sulphurs boil,*
> *They mix a Med'cine to foment their limbs,*
> *With scum that on the molten silver swims:*
> *Fat pitch, and black bitumen, add to these,*
> *Beside the waxen labor of the bees,*
> *And hellebore, and squills deep-rooted in the seas . . .*

Never under the summer sun has work seemed harder, and men
closer in their anonymous part of it to the very nature of the animals
they tend. The marvel is that with means so primitive, and with rela-
tively so few men, and with animals so frantically self-protective, a

degree of efficiency is reached, a job done in its annual cycle for a space of days; and at the end of work, an exhausted and at moments even a rude lyrical humanity returns in the evening to those who have borne the burden of the day.

At the end of the first day of dipping, Don Elizario came from the house after supper as we were all sitting or lying around the coals of the fire where the cook's big enamelled coffeepot kept his brew steaming for our tin cups. The sky was washed with the last rosy light of the west. Our aching bodies sought ease and cool. It was time for sociability.

Don Elizario made a point in such evenings of joining his men, to give them his comradeship as unspoken gratitude for their work. If we were to have entertainment, we must make it for ourselves; and he must do his share. Anyone who could sing a song, or tell a story, or dance a jig, was called on to do so. We left a little clearing between us and the campfire for anyone who would perform by the faint glow, like stage light cast upward. Don Eli sat on an upturned bucket, as his legs were too stiff to let him get down to the ground and up with comfort.

In our first evening festival, Ira the cook—the men called him Irene for their view of him as female in his role as cook, and because of a way he had of shrilling and shooing like a woman when anyone tried to steal anything from his stores of food—usually began the show as someone cried for his fiddle and his dance.

Irene ran to his wagon. He slept there rather than in the bunkhouse and guarded all his possessions in neatness. In a moment he returned with his violin. Making a great act of tuning it, listening critically with the box close to his ear among his wild but sparse tufts of hair, he created anticipation as by an overture to a play. Finally, satisfied, he pushed his crooked spectacles up on his nose, slapped the ground twice with his right foot to announce rhythm, and began to play with a scratchy thin tone a repetitious piece like a tune from a square dance. After one stanza played standing still, he began with the next one to shuffle and stamp and turn to his own music. Turning one way, he was the man, crazily gallant and stiff; the other, he was the woman responding, mincing in exaggerated gentility. Soon we were all clapping hands and whistling encouragement to his music. At this, he would flare his eyes at his audience like a flirt, and then toss his head at our impertinence and beat away at the dusty ground while his mosquito noise kept up with perfect, insane regularity. It was growing dark. Someone threw wood on the fire and light blazed up, throwing the footlight glow over Irene in his greasy rags. He scorned, dominated, and wooed his audience like a great star. Finishing his performance, he slowed it down, and, at the very end, made a deep, rickety, but splendid bow, holding his fiddle and his stick of horsehair widely apart. He created the illusion of a large theatre, transforming our enthusiastic but sparse applause into an ovation.

There was a moment of satisfied quiet. Don Elizario nodded his approval of the show, which he had seen many times. His presence among us was so at home and so easy, yet so sure of its authority, that we were all sure of it too. Nobody was immediately moved to follow the cook with an act, and so, clearing his throat, making rusty little sounds, Don Elizario grandly brushed his profuse mustaches upward with the knuckles of both hands and said, "I will tell you a little story."

Nodding and smiling faintly, he slowly told in his mild old voice a story about a certain Saint Jerónimo—but not the famous Saint Jerónimo, but another less well-known but a saint just the same.

"Did you ever hear of the Devil himself making a saint out of anybody?"

Well, that was exactly what happened in the case of Saint Jerónimo. It seemed that Jerónimo was a ver' handsome young man who had his way with all the fine young beautiful girls in his town (this was somewhere in Spain a long time ago). There wasn't a girl who didn't lie down with him the minute he asked her to. When he made pusha-pusha, they cried out in joy, "Jerónimo, Jerónimo." All the other young men said he had the ver' Devil in him. He had to fight many duels, but he never lost one, and turned up fresh as ever to pick out a new girl.

The Devil got him all those girls, everyone said there were two thousand five hundred and nine of them—Don Elizario with a wheezy little laugh gave the signal for a general stir of carnal laughter, in which all joined—and when it came to number two thousand five hundred and *ten*, the Devil made a saint out of young Jerónimo; for when Jerónimo tried to make pusha-pusha with her, the Devil prevented his *verga* from rising, just exactly at the moment when it was needed. The young lady, who was the daughter of a king, and ver' used to having her own way, slapped Don Jerónimo in the face, saying, "You are good for nothing but being a monk," and went home to the king's palace.

And Don Jerónimo saw the Devil sitting over there on a tree stump with his own *verga* pointed like a carrot and jumping around like a goat's. The Devil was laughing and laughing. Don Jerónimo said, "Ver' well, I will become a monk." And so he became a monk, and lived a long life of good works, and his *verga* never tempted him again, and after he died, he performed many miracles and became a saint.

Everyone stirred. The subject had been raised which was most on their minds, far away from women, tired enough to believe or dream anything, and hungry for any expression of their desire which it was impossible to fulfill; and, too, the possibility of sanctity in any human predicament crossed their minds, however faintly, since everybody believed in goodness as well as evil.

Someone cried out, "Hey, Irene, tell us about the last time you tried to get you a sheep, and what the ol ram did to you for it!"

The cook, in shadow beyond the firelight, tossed his head and waggled his tongue at the question. Everybody laughed at both the questioner and the questioned, and at the inevitable folk joke about those who work with sheep year in and year out. A sort of anonymous comradeship descended upon us all. Sanction, so mildly introduced by Don Elizario, was now rudely confirmed.

Just at that moment, out of the darkness between us and the house in its dome of cottonwoods silhouetted against the stars, Concha came toward the firelight and entered its long rays, which stretched away on the ground between the shadows of the men.

Her husband stood up and said sharply, "What are you doin here? You get back to the house!"

"There is a telephone call," she said. "The Datil operator is trying to get you—"

She turned to go, gathering herself in fear. As she turned, she saw Buz for an instant. He was staring at her with his mouth open. The firelight was on both their faces. The exchange of a look between them was like a bolt of feeling, as if a door had been thrown open and closed on a revelation. Everyone saw this—Don Elizario saw it. He lunged toward Concha and struck her on the buttocks to drive her to the house. They diminished away into the darkness.

"Jesus Christ!" exclaimed Buz softly. "Did you see that?" He asked me, "Who is that? His granddaughter?"

"His wife."

He exclaimed, "Wife!" making the word obscene. He spat scornfully.

The others were all long aware of Don Elizario's marriage, and by now were indifferent to it. They saw no reason for the evening to come to a sudden end. Someone called out, "All right, there, Babyface, now you just give us a song or a story."

This was said in a tone slightly menacing, and the others added their voices. In the air was a threat of hazing the latecomer if he should refuse. Buz shrugged and asked, "Well, is there anybody got a *gui*-tar here?"

One of the Mexican herders handed him one. Buz tuned it even more elaborately than Irene with his fiddle. As he strummed for his own satisfaction, he said, "I'll sing you a song I made up myself."

Stolid silence met this. Finally, in an expert imitation of the show-business singers who broke their voices sentimentally on stressed words, he sang:

> *Oh, my darlin Bonnie Mae,*
> *I said goodbye to you today,*
> *And I wonder if I'll ever see you more.*
> *With your hair so golden bright*
> *And your eyes so full of light,*
> *Oh, my darlin, wait for me I do implore!*
>
> *Oh, no gal was ever sweeter,*
> *If so, I'd like to meet her,*
> *But my darlin Bonnie Mae need have no fear.*
> *As long as stars are in the sky*
> *Then my love will never die,*
> *And my blue-eyed Bonnie Mae will be my dear.*
>
> *Bonnie Mae so sweet and slender,*
> *All her words so true and tender,*
> *I will carry in my heart until the end.*
> *Hand in hand we'll walk through life,*
> *Oh, my darlin little wife,*
> *And nothing from each other shall us rend.*

Slow final chords. Silence. Then, "She somebody real?" asked a voice longing to believe.

"Hell, yes," replied Buz. "Only her name was different."

"Did you marry her?"

"Hell, no. The sorry little bitch ran off with a horny circuit preacher. Them shoutin sons of bitches get all worked up with their Bible whackin, and then can't keep their pants buttoned."

Tom Agee half rose and hoarsely cried out in his weak voice, "Now look here, you little squirt, you just keep some respect in your mouth for the good men who harvest for the Lord!"

"He was a preacher," I told Buz.

"Well, Reverend, no offense," said Buz. "They's all kinds."

But he grinned like a rosy satyr at those nearest him. There might have been a reply, but from the house dimly away came two sharp little screams. We looked at each other and most probably saw the same picture. Don Elizario, done with his phone call to Datil, which would connect his line with Socorro and Magdalena, had turned to Concha and beaten her to teach her a lesson, and, I thought, to chastise himself for what his jealousy had to remind him of.

There was an animal look on Buz's clear little face. If she had made a powerful impact on him, in their lightning-quick meeting of eyes, his excitement, and its nature, were now doubled by the idea of her being hurt physically on his account until she had had to cry out. Someone went to the coffeepot on the coals, which breathed now bright now dim on the light night wind. The pot was empty. It was clear that Don Elizario was not coming back. Tom stood up to signal the end of the campfire hour. Everyone drifted off to bed.

When we were alone in the bunkhouse, Buz asked, "Did you mean what you said about him and her?"

I nodded.

He groaned.

"She's too beautiful to live—especially with *that*. If I could only—"

"You'd better not. He's crazy when it comes to her."

He locked his hands behind his head on the hard uncovered pillow and stared up at the rough beams of the ceiling.

"All my life I said I only wanted to get me a rich woman and settle down and keep her pregnant and then, whoo! I'd be free to do for myself with anybody I wanted to. But when I see someone like that—what's her name?"

"Concha."

"Concha. I don't know. Did you see her lookin at me? —Oh me, oh my. I just bet she'd welcome the change . . . One more look, and it'd be all over."

I remembered Tom Agee's advice to me about Concha; but I did not repeat it now.

Buz had a new idea. "They tell me you are the only one here who goes over to the house."

"I don't know. I *have* been there."

"You goin back?"

"Maybe."

"Yes, Richie. Take me with you! That way, I—"

"I couldn't."

"Sure you could. You could just say you brought your friend to play a game of Crazy Eights, or talk about the weather, it wouldn't matter what, just so I—"

"No. The old man wouldn't have it."

"Well, so how come you get to go there and not me?"

I explained how I happened to be at the WZL.

"Well, I don't have any society doctor to get me in where I belong, but I thought I had a *friend*."

"You do. I just know how things are over there. You wait till the old man asks you. Then I'll take you."

"You sure are the prize gutless wonder!"

I picked up my book and began to read. It was like closing another door in his face. He could not endure being excluded. If he lost me, he lost everyone here. After a while he said, "Where will you go after this job is done? We've got only a little while more."

"I'm staying on till September some time."

"What are you suppose to do here all that time?"

"Oh, odd jobs after the cattle come back and the range men come in, I suppose."

"I bet they aren't paying you anythin. I bet you are just a dude on vacation. *I* have to work for *my* living."

"No, they aren't paying me anything. They are doing me a favor, so they say."

"And you work your balls off for nothing?"

"Listen, I'm trying to read."

He most of all dreaded separateness. He went on, "I get paid off at the end of the dipping. I don't know where I'll go." Expertly, he put pathos into his voice. "Listen, Richie. Why don't you go with me? We'll figger some place to go. Nobody ever turned ol Buz down yet, at anythin. With your brains and my guts—*you* know—why not?"

I remember the power of his confidence in himself, and the appeal this allowed him to exert. His energy was compelling. His color was high, his eyes sparkled, and the flaw in one of them seemed to evoke a vision of a world in which he was all-powerful. His light voice softened with the excitement of conspiracy.

"We'll show the sons a bitches," he said urgently, meaning the world at large.

I had to shake my head.

"But why? Why?"

Saying why took much time and wrangling; at the end of which he was deeply aggrieved, and I was sorry for him, angry with myself, and wondering how I could find a way to be his friend, in spite of everything.

The next evening, Don Elizario was back with us as gently merry as though nothing too real in its revelation had happened the night before. He was ready again for imagined romance, and the rituals of comradely obscenity invoked by men isolated together. Don Elizario cleared his throat.

"I have a song tonight," he said as though to make us forget the night before. We became quiet. In a moment he began to sing. The sound was remote and clouded, in a quavering husk of a voice. I thought of the slowed song of some shelled desert creature—a cicada—created to celebrate the hot and empowering desert light, but now making its last salute to life and creation. That it came from a man full of present regret, and still lively longing, made it, instead of lusty and funny, as touching as shame for that which could not be controlled. He sang:

> *Darling, I am growing old,*
> *Silver threads among the gold*
> *Shine down there on me today;*
> *Life is fading fast away.*

> *Let me feel you everywhere,*
> *Where I'll find your golden hair.*
> *Let us mingle though I'm old*
> *Silver threads among the gold.*

Applause for the boss man was lively; but even before it died down, Buz, gleaming with hard high spirits, took the audience with a song which sounded like a direct reply to Don Elizario's gentle old obscenity. Whacking the box of Pancho's guitar for attention, Buz cried out like a comedian over a boisterous crowd, pressing the unspoken rivalry he dared to feel against Don Elizario:

> *H-o-o-oo,*
> *Will you love me when my batteries need re-chargin?*
> *Will you love me when my carburetor's dry?*
> *When my inner tubes have lost their self-respect?*
> *Will you be satisfied just to bill and coo?*
> *Or will you sit around all day and cry?*
> *H-o-o-o-,*
> *I'll drive that ol tin lizzie till I die!*

He sang it through again, to clapped hands. Don Elizario stood up. When the stanza ended, he said sharply, *"Mañana mucho trabajo, amigos.* So now break it up, break it up."

The circle began to drift away. Don Eli called out, "Bebbyface, you come here."

Buz paused, and then, with a mock-humble skip, went over to the old man, who held out a hand, slightly trembling, with forefinger pointed at Buz. "You stay 'way from my wife, you hear?"

"Yessir. Me? I don't even *know* your wife, Mr. Wenzel. Sure, sir. Anything you say."

But his smile contradicted his respectful promise. Don Elizario waved him off and turned homeward. Buz watched him go, then turned to me, expecting approval. But he saw in my face, apparently, that he had ended forever any chance of his being invited at last to come with me to the house on some fine evening.

"What the hell!" he said defiantly. "There's more'n one way to skin a cat—if you know what I mean."

Like most young people, I was not then fastidious—inclined more to endure what was about me. Through no choice of mine, Buz Rennison was a fixture of my days. In his deceptively slight, neat, clean body, there was something of the confident child, and if self-love and innocence were not the same thing, he made them seem so. He had the intuitive sense of a cat when it came to feeling the mood of another, and like the cat, if he felt himself momentarily rejected, he set out to win fond attention.

"Richie, I've been watching you and thinkin about you. I figger you can help me to find out how to better myself. I said to myself, How does a man get ahead? He don't get all the way there, where he wants to be, just by using his physical culture. I said to myself, No, I said, they have to use their brains. You use your brains all the time, even when you're alone, don't you? You're always readin in a book, or puttin things down in those little pocket books of yours."

"Yes."

"Well, I never went to college, hell, I never finished high school, even, but I've done a lot of livin, and I'm not so dumb. But I figger I've got a lot more to me than I know how to use."

"Everybody has."

"Don't turn me off like that. I want to make a *contribution*."

He mixed pleading modesty with worthy ambition and I had no idea how much he meant any of it; but uncomfortable as I was under the implied flattery and envy of my state of life, I was touched by the other self he showed me, and I was depressed at not knowing how to guide him into ways he sought. It was impossible to tell anyone to begin at the beginning, all over again, and make a new life.

"Will you help me?" he asked.

"I'll have to think about how I can do it."

"Well, for now, that's good enough for me. I knew you would never let me down."

This made me more uncomfortable than ever. If I suffered his worst simply as features of a specimen, I found it more difficult to come to terms with his creature best. I was sure of only one thing about him—never had I seen anyone whose fullest expression was physical, the center of which was blatantly sexual. In act and response, even self-unaware, he revealed this. You'd never see in him any of the humble proprieties of "simple" people. He rarely modified his behavior but enacted his impulses directly. His physical life was intense—even to the way he slept, breathing heartily. Sometimes he kept me awake with this.

One night I had enough of it. Stealthily I got up and pulled on my blue jeans and went out into the cool calm darkness.

The night yielded a waft of wind which slowly turned the windmill, whose gonglike sound drifted over the ranch. The ground was

pebbly, prickly, and I was without boots. I walked with wincing
care toward the salt cedar grove between me and the house. There
was joy in being alone. The waning moon was still so bright that
the stars were paled. The day's ungrateful ground became the night's
pale velvet. Over the house the cottonwoods were modelled like
sculpture—clusters of soft light in relief against caverns of deep
shadow. I savored the natural world so fully that a youthful kind of
ecstasy lifted me out of myself, until the great mosaic of the stars,
and the moon in its decline, united for me the urgency of man's
concerns with the vast impersonal glory of the abiding universe.
Despite promises and longings, I did not know where I was meant
to go in life. And yet there I stood, myself in the center of the visible
world, possessed in my own thought and feeling which united all; I
the vessel of dimensions I could never measure. It was one of those
moments of mystery—or was it revelation?—which came to the young
in terms sublimely dislocating, all the more marvelous because it
was beyond the asking.

It was therefore jarring suddenly to see a figure emerging from
the moon shade of the salt cedars into the moonlight, and to hear a
voice come huskily calling, "*¿Quién es?*—who's there?"

I was not used to night vision, but he was: it was Don Elizario. I
replied softly, "Richard."

I could hear him come toward me, and in a low murmur of relief, he said, "Ah, ah." When we came to stand near each other, he
said, "You are night owl, like me?"

"No, I was just awake. I felt like going out to look at the night."

"Yes," he replied, "yes, I too." He laughed gently. "And I always
come outside by myself to make my water on the ground, you know?
I grew up doing it. There is something about it, I don't know what."

He invoked antiquity in his natural act and pleasure. We stood
looking at the sky. I could see him well now. He wore an old-
fashioned nightshirt with his feet in shapeless masses which I took
to be carpet slippers. With his fingers spread like elongated paw
pads, he pointed in a lurching gesture at the sky and said, "You
know? I come out at night and I wonder why all that goes on"—the
firmament—"and we pass away. If I can see it, and you can see it,
we have it inside us. Why don't we last like the stars?" A pause.
"Well, we are good, and we are bad, but the stars are nothing, they
are just faithful and they are just beautiful, eh? There is no reason
for them to die."

"Well, but they do, sir, you know? After billions and billions of years, some stars do die."

Again his wheezy mild laugh. "It might just as well be forever, then, eh? —How old are you, *chico?*"

I told him.

"Aa-ha. When I was your age—" He stopped, muted by his memories, and so was I, whatever they might be. Presently, "I was married a year younger than you are now. I was a ver' handsome man. Many girls. All I knew was the land, from my *papá*. He told me once, *The land will either kill you or you will make it serve you.* I have made it mine." He waved at the horizon, and the south, where his other ranch lay so far away out of sight. "My sons. There were four. Two are living. They are like me. They live for the work. We are rich and we still work hard. I come out and look up there, and I say I have done all a man is made for." He faced toward me. The immense night had induced in him an impersonal intimacy. "When you have done all you can do—" His voice fell away. The wind stroked the slow turning blades of the windmill. A sheep dog barked once, remotely, loyally. The softest stir went through the salt cedar shadows. His world was speaking to us. His silence was melancholy, but seemed also to carry the content of acceptance. He shivered. He crossed his arms as if to seek warmth. He asked, "You are happy here?"

"Yes, sir."

"Here is where I belong," he said as though to set happiness aside for himself as irrelevant, if he was where he belonged. "Go to bed, *joven*, much work tomorrow. Good night, good night—" He was moving away and his voice faded with him. *"Buenas noches."* My heart came into my throat, why I could not say, as I watched him taken into the shadows of the brake.

But I knew why for certain on a late afternoon when the declining sun was changing color from white to pale gold, and the coming evening seemed as perfect and fragile as an eggshell.

1977

Far from Cibola

(THE COMPLETE NOVEL)

*[A collective portrait of people hungry,
during one day of the Great Depression of the 1930s,
in a small Southwestern county seat.]*

I · UNTIL SUNDOWN

Far to the west, the mountain was shining like glass in color and mystery upon the horizon. Smoke from morning fires vanished against the sky, pierced by the sunlight. In her kitchen, Ellen Rood laid wood in her stove. The children were in the yard, and their mother could hear the noises of their early work. Donald was hacking at wood with the huge ax that wobbled in his grasp. His sister Lena, with delicate childish movements, washed her hands and face in the tin dish that stood at the edge of the well. Mrs. Rood blew upon her fire, and though the smoke rolled back into her eyes, and sparks burned upward to sting her arms, she hardly noticed them. The children sounded happy, and in her own mind there was a strange content, for when the jobs of her household were going forward, she forgot the various halts in her life which made her experience. At least winter was over, and she would have no more strife with cold for many months. The summer would see Don grow a little more, and the farm let into their cupboards a little more food.

But behind such precarious comforts as these, Ellen Rood considered the promise she had made to Mr. Haystead in town yesterday. Everyone she knew was going to be in town this morning at ten o'clock. She had tried to avoid giving her promise to Haystead. Some pride held her back, perhaps it was Haystead's smiling fury, an expression like a threat, that had offended her love of independence. When he spoke of the government relief, his small blue eyes went dry, and a little red. His big hands trembled on the wheel of his car. She knew that his family had suffered, and that he loved his children. It made her scornful to see a man shaken so by the common disasters of everyone she knew. But she had agreed to meet before the Courthouse at ten o'clock. There would be several trucks loaded with food, and a government agent to discuss the sale of crops with the men. Ellen's fire now roared up the adobe chimney.

The children were silent.

She called them, not looking for them through the window. She broke an egg into the coffeepot. Grease exploded in little bubbles of heat in the bacon pan. Ellen said to herself that she was right to make up her own mind. She might go to the meeting, but she would do as she pleased after she got there.

The children hadn't come in. She went to the door. Her eyes were cooled by the light wind. Her breath grew longer in that burdened air of the morning. She called again. She stepped into the sunlight and walked past the house, walls of old adobe with a roof of hammered tin which her husband had made from waste cans a year before he died. A small shed faced her, with glass panes for its front. Here the chickens lived. Walking faster now, she heard a small commotion, a thrashing behind the shed, and Lena's voice chirping with a dry excitement. In a moment she saw Don standing on his bare toes, thrusting a pole at a snake that tried to coil in the shadow of the chickenhouse. Lena's hands were laid over her mouth. Both children were pale. The snake, the color of the ground in shadow, flowed about the pole and retreated, thrusting away the loose dirt surface with a terrible constant strength. Ellen swallowed her breath. A sickness was in her tongue, and she stumbled forward running, her legs unsteady but her eye and her mind strong. She kept her voice quiet so the children wouldn't turn around. She took Lena by her bony little shoulders that shuddered from sympathy at her mother's touch.

"Get the ax, Lena," said Ellen. The little girl crying with a heart full of commotion turned and ran. Don's throat dried and contracted. Ellen heard him choke. She slid her arms over his brown thin arms until she could grasp the pole. Her fingers closed on Don's. She could feel his hard body beat against her own in their joint fight. It gave her a passionate anger. Stumbling together, inspired by her rage, they stepped into the sunlight, forcing the rattlesnake back. In the new light, the snake flashed and dripped with beads of light as if he were wet. The short grasses and the mild dust quivered upward under his lacing retreat. Donald's head was as high as Ellen's chin. His eyes were as sorrowful as her own. Her high cheekbones seemed to have a smile below them always, but her son's mouth, small and delicate, was stern. It resisted threats every day, from hunger and poverty, from natural pride put down by family grief; from private boyish terrors that he might die, and so leave his mother and sister without defense against the trials of living. On Ellen's face there was sweat. Her tongue dried against her teeth. The snake wrapped its golden dusky length against the pole. Lifting her arms, and Donald's, Ellen flung the snake twenty feet away, a streak that became part of the ground when it hit. Behind her Lena's hand pushed against her quivering flesh. Ellen reached back and took the ax.

"Don, stay back with Sister," she said, and drew her fallen hair from her eyes and from the white corners of her mouth. She hefted the ax without feeling its weight, and started forward across the brief grasses, walking with a long pace, lunging jerkily like an old woman. In a little hollow of gypsum stone, white with pure sunlight, the snake rested ready, his arrow's head fixed. His rattles sang in the stillness, like a grasshopper in the weeds by the porch. Behind her, Lena cried shrilly in her throat. The arrow's head moved slightly, side to side. The bright singing of the rattles loudened and stopped. The snake flew. It dustily struck the earth. In the confused shadow of her swinging skirt, where she stepped quickly, Ellen saw the dust-colored body turn again into the coil. Panting out loud, sweating like a woman in labor, she grasped the ax handle with both hands as if it were the handle of a churn, and brought the rusty ax head heavily straight down. It was a thump that wounded the earth, a deep sound. The snake's rattles fluttered. The white belly turned up, and Ellen moved back again. She turned the ax in her hand and clove deep with it, cutting the snake behind its crushed head. A faint stench touched her nose, and entered her mouth, something that smelled damp and yet dusty, like mold, like a foul cistern, yet remote, as if it could be the imagined smell of an illness in herself.

She kicked loose dirt on the snake. The small rain of dust fell back where the body, bled of its smooth power, palpitated slowly to calm. Then she turned, dragging the ax behind her, and walked back to the children. Donald came forward on tiptoe.

"Is he dead?" he whispered.

Ellen took his hard thin shoulders and clutched them with her wet hands. She pressed her mouth shut. She shook the boy with a wild trembling strength. Lena was coming forward too. She began to cry again when she looked up and saw her mother's face, so worn, so familiar, assume the shape of a desperate smile now, while tears ran down its pale brown cheeks. The children understood that their mother was angry with them, and relieved, and fuller of love than she had ever been. The three members of the small, hungry family, three people abandoned by everything but their own ties, suffered a moment that lived as an influence forever after in their lives. The boy forgot it in time. But the weeping love of his mother, as a climax to courage, stayed like a picture with him always. The little girl knew self-pity and generosity, a throwing away of feeling to anyone who would take it.

"Come," said Ellen, turning the children toward the house. She took them to their breakfast. Entering the kitchen, she lifted the old yellow newspaper on top of the scarred sewing machine where she worked at times, and saw that her purse was lying there safe. The children laughed through the sucking breath of the lowering excitement. The purse was a black leather bag rubbed to a worn rust color on the corners. It was a family joke, for Ellen referred to it as the "Black Maria," a phrase she had heard somewhere. Love of independence, and the agency of independence, these were shown the children forever by the frightened concern their mother had for her purse. It had rarely been a full purse. Now it was empty. Yet it accompanied her when she went to the town, and it rang in the mind like a nightmare when it was missing, with incident fears, pallid courage, and childish desire to make achievements to supplant the Black Maria.

The breakfast dishes cooked and murmured on the stove. Ellen agreed with Donald that the snake would not die until sundown; when he thought of that strange fact, his eyes troubled her. Lena shuddered, hating the snake and all mention of it. Her brother let thoughts drift in his mind like dust through fingers, a childhood feeling, which in words might give pictures of the damp hole where the snake lived underground; the gold tracks of its body through sharp grass in the dawn; the eye like a polished grain of sand caught in a drop of milk; the shift of those scales over one another as the body waved flat through the dust; the convulsion of the snake's body all day, the hot day, when the higher the sun rose the more lucent all shadows became, and smells from the desert were forced into the air, while insects made sounds like the air itself, and the snake turned hot and dead to the touch; until sundown, when the smallest grass could feel the cooler wind, and long rays of light bent upward on the horizon, and the dead snake would be at rest, no more treacherous and tried by life.

It was a land where men had to conquer trial and treachery always, the area of New Mexico that shared the plains country and the mountain country, and men deciding to live there chose the small valleys of reluctant rivers, and planted their trees, making a shade over their houses that was the only kind thing for miles around. It was the land of the Seven Golden Cities of Cibola that had wooed the northward Spaniards so long ago. The natural mystery of plains giving back to the sky a second sunlight and of mountains drawing the horizon up to blue pinnacles dazzled men through three hundred years, and led them up the dry beds of creeks and over the heat lakes toward the Cities of Cibola, whose yellow gates they never found. Crossing the very plains and mountains where the terrible wealth was promised to be, they were always far from Cibola; their hope had no strength in it but greed; and legend was only a powerful mockery. What wealth they ever found in that land was created by man with the earth, and toiled for in obedience to the seasons; just as the human graces of shade trees and windmills had to be brought and planted before the land gave any comfort.

In this year, 1933, the marks of comfort were visible, once the town was in sight. The sky was blue in the slow-running irrigation ditches that dragged cool sandy mud from field to field. It was a cloudless April and the winter birds were joined by the mockingbirds of spring, which sang all night long on fences and telegraph wires. In the early morning the air was scented with a sweet burdened wind.

II · SKYWARD

Living nearer to town than Mrs. Rood, the Larks still belonged to the country. Mr. Lark possessed a windmill that turned above his house and his turkey run, shrilling and gonglike, a machine that drew upon the sky to bring water out of the ground. On windy nights, the fury of the turned fan and the complaint of the rudder chains woke Mrs. Lark and visited her for hours like pain. Her husband slept, immense and gaunt, while she held her hands on her breast, hoping to quiet the opinions of anger and disloyalty that arose there and made her heart thump. At such times she hated Lark; yet she could not hate him, for the length of their life together, and the vagaries of humor that kept him laughing or smiling into his old age. He dwelt upon memories, and that made her tender toward him; as a woman of labor and family long scattered, she knew the business of pushing the hours of the present to their fullest use. It was boyish of her seventy-year-old husband to be recalling, always, the circumstances of his boyhood, and the scandals of his early youth, the money he had brought West and lost, the feats of stamina he had performed on the range in winter through snow, or up the beds of dry rivers in the wry droughts of pitiless summers.

Yet Andrew Lark sometimes amazed her by conceiving a plan and executing it at once. In the light winds of the morning, in which his great metal flower turned and whined complacently, the idea struck him that if he greased the windmill, perhaps the next windy night would pass without the clatter that Nona Lark always complained of. He told her he was going up the ladder with a bucket of grease, and asked for his glasses.

"Now, Andrew," she said, feeling short and helpless, wafting her glance across the pale blue sky over them, "you know you're too old to climb them rungs, that's thirty feet to the platform. You wait till Moses comes out next time. You just wait, now."

She saw him walk, the knobs of his joints pulling the tendons and releasing them jerkily. She knew from his hunched shoulder that he was smiling at her. His stubbornness was always irresponsible, a matter of laughter and sly slaps on her old thick buttocks if he chanced to pass her. She saw him go into one of the sheds that he kept so neat out in back. He emerged soon into the sunlight, wearing a wide straw hat and a rope slung across his blue shirt, which was thrust forward by the long bones of his great skeleton. To the rope was fastened a yellow pail full of grease and a stick.

"Andrew," she cried, hobbling forward; her face turned to a bright gold in the sunlight, deepened by parallel wrinkles, and toned by her freckles. "Now, you stay away from them rungs."

Her cats gathered at her ankles with soft rubbings. Lark chuckled breathily and swinging his long arms that were heavy with bone instead of flesh, he passed her grinning. When she called him an old fool, he skipped, grotesquely, almost obscenely, with love of his own contrariness. At the foot of the gray weathered wooden windmill tower, he measured the height with a squint, and adjusted his bucket. He cleared his throat, and she thought angrily that he was about to begin one of his unbearably long monologues, drawing on all his past experience of windmills and their peculiarities. But he stood silent, putting his hands (they trembled, she feared) on the rung at his breast height. Then he started up.

His ascent against the blue broken pattern of sky that showed through the tower scaffold was an unbelievable movement to Nona Lark, standing below. His old legs that passed across the earth with rheumatic trouble, his arms that creaked in supporting a newspaper, were conducting him higher and higher. An absurd flow of pride touched Nona in the throat, and increased her fear. The silver wheel of the mill spun slowly above him, and he climbed to it without pause. Soon his arms were clawing through the square hatch cut in the platform below the wheel. He raised his head above it, and smelled the wind. The wheel, throwing incessant spokelike shadows over this higher world, whistled sedately by his very ear. Looking down, he saw Nona, and waved, as if he had gone on a far journey. A gray sickness crossed his eyes, at the changed colors of his wife, his farmyard, his roof, the bushes and tulips below there. The blood flew away from his sight and his mind. But only briefly. He recovered in time to see Nona wave back, and flop his hand at her whine of worry.

He drew forth his glasses, large black-rimmed circles, and set them on his nose. Then he crawled to the works of the wheel and the center rods, the chains, and the rudder that hummed as the wind shook its silver fin flatness. With his stick, he paddled purple and gold and black gobs of grease upon the bearings of the mill. Turning with the wind, a movement that took a skill of which he was proud, he saw the fan shaft eat the grease and pack it back into the unseen housing where it turned and went soft. He thickened the chains with plentiful greasing where the iron links chafed and squeaked. The wind was melodious in his ears. His zinc windmill with such sharp blades, twisted sailwise to own the wind, filled his heart with pride. Not for years had he been so close to it, for his boy Moses usually came up to fix anything that needed it. The mottled pale blue and silver blades charged and clanged softly as the wheel turned. That was a sweet noise, not one to keep anyone awake, a poor farmer's wife, whose old head was the scene of so many worries, real and invented. Andrew Lark deliberately avoided looking down at Nona, for that might suggest to her that he cared as much as a trotting mare's turd what he thought of her fears. He made a rich and hearty job of the greasing.

When he was done, and the fan turned, the chains quivered, without any metallic sound but only the sound of how the wind was taken and thrust by, he sat down safely beyond the turn of the bladed wheel and pulled out his newspaper from his trousers pocket. He leaned against a corner timber of the tower, and began to read. His incessant habit, it infuriated Nona now, for the unconcern it displayed. She threw her apron up to her face and flashed it down again. She turned back to the house, panting with anger at his absurdity. Once there, it struck her that he was up there to grease the thing as a favor to her, one she had begged to have done by Moses. In her parlor, troubled by the complexities of which her life was made, love mixed with exasperation, and gratitude with terror, she sat down on the ruby-colored sofa of plush, and folded her hands against her lips, and sighed until she felt her gorge rise.

Through the cool dark doorway of the parlor, she could see beyond across the kitchen to the back door, screened. On the screen, haloed with sunlight, the three kittens leaned their forepaws high up, turning their heads sidewise and scratching dimly. The little one, mewing, pressed its pansy face on the screen. Nona left her sofa and went to the cats, thinking the little one was cute's a crab apple. She saw Lark walking toward the shed out in back. Her rising and falling from annoyance and tenderness and fright left her. She was suffused by an inner blush, some reference to their joint past, adventurous and successful. She knew how he felt about going up the mill. It was wonderful.

After breakfast he confessed that he had left his glasses up there on the platform. Her fury was so full at this that she couldn't speak. Her face flooded dark. He laughed. He flung his great flat hand against her breast in playful coarseness. He said he'd get Moses to come back from town with him in the afternoon. Moses would get them down for him. He wouldn't need them, meantime. The silver zinnia hummed and flew slowly constant above the warming yard.

III · TO UNDERSTAND

On the farther edge of town, at the fork of the two roads that fed it, one leading to the railroad junction ten miles away and the other to the transcontinental highway that cut through the mountain, the long low shed of the cotton compress was a grape red in the early sunlight. The shed was so low that from a little distance it seemed to be part of the ground. In the good times, the trucks backed up to the delivery deck charging and ripping the air with exhausts, and the white-and-brown bales of cotton were rolled down the incline in a rich procession, while in the low tower above the shed the steam exhaust pipe blew like a gun, and the furious presses in the cool shadows of the building flung downward on the gray cotton with a wild grunt. Mexicans ran the machine, laboring half naked, deafened by the explosion of the exhaust and the echo like a low thunder in the eardrums, like a shocked blood, when the pressure was released and the baled cotton gorged forth to the waiting truck.

At the north end of the shed was an office, behind heavy doors. Here the clang and thunder and scream of the compress machine were slightly muffled. Yet when the plant was shut down, the silence was more difficult to stand than the boom of industry. No one stayed in the long red sheds but a Mexican caretaker, and the manager, and Heart DeLancy, his stenographer. But the manager was away, trying to save the business for his owners. The Mexican was surly from being underfed and indulgent of his humors, which Heart thought obscene. She was sympathetic of his pennilessness, but the vigilance of her inner eye upon its own woes took all her emotions.

She was twenty-six years old. Her parents who had come here from Texas were dead, after raising her to her teens with intense propriety, naming her Heart out of sentiment for the love they'd had as bride and groom, and showing a long picture over the arc of years of how stubbornness must fail and turn weak when a man's hopes are time after time baffled by the dry earth, disease upon cattle, the escape of the railroad through another town than this, and finally, most astonishing, old age and fatigue. Heart had worked for herself since she was seventeen. The results showed plain in her small brown eyes, which held a wry light, like some drift of fluid over unchangeable opinion. Her face was white, the skin drawn over the bones with a gentle firmness. Her slightly protuberant teeth showed always under her upper lip. When she laughed, it was a cold sound, yet her eyes danced, and a little flush took her cheeks. Her breastbone was prominent, her shoulders shallow. She was slow in her movements, even in her thoughts, but quick in her feelings, and full of desires, many of which she had happily fulfilled by her own enterprise.

The first of these was to be educated. Her Texan parents had both been full of intense but incommunicable opinions about life, the foundation of their experience, the trial at explaining their failure. Heart was convinced that education was the way to conquest of understanding. She had the usual schooling in county schools, and at seventeen, an orphan, had gone to take special work in a business college at Santa Fe. Here she worked as a waitress, supporting herself. Facts poured into her mind and were superimposed upon each other, warming her by their strange presence, and forgotten very soon. But the life she was leading brought her to the conception of another desire, one that she nursed until an inner gaiety arose whenever she considered it.

Seeing the tourists go through Santa Fe, in great cars, with clothes and accents from dim splendid places, she resolved to travel as much as she could her whole life long. She eavesdropped while her diners ate, listening to their tales, gossip, the fall of their speech, not intending to imitate, but desirous only of furthering the boundaries of her life, so bleak in its outline, yet so full of some inherited curiosity and fire at its core.

When she could typewrite and spell, when a little experience had shown her how to behave in an office, she returned to her home, and went to work for the cotton company. Her salary was good. The compress whistled clouds of released steam into the sunlight all day long, for months, years. The warehouse shed space was at a premium. The trucks rumbled off to the railroad ten miles away, bearing cargoes. Sometimes she rode to the junction, named Ramona, and watched the trains, saving her money in her bank account, and her feelings in her mind. At last she had enough money to board the train. She went alone to El Paso, and bought clothes. She went to California. The suffering light in her eyes was lost in her pleasure. She met people easily, talking with men as simply as with women. She spent her entire savings account in a month of investigation of the world. She came back poor, but content, and amazed by her own conversation, which drew authority from the facts she had observed, and sociability from the relaxation of her self-pity.

It was so in the good times.

Now the silence in the office at the north end of the raspberry-red shed was a burden against her head. Heart was alone there. The cotton plants in the wide fields were withered and russet, from being unpicked. There was no one to buy cotton. There was nothing to bale. The engines and the steam were cold and silent. Her boss had cut her salary three times. Then he had stopped it altogether, for there were no letters to be written. Yet he had laughingly assured her that she was still the official secretary and left her her key to the office. Here she came daily, to sit before the typewriter, and compose letters to her friends whom she had met on her trip to California. She looked out of the window and could see ten miles eastward the brushed faint darkness above the horizon that lingered after the train went through Ramona. Between here and there was a tawny space of flat land, green only where artesian wells had been released, or irrigation ditches dug and willows planted. Out of the other window was the mountain, and the highway leading to it, people bounding on fat tires from coast to coast, able to assuage the restlessness that was American in so many of them as a people, and so individual in Heart.

She had been spoiled for the meager design of her destiny, which was to live and die on the Southwestern plains, contributing what she could to the life of those small towns. Turned idle, her fingers unrented for the skill they had learned, she returned to her inner life, yet this time with no possibility of letting it purge itself in action and independence.

In town, opposite the Courthouse, was the newspaper office, with large plate-glass windows reaching almost to the packed-dirt sidewalk. Beyond the window was a linotype machine, which was operated by Rolf Kunkel. When she was successful, Heart had him call for her at the warehouse in the evening, and drive her home in his car. Other times, Rolf's shyness took on the quality of valor, a defiance, covered with blushes and contradicted by some watering of his pale blue eyes. He was nearly thirty, she thought. He was tall, and heavy at the shoulders and waist. His black hair grew in a formal series of waves to a peak over his left eye. She liked his large nose, and the biscuit of his chin, with the long cleft in it. She considered him handsome, and could imagine him in the clothes of a Californian. She was too crafty to investigate his mind, preferring the proofs of his value that she could detect in his body.

Day after day, idle in the office, she dreamed about Rolf. She

passed a succession of plots through her mind each of which ended
with his capture. At first she had thought in terms of marriage. Now,
intense and lonely, without aim, her spirit straightened by poverty,
she thought in dreamy terms of "illicit love." Rolf Kunkel went with
no one else, she knew.

It was a morning like all the others, until the Mexican caretaker
came up to the office door. She knew him by his walk, a step-drag,
step-drag sound that betrayed his lame foot. She hated him, for he
interrupted her empty bliss, and when he walked in she smelled the
reek of his age and indifference, and was angry because he was smiling. She asked him what he wanted.

"*Pues nada,*" he said, "nothing," and cuddled his old brown
hands against his dirty vest, fluttering them against his belly as if they
were captive birds. His smiling went on, and in his throat he made
little moans of announcement and awareness. In a moment, Heart
heard a car, and leaned to the window. Her pale cheeks reddened,
which made the Mexican caper against the wall. Rolf Kunkel was
out there. She watched him climb out of the car and come ambling
heavily down the warehouse deck. His large face was sober, and she
impatiently wondered what made him look so stupid. But when he
saw her at the window, he grinned, and his blue eyes filled with shy
cordiality, a mistiness, and she turned warmly away from irritation,
to meet him, ignoring the Mexican's lecherous imaginings at this
meeting.

IV · THE THREE SONS

If Mrs. Vosz went around saying that she had nothing left but
her boys, then her husband, who was taciturn and opinionated at the
same time, thought the same thing, but said nothing. The boys were
triplets, seventeen years old, tall fellows, with yellow hair, and blue
eyes that darkened with embarrassment or eagerness when they were
filled with ambition or excitement. Their names were Richard,
Joseph, and Franz. It was a matter of delight to their mother when
they left high school to help on the ranch, of their own free will. She
took their hands in hers and wept upon their twisting knuckles,
staring at them out of her weeping eyes with a claim upon them that
was almost unbearable, for its intensity, the references it made to
the amplitude of her donation to their living, and the dues which
they must feed back to her in love. But Mr. Vosz, speaking calmly

behind his curtainlike mustache, returned the boys to high school, and answered the fanciful fears of their mother with a rough tenderness in his touch upon her.

The high school was one of the few eminent marks made by man on the tawny land where the town stood. As the county seat, the town drew business traffic to the Courthouse, and boys and girls from surrounding ranches and villages to the high school. The Vosz triplets were popular in school, where their physical excellence, the thrice-repeated image of men growing out of clumsy sweating boys, whose hands were desirous and timid, whose minds dwelt upon the ripening of information with a secret and frantic intention, impressed the other students though they could not have said how. It was easy enough to admit that the triplets were magnificent athletes, which was true. The teachers sighed over them as much as the girls, for they were famous in their devotion to their mother. It was felt that anyone who was so good to his mother as any of the Vosz boys and was so clever in school, and so furious on the track field, must become a great man.

In the early mornings, Richard and Joseph would get up while a stratum of cool air still clung over the ground, and run a mile, pacing each other, their big chests lifted against the wind of their running, their legs rising and falling like harmonious parts of music. Franz, the other triplet, liked to sleep late. But his brothers got him up and dragged him out with them, making him practice with them for the track meet, which he disdained, knowing that he could do things with much greater ease than his brothers, and that he needed less practice, but only the desire like an inspiration to do anything, to do it brilliantly. Because he was so simply superior in the ease he had over his brothers, Mrs. Vosz often scolded the other two for picking on him. Their bland faces would laugh out at her, as if this were a malicious joke, not to be taken seriously. Franz would thrust his legs impatiently out before him as he sat down, and Mrs. Vosz, seeing how foolishly she had accused them, would begin to cry, begging that they not desert her in her poor fat old age, with her weak heart and her simple needs. This sentimental attack was even more difficult than her nagging. The triplets would crowd around her, stroking her bulging shoulders and back, making impatient sounds of consolation, while she let her head with its topknot of pale thin hair fall against the breast of one of them. If Mr. Vosz found such a stormy woe in progress, he whirled the boys away with his immense hand, and lifted his wife's chin on his wide thumb, looking into her eyes with a sad rebuke for her weakness. She would then control her heart that feared so many unnamable things, and let her love call out for acceptance by baking vast cakes and pies, pampering the boys and their father to excuse their memories of her tyrannical weakness.

But such moments had their weight afterward, when the triplets, abroad with boys and girls in exploration of fun and desire, would lose the sweet feelings of guilt they owned and find themselves hateful for the grief their mother would feel if she knew.

Such things as these didn't show in the pattern of the daily life which people saw of the Voszes. Mrs. Vosz went to her mid-week church parties in town, lamed by the weight her ankles carried, dressed in blue silk that billowed behind as she walked, nodding her head with its party hat that sat high on her faded hair. Mr. Vosz ran the ranch, though no one could sell cows at the price no one was paying. The sheep kept them alive, going at prices which a few years before would have been a rancher's joke. The boys went to school, working afternoons to get ready for the track meet. Richard was a hurdler. Joe ran the short dashes, and Franz ran the mile and did the high jump. The meet was to be held at the high-school athletic field, on the edge of town, a sandy flat with a cinder track. Six schools in the region were entering teams.

But Franz still was too lazy to practice mornings. He could hear his brothers get up, and then the scratch of their spiked shoes in the ground outside his window as they practiced starts. He lay awake, with his eyes closed, then he slept suddenly again, until Dick and Joe dragged him out for breakfast. The sunlight was drifting slantwise across the stove where Mrs. Vosz was busy. The steam from the coffeepot turned a transparent gold in the light. The light bounded back from every clean corner of the room. The smell of breakfast, the virtuous smiles on the faces of his brothers, the unthought-of familiar shape of his mother, made Franz very happy, and he leaned far out upon the table in the kitchen, and thought of the track meet that afternoon; his stomach contracted pleasantly. It was a sensation that reminded him of the challenge to his stride, the fact that he would win, easily, and the simple chance that he might lose; the love for a physical game that kept him and his brothers so busy.

Mrs. Vosz brought the cereal bowls to the table. She set them down and watched the boys pour sugar and cream on. Their big hands, the hungry opening of their mouths, waved across her in a pitiful memory of their babyhood, and she passionately knew they were the same now as then, and that their hearts were untouched by the idea of love, and its consequences, which had drawn her own life down from girlhood to marriage, brief rapture and then devoted drudgery, with her mind losing everything but concern for her family, her body heavying, her fortunes lowering with those of her husband. It was some helpless devotion to life and acknowledgment of it that led her into the punishments she made on herself and the boys when she claimed them, over and over, to her own fidelity. After bearing a large family, now scattered into so many separate lives that touched her only incidentally, though she had given them birth, she had borne the triplets, a last terrible ordeal of her body, and a growing nourishment for her heart.

The boys finished their oatmeal. Their spoons scraped and they licked their mouths, looking to her with trust for the next food she had ready. Their eyes were laughing. She brought them their eggs and bacon and coffee, and then she said, "I know you're good boys, I know it in my heart. A mother always knows."

She knew how they hated any tearfulness, or any of this business about love. Her words therefore sounded angry, for the control she threw into them. Franz slapped the table, and made a joke. They avoided the moment. They remembered times when they had not been good boys. It made them angry now to have such times brought up by what their mother had said. A certain mournfulness, an atmosphere of resentment, drifted over them in the kitchen. It was broken into open irritation when Mrs. Vosz said, "How many of my boys are going to town with Papa and me?"

Joe laid down his fork, and said, "Mumma, you know the meet's this afternoon."

The other two went on eating. But Franz looked up and saw the facile hurt expression on his mother's face.

"Mumma, you've known about it for weeks," he said. "We all three are in it. I'm running the mile."

"So you see, we can't," said Richard.

"What's happening in town anyway?" said Joe.

"Your father has to go to the Courthouse," said Mrs. Vosz. "Your track meet's not till the afternoon. We was going in the morning, and to lunch at the café, but I suppose it's too much to ask for a boy to be seen with his pa and ma."

There was a silence. The morning was recognized as hot, yet with stray tendrils of spring wind in it. The boys hated this sort of rebuke. Their silence, which was one of good judgment, seemed surly to their mother. She laid her plump hands with the smooth shiny filled skin on her bosom under her great rounded throat, and plucked in anxiety, irritation, at the loose flesh there.

"It's perfectly all right to get up before sunrise and get your breakfasts. I suppose I don't need any praise for that. Nor am I wanting praise." The strange churchy sound of the word "praise" took her emotions; it reminded her of God, God is love, and sorrowfully she began to weep. The boys knew it from her voice, for they were not looking at her. Their necks reddened. The intolerable justice of their debt, a debt of life and emotion, made them feel a little wild in their minds. But they went on eating, and their mother went on talking. "Oh no, you'd rather go off somewhere by yourselves or with them kids from school, God knows what you do with them, I pray so hard that you keep good and all, how do I know?" she cried, seeing the inevitable betrayal of her jealousies in the images of the triplets, who carried youth's burdens and needed to be rid of them, a need that contained fear and sweetness, a spending of youngness. "Every chance you get, you run away from us, you leave your home, God knows 'tain't much: your papa has done the best he could: and so've I, not that you care, with your track meets and all: what is this crazy track meet: you ought to be on the ranch helping your papa instead of running to school with them girls . . ."

Richard pushed his plate away and arose. He went to his mother and touched her shoulder.

"Now, Mumma," he said.

She sobbed and refused his touch.

The other boys, with a heaviness in their hearts for the humiliation of their spirits, and yet knowing a necessity of assuaging bitterness, went to join Richard. They gathered around Mrs. Vosz and playfully talked to her; they made jokes, and agreed that they were poor dumb johns, and didn't deserve all she gave them. She admitted that her heart was sore from things that she couldn't define, and that her temper ran away with her. She kissed them all, and said she was sorry for thinking mean things about them: she knew they were good boys, in her heart, she said. They blushed. Franz, in confusion, said that he would go to town with his father and mother, and after lunch, he would go to the track meet. The other boys, he said, were going to spend the morning at the field, practicing. He wouldn't need the practice.

"I'll go with Poppa and Mumma," he said to Richard and Joe. "You johns better get to work. I don't need the practice."

They all laughed together, and a new geniality came up. Mrs. Vosz kissed Richard and Joe, forgiving them for not staying with her. It was Franz, who did everything so easily, the handsomest, the sweetest, she knew, it was he whom her secret heart loved as the son of whom the three boys were the triple likeness.

V · INTENTIONS

Fat's Café was across from the Courthouse, and a couple of doors down from the newspaper office. It was the place where occasional transcontinental motorists stopped for lunches and suppers, and where all five of the high-school teachers went now and then for a festive meal. In good times, when the movies were showing twice a week in the Imperial Theatre down the street, Fat had crowds for supper. When the cotton compress was running, the truck drivers and the foremen, the visiting ranchers and farmers all came to eat with Fat. He composed affectionate little ads for the paper, "Fat's Café, The Lunch Grand," and "Elegance and Home-Cooking, Fat's Café," which brought his appearance and his voice before the reader's eye. Fat was the owner of a sad face with a fastidious expression. His flesh flowed in a widening line from his ears, the button of his chin, his buried jaws, down upon his breast and back. His arms were pink and delicately modelled, in spite of their grossness. His hands were small. With them, he worked over his hooded stove, and served his customers, smiling with his mouth, that never lighted his eyes in the same expression. His thoughts were always emphatic, but his voice was thin and high, a prayerful tenor that made him sound bewildered. His most constant thought about himself was that he needed to be hard. He would shriek at high-school boys who tried to charge their cups of coffee and doughnuts. They would smile, and walk out, and later pay him, making him feel that some strength was missing somewhere in him. But the air of steam hooting softly above the range which he kept so well shined always restored his happiness, and he forgot the necessity of being as skeptical, as narrow-eyed, and as "hard" as the men of the town whom he knew as a fellow citizen. His pride lay in his Café, in the accomplishment of every small order with as much elegance as he could put into his cooking and serving.

That was why he had a waitress; it was, he said to himself, why in such disastrous times as these he still employed a waitress, though the crowds were thinned down to the old level of his early days, when he had been sufficient to cook and serve too. Every morning at seven o'clock, Mrs. Rocker arrived, and she stayed until ten at night, leaving Fat to close up at twelve. She went home to her naked boarded house that had one room and three beds for herself, her husband, and their six children. Fat had called for her once in his car, to take her to work. The sight of the bedclothes, the collapsing white enamel and brass beds, the hardened and shined and worn plaster of dirt on the floor, the happy, lousy children, the dogs and cats who slept and ate in the quilts and the dishes with the family, the smell of old lazy animals that filled the Rocker house, turned something in him to disgust and then pity. Mrs. Rocker had been so cheerful always, so unexcited about her way in life, that he'd assumed her to be well taken care of. After that, he couldn't pick her up, and for weeks he struggled to be hard, and discharge her, for the place she came from must certainly threaten the cleanliness of his Café. But if she saw his sullen agonies of intention that failed to crystallize in act, she said nothing, but smiled at him all day long, rubbing the counter with rags, sweeping corners, pulling her hair out of her eyes, and laughing through her lips that shielded very few teeth. Fat remembered in despair the beautiful girls who waited table in El Paso, with their eyes painted blue and lashes black, their cheeks shading from high crimson on the bone to plaster white at the neck, their mouths rouged, their hair bleached. He often comforted his soul in bed with the scheme that he might one day marry such a person and bring her to his bed and his Café. In the meantime, Mrs. Rocker found things to do all day long in the Café, smiling with trust upon him, never questioning his rightness, and taking her small wages from him with an agonizing, flattering humility. She was simply dependent upon him: and too, her husband, the children, the cats, the bitch who trailed complacent dugs to feed the litter for whose mother the Rockers could spare a little out of even their own needs.

Yet as the months went past, and spring approached, with no better trade, the grocery stocking fewer dainties, the teachers staying home at their boardinghouse when the county passed up their salaries, Fat knew he must discharge Mrs. Rocker, for there was nothing to pay her with. He could do the work himself. It would be a relief. In the afternoons, when great dinners should have been mingling their rich fumes on his stove, with Fat himself tasting and planning, the stir of spoon in stinging messes, and deep content of filling up kettles with most edible stews, he had lately been sitting at the counter staring at newspaper pages, not reading, only watching pictures, while he grew drowsier and drowsier. The light changed and ebbed from his long narrow Café, while the polished light brown of the counter vanished way back in the room to shadow. The row of six tables opposite the counter receded like a darkening checkerboard. It would take a cup of coffee to wake Fat up at four o'clock. Waking from his unsleepy daze, he would see Mrs. Rocker beyond the stove sitting on the packing box which was her own domain and smiling at him, as if she were waiting for him to awaken and take her smile. Fat thought angrily that she looked at him like an old fool-hound dog bitch. But he could say nothing.

In the morning he went out to the grocery, and returned with a number of extras. Good times or bad, there was no difference to Mrs. Rocker. But he knew that the track meet would bring a lot of visitors, and he must be ready for them. He could take in enough to give Mrs. Rocker a week's wages and tell her not to come back. He had just spent every dime he owned in cash, and still owed the grocery. The morning was brisk and sunny. Mrs. Rocker left the door open to smell the wind off the plains, while she scrubbed at the large mirror facing the counter. Her cleaning stroke left rubs of light soap. Fat dumped his provisions on the table beside the range, and got hotly to work. Every time he turned around, she was smiling at him in the mirror, clouded and turned witchlike through the soapy reflection. His fat hands flew, shaking the upper arms. His skill revived; his knife flashed in the steamy sunlight around the stove. His spice boxes of green and red with gold exposition labels flourished above the copper pot and the rubbed aluminum vat where the soup bone protruded, boiled blank of succulence.

Presently Mrs. Rocker moved back of the counter. To pass Fat she had to squeeze against the counter, and he had to tiptoe and lean over the stove. It made him blush with exasperation. Who wanted her here anyway? She was in the way! She bent under the counter to get her sugar sack to refill the bowls. Her buttocks touched Fat behind his leg. He turned, ready with a fury that he couldn't explain. But Mrs. Rocker, innocently straightening up, moved down the counter at her work. She poured the sugar into the glass bowls with hinged metal tops. Fat said to himself with the emphasis of his opinion, "God damn it!" and went on working. Pretty soon, the old mood came on him again, and the mixture of his vapors, the ingenuities of his baking and his precision, satisfaction at applying the knowledge he had found out for himself and turned to use, let him begin to sing. His voice, so short of speaking, was expressive in song, and an original melody he had sung for years at his work, over and over, without change, rose from him and vanished up the tin hood of the cooking range, a sound like a part of the morning.

Later, Mrs. Rocker came back from the front of the Café and showed him an empty catsup bottle. Her expression assumed openly that it must be filled, and that Fat, who had everything so excellent, would see to it at once. He looked at her toothless smile, the dancing, familiar content of her blue eyes. Unable to name it, and so argue it away, he saw again his obligation to her, which he must meet or admit failure. How could he tell her there was no money at last? You don't buy catsup for nothing. Maybe tonight if there was a crowd in, there would be money for that. Also, money to send Mrs. Rocker away with.

She set the bottle down and went back up the aisle behind the counter. He felt again the severe need to be hard. It was not his fault that the Rockers would starve together, the old man, the kids, the cats and dogs, anything else that lived in that shack. He turned back to his stove. A rattling noise from the front of the Café made him turn. He threw down his butcher knife and shrieked with all his confusion, dividing his small voice with his unfamiliar vehemence, "Y' old fool, quit disturbing all that!"

Mrs. Rocker, who had been rearranging the Chesterfield cigarette cardboard displays, turned back to look at him, amazed and a little frightened. After staring at the sunlit window space, her eyes were dim until she was used to looking down the aisle of the Café. She saw, in a moment, that her fright was foolish. Fat was standing there, wiping his knife against his apron where it rounded across his stomach. He was smiling at her, his face was a heavy red, and the idea that he had sounded mad at her was lost in the new idea that he must have been joking, for he laughed a little before he turned to his meat block and began to slice chops.

In a few minutes the sheriff came in for a cup of coffee. Mrs.

Rocker served him, for that was her office; and when it was done, Fat strolled down the aisle and leaned on the counter where the sheriff was, and the two men without speaking greeted each other by staring into each other's eyes, long and with unchanged looks on their faces, the sheriff looking above his tilted cup and Fat leaning on his palm; neither having anything to say, yet mindful of the custom of sociability.

VI · COWARDS

In the road camp eight miles from town, Leo was awake when dawn began. He always woke up before sunrise, with a cold abandoned feeling in his stomach. He wrapped his thin arms around his chest, shivering at the fleshless articulation of himself, and watched the sky send reflections of light on the hazy brown earth. When the sun was up, the road camp would awaken. He would drink coffee, and thank the men for letting him sleep all night with them. Then he would start off again, walking on roadsides that had small stones in their dirt. When he stepped on a small stone, the jolt shocked by relay all the way up to his neck, and his head, a small head with white cheeks and reddish eyes, rolled with an ache. Cold and dismal though he felt the dawn to be, though it was early spring and an occasional smell full of sweetness and promise touched his nose, he closed his eyes and inched into his blanket, planning in his mind how warm and happy it would be if he could stay all day, sleeping in the blanket in the little tent. But this was a positive desire; his strength, physical force and private will, were all gone. He hardly possessed opinions any more, saving only that one which let him believe in his heart that life was altogether miserable, a thing that could just as well be denied and ended, in spite of the strange gripings in his stomach that made him beg food every day, or in his mind that kept him toiling toward California, on alien roads in the company of no people but other aimless paupers like himself.

The sun now showed, after silent trumpetings of gold rays above the waving line of hills. A blur of gold that looked wet as melted metal grew along the horizon. An intimate light turned the sunward edges of all things in a brief golden beauty, cactus bushes, small pebbles, the poles of the telegraph by the road, the small tents of the camp, the barred and chained bodies of the trucks, any growth.

Then the light became suddenly equal, and shadows faded, while a returned chill smote the air that had been briefly warmed. Distant hollows in the ground lost their blue mists of broken light, and clumps of trees came out from obscurity, and the town eight miles away in the sharp early light had a clean toylike look.

Leo was fogging his memories in a returned sleep when the boy in the tent with him sat up with an explosion of breath, and a yawn full of noise like the sound a dog made when yawning. Leo's nerves sickened tight at the disturbance. His tent-mate crawled out into the light and went to wash. He was greeted by a dog. There was one more moment of stillness in which the humming of messages on the roadside wires travelled clear, and then the camp seemed all at once to be awake and busy. Cooking smells drifted to Leo's nose. The mucus wept a little at this stimulus, and rolling his head with weak desire to arise, Leo felt the saliva run down his mouth and choke him. But he came to his crawling position, and left the tent. His feebleness made him seem old, though he was twenty-six. His smile of ingratiating thanks, of willingness to help with anything, made him look like a sneak, for a scar held one corner of his mouth down, and any pleasant expression turned to a sneer on his face, while in frown or repose his face had a thin starved dignity, under the bald rise of his round forehead that bulged and made his head so much too big for his neck and shoulders. The camp boss told him to sit down and wait for breakfast, impatiently, embarrassed by the weak murmur of Leo's voice, and the tragic affability he so hardly managed.

At last, holding a tin cup of coffee that burned his fingers, he knew a tide of courage run through his aching tripes, and he told the men eating with him that he was moving on to California that day. He had been, he said, without work for fifteen months. He did not add that he suffered from tuberculosis of the lungs.

"In California I know plenty of people. I have an uncle who is a lawyer. The climate will be easier on me, too, than the East."

He spoke with a precision of word and tone, making reference to his past, which included education, ambition, content, and no plan for such a present as he owned. He told them he would make it in another week at the outside. From New Mexico to the coast was an easy route. The coffee, having shocked him into well-being, now cooled in him, and indigestion returned, his mood faltered, and he

grew silent, weakened. The men ate stolidly, silent except to comment on cars that went by on the road, a few in series, then none for
a long time. Leo looked after the cars.

"Damn their souls," he said.

The camp boss looked at him curiously.

"I had a car once," Leo continued, a pale flush showing on his
cheekbones. It was a weak whimper that he made, and the boss in-
differently turned back to his food, easily certain of what to think
of cranks who magnified their hard luck into a whole attitude toward
everybody else. But Leo went on talking, his big head shaking on its
poor neck, making the only protest he knew to make against the
circumstances of the life that let him lower every day into helplessness. It was a murmur, almost impersonal because of the feebleness
of its delivery, against the larger lives that survived while his own
faded. Everything he said referred to money, and its absence from
his pockets. The men let him talk, hardly listening any more than if
they were listening to the crying of a cat. Nor did Leo expect them
to listen, for he was talking to himself. It was a rehearsal of the
thoughts that made him dream at night. He presently fell silent,
knowing no conviction from his breakfast or his tirade.

The men got up. The cook watched them dump their dishes into
the big tub for washing. They went to the trucks, and soon a wild
firing of the exhausts sounded out. The trucks lined up on the road
heading east. The boss told Leo he was sorry he couldn't offer a lift
on the road but the trucks were all working in the opposite way. Leo
said it was all right; he thanked the boss for the night's shelter and
the breakfast. The affability in his eyes touched the older man, and
as Leo turned to walk off to California, stumbling slightly on the
rutty roadside, the boss had a feeling of pity and half-comprehension,
which if he could have said it would have told that every scale in
life had eagerness to exist, and that to see this eagerness defeated by
forces beyond control was pitiable.

Walking slowly, Leo had travelled over a mile when a car pulled
up beside him. It was already hot in the open country, and the sparse
sweat that his body could produce showed on his face. The man in
the car said that a man he knew, the road camp boss, had told him
to pick up this guy. Leo got into the car, breathing through his
mouth. He smiled his unalterable sneer, and settled back on the seat.
The driver was a fellow about thirty-five or so, Leo thought, heavily
tanned, and thickly built. He was smoking a pipe. His face was

bland and almost merry. The car was an old coupe, travelling with loud winds of mechanical maladjustment. Yet it was cool in the car, and Leo felt a kindness toward the day that brought a sensation of strength with it.

His driver said he was coming down from his filling station in the hills to town, and could take Leo as far as that. He claimed to be always willing to give a guy a lift. He spoke with a Southern accent, and presently revealed that he was from Georgia, and in a rush of confidence that surprised Leo, he sketched his past with an assurance that it must be of interest to anyone. He'd been in the navy during the war, and after that had a job with a bank that didn't pay enough, and it was a raise to drive a long-haul freight truck in Alabama. That didn't last very long. The Texas oil fields looked good, and when they cut down, he drifted up to New Mexico and got a job helping in this filling station. He enjoyed talking about himself, contented with his past, and requiring little of the present. Leo thought him an enviable person, for the bodily strength he had, and because life to Leo had become the necessity of wanting what others had. Facts about Leo didn't interest the driver. He gave no time for any confession. The first interruption in his agreeable reminiscing was a blowout. The left rear tire gave out, and the rocking car slid on loose gravel for several yards before it was halted. The driver sat still for a moment, humorously nodding his head.

"Wul, Gawd da-yum!" he said.

Then he shrugged, and got out, lazily, stretching his arms after tucking his pipe away. He knocked the seat cushion out of place, and dragged out the oily dusted tools. Leo stood by him, wanting to help. The driver threw him a wrench to start loosening the nuts on the rim, while he himself jacked up the axle. Leo set the head of the wrench over a hexagonal nut, and threw the force of his body against the lever's force. Up his arms went pains with a fluid swiftness. He smiled and tried again. A little gray caked dirt fluttered to the ground from the wrench head. He couldn't turn it. His chest began to hurt. He coughed, slaking his dry mouth. In a moment, the driver came around beside him, and then saw that nothing had been done, he grasped Leo's arm with a lifting grab and set him aside, making a disposal of such a puny wretch. Leo stood by. Rage boiled in his throat. In a few twists of the wrench and an easy slide of muscles, the driver had the nuts off the wheel, and the tire bouncing on the ground as he leaned it against the running board. While he worked, the driver whistled a tune. Now and then he looked at Leo, who was sitting on the shady side of the car. He thought Leo was laughing until he saw that it was shivering that made his head wobble and his shoulders tremble. But there was nothing to shiver about, and he ignored it, turning back to the new tire which he was screwing to the wheel.

Leo was shivering from injustice. His arm was bruised where the thin flesh had been rubbed against the bone by this man who had set him aside like so much tumbleweed. In his heart was a need to refuse further help from such a man. He stood up. The driver began to let the jack down. The car settled on to the new tire and the driver withdrew the jack. Leo watched the spare tire flatten down almost as low as the punctured tire had been. He waited for the driver to see this. He pointed it out to him, smiling with a timid return of friendliness. The scarred lip showed his teeth. It looked like a sneer, a delight in this foolish hard luck. The driver looked at the tire. He kicked it. He turned back to Leo and said, in a roar of sudden exasperation, "Well, wap off that Gawd da-yum smahl!"

He went to the front of the car and pulled out an old tire pump, and set to work. It was slow going, and the tire rose imperceptibly. Leo sat watching a Negro approaching them from down the road. Making a small cloud of dust with his kicking feet and swinging his hips from side to side as he walked, a mincing, muscular stride, the Negro approached, and Leo could see that he was young, and of medium height. His eyes were sleepy. He was smiling. In his hand he carried an old stick. The driver didn't see him coming, but when the Negro said, "Mownin' boss," he turned, resting his fist on the pump handle.

"Whey you come f'om, nigga," said the driver, in an exaggerated accent that Leo coupled with the fact that he was from Georgia.

"F'm down de road," said the Negro, leaning in a friendly way against the rear of the car. "Havin' tah trouble?"

"Git a holt hah," said the driver, throwing the pump handle toward the Negro, who smiled like a pickaninny with candy and did nothing. The driver tightened his stance on his spread legs. He looked at the Negro waiting. The Negro laughed out merrily, full of sunshine and goodwill on the morning when the wind blew so gently and so freshly. He crossed his legs, standing with a certain natural elegance, a racial and physical ability to express his mood with every change of his body.

"Did'n yoh heah me, nigga?" said the driver. Leo saw that his face was a deep plum red. His own mouth turned dry suddenly, when he saw that the driver was angry. The Negro closed his eyes and shook his head, shaggywise, spilling out the mood of comic happiness he held.

"No zah, boss," he said in a rich voice, hoarse with comedy. "Ah don' want pump no tahs . . ." exploding into a hooting laugh that assumed universal amusement at the situation. Leo saw the red fade from the neck and head of the driver, and relaxed, thinking that his anger was gone. But stooping quickly to the ground, the driver picked up in each hand a small stone that would fit the closed fist, and with a blast of breath from his nostrils, he bounded forward and hit the Negro twice, once with each fist, against the temple and on the jaw. The Negro's eyes fell open, and he choked on his laughter. He dropped his stick. He fell against the car and rubbed his head. In his hoarse voice, roughened first by amusement, he began to wail, making no words, but only doleful syllables. Before him stood the driver, boxing the air, and leaning and leaning with his body, and smiling with the simplest face of pleasure. There wasn't the slightest look of fury about him now. His merry eyes were lighted with fun. The rhythmic, slow spar of his hands had a gaiety in them that was full of grace. He turned his body at the waist, swinging rapidly. He waited for the Negro to recover his breath, and to lose his amazement of pain.

The Negro lowered his hands from his head, with his enormous fingers spread out. Leo thought it was like a monkey in a zoo lowering his paws from his puzzled head when he had a headache, a thing he couldn't explain or touch, some alien menace.

"Come ohn," said the driver. His voice was teasing and humorous. "Hit me: hit me, nigga."

He backed off as the Negro lunged forward on his feet. Blood was curling down the Negro's face from the cut temple. He shook his head. The driver poked out with one rapid arm, and cuffed the Negro's ear, a stinging and taunting hit. Leo sat down on the running board suddenly, too shaken to stand. He tasted the coffee from breakfast as it regurgitated into his throat. He swallowed with control. The Negro was weakened by astonishment. Leo clenched his mouth and hoped the Negro would hit the driver.

"Hit him!" screamed Leo suddenly.

"Ah'll hit 'im," said the driver, lazily looking at Leo with appreciation, and instantly thrust his fist into the Negro's belly. The whimpering stopped. The Negro took in a series of shocked little breaths through his mouth, making a sound. Then he skipped out from his position against the rear of the car, and dancing wildly on the road, he gave an appearance of having his tail erect, with his head up and his back curved in. His hands played across his front. The driver glowing with delight danced around as the Negro's eyes cleared and watched for an opening. It came, and the black hands drove to the pink jaw, which jerked away. It was the last blow the Negro landed.

"Oh, yeah?" said the driver, and clutching his stones till his palms sweated against them, he swung right and left against the Negro's head, his body; breaking the left ear and ripping teeth down into the bone with a remote crackling sound. He beat the Negro back to the side of the road. The stoned fists cracked against the black skull. They drove into the Negro's belly, rising up under the heart and the ribs. Leo saw the Negro stagger and fall into the ditch, and ran forward from horror. The driver leaped down into the low ditch beside the road and picked the Negro up. He stood him on his sway- ing legs, and knocked up the Negro's arms, making an insolent de- mand that the Negro defend himself, guard his body before the new attack. Blood ran down from the Negro's eye, looking pink upon the grayed flesh of the face. The driver grinned. His pink jaws were widened by the pleasure of his blows. The pain of the Negro's first blow on his face was something exciting and stirring, like the quickest delight imaginable. The Negro wandered in tiny circles, hardly standing. Along with the sedate and narrow welling of blood out from his lips came a whispered wail. The driver leaped once more. He drove one hand to the Negro's mouth, closing the fat lips and whitening them. He struck with a wet accurate sound at the jaw with the other hand. The Negro's eyes rolled upward, and the lids stayed open, and the eyes showed white. Bleeding slowly, the Negro fell to the ground in the ditch, where it was half shady. His breath wheezed with wetness. The driver threw down the small stones from his hands and spat on the ground. He looked cheerful. He stirred the Negro once with his foot, almost gently, and watched for any awakening. There was none. Scratching himself in the crotch with an easing sensation of triumph, he went back to the car and slapped Leo on the shoulder.

"Ol' nigga get fresh wid me," he said with a certain tender simplicity. He laughed softly in his throat, and leaned down and picked up the brass tire pump. He bent his back up and down over the pump. The tire rose slowly again.

Leo went to the side of the ditch and looked in. Half in sunlight, the beaten man lay like a large baby, his knees bent, his forearms bent back and the hands lying with relaxed curled fingers above his shoulders. His head was rolled to one side, and the red-and-white issue from the mouth flowed slackly to the ground. The eyes looked dead. But threads of tortured reflex tightened in the body, and it quivered every few seconds, accompanied by a windy grunt from the working throat of the Negro.

Leo sat on the edge of the ditch to gasp. He could taste his own illness in his mouth. He sat without ideas and forgetful of words. In his heaving were flashes like blindness that showed him how much he hated the driver and his acts. He felt hatred for himself, who had stood vomiting and helpless while the Negro had been beaten down to a ditch. He saw the body stir now, slowly, as if awakening from some hibernation. But it quieted again at once, with only the shocking quiver tightening and loosening in the torso and along the legs.

The driver threw down the pump and kicked the tire.

" 'At's O.K.," he called to Leo. He unscrewed the pump hose from the tire valve, and threw the pump into the seat with the other tools. He replaced the seat cushion. Then he walked over to the ditch. He chuckled, and said as if he liked the Negro, "Ol' nigga be 'bout an hou' comin' 'roun . . ."

Leo set his wrists against his eyes to stop his weeping. He stood up.

"Time we got goin'," said the driver, and turned back to the car.

"You're going to leave him here?" said Leo.

The driver stopped. He laughed generously.

"Fo' Chras' sake!" he said, and then disdained further answer or comment. He clambered into the car and started the engine. He called to Leo to hurry. Looking again, Leo saw the Negro there, whose life slowed in the black body. Then taken by a strange panic in himself, Leo turned and ran to the car and clattered in beside the driver. They drove off. The wind cooled them. Nothing could cool the burning shame Leo felt, to be riding here now. The driver lighted his pipe and sighed, for his body was contented with the spend of violence it had made. He smiled dreamily. His mouth moved around the stem of his pipe as he talked.

"Ol' nigga," he said, with amusement. "He sho' made a mistake
to git fresh wid me! Eh?"

He turned to Leo.

"He sure did," said Leo, loathing himself.

"Sure beat up on 'im, didn' I?"

"I'll say," said Leo.

"See 'im try to hit me?"

"Yeah," said Leo, and laughed. The droll pity in his voice satisfied the driver. Its cowardice set Leo trembling in his breast. He
closed his eyes, looking inward upon himself. All he saw was a tired
soul, begging sleep.

VII · UNDER THE WIND

The Courthouse stood in the hot sunlight, with shadows of the
tall trees washing over its yellow brick front. The building was two
stories high, rising toward a roof of chocolate-colored slate. In front
was a tower that rose a third story, and ended bluntly, in a cluster
of dormered windows. All the windows of the building were tall and
narrow, with rounded tops. Their edges were trimmed in gray stone.
The window woodwork and the doorways, the glimpse of cool hallway inside, were finished in dark varnish, brown with a glow of red
beneath. The Courthouse rising from a country of dust had something of dust's color in all its parts, except where the shadows waved
like a cool wash across its front, in blue leaf echoes. The trees were
great cottonwoods, planted forty years before, watered in their early
sprouting by the ditch that used to flow from the river; grown in their
middle years to be large enough for hangings after posses returned
with human trophy; now stately, like patriarchs whose wisdom lives
in their mere physical presence, after all sight and mind have been
feebled.

On the thin scatterings of grass before the Courthouse, the crowd
grew as the morning went on. Shortly after eight they had begun to
assemble, leaving their cars, trucks and coupes and sedans, touring
cars, around the corner and down the main street, parked in front
of the newspaper office and Fat's Café, a line of various cars spreading as far as the garage at the point where Main Street became highway. They came with lunches wrapped in paper. They came with
empty stomachs and fearful breasts. Their greetings were lively and
happy, as the eddies in the crowd changed and distributed the indi-

viduals. Coming together for a common purpose, the people of the town and the country were easy in their meeting, like people who have for generations drawn comfort from the camp meetings and revivals of the plains. They made a texture of gossip, walking and glancing at the Courthouse under the trees. High in the yellow-green boughs the wind turned coolly.

From the throng rose a sound, broken yet sustained and overlapped, like a murmur of bees, heard closely. They talked about the troubles that touched them all equally, in common. There was no money and since there was no money, often there was no food, and certainly no good clothes. As individuals talked, their private and separate prides appeared, and though they had come like everyone else to demand and receive help from the government this morning, their eyes and their voices carried hints from the past, when the ranges were cropped by great roving herds of cows that moved like the mottled shadows of clouds over the tawny unchanging land, and money rolled into the bank in town; when the stock corrals at Ramona, painted white at the railroad side, were always full of the rich herds waiting to be pulled East to market; when there was a vast cotton market waiting to buy the white burst pods from the local fields; when oil was predicted between here and Ramona, and the drilling crews came, setting up derricks that worked all night, with great white lamps flaring so they could be seen for miles . . . A past unmindful of hope, for the great plenty and occupation of its time.

Now in the morning that grew hotter as they waited, stirring uneasily because it was after ten and nothing was done yet, the gossip enlarged itself from mouth to mouth. It was true that the representatives of the government had arrived from Ramona a little after eight, coming by the seven forty-five train from the North. They were seen in the Courthouse, going over the files of the local emergency committee with the sheriff. In the meantime, rumors grew. The government had sent money in bags. There was food in boxes inside the Courthouse, held safe in the vault, where the gold was, in its bags, a safe enough place since the bank had failed. A thin girl with a prominent breastbone, and excited eyes with a wry light in them, moved forward through the crowd, holding by the hand a tall heavy man who grinned foolishly at being dragged along so. Her voice was shrill, telling anyone that it was time to get help from the government, and that it was also easy, with the gold in the Courthouse vault that had been moved in during the night, for safety.

"Did you hear that?" exclaimed a heavy old woman who sat on a bench near the front steps of the Courthouse. "They brought gold in during the night, in the Courthouse, during the night, they was attacked during the day, so they brought it during the night."

The news roved and crackled through the people, several hundred of them.

The door of the Courthouse was open, and they could see the dark hallway running the whole depth of the building, a brown tunnel with cool light at its far end. Now and then a door would open in the corridor, and a clerk would walk across to another office. Each of these small events caused the crowd to stir and shift, pressing closer. The people in front thought the people behind were crowding them toward the building, leaving plenty of space back there near Main Street. But the space near Main Street was filling gradually, as more people came. Old men and women grew tired, and their limbs began to tremble. They sweated and wiped their faces. At the far edge of the crowd, a small man with a heavy head on a thin neck lifted himself on tiptoe and craned for a look at the Courthouse door. He could see nothing. Slowly, with heavy breathing, he began to slide his way through the crowd. His voice, begging passage, was high, a whine, like a cat's.

At the front of the throng, a little girl, tired of waiting, ran up the steps and into the door. The crowd laughed, seeing their own desires so frankly acted out for them. An inner door opened, and a strange man led the child back to the sunlight, smiling with an official frown at the crowd. He stepped back in the building and closed the doors. The little girl began to cry, from petulance. The crowd was silent, totally, in a hush like the air in the treetops. Then sounds broke, they let their opinions out, and the press of each person upon the next, the hot morning, the desperation of their needs came together and lifted the sounds of voices into a low menace. Suddenly the bodies were pushed together. A witless agreement made everyone surge toward the doorway. The old woman sitting on her bench near the steps was overturned. The bench broke down, and she cried out in distress. Her son was somewhere else in the crowd, and her husband had been talking to a tall old man under the far tree. The people stopped and helped the old woman to her feet. They set the bench up again. Someone cried out, "Stop pushing!" and the tension relaxed. They breathed apart again. Perplexity grew, wondering what in the world could be going on in the Courthouse. A youth, bright with eagerness, ran to the trunk of the tallest cottonwood, and clamping it with his arms and knees, he climbed up. He walked out on the heavy branches toward the windows in the front of the building. He laughingly peered down, and the crowd looked up at him, delighted with his audacity, the scheme for seeing what was going on inside. He sat down on the bough and swung his legs.

"Can't see a thing," he called.

The old woman on the broken bench looked up and saw her son. She cried out to him to come down. He laughed. He turned and ran back along the bough, balancing with his brown arms outstretched, running on his toes, his yellow head bent to avoid the small branches about him. The leaves shivered at the impact of his feet on the bough. When he came to the trunk, he reached up for a higher branch and swung on it with his hands. He turned his body in mid-swing, and hooked his legs over the branch. Then lazily he swung himself up to a sitting position there and sat looking down on the crowd which had forgotten him. He was panting; his pink breast rose and fell under his rough blue shirt. He was thoughtless and contented with muscular play.

Shortly before eleven, Do Miller drove into town from Ramona, where he had been to pick up a part for a car he was repairing in his High Way Garage. The street choked with cars surprised him, but he remembered the meeting, treating it mentally with great skepticism, having heard at Ramona that the government people were coming down just to make a survey, and see what had to be done, and how to do it. He drove his service truck as near the Courthouse as he could, and then walked half a block to see what was going on. He saw the crowd, stirring in the heat of approaching noon. Nothing seemed to be going on. It was sure a big crowd. Most everybody in town was there. He recognized dozens of people. He laughed at the expression made by the backside view of the fat man on the outskirts of the crowd, who was dancing on tiptoe, with his dimpled arms raised, in airy efforts to grow tall enough and light enough to see through the crowd, or above it. Do Miller rubbed his forehead with the back of his hand, habitually mindful of the motor grease that might be on his fingers, and turned away. The spider gear he had got needed installation. So far as he could see, there was just a mob of people waiting there for nothing. Touched by his own vague approaches to philosophy, he swelled his chest. Then he felt sorry that so many people would be disappointed if the government people really had nothing to give them. He drove his truck back to the High Way Garage and went to work.

In the cool stucco interior of his garage, after a while, he could hear the noise. He sat back on his heels, setting his wrists on his knees, to keep the greasy touch of his hands off. In the whole stillness of the day, with the town deserted in favor of the meeting, no cars moving, or bodies passing, the noise grew and expended itself without stopping. The crowd was yelling. Do walked to the open double doors of the garage and looked down the street. He could see nothing. But the sound was angrier, and his mind made sudden pictures for him of who was yelling, the people he knew so well. He couldn't picture Andrew Lark screaming at a blank building, or Mrs. Vosz or old Fat. Mrs. Rood, whose car he had sold for her for sixteen dollars, would not raise her voice like that. Mrs. Lark was a proper little old woman, with the most modest eyes he had ever seen, always downcast, except when she said something fooling, when they were raised for a sly look. He threw down his tools and stuck his pipe in his mouth. He started to walk back toward the Courthouse plaza. In his middle was a slightly sick feeling, for the unrecognizable sort of noise the crowd was making. He thought he could begin to hear words, the closer he got. But they just eluded his ear that would sort them out of the confusion. When he climbed on top of one of the battered trucks driven in by a farmer, he saw the waving arms, the shaking heads that roused the howls. He stood in the sunlight, which was almost straight above him, intense and palpable.

Suddenly the noise from the crowd lowered.

A softer sound, the panting of all the breaths, made an expectant pause. The door of the Courthouse shook in someone's grasp again, and then it opened. The double doors were thrown open. The crowd slacked off a little. Air spaces widened between the figures. On the stoop of the entrance, the sheriff appeared. Someone called out his name, and he waved his arm, genially, yet his face was cross. He rested his hand on his hip and slouched one leg. His voice was hardly audible, yet it was firm and impatient.

"We are doin' the best we can in here. It wasn't our idea to have any mass meetin', anyway."

Someone called to him, "Cheer up, Sheriff!" and the crowd laughed, nervously. They didn't know what his words meant. He opened his mouth as if to speak again, but changed his mind, and looked across the faces once or twice, and then backed into the doorway, which he left open.

From the rear of the crowd down to the very front, wriggling his way and panting, touching people's necks with his wet cold hands to make them give way, Leo struggled forward. He was possessed by a desire to be a part of the crowd. When they murmured, now, at being abandoned again by the sheriff, he lifted his voice with theirs, making no words, but only a dutiful meow of menace that was absent-minded, bent as he was on reaching the front row of the impatiently waiting people. He knew no one around him. The driver had left him at the edge of town, hours earlier. Leo wanted to be washed; he felt that some atonement must be done by him before he could be again a human being, after the events of the early morning on the roadside. He let himself into activity, instead of thought. He crawled against the resistant bodies of the crowd, trying to pass them and be one of them. His face was white and his eyes fired with exhaustion.

On the outside of the throng, Fat rose again on tiptoe, keeping his balance by lifting his arms. He could see nothing. But in a moment he heard a sigh go up, some greeting, and knew that the people were busy with something. He became suddenly angry at being so ineffectual. He felt, in a quick minute of recognition, the core of something hard in him at last. With a fury like pleasure, he began to beat his way forward, not caring for his neighbors, and determined to find out why nothing was done for a starving country.

Down on her bench, Mrs. Vosz settled her arms on her bosom. She looked up to the stoop, and nodded her head with a vague matriarchal dignity. In the doorway, pausing briefly, was a strange man, who smiled at the crowd, and then walked slowly forward to the top step. He was followed by the sheriff and another man and a woman who was taller than any of the men. She was dressed in a blue linen suit. She wore glasses and turned her head from side to side, smiling with her upper teeth exposed. The crowd made sounds of expectancy, and satisfaction. They turned to each other, saying, "Well, at last." The sheriff lifted his hand, and indicating the first stranger, he said, "This is Major Drew, and he will say a few words to you."

Drew smiled to the sheriff, and bowed, with a platform courtesy that seemed out of place. He turned to the crowd, and raised his shoulders and dropped them, settling his arms behind his back like an orator. He lifted his neck out of its collar a little, and cleared his voice. He had a large pink head and raised eyebrows. When he talked, they couldn't hear his voice at the rear of the crowd. He said that he and Mr. Edwards and Miss Molton had made a preliminary survey of the needs in this county. So far as was possible, they had read every report of complaint and request filed in the Courthouse. Maybe he should explain, said Major Drew, that the government, in these matters, always required a preliminary survey, which was to be followed by a routine relief agency, where food and clothing would be issued as needed. He hoped it would be possible to establish this agency here within a month. In the meantime, he wished to say that the interest exhibited in the work was very gratifying.

Major Drew paused and brought his hands around from resting on his rump. He folded them in front, and cracked the knuckles, stretching his arms downward.

Miss Molton glimmered with her glasses and her teeth at the crowd. The blood was pounding in her throat, and her mouth was dry. Her smile was a twist of strain on her face, for she watched the crowd, and their quietness was strangely terrifying. Major Drew looked at her for understanding. The crowd had listened, but said nothing, and seemed to understand nothing. They simply stood, waiting, in the dusty heat of noon, under a somewhat risen wind flying faster over the low buildings of the town.

Major Drew nodded his head paternally at the near members of the crowd, and began to speak again.

"We find that your conditions here are very uncomfortable, of course," he said. "It will be our aim to bring help as soon as we can. But I *will* say, I *must* say, that up in the northern counties, the suffering is far worse than yours here is. We have been working night and day, nigh-tan-dday, up there."

"When do we get ours!" cried a voice from the crowd.

The crowd let itself down with a noise like wind. Here it was, the question, at last. Many voices brought it up, now, and full of self-pity, some of the old people began to moan and weep, holding forth their thin arms where the bones showed against the skin like the stems in a leaf, waving their arms vaguely at the group on the steps. Major Drew stepped back a pace and then forward again, as if he had made a mistake to retreat. He extended his arms.

"Please, please," he said. "Let me explain."

The news travelled back through the crowd to the rear, which had not heard, that the relief agency was a lie. There was no help. They talked about investigating and reporting, and so on. As it passed from unminded mouth to angry ear, the news lost all reality, and became merely something to defy. Knowing hunger, and remembering a winter of sharp helplessness, the people heard rumors inside themselves as clearly as they did the words from the steps.

Miss Molton was talking now. Her voice was piercing, and every ear could hear. Her words trembled from the strain of her sincerity. Her tongue clove to her mouth from nervousness. It made her sound guilty, and the crowd hated her for her hesitations. She told them that when the relief station was opened, it would run as long as it was needed, with herself in charge. She said she was sorry that the news had leaked out that the officials would be here today, because they were not prepared for any meeting, or to give out any food. Or money. Whatever had brought them together, she was glad she had a chance now.

"I'm glad I have a chance now," she said, wringing her bony hands upon her breast, "because I want a chance to tell you all how much everybody understands how brave you all have been in these hard times and they have been hard, and they might go on being hard times for a little while longer, and, but, the idea is that we have all got to do our best for each other. So now that we understand the situation and all about how it is here, why, Major Drew and Mr. Edwards and myself, we are all going to see that things, your problems and things here, will be taken care of. As soon as possible. The very first minute."

She opened her mouth to say something again, but she had no saliva, and she swallowed painfully. A bright wetness stood in her eyes, from the strain of speaking against the will of the crowd, which now crept forward thoughtlessly, its faces strained and blanked by the effort to realize the fact that there was no relief about to be given out. There was no gold in the bags in the Courthouse vault, or trucks of food. Miss Molton coughed, and then turned abruptly back to Major Drew and Mr. Edwards.

The atmosphere over the plaza seemed to grow closer and hotter. A mood like the warming of the day ran over the heads. For a moment, a bated interval, there was nothing. And then on a wail, a woman's voice rose, screaming, "We want money!"

"—Food!" declared another voice.

They had stood most of the morning, waiting.

Without a summons, they had gathered from all their places to come, and once together, to receive.

They awaited leadership. They stirred from foot to foot, imploring one another with blank eyes.

The wind, like something in that human weather before the building, sang dismally against the trees, and the air darkened a faint little as the fine dust of the surface was stirred and turned.

The voices were talking against one another, yet with the same burden behind them. The relief committee on the stoop could not be heard. They nodded, with pleading expressions on their faces. They shook hands with the crowd in pantomime, and failed to believe that a temper was gathering into a unanimous strength. To look at them, the people were kind and honest, average. Already one or two at the outskirts were beginning to drift away toward the waiting cars. Miss Molton nodded to her companions, and they turned. They went into the building. The sheriff stared at the way the crowd fell back upon itself as the doors swung shut. Then he heard the wave begin to rise.

The mob tightened instantly. Small eddies of people in parts of the crowd turned against itself. In one of them, Heart DeLancy began to shriek an address at her immediate neighbors. She worked until her arms were free of the pressing people, and then above her head she waved them like brands. Her words tumbled out in a shrill line, and Rolf Kunkel, standing behind her, pressing upon her in a public intimacy that flushed his veins, heard a mad eloquence stream from her. Heart was wild in his eyes. Her strength was amazing. As she turned to free her message of discontent and desire, she struck him on the shoulder with her arm, and the blow hurt with a dull energy. It enflamed him to see her staring at him and screaming, as if she hardly knew him, yet had to convince him. She was convincing others. The crowd settled close around her, waving their arms. They called out agreements with her. There was gold in the vault, and it might as well help lives now as later.

She turned and pointed to the door of the Courthouse. There was a low silence, while the crowd paused, and the voice of an old man rose up saying a prayer. Awed and happy, the crowd knew its strength. They began to sway slightly, and Mrs. Vosz's famous contralto voice was lifted in a line of song. Under the tallest cottonwood, Ellen Rood heard herself singing also, a pale troubled voice that came back to her ears with all the force of her despairs that she had never yet yielded to, as she was yielding now. The old man praying was Andrew Lark. Every sentence he spoke ended on a rising inflection. His eyes were closed, and he was trembling, transported out of himself.

It was a short pause, filled with the breath of exaltation. Heart cried out again. There were echoes. They began to push against the bodies of each other, and as they moved, together, their voices roared. They started across the sidewalk to the foot of the steps. Leo was turned and rolled like a log in the current, rubbed against the trunk of one of the great trees.

"O Lord?" declared Andrew Lark, "where Thy steps take us, so there shall we walk? Lord. Amen: amen? Oh, Thy steps, Lord? We shall walk in Thy ways? Glory?"

As she murmured a faint melody, vague and hopeful, Ellen Rood admitted a strange peacefulness to her breast. Her heart seemed to be overflowing with richness, for she was at one with the people around her, and she remembered the revival times when the bleak sorrows of her little family had been made to glow with some fine life in the flood of prayer. So she felt now, clasping and unclasping her fingers; her eyes stared and her voice trailed uncertainly in the wake of her joy. It was escape. She was forgetful of herself, her children, the dangers of the morning, and the emptiness of the future. The crowd around her were moving and tightening toward the Courthouse. She raised her arms and imitated the threatening gestures of those around her. Her face was changed. She would not have known herself.

Mrs. Vosz struggled to her feet as the crowd closed about the bench where she'd been sitting all morning. The fervor of old Andrew Lark's prayer had started her singing, and she could see his face, tilted back and free to the windy sunlight. The slyness was gone from his leathery wrinkles. His eyes were dropped half shut, and he prayed with his mouth slacked, biting no labial words, only letting his tongue articulate in his mouth. Except for the dim movement of the tongue, he looked like a man dead, whitened by sun and sightless. His voice continued with a curious power. Mrs. Vosz began to weep at the beauty of her singing, which rose and fell in a mournful strident sound, hollow of music but charged with meaning for the crowd.

Heart DeLancy was steady in her effort. So much in her was being fused to purpose that her influence travelled through the crowd. At one point she saw Leo fixed upon her with his immense eyes, and in a recognition that belonged to the genius of the moment, she knew his hysterical strength, and she grasped his thin hand over the heads of those near, and burning with a power that depleted itself only in action, they cried out and charged forward, making shocks and impulses that bruited from body to body and mind to mind. They moved. The singing of the women, the prayers from the old men were submerged.

Do Miller had about decided to go back to the garage when he saw the crowd tighten and heard the praying voices rise. He laughed to himself, at the inappropriateness of the sounds. He was moved again by the peculiar feeling that people he knew well, every day, seemed now like strangers, as parts of the crowd. He saw little old Mrs. Lark biting her lips together with an expression like a taste of vinegar, and beating her fists against the air, as she shuffled forward with the mob. With a red face oiling itself in sweat, Fat, the proprietor of the Café, had beaten his way through the crowd and now stood looking with an expression of stern virtue over all the heads near him.

Do was simply conscious of the changes he saw.

There was a shock through the crowd, some physical tug like the pull that goes down the line in a freight train from car to car. The crowd started up the steps, and at the same moment a loose stone sailed through the air and wrecked a window in the left wing of the front door.

Do Miller jumped up again on the truck where he'd stood watching before.

The glass chimed to the stone stoop. Men began scrambling on the ground for loose dirt and rock to hurl. Heart found a brickbat and threw it. It struck the stone trim of a window and fell feebly. They engulfed the steps.

The doors opened quickly.

The sheriff stepped out holding his gun. With his left arm he motioned the crowd back, frowning sickly. These were his townsmen. He raised his arm over the charging mass. He fired three shots in the air, at random, and a few clipped fresh leaves spiralled slowly down from the cottonwoods. The three shots broke the noise with silence. The people stopped.

When the silence was complete, the sheriff said, "I'm sorry to use a gun against all my friends. Now quit, and get home out of here. We've had it hard all year, and 'tain't any easier right now. But it's going to be, soon's possible. They ain't any gold in here, nor food, nor the like. We can manage for another two weeks. Now we got to hold on. Now break it up."

He watched in silence then until he saw the first falter in the crowd. The sound of his three shots, fired over their heads into the air, seemed still to echo. Someone sobbed once, with fright and fatigue. It made a sound suggestive of shame. The crowd loosened. Some shook their heads. They returned as if from a dream to the direction of their ways, the separate lives that had been so intensely merged and shared.

With a scowl of friendly approval, the sheriff nodded, and turned back into the building, leaving the door open, the way unprotected, for he knew by feeling that the menace was relaxed. The people moved out to the street from under the shade of the great trees, breaking up into small groups for talk, reassuring one another, and divided between shame and indignation at having been fired upon. They found their cars. How much longer they would be able to buy or barter gasoline and so keep the ability to move from farm to town, they could not know.

From behind the Courthouse, they saw the sheriff's car appear with the government officials in it, heading toward Ramona to catch the afternoon train.

Mrs. Vosz stood by her bench waiting for Franz and Mr. Vosz to get her. She was weak from the excitement of the day, and the tears still rolled down her cheeks from the commotion that her singing, her yielding, had made in her. She saw the crowd thinning. They stirred the dust. The wind picked up the dust and made a dull gold haze in the air. She saw Mr. Vosz moving toward her slowly; his sober stride contracted her emotions. She knew how he hated fuss. She wiped her eyes with her shiny fat wrists, and pressed her bosom to find control. She began to smile for him, when someone screamed "Look!" and she turned to see.

Among the branches of the tallest cottonwood there was a slow rustle. She saw two swinging legs appear below the bottom branch, and then the fall of a body, which rolled on the dust and fought against stillness by cramping its knees upward. She saw the face of her boy Franz smiling with absent-minded pain. On the white breast through the blue shirt she saw a well of scarlet. The remnant of the crowd closed about him. She fancied she heard him call her. Whenever she needed it most, strength came up in her. She gave the back

of the bench a shove for impetus, and walked with a violent weighty
stride to the shade of the tall tree. The people opened for her. She
knelt down with gasps of effort for her immense fat legs and body.
She gathered Franz delicately into her arms and tried for his pulse.
She had no tears, and she knew from the blue veils of his eyelids, the
whiteness of his mouth, and the inertia of his body that he was badly
hurt.

"It must have been the shot," said someone in the crowd. "He
fired them into the trees."

Franz opened his eyes and with an ashamed gallantry at his suc-
cumbing, he nodded and smiled that this was so. They saw the flesh
eaten from his palms by the bark of the tree, where he had clutched
them to keep from falling at once. His face was scratched by twigs
and little branches. The blood rolled out of his breast and sopped
the handkerchief his mother was holding against him. Mr. Vosz was
suddenly beside her. In a low voice she ordered him to back the car
into the plaza. People drifted close shaking their heads, and a new
resentment against the sheriff arose. Trembling, Mr. Vosz got into
his car. Franz was dying, he could see it. How could his mother bear
up so! They lifted the boy into the car. Fat had run to his Café
across the street for clean napkins. They made bandages. Mrs. Vosz
saw in her mind a surge, a threat of all that this life would cost; she
bent down to slake the wound, rigidly staring at the bullet hole with
its pale-blue bruised rim to keep herself conscious of what must be
done. They drove slowly to the street. Mrs. Vosz called out to Fat
to send the doctor out to their place at once. Ellen Rood got into the
car with Mrs. Vosz. The boy breathed with a short, slack sound. He
seemed to fall lower and lower against the two women who held him.
He kept licking his white lips. In a voice that was stern, his mother
spoke softly to him, "Be still; we will get you home; everything will
be all right."

Ellen Rood saw how frank and delicate was Mrs. Vosz's touch
upon the pack bandages that had to be changed constantly.

The road lay ahead of them in a straight line of dust. Though
their house was one of the nearest farmhouses to town, they could
hardly see it for the stirred cloud of dust that drifted low on the land.
Mr. Vosz gripped his steering wheel and asked a question, how
Franz was, but his voice made no sound. Pictures returned to him
of the times of crisis in his family. Always it was his querulous wife

who turned with a heavy strength to meet emergency and trial. He was weak in adversity. He thanked God that he had something to do, such as driving, though the wind carried fine gritty dust into his eyes, and pitted his cheeks, and rattled faintly upon the faded surface of the car.

As they neared the house, Franz opened his eyes with a look of inquiry. His legs stiffened against the women's for a moment, a soft tremor that seemed to press for reassurance. He shook his head a little, as if to shake free some puzzling thought. Inspired by Mrs. Vosz's majestic and serene control, Ellen Rood said, "There!" to the boy, and at once began to weep. He shut his eyes again and the trembling pressure of his body was quieted. By a secret hysterical suggestion, Mrs. Vosz thought of the track meet where his brothers were running and jumping. Her hands on his shoulders heavied with a terrible resentment that Franz was wounded rather than one of the other boys. She inhaled sharply in rebuke for the thought. The three boys would all gather again at the high-school field. They would! They would!

The events were slow in starting, and the contestants strayed over the center of the field, a grassy place which was enclosed by the running track. In the white sunlight, which was filtered by the haze of rising dust, the athletes made a pattern of brilliant color. Their trunks and jerseys were spots of orange, vermilion, yellow and magenta, and white, blue, green, and maroon. Their bare arms and legs drew color from all these tints of cloth. The grassy plot was already green, and moving against that and upon the black cindery track, the boys' shapes and colors leaped to the eye. They pranced like horses, limbering their legs for the events. They knelt and practiced starts. Running backward, they danced against the wind, serious and intent upon the science of preparing for races. The two Vosz triplets paced each other, grunting under their breaths. They were watching absently for their brother.

At one o'clock, the starter's pistol sounded, cracking down the wind, which was rising continually, making it hard for the runners to breathe comfortably. The spectators were ranged upon unpainted bleachers. They were mostly boys and girls from the competing schools in the district, though a number of people from town had come from the Courthouse meeting to watch the contests. They sat facing the mountain, which was disappearing from its base upward, as the plain let its surface into the air in a wind of dust. The sky at the horizon turned a gray-white. Above, it shone blue and brilliant where the sun stood.

Richard Vosz was announced for the high-hurdle event. He trotted to his place in line. At the sideline stood his brother Joseph, watching him. Dick scraped the cinder track with his cleated shoes once or twice, and spat on his fingertips, a gesture of confidence rather than utility. Joe nodded at him. The starter raised his stubby pistol. He glanced at a small crowd of spectators who were just arriving, having parked their cars at the gate. He glanced down at his stop watch, and cried, "On your mark," "set," and fired.

The boys leaped ahead. Excited, the new spectators ran forward to see the hurdle race. They leaned down the track. The hurdlers ran with their heads up, rising with legs spread like wings to take the hurdles. Joe heard his brother's name from one of the newcomers. He glanced, and the speaker turned, and saw him, staring with a peculiar reluctance. Joe looked back at the race again. He saw Dick, yellow head and green jersey above white trunks, take the last hurdle far down the straightaway, and breast the tape in a final lunge. He started to run down the trackside to Dick, when someone took his arm, and looked at him, again strangely, and said, "Joe, did you know about Franz?"

"No, he's late. Where is he?"

"They took him home."

A sensational communication that ran through the people spread to the bleachers. They began to rattle down from the board seats, and cluster around Joe, watching his face to see what he would do. They felt sympathy, but their curiosity was more powerful. Joe looked at the faces around him, where obscure messages were implied. He was suddenly turned by suspense, like fear.

"What about him?" he demanded.

"He got shot."

Heart DeLancy leaned forward, and came between two people to speak to him. She put her hands on his arm, and mindful of how much he looked like his brothers, she was excited so that her voice quivered.

"He had an accident, Joe," she said, turning to see the proper understanding of her tact in Rolf Kunkel's face. Rolf nodded soberly at her, and Heart continued. "He was sitting in a tree before the Courthouse, and the sheriff fired at the air, above the crowd, nobody knew Franz was up there in the tree. The bullet hit him, and he stayed there. He sat there, I mean he hung on until the crowd was pretty nearly gone. He fell out of the tree after that, and your mother was there. And your pa. They took him home."

Joe looked at her in a wild silence.

She said, "I don't know how bad it is."

Joe felt her fingers on his arm, and saw the faces around him echoing his own expression of fright. Their eyes opened like his, and their mouths dropped. They had seen what they came to see. He flung Heart's hands away and, turning, ran down the trackside to meet Dick, who was walking slowly back to the starter's line, pigeon-toed, breathing hard, flushed with his victory and modestly hanging his head with a heavy grace as he walked. He was listening to the poured praises of his schoolmates without acknowledging them. Joe ran up and struck him on the breast, a heavy blow.

"Dick," he said, choking on his dry throat, "we got to go. Franz is hurt bad."

Dick paused a second, then without asking details, he fell in beside his brother, and they ran to the gate, past the crowd, Dick pausing only to grab up his sweat suit. He struggled into the upper half of it as he ran. They started through the gate and down the road that led to town. But Joe stopped, and said, "We can't run all the way . . ."

Rolf and Heart were hurrying toward his car. They waved to the boys to wait, and climbed in. The engine started. Rolf backed and turned, and overtook the boys, flinging the rear door open for them to get in. Dick threw himself on the seat, and lifting his legs, pulled on his sweat pants.

Rolf drove to town, where Main Street was thronged. The crowd had broken into small groups. Men stood with men and women with women, among the cars, talking. They seemed to be excited. They shook their heads, and as each little group separated and went to its various cars, there was an attitude, common to all, that contained grief and anger. Rolf drove slowly through the crowded part of Main Street, and then crossing town headed out to the open country on the other side. Joe sat forward gripping his hands. Dick sat sidewise, listening with him to another telling of the story by Heart. There was bitterness mixed with her sympathy. She leaned over the back of the front seat to talk to the boys. Her excitement of the morning was gone. She remembered her actions with a detached shame, and flushing at her own hysteria among the crowd, she told how the people *had driven themselves* into a riot, and that Franz had gone up in the tree before any of it started. They had seen him run out on a limb and try to gaze into the Courthouse windows. He laughed and ran back and had climbed higher. They had forgotten him. The sheriff fired into the trees. She remembered seeing some leaves fall, and hearing the strike of the bullets among the thick branches. In some awed fashion, she made an eloquent story of the descent from the tree, until the brothers writhed from concern and excitement.

Rolf sat, large and troubled, driving. His big face with the weak blue eyes was puckered in an agony of sympathy. He swallowed several times, for the lump of sorrow in his neck. The dust, twisting into the car by its speed and the wind, got into his watering eyes. Ahead of them, the sand blew in thickening clouds. They could see nothing, and now found it difficult to hear Heart speaking, in the increased wind. They rode swiftly along in a void of blowing dirt, anxious and impatient. Dick suddenly leaned and hit Rolf on the back, and said, "God damn, can't you hurry, Rolf?"

Rolf said nothing, too amazed that he should be abused at a time like this. Heart turned back to the front, knowing she must not look at the fear on the boys' faces. Rolf leaned over his wheel, and the stupid suggestion of him that his body made filled the boys with despair. But he stepped harder on the throttle, and the car, groaning and cracking as it bucked the wind, leaped a little as it took new speed, and the boys sat back, and sat at once forward again, watching for a first glimpse of their house far down the road, which was hazed by the blowing drift.

Now thicker, the sand rose high enough in the sky to obscure the sun, and the light turned yellow, softening everything, and bringing a sharp drop of temperature. Off the plain below the mountain, the wind rose and carried sand, pulling it in a great veil across miles of ground, so that the town could not see the mountain, and the spring morning disappeared with its freshness under the choking afternoon, that swept its new atmosphere across the whole valley, obscuring everything.

VIII · SUNDOWN AND AFTER

Closing the hidden afternoon, dusk found the wind dropped, and the horizons clear, and a stillness in the air that was welcome after the choking storm. Ellen Rood reached her home just before sunset. She was left there by the doctor, driving back to town from the Voszes'. As she entered her yard, she called out for the children; and presently they came, meeting her with excitement, confusing her with news of the day's events, none of which she heard, content to know the comfort they gave each other by being together.

The sun was vanishing on the edge of the plain, warming that black shelf of the world. Donald suddenly squeezed his mother's arm, and holding his breath from regret, he turned and ran back of the house, where the failing light lay even. Twenty feet past the chicken-house, he stopped running, and walked on tiptoe, bent like an Indian. He went through the dusty open places he knew among the scrub bushes and grass. His eyes were fastened on the snake. The closer he came, the more strictly he knew that he was too late. He had missed it. The moment toward which he had been working all day was gone. The sun was gone, and the twilight turned softly dim. The snake lay quiet, never to quiver again, as he had seen it quiver at intervals in the hot morning, and shudder under the sweep of the windy afternoon.

But if he had missed watching the snake's sundown death, he need no longer be afraid to touch. He went closer, and turned the snake over with his foot. The wavy coils slid and changed so suddenly, with such a heavy fluid weight, that he jumped back, scared by an echo of life. Then he laughed hoarsely at himself, a catch of breath in his mouth, and toed the snake once more to prove that he was not afraid. There was no quiver. The sun was down. The old snake was really dead. He kicked a few scoops of dirt against the long body, and trotted back to the house, where the light of a lamp in the kitchen made him shiver with awareness of the evening's coolness. The green-yellow flare of the gasoline lamp through the window was something that made him feel all of a sudden like a very little boy again, and at the same time charged him with responsibility, like a man. He quickened his steps, running to the door, needing to be inside, where the yellow lamp shone with quiet clarity upon everything he knew and loved.

Ellen, too, possessed some feeling of restored security in her kitchen. She laid the Black Maria on the sewing machine and covered it with the newspaper properly. Then leaving her hat and coat, she bent down and pinned Lena's hair up on top of her head, making the little girl resemble a tiny adult. The child squealed with fun.

The heaviness in her breast began to melt, Ellen thought. She felt tired and no longer desperate, or lonely. When Don came in, swaggering a trifle, she wanted to laugh out at him for his assumption of importance. She sent him for water, and began to gather the sparse ingredients of her family's supper.

Moving at her familiar concerns, her mind became pleasantly empty. The children helped her. They ate their supper without talking, though thought returned to Ellen when she watched the children eat, with hunger and satisfaction in every gesture of their spoons, their mouths, their licking tongues and working cheeks.

After supper, they turned the lamp a little higher, and gathered in front of the kitchen stove, where vestiges of fire still bloomed through the velvet ashes. Lena lay in Ellen's arms and Donald sat by her feet, facing her, while she read aloud to them in halting voice that wavered now and then from fatigue. The story was from Grimm's fairy tales, an ancient copy on gray paper with rubbed binding of faded red. The world of swans and forests, deep and treasured obligations in the hearts of princes and swineherds, was a simple and real thing to Donald. His little sister always dozed, breathing like a puppy, with hot nose and petulant little sounds. Ellen read with a monotonous inflection, an expression something like the doleful and vague aimlessness that her singing in the crowd had that morning. But the story always filled her with feeling, and some transfer of that touched Donald.

The evening latened. It was fully dark outside now, and the strange day was ended. Lena lay sleeping behind the fairy book. Don rubbed his eyes to stay awake, and Ellen had briefly forgotten the ride of the afternoon, charging through the dust storm with the heavied body of Franz Vosz held by her and his mother. Ellen knew before Mrs. Vosz that the boy was dead. Waiting for her to discover it, Ellen wondered wildly what to do. The car jolted on, beating against the crossroad wind. Presently they saw the Vosz house through a rift in the dust cloud. Mrs. Vosz petted Franz to encourage him. She found out then.

Small red embers sifted down the grate of the stove. Ellen's voice fell away. Like her children, she seemed ready and willing to succumb to tiredness. Around her, for this moment, were all of the things that let her have peace, however humble they might be. The room was crowded with possessions, none of which had value yet all of which were valuable to her for the impulse she had to gather them and hold them, some attempt to make up with profuseness what she lacked in worth. Her mind wearily and in content turned upon the troubles she faced, along with the rest of the people in the valley. But aside from a feeling that someone was responsible for her, and must help her, must help everyone in difficulty, she was happy. The kitchen was warm and the children were by her. The lamp faded gradually, as its air pressure in the gasoline bowl lessened. She saw with an intimate pleasure that a pot of beans was soaking on the floor beyond the sewing machine. It was a kind of happiness to feel tired, and to give in to it. She sat with her eyes closed. Her high cheekbones preserved the illusion of a smile on her worn face, though her mouth drooped. She forgot the Voszes.

IX · S O L A C E

By sundown, Franz Vosz was properly arranged in death. He lay in the front room on an ancient sofa. His face astonished everyone with its difference: he looked hardly like himself, they thought, not perceiving the absence of beauty, the famous splendor which all the triplets had in almost equal measure. Now, with color fallen out of his cheeks, and his eyes shut, his mouth stiff against his teeth, it was possible to see that the boy's features were anything but distinguished, and that bereft of its character, his face and body, impersonal, should fail to echo the things in him that had been loved. All the evening, people came to look at him in the parlor, and were shocked by this trickery of death. They would look at the ageless face, and then consult their memories, and then turn to see the surviving brothers, to recover some image of that dead boy that would be recognizable. It was Franz's memorial that the eyes of the living should reject his dead likeness as faulty; and seek for some less real thing than the facts of his bone and still flesh, the architecture of his person, and demand as vestige any reminders of his spirit, made of laughter, loyalty, wit, strength, and easy vitality and rich temper.

His father remembered him best.

He remembered exactly the difference in this son from his other triplets, which was a sly, childish pleasure in excelling them at everything, and a modest refusal to do so very often. He remembered that Franz had been cleverer with people than his brothers, and that he had also been, so, more inclined to tell lies, and evade bothers, all with the greatest and most charming blandness. Mr. Vosz had wept, in silent spasms, when he had driven in to his own porch and been told by his wife that Franz died about three miles back. He had carried the boy in the house, concerned in his mind with stopping his sobs, a first concern of duty and self-consciousness. In the early evening, he received the people who came to call, unable to say anything, but he shook their hands, and suggested with an embarrassed wag of his head that they were to go in the front room and see the body. He was divided between thanks that people should be so kind as to bring sympathy, and resentment that his private grief was so exposed to anyone who might come.

Mrs. Vosz, on the contrary, though she would see nobody, lying inert on her great bed and swelling its shape with her shaking body, required Richard to report to her, whenever anyone came, who it was, what they said, if they had messages for her; her mind trivially busy with the social aspect of death in the family, while her heart slowly grappled with the grief that sat there. Her fat hands were fretful, wandering to her lips, or her temples, holding handkerchiefs and pressing her heart. In her eyes, behind the tears that streamed ceaselessly like a veil to keep her from seeing too clearly, was a latent spark of comprehension, a little force that would grow with her memories until she would know the real size of her loss, a deprivation that was the greater for her years of wildly building up its meaning and value.

She heard cars come and go; the low voices of consolation, the shriek of some uncanny dog in the yard. She commanded her mind to invent tasks. Her hands travelled with her thoughts, and lying in tears upon her bed, she seemed more active and restless than if she'd been on her feet at housework. Finding things for Richard and Joe to do, her voice told them in hoarse groans. Behind all these devices of evasion moved images of Franz, of her three sons, whose epitome he was. She saw him run down the yard as a tiny child, with yellow hair, and trip, falling, returning to her with bleeding knees, and a little face ugly in rage, his tears mingling with the run of his nose; she remembered his boyish cruelties to dogs and chickens with a perverse tenderness; how he looked asleep when his brothers had carried his cot one summer dawn out to the yard and brought her to see the joke of his not awakening; she called back family scenes in which her favor for Franz was clear, like accusation; and at this a new weight fell on her heart, and she half-sat up in bed, calling for Richard and Joseph, who came at once, scared by the terror on her great face that was wet with grief. She put out her hands, and took theirs, staring at the boys with flooded eyes. They held her to a sitting position, and murmured to her, soothing her, knowing that she was wanting to speak to them through the suck of the sobs in her throat. They exchanged looks, adult in their intuition; perhaps this was something worse than sorrow? Mrs. Vosz dropped her head, and said, at last, "My boys must hate me, but don't ever leave me, he is dead, and I love you both just as much . . ."

They were astonished. They hushed her, speaking tenderly, and she refused their efforts to quiet her.

"Maybe I have been a bad mother; I loved Franz and petted him, and you boys used to know it. Papa always said he was my favorite; oh, Dick," she cried, "maybe I have been unfair? Joe? You won't leave me?"

The boys blushed with wretchedness. They read in her eyes the fear that she might be abandoned by everyone now. It was less remorse and love for them than it was a feeble and pitiful fright lest the two sons she had slighted now feel free of her. Her body, working in the bed with restlessness, her reddened face, touched them with some humble return to the time of their dependence upon her, and they promised with a moved enthusiasm never to leave her. They convinced her, and she fell back again to weep and deny the pictures her mind made for her.

She finally let them go to see who had just arrived, and who was leaving. Outside her door, the boys looked at each other with an emotional shyness. A feeling like shame took them both. They went in and looked at Franz, seeing with memory the neat bullet hole in his chest, dark, rimmed with blue that faded to the white flesh. The visitors made the proper clucking sentiments around them. Their father hung his head and shuffled his feet by the door. Andrew Lark, in the corner, rocked faintly in the walnut runner-rocker, and declared to anybody who neared him that Franz Vosz had been a fine lad and a proper; and the brothers stood knowing without thought or word what missing Franz would be like, all things from their birth having come to them equally and with the same meaning for all three, having grown up closer than together. They shivered within their best clothes. By staring long enough, they could imagine that Franz breathed.

Andrew Lark stirred and rose, slowly, when his wife told him they'd better be going. She was mindful of the proprieties, and they'd

been there too long already. The old man paused again to look at
Franz, and knew a recognition like joy flood his mind; he saw a self-
image at the same age, and passing Mr. Vosz, at the conviction that
Franz was a fine and proper boy, Lark was heartier than ever, in his
ancient way, going out with his wife and feeling a curious exhilaration.

But as he was leaving, a car drove into the yard, and the sheriff
came to the porch, and Lark turned back to see.

The brothers held the door against the sheriff, instantly speech-
less. Their minds cleared, and they saw how soft and silly they had
been all their lives. Their grief found its true nobility in a masculine,
animal rage. It was the man who had killed their brother. They
began to growl and whisper promises of what revenge they would
invent and commit. The sheriff put his hands against the screen
door, and said softly, "Now listen, boys; listen"; and the limited
commotion brought their father to the door.

Vosz thrust the boys away and opened the door. He grasped the
sheriff by the arm in a painful grip. Without speaking, he brought
the sheriff into the front room, through the dwindling crowd of
visitors. They stood by the old couch and they both looked down.
Vosz was a reasonable man; he hated the man beside him, and he
knew any blame was foolish. He watched the sheriff, who looked at
Franz. Perversely, Vosz was angered when the signs of genuine grief
showed in the sheriff's face, and he felt this to be some intrusion
upon the privilege of those whose loss it was.

The boys had gone to their mother's room, furious with the
news. Mrs. Vosz opened her mouth, a shape of outrage. Now Mr.
Vosz came in and said the sheriff wanted to see her, and here he was.
There was a shuffle of feet at the bedroom door, as Vosz stood aside;
and the sheriff came in to stand at the foot of the immense bed and
feel his tongue cleave to his dry mouth as he gazed at the mother of
the boy he'd killed. The brothers stood at the head of the bed.
Richard was in the near light of the lamp, and his body cut off much
of the light on the figures in the room. But Mrs. Vosz, struggling
against her pillows to sit erect, was bathed all down her left side by
a gold flow of light that spilled on cheek and loose bosom, and the
white of the bedclothes. Dark shadows lost her other side and put
shapes on the wall. The silence in the house was full. Mrs. Vosz
stared, shaking her head with the slightest movement at the sheriff.
The tears ran silently down her face and into the hunched hollows

of her neck. She seemed to be sexless and without age, in the beautiful strange light, and in the attitudes of astonished grief she held, an almost impersonal embodiment of emotion, and without being able to say it or imagine it in words, the sheriff thought that for the first time in his life he was looking at the face of suffering, and he felt a new sadness for the messes into which people got through no fault of their own. He looked at the brothers, who were pale in the lamplight with hunger for vengeance. Vosz stood beside him, saying nothing.

The sheriff said, hesitatingly, "There's hardly nothing I can say, Mrs. Vosz. I *have* to say I'm sorry, and you know and I know and his father knows it was an accident. But we all know *that* don't help matters none. But I *want* to say that I'd trade places right now with that boy if it'd do the good of giving him back to you. I *swear* I mean it, ma'am?"

His voice was rusted with confusion, and his words coming slowly had the dignity of entire sincerity. He let his fingers rest on the foot of the bed. Mrs. Vosz closed her eyes and allowed her head to fall back so that her thick neck swelled out at the sides. The loose hair drifted down to her cheeks. She made no sound. The brothers leaned to her and put their arms against her back, to support her. The sheriff was made mean in feeling, to be so ignored, and he spoke again, with pleading rough tones.

"I maybe was out of place to come here, ma'am? but so long as I didn't come to pay my respects, I figured it was worse than coming where I'd be mighty unwelcome."

She opened her eyes and stared at him again. Her lips drew in against her teeth, as if to make her silence more terrible, more accusatory than ever. No one in the room took her eyes off her. There was a groaning splendor of grief about her shapeless body and her blotched and quivering face. In the front room, the visitors were as still as the dead, their eyes glistening toward one another as they strained to hear the furies that must be loose in the bedroom.

"Anyway," said the sheriff, moving back from the carved walnut of the bedstead, "I can't tell you how *I* feel, but I know how *you* feel, Mrs. Vosz? and I swear to God A'mighty that . . ."

He could not say what he would swear.

He was sorry? The word was too little. Guilt? But his crime was not a crime. Mrs. Vosz leaned forward a trifle, as if waiting, extracting, the full dues of his misery. Her eyes went sharp, behind the run of tears, and she fatly stirred in her bed to await the avowals that were so hard for the man to make. The sheriff turned to Vosz and shrugged. He ran his thumb up and down the lapel of his coat. He turned back to Mrs. Vosz, and saw with a fresh eye the ugliness of her abandoned body, and his feelings rose up in him with resentment that she should so refuse his poor offer of sorrow; he shook his head at her, and dropped his look, while the heat blurted into his eyes; he swallowed his breath. Mrs. Vosz leaned sharply, to see these signals of feelings. He turned and left the room in the same appalling silence she had met him with. He was followed by Vosz, who saw him to the front door. The visitors had retired to the shadowy corners of the front room and they saw the departure through the hall doorway. The front door slammed, and the dogs on the porch whimpered. They heard the motor start, and saw the headlights switch on through the windows. The backing and turning car threw an arc of light across the windows, printing shadows of lace curtains upon the peering faces. The whine and settle of the changing gears receded. It was silent again.

But only briefly, for rising in a sob of lost control, they heard the voice of Mrs. Vosz break forth in a storm of volubility.

She was sitting up, clutching at the strong arms of Richard and Joe, pouring out an almost wordless fury of sound. They could recognize in her thickened speech references to the man who had just left; they could perceive snatches of pictures in it, as if memories suddenly showed among the rages in her mind, and demanded expression. They squeezed her arms and stroked her hair, calling her to be quiet. The tears ran from her eyes and the saliva poured from her lips. She sweated and strove with her hands to say what was in her heart.

The sounds of this fury came to the front room as something terrifying, and a few of the women tiptoed to the bedroom door, full of an awed courage that demanded a sight of such grief. What they saw made them feel either sick or hysterical. The two boys grew frightened and exchanged impassive looks that included the notion of flight; but they would have denied it, and they heard the voice of their mother change, taking on the noble and witless sonority of one who prayed at a camp meeting. She made the shapes of visions in the air with her hands, and her voice became solid over the caught gasps of the sobs, and her husband came into the room to see upon her stained and wretched face some light like the light of those who receive the Holy Spirit, and he knew that she had found occupation in the old assurances of her baptism. Her voice rolled on, like the river of a sermon. He fell to his knees by the side of her bed and put his head on the bedclothes and began to weep. Her hand descended upon his skull, and he felt its vibrant obsession.

Richard and Joe suffered for the way their parents had let go. They started to withdraw. But the mother embraced them with her rich tide of wrath and redemption, making them kneel too, rising in some majesty of strength above the shames and the griefs of her men. The voice poured on, filling the air with threats and judgments, phrases of hatred and promises of peace, the blood of the Lamb and the fires of Hell, with amen and amen and alleluia.

In the front room, Andrew Lark once again brought his wife to the door. The evening was clear, and as they drove away, the harangue of sorrow and comfort was still going on.

X · SURVIVAL

From far down the road, Andrew watched for his mill, and when he saw it, sharply edged against the last sheets of light that faded down from the deepening sky, he felt an uprise again of the exhilaration that had possessed him back there as he had gazed upon the dead boy. Mrs. Lark rode beside him, her hands folded in her lap, her eyes working right and left, right and left, as she told over in sympathy the terrible meanings of the house they had come from. She could tell herself that everyone had their time; it was best to meet it without terror; but when a grief so monumental as Mrs. Vosz's got loose, it went extra deep into hearts that before had known few doubts.

They rode, the old couple, bouncing in unison as the old Ford bounced. It was an ancient car, with a spidery look to its thin axles, its steering gear, the supports for its wind-rattled top. If anything could make it look more precarious and tentative than it really was, it would be to see Andrew Lark, himself so ancient, driving the Ford at its fastest speed, an old engine of potential destruction, driven by an old man whose steps must surely be numbered.

Beside him, Nona was murmuring the slow words of one concerned with proper misery. He hardly heard her. He sat driving, his eyes fixed upon some point farther than the road, his sharp old mouth that bent in the middle with a look like a lion's snout grinning with content. When he turned into their own yard and brought the Ford to a creaking halt within its shed, he heard Nona sigh heavily and watched her walk across the yard with her rheumatic, rolling gait. By himself, he stood in the cool yard. The wind had dropped. Above him the mill hardly turned, and he was thoughtless of it. In the late dusk, he stood like some old tree. When he saw the lights from the lamps catch and increase from Nona's match, he cleared his throat, and brought himself out of the curious haze of joy that had possessed him at the Voszes', and went to the back door where the cats were clustered hungrily, mewing and climbing against one another, and purring when Andrew opened the door and let them through the shuffle of his feet.

He dropped his stiff black felt hat on the kitchen table, and went to the front room. There was his newspaper, all set right by Nona on the table. The lamp made a live world of a circle of light, cutting across the red plush of the sofa, dropping to the green-and-brown carpet, crossing the black boards of the floor, the seat of the gold cane chair, and the dusty black of the coal scuttle. He heard Nona talking to the cats. He sat back in the Morris chair, which had adopted his shape like a shell, the green corduroy cushions hollowed for the curve of his long back and the settle of his bony rump. He heard Nona begin setting supper ready. He admitted he was hungry.

He went when she called him, and sat with her at the kitchen table, and as the evening advanced with his silence continuing, she began to worry about him. He was looking at nothing, only smiling, as if for himself, eating his eggs and scraping his porridge spoon and wetting his chin in silence. To make up for this strange look of his, she began to chatter, lamenting that such things could happen as happened today; she spoke of the time her son Elbert had died, as a child of three, and she said she could feel for Mrs. Vosz; to lose a child not yet grown, hardly, was so sad; she heard Andrew chuckle, and raised her eyes to him. He seemed to be alive with pleasure, some happiness which dismayed her.

"Andrew:" she said, putting her freckled old hand to his arm, "what's got *in* you!"

He shook his head, and shoved his chair back, and returned to the parlor and his big chair. In the orange glass miniature of a top hat he found toothpicks, and took one, and began raking his blood-less gums with it. She came and peered through the door at him, ankled by her cats, and was alarmed to see him lying back with his eyes shut, smiling and working his toothpick. She saw the paper at his elbow, ignored; and the change from his habit of hastening to read after supper filled her breast with a breathless fright. She went in and picked up the paper, and laid it on his lap, speaking to him. He scrambled for the paper with his fingers, and didn't open his eyes, only nodding. She left him, troubled by strangeness. In the kitchen a new fear took her, and she remembered that he had left his glasses on the windmill platform that morning; that Moses was supposed to have come out that evening to bring them down, and that the events of the day had prevented their seeing Moses. She thought, If Lark goes up there at night . . . he'll fall . . . And she folded her hands for the fool she had been in reminding him of his paper, for he would need his glasses for that, and in his musing and smiling, he could sit forever without them.

She silently went to the back door, and walked to the foot of the windmill. Her face was hot with a wild courage, but she looked up at the clear towering lines of the timbers, and said to herself, with feelings like weeping, "I could never climb it." She put her hand on the low rung of the ladder, as if to test her strength. The mill softly keened above her, and she looked up at it, seeing its blades against the chilling sky where the stars were brightening against the darkness. She shivered; it would be another cold night, and embracing her shoulders, she went back to the kitchen. Andrew was motionless. She went to her work of clearing up, listening for the moment when he would sit up and clear his throat, and declare that he must get his glasses down from the platform.

But her fears were stretched over the whole evening.

He sat, content and silent, in his big chair. When she came to sit with him and do her sewing, he looked at her. His eyes were remote and milky with odd meanings, and she decided not to ask him what he was up to. He could not have told her. He only knew that an inner sensation of power and life possessed him. It had arrived in him in the late afternoon, when he had looked down at the dead Franz Vosz, and seen so young a man, with so appealing a face, with such a strong body, laid useless forever; while he, Andrew Lark, who would never see seventy again, was alive and could feel the blood flooding his veins; and the things he knew filling his mind; and the things he saw coming into his eyes. He had shaken his head over the dead. And then he had admitted to himself that he was proud to be alive. He had thought of himself at Franz's age, looking at the boy. The whole chain of things that had happened to him in his life began to come back to him. His memory was prodigious. He saw how fortunate everything had been. If there had been any deviation from the line of his history, how different everything might have been!

But it wasn't.

He was conscious of his old age. The only triumph of old age, which is survival, lived in him too. He sat and mused all evening, shaken and enlivened by the happy selfishness of his own thoughts. The boy was dead, and Andrew felt an unmalicious satisfaction in finding himself still living. He forgot his paper. Every time he looked at Nona, when she recurred in his chain of memories, he wondered why she looked so perplexed. He would chuckle at her, and she, still possessed by thoughts of grief and worry, would be shocked at his levity, not knowing how he was welling with contentment, a sense of integral being.

He thought once of mentioning what was in his mind to Nona. But he sensibly decided that she would never understand him, and he closed his mouth again, after frightening her by holding it open for speech for a long moment. He only shook his head at her fussy inquiries, and sank back into preoccupation with his content.

The cats came suddenly to life in the kitchen, and raced out from under the stove when the clock struck ten. The day was over, and Nona was relieved at last, for he would never climb the ladder now, it was too late to read. It was bedtime.

She went to the kitchen and let the cats out for the night. They paused on the doorstep while she held the screen door open. They tasted the night, turning their heads, whose little faces were hooded by ears and neck. Then, with silent accord, they turned and became parts of the shadow along the house.

Andrew rose from his chair, obedient to his nightly ritual, reflecting that it was just such regularity of habit that had brought him this far and that would take him years and years farther. He guessed he hadn't missed a minute in years from getting ready for bed at ten o'clock. Nona, in the bedroom, moved against the area of the lamplight like a sleepy and comfortable shadow. He appreciated dimly the wide and the heavy bed where so much of his joy and content had come to pass.

The yard was cleaned by the wind of the day. In the chill moon-light, he looked around, as he had looked around every night for so long. He spread his legs and began to make his water, yawning sleepily. He made a little river on the swept ground. He shivered, feeling the cold strike into him, and anticipating the warmth of bed. Inside, Nona, hearing his nightly watering of the ground, shrugged with impatience, her delicacy offended, reminded by this of all the little things that a lifetime with Lark had never reconciled her to. But they vanished from her mind out of habit when he returned to the house, chuckling and peering at her sidewise, saying that he'd forgot to get his glasses down off the windmill. Nor had he missed them till now. Now what did she think of that!

He trundled by her, pulling at his shirt with little grunts. She thought with an almost shamefully girlish notion how foolish he was, how much doing-for he required, and, remembering the Voszes, how if his need of her should be broken by death, she would know noth-ing to do but wait.

He let himself into bed, which creaked. He held up on one elbow, listening intently. An idle night breeze was about, and he thought it might be enough to make the mill swing around and screech. But he nodded his head with satisfaction when all he could hear was a constant, airy w'anging from the metal blades that turned slowly, and the metal fin that strove always to be parallel with the wind.

XI · FALLEN IMAGE

The evening rush was over by the time Rolf and Heart pulled up at Fat's Café. The light from the restaurant streamed across a limited area of sidewalk, with a golden spill that suggested warmth after the sharp and coldening evening. They went into the Café and Fat waved at them with his bare arm, a figure of buoyant good feel-ing, addressing them as Folks, and piping in his oily voice. He came around from behind the counter himself instead of letting Mrs. Rocker take their order. They sat down at a table opposite the shining coffee urns, and looked up at Fat hungrily.

"I've had such a rush," said Fat, "don't know hardly what's left; but you can bet, you can just bet on it, I'm gonna feed you."

He cocked his eyes at them, looked at them shrewdly, a regard

that made Heart drop her eyes and inwardly admit the embarrassment and the confusion in her breast. Rolf told Fat to bring them
whatever he had that was *good*, and turned back to Heart.

She looked straight into his eyes, and pulled a blush from his
veins. They were both breathless; when they started to speak to one
another, their words had a catching pulse under them. She laid her
hand against her breast, thinking that was where her desire lay; but it
eluded her touch, and she stirred in her chair with the possession of
her feelings. Rolf hung his head. They had been driving in the car
ever since they left the Voszes'. Without saying much of anything,
the two of them had arrived at their conclusion, and Rolf knew it
was Heart's strength that she had excited him, and with caresses and
no words, had proposed to him the things that would happen after
their supper.

It was warm in Fat's Café. The steam rose and whispered above
the hooded stove. Presently Mrs. Rocker came with the thick white
bowls containing the soup, flanked by crackers, that always heralded
Fat's "club menus." She walked with exaggerated care, her miserable
slippers creaking and yawning at her every step. She bit her un-
toothed lips with a grin of pride and caution, and at last set the
steaming soup down before them, and retired behind the counter to
consult Fat with one of her willing looks that so enraged him.

But tonight he sang in his heart. He seemed beyond rage, for
that was the sign of a weak man who was not master of his world, and
therefore of his temper. Fat was hard tonight. He narrowed his small
eyes, and squinted into his stew with pitiless and rocklike character.
He turned to instruct Mrs. Rocker to set some celery on the table
for the guests, and lifted his eyebrows at her in an elaborate threat
which she failed to recognize as such. Hard? Tonight. He would
fire Mrs. Rocker tonight. The crowd from the track meet had filled
his cash register. "Mrs. Rocker," he thought, "here's your wages and
a little over. Goodbye, git. Git out, Mrs. Rocker, I said. Go on, git
now, I said. You old fool, can't have a smelly old woman like you
round here no more, I said. Waagh! whoosh! I said, and don't try
no cryin and weepin and caterwaulin, I said, on me, I said, it won't
do you no good 'tall. I said, I put up long enough with your cussed
foolery, and wastin time, and taking my wages week in and week
out, I said. Go on, I said, git!—"

He sliced some bread, warmed and enriched by this mental
achievement of a scene he was waiting for with relish. He sent her to

the table with the bread, and then leaned on his immaculate counter to watch the diners. His fat arms and pink elbows flattened out on the light yellow wood. Feeling hard, serene, a master of all situations that might touch him, he prided himself tonight on a keen, even a relentless understanding of other people. They might have secrets from home, but not from him. His own secret was so well guarded that no one would ever know it: who had seen him? In all that crowd? Nobody. He had picked up a brick, a loosened brick from the edge of the walk in the Courthouse plaza, and in a moment of glorious inspiration, he had risen above the crowd and hurled the brick at the doors, smashing the window, creating a leadership in destruction that through no fault of his own had been put down. But he, Fat, was the single hero of the day's events, though nobody knew it but himself; which was enough. His private virtue flowed throughout his immense and dainty body, a masculine elixir.

Heart and Rolf ate their supper in half-silence, consulting one another with small sounds and quick glances. Their breath lay under their words with soft laughter, and Heart could hardly eat anything. Rolf consumed everything as it came before him. She watched him eat, feeling possessive of him already, and noticing with a strange intensity such things about him as might at other times have disgusted her, his clumsy table manners, chewing with his lips open, packing his food with his knife, ways that were un-Californian. But to her, a preciousness seemed to cover everything about him; and in his mind, as he inarticulately preserved the heat that had them both, was some tenderness that covered his resentment at having been so obviously trapped and excited by her.

Fat played his fingers along his mouth, leaning on his palm and watching them through drooped eyes. There was solicitude in his heart, as he made idle and lascivious dreams about the two young people. He felt like offering them congratulations, with sly winks and tribal pokes in the rib for Rolf, and a shared reference to their common valor as masculine achievers. But he only hummed his little tune, and stored up the interesting moments, imagining voluptuously what Rolf and Heart would do when they went away alone after supper; leaving him alone with Mrs. Rocker, who would then be canned with grandeur.

He looked around from the diners when he heard the front door open slowly. He left his chin resting in his palms, his elbows planted in rings of their own fat upon the counter. His eyes narrowed, with

the keen feeling he had had since noon. The door closed slowly and
respectfully after a thin shaking man who walked down the aisle
between the tables and the counter. His large head was unsteady
upon its small neck. He was smiling, his lip lifted off his teeth by a
scar. In his hand he held a scrap of a hat. Fat watched him approach,
saying nothing, only turning his head to keep his eyes on him. Heart
looked up, but didn't recognize Leo, and forgot him.

"Excuse me, mister," said Leo, in a breathy whisper, shaded with
an attempt at charm and culture, party manners, "is there anything
you could spare me to eat? I'm broke, and pretty hungry, I can tell
you."

Fat drummed his fingers against his teeth. A flush like a smile
rose around his eyes. He said, with a lazy mildness, *"Nuh-uh,"*
meaning no by it.

Leo stood. His constant sensation of quivering showed a little in
the way he moved his arms in a motion of appeal, as from one man
to another.

"I won't need very much," he said, looking around at Heart
and Rolf, and then at Mrs. Rocker, with a smiling abandonment of
pride and independence, a public resignation of his only birthright.
"I'm hitchhiking my way to California, where I have relatives; my
uncle is a lawyer there, and once I get there I . . ."

"Nuh-uh," repeated Fat, yawning artificially behind his hands.
Mrs. Rocker stared at Leo with compassion. Her hands worked
under her apron.

"Once I get there," continued Leo, "I could probably send you
some money for what I might maybe owe you. Boy, I'm *hungry*."

A hearty idiom like that, coming in Leo's faded voice, brought
tears to Mrs. Rocker's eyes. She was astounded when Fat stood up
suddenly, leaning across the counter, and bawled in his thin forced
voice, "Nothing here for panhandlers and handouts! Now git!"

Fat subsided back of the counter, and turned his back, inventing
business with sweeping the crumbs off his meat block, where he also
cut bread.

Leo turned around. The scar was frankly part of a snarl now,
and his smile showed dry as the lips stuck to his teeth. He shuffled
down the aisle toward the door. There he paused, having a ridiculous
trouble in getting the knob to turn and the latch to open. Heart and
Rolf lifted their heads, and Mrs. Rocker encouraged the temper in
her heart. Fat scraped the crumbs over and over into separate little

mounds. At last the door opened and Leo went out. The door slammed after him. Mrs. Rocker saw him turn up his collar against the cold night and move off into the shadows. She looked at Fat. He refused to look at her. He was saying to himself, over and over, "That'll show them," not knowing whom he meant or what was to be shown, except that he was tired of being imposed on all his life by people, confusing his weakness which came from within with impositions which came from without.

Three minutes went silently by. Then Mrs. Rocker rolled off her apron and dashed to the door and into the street. She stared up the walk after Leo's direction. Fat turned and screamed to her, "You come back in here!" hating her for acting upon the impulse that he had denied. She moved out of sight. Everything changed for Fat. The image toppled. He said to Heart and Rolf, "I'd have done it, only if I feed one, I feed all. God knows I hate to see anyone go hungry . . ."

Heart shrugged, a sophisticated gesture that was unconscious; she was thinking of nothing but herself.

In a moment Mrs. Rocker came back. She was remembering Leo's smile, a vehicle for hatred. She said she couldn't find him. He'd disappeared. He sure had looked hungry. She looked at Fat, shyly, with a trusting simple smile. He scowled at her and then sighed. He went flabby and weak again. Everybody else did what he wanted to do, and should have done. There she stood, not even thinking badly of him because he had turned away a starving hitchhiker! Her watery blue eyes never concealed any opinions. If she had been momentarily furious, needful of feeding Leo, it was all gone now. She watched Fat for her instructions, and took every little idle movement or expression of his as a signal of some kind for her.

She went to get the dishes from the table, and prepare for dessert, which Fat set out on the counter: two pieces of pie, cherry pie, of his own make, with thick juice running slowly from the crust to the plates. He laid squares of cheese on each plate. But Heart suddenly stood up, and Rolf stood with her. They said they didn't want any dessert. She smiled. Able to conceal nothing, yet secure in their sphere of excitement, they left the Café. Fat put his pieces of pie back into the icebox. Mrs. Rocker performed her nightly tasks before closing up. At last, when he stood waiting for her to get into her hat and coat, his pockets full of the money emptied from the cash register, he looked at her and dropped his look, knowing he would never fire her; she trusted him; she relied on him; she thought he was O.K., even after Leo; she made him sick of the sight of her. He held the door open, and she walked out. He locked it, testing the latch a time or two. He felt abandoned, knowing it was his cherished self that he had abandoned. Mrs. Rocker walked her way, opposite to his. He turned and ambled up Main Street. The few stores were dark. The money clinked and rustled in his pants pockets. He was lonely and lowered in his own eyes. There was only one way in which to regain himself, to lose himself. Thinking pitifully of the waitresses in El Paso, with their blue eyelids, their black lashes, the fiery rouge that bloomed on their cheekbones and faded to the neck in a powdery plaster white, their yellow hair, their amiable hips, he left Main Street and trudged through the dust and leaves of the back streets, walking under the great hooding cottonwoods that strained the cold starlight, and came to the faded green board house that sat low behind a rotting fence. The windows were heavily curtained. There was no sign of life. But he walked to the door and rapped. In a moment, with a final question of folly in his mind, he was admitted.

XII · CONVICTIONS

The darkness was pungent with the smell of printer's ink and rolls of newsprint, mixed with years of dirt swept into the corners of the newspaper offices. In the middle of the rear wall was a door that had a window in it. The glass was filmed with a pearly dust. Through this the faint moonlight filtered. There was no other light. Heart moved to the door and tested the key in the lock again, to be sure the door was fastened. She heard Rolf stir and breathe where she left him, sitting on the long bench that was covered with her coat. She felt again the loving clumsiness of their hands, meeting and offering expressions of what was inside their hearts. Standing in the moonlight away from him, she saw her fierceness go, and marvelled that his should survive, should even grow so that his embraces seemed to her shameful in looking back on them, though she had desired them and brought them to being.

He called her in a whisper to come back beside him.

She walked slowly over to the bench and sat down. They could see each other like shadows, in the dimly distributed moonlight. He was not replete yet, not content, though from the moment of their slipping into the dark printing room, using his key at the back door, her abandon had asked physical questions. Not seeing her in the dark, she seemed to him a stranger, losing the sharp diffidence, the resentment in her eyes. He had not expected such wild tendernesses as she gave him. But now they had been given, she was again changed; and sat beside him on the bench in propriety, some seriousness that perplexed him and inclined him to anger. After all: he thought: there can't be any airs or secrets any more now.

"What is it:" he said to her, setting his large fingers on her breast.

She shook him away.

"Oh, I don't know," she said, in a wretched whisper.

"Aren't you glad?"

"You hurried me . . . I couldn't think."

He sat away from her, wondering if she really thought that. The sound of a soft sigh convinced him that she did. Compassion and pride bloomed in his breast. He leaned to her again, and this time his touch was delicate and mournful.

"I couldn't help myself," he murmured, relaxing finally from his lust, taken by the new emotion of being a slave to his passions. She sighed again, and in a throe of tenderness and weakness, put her head on his breast. She resigned herself. She felt that she had a right to be weary, for the months she had been in bringing Rolf to this night. He stroked her hair, richly confused by feelings of desire and protectiveness, warmed by one and inspired by the other. But nothing he could say, his murmurs about the joy it would be to have other nights, the fact that they were not lonely any more, could make her stop her faint distress.

"What is it:"

"What have I got to look forward to now:" she said.

"What do you mean?"

"You know, well enough . . ."

"No, really I don't."

She pulled away from him.

"Well, I know . . . I know just what I mean to you now, after this."

He remembered that there had been no words of love exchanged.

"Oh, come on," he said. "You know you'll mean more than ever to me now."

"Oh, I know that," she said. "But in what way: any girl will know the same thing."

"Well, if you mean will I go looking around after other girls, you're just crazy."

"... not what I mean."

"Then what:"

"You won't have any use for me but in one way, now," she said, feeling sincere in the ancient ritual.

"Oh:" he said, his voice hushed as he realized his obligation. He hotly thought that she had led him on, God knows she did that. All afternoon, talking and hinting, and working on him, with her hands, and then being silent, she certainly had led him on. Her voice cut against his secret accusations.

"What could I do, Rolf darling? You knew I couldn't fight against you, you knew that. The trouble is, I love you, if I hadn't loved you, it would have been easy to turn you down. You know that."

Here it was. In terror, he stated that he loved her. He said that was why he had done what he had done. She embraced him gently, and waited for the other avowals to follow. She shuddered against his breast, making whispered references to his powers, the fact that he was overmastering, and even dangerous. In the intimate darkness, surrounded by the familiar atmosphere of his job, printer's ink and the acrid scent of linotype metal, cooled, everything she said seemed likewise familiar and believable. Perhaps, no, certainly he was over-mastering. It seemed to him intelligent and logical when he declared, later, that they would be married right away. He told her he wouldn't hear of any objections, there was too much nonsense nowadays about women and freedom.

Heart closed her eyes, clutching his large shoulders. She had known her advantage and used it. He was convinced, even if she was not. She knew how he would act the husband, and that she would spend her life preserving for them both the illusion that he was a delicate tower of strength, whose control was capricious and dangerous. He would believe this himself, for it was only human to drink in a heartening belief about yourself, she thought; she also thought, closing her lips upon him to deny it, that her various inner convictions of truth and plan would accompany her, disappointed, though happiness could live over that. Holding each other, delivered to one another, they sought terms in which to declare their shared lives.

XIII · CONVIVIALITY

Hazel brought Fat out of her room into the sitting room at the back of the house. She walked in front of him, sighing with a comfortable propriety, and closing her thin kimono about her loose body. He followed her, sorry for passion vanished so soon, and stepped through the portieres in the doorway. Hazel threw herself on a chair and crossed her legs, waving Fat to a chair at the table where there were a bottle of whiskey and several glasses. Two men who were sitting at the table looked up at Fat in a moment of silence. He recognized one of them as Do Miller, and said hello.

"Hi, Fat," said Do.

Do turned back to his friend. Both Do and the other man were sitting at their ease, in their undershirts, with their belts loosened, their shoes off, and their shirts and coats hanging on the backs of their chairs. The stranger had a cigar which got in the way of his words. But he spoke in a continuous stream of interest in himself, and what he had done, and was going to do.

Fat poured a drink and listened. Hazel yawned, and lighted a cigarette, smiling at Fat through the tears of smoke and fatigue. He felt suddenly very fond of her, and saw her with new eyes, as if she were someone whom he'd met in somebody's home. Remembering his half hour with her, he blushed. He turned his nose into his whiskey glass to hide his feelings. The liquor was sharp, a cheap grade of white mule. It made him gasp for a second. But with Hazel and whiskey, he was full of comfort. He belched loudly, a surprising thing for Fat to do, and Hazel, knowing him in his Café, knowing his elegance, the daintiness of his ways, laughed aloud at him, and stood up, pushing her hair over her forehead with both hands.

"Great big boy," she said, in a teasing voice. She turned and ran her arms down across his shoulders from behind. But a rap at the door interrupted her, and she squeezed his breasts and left. Fat settled down to listen. The stranger turned from Do Miller, whom he had been tapping on the chest to punctuate his stories, and looked at Fat with a friendly smile, as if to include him in the audience. Fat smirked. He heard the front door open and close, and then the sound of walking down the hallway, and another door.

"I tell yoh 'baout dis mawnin?" said the stranger.

Do shook his head and drank from his glass.

"Baout dat nigga?"

"*Uh*-uh."

"Boy howdi!"

The stranger dropped his head and laughed weakly, flopping his hand at Do as if to defy him to think up anything better than what was coming.

"What nigger?" said Do.

"Dis mawnin: I was pumpin tah up, lost all the air outa my spah tah, and nis nigga came along. I reckoned he was one onnem hitchhikin niggas, and I figga givem a rad to town. So I tolm get aholt onnat pump, pump up my tah for me."

Fat leaned out on the table, flattered by the way the man's eyes sought his every now and then, dividing his story between Fat and Do, seeking in vanity for the applause of both.

"Well, ol nigga stan nere, and tell me he won't pump no tah. I looked at im, I said get aholt. Nigga begin to grin and laugh, and said he didn want pump no tah. Boy! Bam! did I hit im! zowie! I hit im so fast on each side of his jaw, he didn know what's coming or goin. I backed im up against the car, and I hit im again, swingin low, and he begin to cry. He cr-y-y-y, just like a puppydog. I told im, nigga, I says, put up yoh hands. You hit me, I says. Come ohn, hit me, nigga! Should of seen 'at nigga *try* . . . Hit me, I says. An' I let im have it again."

The man took his head in his hand, closing his eyes and wagging, voiceless with amused memory, and full of sociability. Do Miller grunted in his chair, a sound of appreciation, and slumped lower to be comfortable. The stranger looked at Fat with dancing eyes, and Fat winked at him, and slapped the tabletop with a crash of his fat paw, drawn into the world of men who destroyed insolent Negroes, and enjoyed the membership.

The talker threw himself back against his chair again, and stretched out his legs, scratching his groin, a gesture of self-congratulation.

"So, nigga, he try to hit me. An nen I get sore, well, not sore, but it made me mad, to have at nigga try to hit me. So I backs im up towards de ditch, and boy! howdi! did I let im have it! I knocked him down wid one blow, and nen made im stand up again." He smiled with modesty, his red handsome face looking strangely younger. "After he stands up, I knocks im down inna ditch, an boy! he's inna ditch for good! Knocked im out pretty as you please! He was a young nigga, musta been baout tweny-tweny-one. He had a good build on im too. Be a good nigga, if someone just teach him his lesson or two. Like I did."

He chuckled affectionately. Do splashed some more white mule in their three glasses, and they drank together, full of a common excellence, a power that made them enjoy one another, and that gave them a common point of view. Fat was flooded by sensations of ease and ability. Clearing his throat, a test of his thin tubular voice, he leaned forward and with exaggerated caution began to tell a dirty joke. Do and his friend leaned forward to catch it. Fat knew they liked him. Their eyes and mouths echoed his own expressions as he told the story. They hung on his lips. When he finished, telling the end through laughter that he tried to control, they all threw back their heads and barked and coughed with amusement. They had found their common tongue. They sat drinking and smoking, solemnly rotating their turns to tell jokes. Each one was finished with the same raking laughter. Fat kept thinking, It does a man good to let go now and then.

Presently the portieres were held up and a new girl came in. Her face was chalk-white, with rouge spots on the cheekbones and blue shadows on the eyes, and a bowed mouth whose painted outline left the natural one. She had a bony nose, which looked as if it had once been broken, and which gave her face the look of a parrot, when she rolled her eyes and shook her yellow hair. Fat had never seen her before, but had heard there was a new girl at Hazel's.

She walked to the back of the stranger's chair, and leaned down over his shoulder. Fat watched her with a quiver of envy and admiration. She reminded him of the waitresses in El Paso. Her voice sounded now, a smothered sound as if her broken nose interfered with her speech.

"What're you doing?" she said, rolling her eyes at each of them in turn.

"Telling stories," said Do. "Do you know any good ones?"

"I know plenny bad ones," she said, and squawked. "But I never tell them to gennamen."

She uttered this with tones of refinement. The stranger smiled up at her, and she patted his cheek. It was like a little passage between married people.

"Where's Hazel?" she said, with a restless sound in her voice.

"Somebody came in, she went back there with him," said Fat.

"I can't see it," said the new girl.

"See what?" said Do.

"Hazel: can you? How any man could *look* at her, she's so *ordinary*-looking, I said to myself when I *come* here, My God, do you have to work under the same roof with *that!* She's so ordinary-looking!"

Fat was startled. But, unable to make an opinion for himself, he began to view Hazel in his mind from this new angle. All he could remember was her general friendliness, a thing that always appealed to him. But he would never feel the same about Hazel again, having heard a doubt expressed about her. The new girl seemed somehow superior now, and he leaned forward to get her eye, and began to tell her the first story he had told the men. She listened to him, shifting her gaze from his eye to eye, breathing with her mouth open, waiting with short breaths and widened nose for the point of the story, an image of appreciation and encouragement. Fat blushed with content. His voice rose. When they all lost themselves in new laughter, he lay back in his chair drunk and reassured.

XIV · TO CALIFORNIA

The moon rode high, unharried by the wind and the cold that played along the ground. The road banked with the hills, far, far in the distance, and rose invisibly toward the mountain passes. The mountain itself was a shadow against the lighter shadow of the night sky, and Leo looked ahead now and then, trying to set his gaze steadily upon the dense and inscrutable darkness where the mountain opened and the road entered, a place where his steps must eventually carry him, though he murmured to himself in a little high moan that he felt so tired and hungry . . .

It was the shocking coldness of the night that made him begin to wonder at his decision to take to the road, trusting for some kind of hitch to carry him nearer California. The afternoon had been whipped by wind and blown sand. But the morning, with its heat, had told of spring. Tonight there was an edge like winter in the air. He leaned into the direction he was taking, and breathed against his turned-up coat collar, making a warm mist of spittle. His hands were folded inside his shirt on his breast, and the fingers moved constantly, crawling over one another on his bony arch. His lips moved to the tune of the thoughts that rolled in his mind. (He had the conviction that he was striding firmly toward the mountains; that he would walk into the dawn somewhere beyond the dark canyons of black pine; that his promised land of California awaited him with warmth and money, kindness, a job, security. It was the place where his uncle lived, and all the movie women, where life was a thing of easy solutions and sunshine on the seashore and beauty that was cheap and available. He saw his arms swinging and his head thrown up. The road was a river of moonlight.)

Moving by the ditch side, Leo's feet hardly travelled. He was shuddering within his loose black coat. The strain of his eyes to watch for the beam of a car's lights, a car that might pick him up and let him sleep to the rumbling rhythm of tires on a graded road, the feeble cracking of his fingers against his chest, the way he was turned and worried by the fall of the cold air on the mild wind, all these made him look like a scarecrow blown fitfully, an image of public humor and no significance.

No cars came and went. The high moon softened all objects with a silver pour. Leo's eyes watched the fence posts, his feet trembling after one another as he walked. It had taken him hours to get so little beyond town as he was now. He imagined that he could see strange things in the richly shadowed ditch above which he was walking. Thoughts of fear intruded among his sensations of speed and accomplishment. But he would bite his tongue and widen his eyes, remembering that he was from a good family, with a good background. He was an educated man. He had ideals. He was practical enough to go out after them, he told himself. Hence, California.

Suddenly he found himself sitting on the edge of the ditch, retching emptily against his palms. He was tossed on his back by the strain of convulsion, and then he sat up again, feeling strangely more comfortable, and with a cleared sight. He looked around him and winced at the cold that fingered his skin through his clothes. He thought of lying down in the ditch to be out of the wind; and he crawled down into it, but it was capriciously filled with tumbleweeds by the wind of the afternoon, and he recoiled from the sharp burrs and thorns of the billowed, brittle bank. He pulled himself erect by a fence post. There was a dark shape in the field beyond the fence. He leaned on the post and focused his eyes. What he saw was the body of an old Ford, a burned-out wreck that sat on the ground without wheels or top, no fenders or doors, only the rusty and dull black shape of the body, and the shapes, inside, of the front seat and the back seat. On the ground were scattered bits of debris from the wreck, old fenders, a lamp reflector, a shattered door, a broken wheel. In the pouring moonlight, these things shone clear.

"A car," said Leo to himself aloud. He raised himself to look better. He said that it would at least break the wind. He could lie down in the back seat and be out of the cold wind. There would be some protection under the curving back of the car's body, and there was no danger that he might be run over in that field, as there would be if he lay by the road to rest.

Feeling joyful, he decided to climb through the fence and go to the wreck. He lifted himself a little, raising his leg to climb over the barbed wire. He fell to the ground, astonished by his weakness. He could not pull himself up to climb the wires. He began to whimper, fearing that he would never reach the wrecked Ford, where he would spend the night. It had become the image of haven to him. He was too tired to change his plans. Bitterly setting his hands against the ground, he began to roll and crawl nearer the fence, and with a faint warmth of success, rolled under the lowest line of barbed wire and saw himself free in the field. He came to his hands and knees, and then arose, slowly, standing airily. He picked his way among the flung junk of the wreck, and reached the body. He rejoiced to discover that the rear seat cushion was there, left by the owner because it had been half burned up. There was still an old smell of fire about the wreck, and where Leo touched the metal and the charred upholstery, his hands came away black. Rust had followed fire. The wreck had sat in the field for weeks.

He clambered up into the tonneau. He lay down on the rear seat, and pulled his knees up to his belly. He heard the wind sing like a low gong as it stroked the charred fenders that lay beside the car. The wind passed over his head, and he gratefully lowered his chin to his shoulder, feeling a flow of self-comfort like a little child, while his hands kept on shaking and his touch on his own face was too chill and remote to be felt.

He had the idea that lying here, he was able to rest for the night, and still be headed right in the morning, for California. He was comforted by the fact that he was below the level of the wind. Nor could anyone see him, from the road. There was nothing to disturb him. He was half aware, later, of a car going by on the road, whistling against the cold with its speed, and touching roadside objects with vanishing light as it passed. (It made him think briefly that his own car, where he was lying, was moving swiftly down the road to the mountain. But he laughed at himself and repeated that he was not riding, he was walking.)

While his body, curled against itself and stiffening with cold and sleep, lay dark in the tonneau of the burned-out Ford, his dreams picked up from his thoughts and went on. He was walking toward a sky that was like sunrise and sunset. It was warmth to wrap himself in. (His face quivered and his eyes let a little stream of liquid that glistened in the vast moonlight.) He dreamed that the sea was breaking at his feet on a shore of warm sand, and beautiful women crossed his dream, familiar in the black-and-white of the movies; American goddesses never before within his grasp. The dream's unreality was his only strength, but it was sufficient, against the night that grew colder as midnight passed and the still late hours followed. Sometime before dawn, Leo's dream ended.

He lay in his car, in some way a responsibility of all the lives he had ever known; though when the farmer and his hand found him days afterward, it was with simple expressions of wonder and curiosity, deciding that he had died of exposure on the night the frost had cracked down on the valley.

1936

WITHDRAWN